Creativity and Children's Literature

The role of books whether for children or grown-ups [is] to expand our horizons, to tell us more than we had henceforth ever imagined, to give us a sense of life's exhilarating possibilities, to influence our moral outlook and to help determine what kind of people we strive to be.

Selma G. Lanes
(*Horn Book*, Sept./Oct./ 1996
Vol. LXXII, No. 5, 558)

Creativity and Children's Literature

New Ways to Encourage Divergent Thinking

Marianne Saccardi

AN IMPRINT OF ABC-CLIO, LLC
Santa Barbara, California • Denver, Colorado • Oxford, England

Library of Congress Cataloging-in-Publication Data

Saccardi, Marianne.
Creativity and children's literature : new ways to encourage divergent thinking / Marianne C. Saccardi.
pages cm
Includes bibliographical references and index.
ISBN 978-1-61069-355-4 (paperback) — ISBN 978-1-61069-356-1 (ebook)
1. Children's literature—Study and teaching (Elementary)—United States.
2. Creative thinking—Study and teaching (Elementary)—United States. I. Title.
LB1575.5.U5S33 2014
370.15'7—dc23 2014009411

ISBN: 978-1-61069-355-4
EISBN: 978-1-61069-356-1

18 17 16 15 14 2 3 4 5

This book is also available on the World Wide Web as an eBook.
Visit www.abc-clio.com for details.

Libraries Unlimited
An Imprint of ABC-CLIO, LLC

ABC-CLIO, LLC
130 Cremona Drive, P.O. Box 1911
Santa Barbara, California 93116-1911

This book is printed on acid-free paper ∞

Manufactured in the United States of America

To our granddaughter, Stella, and to children everywhere.
Know that the future is in your hands and that your
divergent thinking will create a better world for all of us.

Contents

Acknowledgments

This book is, in so many ways, a team effort. My thanks ring out to:

My husband, Thomas, who refused to let me abandon the concept of divergent thinking. This book would not have been written without his constant prodding and encouragement. I am also grateful to him for the hours he spent photographing fourth graders at work in Julian Curtiss School.

Trish McGuire, principal of Julian Curtiss School, Greenwich, CT, who graciously allowed me to partner with fourth graders in her school.

To fourth-grade teachers Valerie Viscome and Elizabeth McMillan, for opening their classroom to me and giving generously of their time and ideas in planning and teaching the unit on air pollution.

To the fourth graders in Valerie's and Elizabeth's class. Your enthusiasm, hard work, and innovative ideas awed me. Keep those ideas coming.

To Sam Samiperi, environmental analyst at the Connecticut Department of Energy and Environmental Protection, for making the trip down from Hartford and spending the morning with our fourth-grade students.

To my son, Chris, for collecting, labeling, and sorting files and for talking me through many computer glitches. Thanks for your "Sure, no problem, mom" attitude.

To my son, Dan, for constantly leading me to TED talks and keeping me abreast of new innovations and technology, and for his help with computer issues.

To my editor, Sharon Coatney, for her kind words, patience, and gracious willingness to keep track of cover image files.

To the many children's book publishers who allow me the privilege of reviewing their books and the dedicated children's book authors and illustrators who provide the books that offer us so many joys and insights.

Introduction

The children we are teaching today will, in a few short years, be the human service providers, the laborers, the lawyers, the business people, the doctors, the CEOs, the homemakers, the political leaders of our country. How they meet the complicated challenges and recognize the vast opportunities before them will depend largely upon the kind of thinking we have trained and encouraged them to do in our classrooms—thinking that will lead them beyond the ordinary to the unexpected. But can creativity really be taught? Can we teach our students to arrive at that "out of the box" divergent thinking that results in innovation? In her insightful article, "Learning to Think Differently" (February 9, 2014), Laura Pappano states that while it was "once considered the product of genius or divine inspiration, creativity—the ability to spot problems and devise smart solutions—is being recast as a prized and teachable academic skill" (8). In fact, a survey of 1,500 chief executives in thirty-three industries taken in 2010 by IBM found that "'creativity' was the factor most crucial for success" (Pappano, 8). And so we offer this book about thinking, about teaching our students to think creatively and divergently, and about a rich resource we teachers have readily at hand—literature written especially for children—that can be mined daily to help even our youngest students begin to focus in new ways

The Common Core State Standards for English Language Arts and Literacy certainly require student understanding of fiction and informational texts and the ability to express their ideas well verbally and in writing. Yet, as the Core Standards stress, our teaching should not be limited to just the fundamentals: "While the Standards focus on what is most essential, they do not describe all that can or *should* (emphasis added) be taught. A great deal is left to the discretion of teachers and curriculum developers" (Common Core Standards, 6). In fact, preparing our students to become productive members of society in the 21st century actually demands that we stretch the limits of our curricula. What we want children to do is burst out of the ordinary to consider the improbable, the impossible, and in their reaching beyond the "limits," come up with ideas that work. We want looking for the extraordinary in the ordinary to become the way they live and breathe. We want to create an atmosphere in which children can develop, as Mark Edmundson (*NY Times*, OpEd, A8) puts it, "hungry hearts," eager to learn and try new things even when failure is a possibility. A four-minute video on YouTube (http://www.youtube.com/watch?v=W19kzJQwOJo) conveys quite powerfully the new world in which our students are living and the skills they will need to take their places as productive members of 21st-century society. It is important viewing for anyone working with students, and it echoes the kind of teaching and learning strategies we stress here.

We live in complex times. Doctors and scientists have devised new technologies and medicines for the diagnosis and cure of diseases considered fatal just a few short years ago. Yet millions of people do not have the health insurance they need to pay for such sophisticated and expensive treatment. People are living longer than ever before, but the cost of caring for the elderly continues to escalate faster than the means to pay for it. Ever-faster modes of travel have brought even the most remote regions of the world within reach and opened new markets for trade. But these new opportunities present the challenges of increasing productivity in our factories and businesses while keeping costs and profits in balance, and safeguarding the environment as well. The Internet, now available to us in devices small enough to fit in a shirt pocket, makes the latest information available at the click of a button, and social networks enable us to spread that information instantly—even to remote parts of the world. Yet so many of us caught up in this information craze often neglect to reflect on it or research its authenticity, and hence, are sometimes led astray. The increasingly diverse population in the United States provides us with many talents and viewpoints as well as the enormous task of eradicating the strangling tentacles of racism. Indeed, C. Ronald Petty states, "One of the most perplexing problems faced by American executives today is diversity and how corporations should address it" (Petty, 1996). The constant danger of terrorism throughout the globe has resulted in war; thousands of deaths; destruction of property; increased security and surveillance procedures; the expenditure of billions of dollars that could be better used to improve the lives of so many; and a general unease that often brings about a dependence on medication to alleviate depression.

Writing about world problems such as those discussed above, Warren Buffett's son Peter calls for systemic change in the way philanthropies try to alleviate them (*The New York Times*, July 27, 2013, A19):

"It's time for a new operation system," he states. "Not a 2.0 or a 3.0, but something built from the ground up. New Code. What we have is a crisis of imagination. Albert Einstein said that you cannot solve a problem with the same mindset that created it. . . . Money should be spent trying out concepts that shatter current structures and systems."

A Definition of Divergent Thinking

How will our children contribute to solutions for these and future dilemmas as they begin to take their places in society? We suggest that they begin now to engage in divergent thinking, a kind of thinking described by Carnevale et al. (1990) as "a process for expanding the view of a problem. It involves thinking in **different** ways about the problem as a whole without necessarily trying to solve it. In divergent thinking, a person tries to connect ideas for which connections are not apparent; the resulting combinations may lead to a previously unsuspected solution to a problem" (201). This definition suggests that divergent thinking goes even beyond the creative. It requires one to see outside the problem at hand; to reach for more than logical solutions; even to dream the impossible. It is this kind of thinking that can make the unfeasible a delightful reality. Serendipitous surprises are the common lot of divergent thinkers. These are the entrepreneurs, the creators of art in all its forms, the people who make a profound impact.

Our challenge is to endeavor to expand our students' horizons, notwithstanding the pressures we all face in the classroom. With the current emphasis on high stakes testing, and now testing to the Common Core State Standards, where school districts and individual schools, principals, and teachers are being judged by students' test scores, it is tempting to focus solely on material that children will face on these standardized tests. Lisa Jeschke, a fifth-grade teacher in Poestenkill Elementary School in upstate New York, states that, "when the faculty is prepping students for state tests, the lessons are more about formulaic ways to write essays and answer questions, because that's what it takes to score high. There's less opportunity for teachers or students to try fresh, original thinking" (Jehlen, April 1, 2012). Wendy Lecker's op-ed piece, "Testing the learning right out of schools" (2012, A23), is equally disheartening. She recounts what students have told her about computer-graded writing assessments on standardized tests:

> The computer requires an essay with three supporting points. As long as the computer sees three points, the students can get the highest score. Knowing that, students choose any three points—weak, dull, it doesn't matter . . . The goal is not to write well, but rather to attain a high score. These 13-year-olds know the game.

While this kind of teaching may produce marvelous results at test-taking time, the cost in human potential will probably be too great to bear. We may, in the end, have a generation of automatons unable to think beyond multiple choice responses or three-point essays. We may have a generation of children who are unable to engage in the kind of thinking their living in a complex world will demand.

Will the Common Core curriculum and the standardized tests now linked to it raise the bar by requiring more sophisticated thought and analysis from our students? Will it graduate students more able to compete with their peers throughout the globe? We certainly hope so. But as educators Andrew Hacker and Claudia Dreifus contend in their article "Who's Minding the Schools?" (*New York Times*, Sunday Review, June 9, 2013), "the Common Core takes as its model schools from which most students go on to selective colleges. Is this really a level playing field? Or has the game been so prearranged that many, if not most, of the players will fail?" (7). Rather than give students space to think in their own divergent ways, the tests that evaluate their knowledge of the Common Core curriculum require that students and teachers across the nation perform in a uniform way. Yet, says Alan Starko, "We want our students to have zest for life and hope in their capacity—and we want them to have those things in school" (5). Perhaps thousands of students drop out of school every day because they don't have that joy in learning, that freedom to think and create.

Despite these caveats, children in most states will likely be tested on their knowledge of curriculum material related to the Common Core Standards, and teachers will likely have to teach this curriculum and prepare their students well. The good news, according to Gillian Engberg, is that "While the standards' specific structure may be new, their goals are familiar in vibrant classrooms: to expose students to complex texts, encourage close reading and inquiry, and support students' abilities to analyze, imagine, and communicate ideas" (*Book Links*, April 2013, 1). The activities and discussions suggested in this text promote just such complex and close examination of the books included in each chapter.

The books discussed throughout this text are by no means meant to be exhaustive examples of a genre. They are only a sampling to get you started. Once you begin to use these books, engage in some of the suggested activities, and observe your students' reactions, it is my hope that your enthusiasm for them will increase, and that you will find many more titles on your own to share with the children in your life. If we invite divergent thinking from their earliest years, if we leave room for trial and error and trial again without reprisals, we can be confident that our students will continue to think in new and exciting ways as adults.

Characteristics of the Divergent Thinker

What is the divergent thinker like? Synthesizing many research studies, Alan Starko (2012, 87–102) lists several characteristics of creative or divergent thinkers. He divides them into cognitive and personality traits.

Cognitive Characteristics:

1. Metaphorical thinking, or the ability to find parallels between dissimilar ideas
2. Flexibility and skill in decision-making, or the ability to look at a situation from different points of view
3. Independence in judgment and the ability to be mindful of the consequence of such judgments on individuals and society
4. Coping well with novelty
5. Logical thinking skills
6. Ability to visualize what is unseen
7. Ability to escape entrenchment and consider things in new ways
8. Finding order in chaos

Personality Characteristics:

1. Willingness to take risks, that is, express a different opinion or try out an idea that might fail
2. Perseverance, drive and commitment to a task
3. Curiosity
4. Openness to experience and receptiveness to the complex input of the senses
5. Tolerance for ambiguity
6. Broad interests
7. Value of originality
8. Intuition and deep emotions
9. Being internally occupied or withdrawn

While creativity is a complex concept involving often contradictory characteristics or characteristics that have different manifestations in different fields of endeavor, Sarko's list is, nevertheless, helpful for educators to keep in mind as they seek ways to help students develop as creative, divergent thinkers.

Marzano et al. (in *Workplace Basics*, 192), describe the creative or divergent thinker as one who pushes the limits of knowledge and ability, is intrinsically rather than extrinsically motivated (what implications does this have for the awarding of gold stars, etc.?), is able to reframe a problem in order to see it in a different light, and can block out unproductive distractions.

Recognizing the need to help our students develop more complex thinking, Lorin Anderson, a former student of Benjamin Bloom, worked with David Krathwohl, to revise Bloom's famous taxonomy. She changed her mentor's category names from nouns to verbs, emphasizing thinking as an intrinsically active process. More importantly, she raised the stakes, making "create"—that is, coming up with completely new ideas and products—the ultimate goal of higher-level thinking. This new taxonomy is more in line with the needs of a complex world, a world that will demand new solutions, to the problems and challenges at hand. (See http://www.utar.edu.my/fegt/file/Revised_Blooms_Info.pdf for a compari son of the old and revised taxonomies.)

More recently, Andrew Churches took Bloom's taxonomy even further by devising a digital taxonomy (see http://edorigami.wikispaces.com/file/view/bloom%27s+Digital+taxonomy+v3.01.pdf), advocating the use of modern technologies to facilitate learning and thinking. Today's students spend ever-increasing amounts of time using digital devices, and it is important for educators to understand how to bring these technologies into the classroom in meaningful ways that promote divergent thinking. These tools make it possible not only for students to generate new ideas but also to share those ideas with others, receive almost immediate feedback, and then refine their thinking even further. These tools make it possible to break the barriers of classroom walls and view a problem or challenge from multiple perspectives around the globe. What an exciting way to channel students' natural affinity for technology into collaborations that result in hitherto undreamed of solutions. Several suggestions for integrating technology into projects appear throughout this book. Keep in mind, however, that since technology hardware and software change and update almost daily, some suggestions that appear here could easily be supplanted by the use of more recent tools. Students will likely be wonderful sources of information for ways to use technology in the classroom.

Problems Solved in Unexpected Ways by Divergent Thinkers

Divergent thinking may sound like a time-consuming exercise with no practical results. However, Henrique Fogli states, "though . . . forc[ing] yourself to see different aspects of the situation, using unusual points of view, *no matter how abstract or absurd they seem at the first place* . . . might sound like a waste of time, many corporations have found appealing answers to their problems by using such method" [*sic*] ("Divergent thinking," http://creativegibberish.org/439/divergent-thinking/). Here are just a few examples:

Recall the challenge presented in a previous section regarding the need for companies to be increasingly competitive, productive, and profitable to succeed in ever-widening markets? The logical answer might be to require employees to work longer and harder at what they do. Yet, in 1948, in the midst of a feverish post-war industrial heyday, the 3M Company decided to do just the opposite—give everyone, not just the scientists, but everyone—15 percent company time off to pursue their own interests and ideas. Gaining more by asking for less work time seems ridiculous at first glance. But the result was as surprising as the initial proposal. Such innovative products as Post-it notes, a painter's tape that can stick to walls without damaging them, a sandpaper that acts like a cutting tool—and many more avant-garde inventions—have been devised by employees using their 15 percent time. Giving their employers space to think and create, as well as supporting them even when their ideas do not always succeed—has been the key to 3M's long-time position as a world-class innovator and its ability to attract an enthusiastic work force. (For the full story, go to: http://www.fastcodesign.com/1663137/how-3m-gave-everyone-days-off-and-created-an-innovation-dynamo.) Other major companies have followed 3M's lead in recent years. Google's 20 percent off time has resulted in Gmail, Google Earth, and Gmail Labs.

Tina Seelig (*Ingenius*, 2012, 26) describes how shifting their thinking to look at alternatives resulted in a boost in sales for the Tesco food company in South Korea. Company directors realized that people were so busy they were unable to find time to shop in their stores. So they posted photos of their food aisles in the subway and enabled shoppers to shop by sending photos of the QR codes (that is, a Quick Response Code designed for use on smart phones and other devices with cameras; these codes provide websites and other helpful information to users) on products via smart phones and paying by credit card. The food was delivered when they returned home.

Problem: Many small merchants lose business because they cannot process customers' credit card payments and still make a profit. Enter Jack Dorsey, CEO of Square. After some false starts, Mr. Dorsey developed Card Case, a Smart Phone app that allows consumers to "pay for their items just by giving the cashier their name; the app activates the charge to their stored credit card . . . [It] can also show . . . your payment history, what's for sale in-store, and nearby places that take Square" (McGrit, *Fast Company*, 84). In addition to simplifying life for busy consumers, Square's flat 2.75 percent processing fee per swipe makes the process affordable even for smaller businesses. An important added bonus: "Giving people a fast and free way to start taking payments creates businesses . . . and that means added jobs" (85). Following Dorsey's success, many divergent thinkers have now devised apps that make paying for products fast and easy.

In 2007, *Time* named William McDonough and Michael Braungart to their "Heroes of the Environment" list. The two men work with corporations to enable them to do what had hitherto been considered impossible: produce a high-quality product, protect the environment, and make a good profit. Contrary to the predominant practices of our throw-away society that finds it easier to demolish buildings rather than to restore them or to dispose of medical supplies rather than sterilize and reuse them, these visionaries believe that waste is unacceptable, that manufacturing plants need not have a waste product that pollutes, and that all materials used in the creation of a product can be safe for humans and the planet they inhabit. Through their unique designs, they have created buildings and factories that are efficient, a delight to work or study in, and cost effective. (For more detailed information about their fascinating work, view the YouTube videos found on http://www.youtube.com/watch?v=vyciEjLtiCM and http://www.youtube.com/watch?v=VO-oO7uULcc.) With their help, Rohner Textiles in Switzerland supplies textiles that are completely safe; Nike makes rubber that contains no polychlorinated biphenyls (PCBs), without sacrificing the quality and performance of their shoes; and the Ford Motor Company now manufactures cars that are 85 percent recyclable and that contain environmentally friendly materials. In fact, Ford has "saved approximately $4.5 million by using recycled materials, and diverted between 25 and 30 million pounds of plastic from landfills in North America alone." (Media.Ford.com, http://media.ford.com/article_display.cfm?article_id=32474. Accessed April 10, 2012.)

More than a half million women die in childbirth each year, most of them in developing countries. While many of these deaths are unpreventable, Dr. Laura E. Stachel, through her extensive work in Nigeria, discovered that all too often, doctors cannot provide the necessary procedures to save lives because "sporadic electricity impairs the operation of surgical wards, delivery wards, essential hospital equipment, and hospital communications" (wecaresolar.org/about-us/). "Without a reliable source of electricity, nighttime deliveries were attended in near darkness, cesarean sections were cancelled or conducted by flashlight, and critically ill patients waited hours or days for life-saving procedures. The outcomes were often tragic" (wecaresolar.org/about-us/our-story). So, with her husband, Dr. Hal Aronson, she founded We Care Solar, a nonprofit organization committed to solving the problem. Dr. Aronson created a suitcase-sized solar electric system that can provide enough power for operating rooms and medical equipment in areas that would otherwise be without sufficient electricity. Doctors Stachel and Aronson are now working to make the solar units as affordable as possible and to distribute them in ever-increasing numbers.

A Classroom Environment That Promotes Divergent Thinking

Practice in divergent thinking must start early, even in our preschool classrooms. Susan Gelman, in a review of the research on the young child's thinking abilities, states that children as young as four years of age can see beyond the obvious, that they can "make inferences from whatever information is available to go beyond what is most immediate" (Gelman, 1998, 21). Opportunities to engage our students in divergent thinking present themselves continually as we face the social and academic problems that arise in our classrooms and strive to solve them together. In addition, there are sometimes contests in which we challenge young people to come up with new inventions to answer a specific need. Science fairs also provide outlets for students to display new scientific ideas and research. So what can literature contribute to the process? And why another book about children's literature? Because the goal here is to help teachers look at books, even those they may have seen and used before, with new eyes. Certainly, we should enjoy the stories for themselves *first*, as delightful sojourns in the world of literature. But we can also help our students look at characters for what they have to tell us about how to live and grow and contribute to the world around us. Louise Rosenblatt states, "Whatever the form—poem, novel, drama, biography, essay—literature makes comprehensible the myriad ways in which human beings meet the infinite possibilities that life offers" (Rosenblatt, 1976, 6).

References

Buffett, Peter. July 27, 2013. "The Charitable-Industrial Complex." *The New York Times*. OpEd. CLXII (56,210). A19. Buffett calls for a new paradigm in the world of philanthropic giving.

Carnevale, A. P., Leila J. Gainer, and Ann S. Meltzer. 1990. *Workplace Basics: The Essential Skills Employers Want*. San Francisco: Jossey-Bass. ISBN 978-1555422028. The authors present the findings of a three-year study regarding the preparation of a workforce that meets current business requirements.

Churches, A. 2008. "Bloom's digital taxonomy." http://www.techlearning.com/studies-in-ed-tech/0020/blooms-taxonomy-blooms-digitally/44988 (accessed April 11, 2014). Churches emphasize the need to use digital technology to enhance collaboration and provides many examples of such use.

Edmundson, M. 2012. "Education's Hungry Hearts." *New York Times*, OpEd. April 1, A8. The author argues that it is more important to be eager to learn than to have the highest SAT scores to get into college.

Engberg, Gillian. April 2013. "The Fourth R." *Book Links* 22(4): 1. The author asserts that good literature helps children grow into curious thinkers able to solve 21st-century problems.

Fogli, H. "Divergent thinking." Creative Giberish, http://creativegibberish.org/439/divergent-thinking/ (accessed April 11, 2014). Fogli describes divergent thinking and suggests ways to improve thinking skills.

Gelman. S. A. 1998. "Research in Review. Categories in Young Children's Thinking." *Young Children* 53(1): 20–26. The author cites research that shows even very young children are capable of higher thinking operations than previously acknowledged.

Hacker, Andres, and Claudia Dreifus. June 9, 2013. "Who's Minding the Schools?" *The New York Times*, Sunday Review, 1, 6–7. The authors discuss the merits and pitfalls of the Common Core curriculum and the tests that evaluate students' knowledge of this curriculum.

Jehlen, A. April 1, 2012. "Keeping Classroom Creativity Alive in the NCLB Era." http://neatoday.org/2012/04/01/keeping-classroom-creativity-alive-in-the-nclb-era/ (accessed April 11, 2014). The author stresses the drawbacks of NCLB and highlights a school that eliminated test preparation for a week.

Lecker, Wendy. 2012. "Testing the Learning Right out of Schools." *Greenwich Time*, OpEd, June 17, A23. Lecker describes how students merely include any three points in a computer-graded essay to obtain high scores on standardized tests.

McDonough, W., and Michael Braungart. October, 1998. "The Next Industrial Revolution." *The Atlantic*. http://www.theatlantic.com/magazine/archive/1998/10/the-next-industrial-revolution/304695/ (accessed April 11, 2014). The authors advocate for producing materials in ways that create no pollution, even in their eventual disposal.

McGrit, E. 2012. "For Making Magic out of the Mercantile." *Fast Company* 83–85, 146–47. McGrit describes the innovative app created by Jack Dorsey of Square Company.

Media.Ford.com. "Ford Is Making Greener Vehicles Through Increased Use of Renewable and Recyclable Materials." April 20, 2010. http://media.ford.com/article_display.cfm?article_id=32474 (accessed April 17, 2012). The article outlines the Ford Motor Company's use of environmentally friendly materials in the manufacture of its vehicles.

Pappano, Laura. 2014. "Learning to Think Differently." *The New York Times*. Education Life. Feb. 9, 8–10. Pappano discusses many courses designed to teach students to think creatively and describes some innovative student inventions.

Petty, C. R. 1996. "Companies Should Work for Social Change." *The New York Times*. Op Ed. Nov. 16. Petty argues that corporations should promote diversity.

Rosenblatt, L. M. 1976. *Literature as Exploration*. 4th ed. New York: The Modern Language Association of America. Rosenblatt discusses the transaction between the reader and literature.

Seelig, Tina. 2012. *Ingenius: A Crash Course on Creativity*. New York: Harper One/HarperCollins. ISBN 978-0-06-202070-3. The author offers practical suggestions to awaken the spark of creativity she asserts is in everyone.

Starko, Alane Jordan. 2010. *Creativity in the Classroom: Schools of Curious Delight*. 4th ed. New York: Rutledge Publishers. ISBN 978-0-415-99707-2. Starko links research in creativity with classroom practice.

1

Poetry: "Words . . . That Rub Together with Small Explosions" (Karla Kuskin)

Poetry lets us experience the world with joy

—Joyce Sidman (*School Library Journal*, "Why I Write Poetry")

It has long been a practice in schools across the country to set aside the month of April each year to celebrate poetry. Publishers of children's books disseminate special activities and events on their websites and even release poetry books to coincide with Poetry Month. There are poetry readings, poetry writing contests, school visits by poets who write for children, and classrooms humming with verse. But poetry is too important to be relegated to a single month and then tucked away until the following year. We need its rhythms to seep into our students' minds and hearts and become grist for their own speaking and writing. Even more relevant to our purposes here, poetry is essential for helping our students think in new ways; to see possibilities where none initially seem obvious; and to make connections that can result in innovative ideas. In fact, several of the characteristics of divergent thinkers listed in the Introduction (p. xiii), namely, they can engage in "metaphorical thinking and find parallels between dissimilar ideas"; have the ability to "visualize what is unseen"; have the "ability to escape entrenchment and consider things in new ways"; have "curiosity"; have an "openness to experience and receptiveness to the complex input of the senses"; "value originality"; and have "deep emotions" speak directly to poetry. It was, therefore, a deliberate decision to begin this book with a chapter on poetry. Children need to experience and understand how poets observe the world with minute attention to details and how they surprise with unlikely connections that work so that they, too, will be able to break out of the "expected" into unknown and possibly life-altering territory.

Helping our students fall in love with poetry and reap all its benefits requires daily exposure during which analysis plays a minor role and reveling in the music of poetic language and its often stunning images is front and center. Fortunately, selecting appropriate poetry is easy, because publishers provide a rich variety of anthologies and even picture and board book editions of poetry collections. Contained within these volumes are poems that will appeal to every taste and age. Teachers will also find poems to complement just about every subject in the curriculum.

Poetry: "Mak[es] Familiar Objects Be as if They Were Not Familiar" (Percy Bysshe Shelley)

As poets walk through the world, they see what is around them not only with their physical eyes, but also with the eyes of their imaginations. When Carl Sandburg writes, "The fog comes / on little cat feet" (In Hoberman, "Fog," 2012, 93) (see also Starko, 2010, 88), he sees the fog as more than a low cloud of mist hovering over an area. He sees in his mind's eye the stealthy creep of a cat as it moves low to the ground and silent—a perfect metaphor for the way in which fog can creep up and catch us unaware. This juxtaposition of two seemingly unlike things is one of the most striking characteristics of poetry. Poets seem to breathe in metaphor and it fills their work. The poet Joyce Sidman says, "metaphor is at the heart of poetry" (*School Library Journal*, 2012, 34). What does this have to do with enabling our students to be creative, divergent thinkers? Alane Starko, whose *Schools of Curious Delight: Creativity in the Classroom* (2010) is all about teaching children to be creative, provides the connection:

> Creative people are often able to find parallels between unlike ideas. They take ideas from one context and use them in another context to create a new synthesis, transformation, or perspective. Metaphorical thinking makes it possible to use one idea to express another. (88)

The poems discussed in this chapter bear out Aristotle's assertion that "it is from metaphor that we can best get hold of something fresh" (in Sidman, 2012, 34). As we begin to suggest activities and lessons that might accompany the enjoyment of these poems and the other genres throughout this book, it is important to keep in mind that children, especially as they advance through the grades and on into high school, should know why they are engaging in such activities. Why is it useful, for example, to be able to link unrelated objects to form a new image as suggested in the preceding paragraph? Such an ability can help students make connections in their learning so that they can, for example, understand how an event in one part of the world might impact places thousands of miles away. It can help them see how seemingly unconnected ideas can be useful, when the good points of each are brought together, to solve a difficult problem. Children who complain, "I don't know why I have to learn this" might be more eager to dig into projects, to enlarge their horizons, when they see how divergent thinking can have an impact on their lives and the communities in which they live. Remember the invention of the 3-M Post-It note mentioned in the Introduction (p. xiii)? This is a perfect real-world application of metaphoric thinking. A scientist is trying to invent a super adhesive. Instead, the formula he comes up with is actually weaker than the adhesive already manufactured by his company. So the results of his experiments lie dormant on the shelf. Years later, another scientist at the company makes a connection between the paper markers that keep falling out of his choir book at church and that weak adhesive previously devised by his colleague. Voila, pieces of paper large enough to hold jotted notes or mark places in a book, can adhere, and yet be pulled off without damaging the pages, become one of 3-M's most popular items.

Give Yourself to the Rain (2012) is a wonderful collection of poems for very young children by one of our most beloved children's book writers, Margaret Wise Brown. In "Green Grass & Dandelions" she treats little ones to a different view of dandelions:

Bright yellow
Constellations
Brave little lions
Suns in the grass
Dandelions

Eugene Field's well-loved *Wynken, Blynken, and Nod* has been beautifully illustrated in recent editions by both Giselle Potter (2008) and David McPhail (2009), the latter now available as a large board book. Three nighttime travelers sail off in a wooden shoe where they catch herring fish in a beautiful sea. Only toward the end of the poem do youngsters hear that the three fishermen are really metaphors for the sleepy eyes and nodding head of a little child tucked into bed (the wooden shoe) while stars (herring fish) twinkle in the night sky (the sea). Another child views his bed as a boat that he boards at night as he says farewell to "all[his] friends on shore" ("My Bed Is a Boat," 34) in Barbara McClintock's illustrated collection of Robert Louis Stevenson's *A Child's Garden of Verses* (2011).

Most of the very short poems in *Silver Seeds* (Paolilli and Brewer, 2003), are metaphoric riddles, and as an added bonus, the beginning letter of each line forms an acrostic that provides the answer:

Huge elephants
In a row,
Lying
Low and
Sleeping.

Other poems in the collection help children view a leaf as a "loose brown parachute" ("Leaf") and stars as "Silver seeds" ("Stars") "Tossed in the air / And planted in the sky."

A Children's Treasury of Poems (2008) is a collection of familiar poems for very young children with charming illustrations by Linda Bleck. In "The Man in the Moon," the anonymous poet says that "as he sails the sky / [The Man in the Moon] Is a very remarkable skipper." In the poem "A Good Play," Robert Louis Stevenson delights children with his description of a ship built "upon the stairs / All made of the back-bedroom chairs" for lots of fun sailing the make-believe seas.

Read some of the excellent poems celebrating outdoor play in Marilyn Singer's *A Stick is an Excellent Thing* (2012). In the title poem (28–29), children pretend a stick is, among other things, "a scepter for a king" and "a magic wand." In "Bubbles" (8–9), a young girl sends a "parade / of small bubbles—a whole fleet—/ that is sailing right behind [her brother]." Even very young children are capable of making such connections between unlikely objects in pretend play similar to the games engaged in by the children featured in this poetry collection. Youngsters have no difficulty seeing a broom handle as a horse, an oatmeal box as a drum, or a sheet as a camping tent. Preschool and early childhood teachers can encourage such play; listen for and celebrate the connections children make in their ordinary speech, especially on the playground; and model such speech themselves. They can make a list of metaphors that come from the mouths and actions of their students and occasionally call children's attention to them. After enjoying the poems described earlier for several days, we can help slightly older children begin experimenting with the creation of simple metaphors by considering the objects in their classroom or the world just outside its windows in novel ways. Ask students to help you make a list of things in the room such as pencils, board erasers, books, markers, etc. Then, just as the poet called a leaf a "loose brown parachute," a metaphor that aptly captures the characteristics of a falling leaf, how can they visualize some of the things on their list in ways that encapsulate the properties of that object? For example, the classroom door could be called "a gateway to discovery"; a book could be "a word holder." Perhaps alert students will realize that, if there is a computer in the room, it likely comes with an accessory that is itself a metaphor—a mouse. Discuss why this is so. Take a walk in the school yard and/or the neighborhood, make another list of objects, and create metaphors for them as well.

How fortunate we are to have a recent compilation of some of Lilian Moore's poems about the city for young children: *Mural on Second Avenue and Other City Poems* (2005). In these seventeen poems she revels in the simple joys of city life. The language is straightforward enough for young children to understand, and filled with lovely images as well: A "comma of a moon" brightens the "Winter Dark"; "Corners are surprises" ("How to Go Around a Corner"); and rain "litters / the street / with mirror splinters" ("Rain Pools"). Lee Bennett Hopkins also celebrates the city in *City I Love* (2009). In the poem "City," "skyscrapers are . . . trees / . . . A hydrant is [a] swimming pool." "From the Ground" is a poem in which watching from the ground as workers build a skyscraper is "like watching / a razzle-dazzle / rassmatazz / three-ring / steel circus / performance." In "City Summer," "even / the fiery / orange-red / sun / wears / a / sweatband." Enjoy the poems in these books and talk about things the children enjoy in their neighborhoods. What metaphorical expressions might they use to name objects in their environment—a favorite shop window, a street sign, a delivery truck, for example?

Pat Mora's haiku poems in *Yum! ¡ MmMm! ¡ Qué Rico! Americas' Sproutings* (2009) celebrate foods native to the Americas, and the accompanying illustrations are filled with

vibrant color. A "Chile" is "green mouth-fire"; "Corn" leaves "sprout [a] silk-snug house"; and a "Cranberry" is "Scarlet fireworks." Each spread in this visual feast includes a paragraph about the history of the plant and other interesting information. Children can work in groups according to countries of family origin, research the different foods native to those countries, and write metaphors for those foods.

The jacket flap of Heidi Mordhorst's *Pumpkin Butterfly: Poems from the Other Side of Nature* (2009) states, "Look closely at the world around you, and you may see another world—a world where butterflies are the ghosts of pumpkins." Surely young children have seen piles of autumn leaves, but have they ever considered them as "fires without flame / smoldering among the roots of / a monumental oak"? Or have they ever thought of a falling leaf chased by their cat or dog as "a little candy bird flapping / cellophane wings"? This is a beautiful collection that will surely prompt a walk in the neighborhood looking for familiar sights that aren't so familiar after all.

Another invitation to look closely at the natural world presents itself in Jane Yolen's *Shape Me a Rhyme: Nature's Forms in Poetry* (2007). The poems, illustrated with gorgeous photographs, focus on shapes in nature and while some, like the round ball of the sun, are obvious, others, like the triangle that forms an alligator's head and snout, are not. "Since," as Yolen states in "Square" (17), "nature rarely / Seeds a square" she presents readers with the square formed by a shadow on a frond. For each shape, there are additional synonyms. For example, on the spread for the illustration and poem about "coil," the words "curl," "curlicue" "twist," and "spiral" also appear. Even in the poem for the obvious shape of the crescent moon, Yolen helps us look at it in a different way: "Your shape, like the side / Of a copper cent, / Out of pocket but / Not yet spent" (30).

Looking closely takes on a whole new meaning in J. Patrick Lewis's incredible *Face Bugs* (2013). Large colored photographs provide close-up views of bug faces as students may never have seen them before. Huge, bulging, many-faceted eyes, gaping mouths, hairy legs, and antennae appear opposite the poems while comical line drawings show the bugs interacting with one another and the reader. The vivid metaphors Lewis uses in his poems so aptly express the essence of these creatures' appearance and habits that they will entice students to create metaphors themselves for the insects they are studying. In "Eastern Carpenter Bee" (8), Lewis gives the bee a "football-helmet head." The "Nursery Web Spider" (11) has "eight round eyes in [the] dark crawl space" that is its hairy face. The two faces on the "Dogday Harvestfly Cicada" (13) are "a

head-on / Insect wreck." And the "American Horse Fly" (14) is wonderfully called "The Clydesdale of all flies." Truly, as the opening poem, "Grand Opening: The Face Bug Museum" (4) states, "you never really know bugs til you look them in the eye." Don't miss a chance to meet these insects face-to-face.

Outside Your Window: A First Book of Nature by Nicola Davies (2012) is a big, gorgeous book of poems. It is divided into four seasons and features the special sights and sounds of each. "Cherry Blossoms" (23) are "pools of pink"; Shells ("Shell Song," 46) are "Pyramids and angel's wings / lying in the sand." When Davies writes about tracks in snow ("Snow Song," 92), she offers this stunning image: "In the morning, you'll find the snow has kept a diary / of things that happened when you were asleep." In *Once Around the Sun* (2006), Bobbi Katz writes a poem about each month of the year. "March is / when a cheerleader / no longer / cartwheels / inside your chest / because the forecast is / 'SNOW'," "October is / when night guzzles up / the orange sherbet sunset," and "December is / when greedy night / grows fat, / gnawing / away the day / until all that's left / of afternoon / is a small bare bone." For his collection, *Sharing the Seasons: A Book of Poems* (2010), Lee Bennett Hopkins has chosen the poems of many famous poets to celebrate the four seasons. Tiny bugs take up residence in lilies and magnolias, their "summer bungalows" in Carl Sandburg's "Small Homes" (32). With the sun shining on his straw-golden hair, the scarecrow becomes a prince, "Royal Keeper of the Corn" in Terry Harshman's "The Scarecrow Prince" (44). Paul Janeczko also anthologizes a collection of poems by many noted poets who help children view the unique characteristics of the four seasons in *Firefly July* (2014). In "A Happy Meeting," Joyce Sidman describes a summer rain as it meets the earth with "soft, cinnamon kisses. / then marriage: mud" (17). In "Sandpipers," April Halprin Wayland speaks of the sharp "needle" beaks of sandpipers "hemming the ocean" (19). All of these collections are perfect accompaniments to a study of the seasons. After children have enjoyed many of the poems, encourage them to talk about the ways in which they experience the different times of the year. Are there new ways to consider the burgeoning life of spring, the heat of summer, the colors of autumn, the brisk cold of winter?

For students studying trees, Douglas Florian's *Poetrees* (2010) is a treasure of word play and creativity that will enable them to consider these giant plants in ways they may never have considered. The "Baobab (15) is a 'jug tree. / Hug tree . . . / Bottle tree . . . / Bubble tree'." "Giant Sequoias" (18) are "Ancient seers . . . / Friends to the sky." And the "Bristlecone Pine" (30) is a "master of longevity." Divide the students into groups and ask each group to divide a piece of paper into three columns. In the first column, they should write the names of all the trees they have been studying, skipping several lines between each name. In the second column, write some characteristics of each tree: leaf shape, kind of bark, seeds, size, and so on. In the third column, turn the trees' characteristics into suitable metaphors. When the groups have completed their work, which may require several sessions, bring them together to share their metaphors.

"A Tomcat Is" by J. Patrick Lewis (*A Foot in the Mouth*, 2009, 34) is filled with metaphor. The cat is "night watchman of corners," a "bird-watching bandit," and even a "dude in the alley." In his "Home Poem Or, the Sad Dog Song" (35), the dog narrator calls pie "the home of the fly," and me [the dog] the "home of the flea."

Students will never see feet in quite the same way again after enjoying the poems in Stefi Weisburd's *Barefoot: Poems for Naked Feet* (2008). Throughout the poems, feet are called "bolts of lightning" ("Shocking," 8); "bulldozer[s]" ("What's Afoot at the Beach," 18); and "two puckered old me" ("Bathtub," 22). In the poem "A Ride in the Country" (23), Weisburd actually turns feet extending out a car window into a dog that "pant[s], lick[s] at air," and whose fur is "flung by breeze." Most fascinating of all is the poem "Vacant Houses" (10–11), in which descriptions of different kinds of shoes read like real estate ads; for example, "High heels / cliff-side beauty on stilts," "Flip-flops / great lakefront property," and "Boots / sturdy brown brownstone." Can students take a part of the body: hands, heads, and so on, or an article of clothing, and work in groups or as a class to come up with metaphors for them? Might they wish to turn these metaphors into poems?

If your students are studying pond life, Joyce Sidman's *Song of the Water Boatman & Other Pond Poems* (2005) will greatly enrich the unit. If not, the poems and illustrations in this beautiful collection will have them clamoring to do so. Sidman's poems demonstrate that ponds are places that teem with animal and plant life. In "Caddis Fly" the poet describes the animal's habit of camouflaging itself with pond debris as donning a "sleek suit [that] measures less than an inch." Duckweed ("A Small Green Riddle") is a "water-carpet" that grows "daughters like ears." This plant is "no bigger than a splatter of paint." All the poems are illustrated with lovely colored woodcuts and accompanied by additional scientific information. If the wider world of the ocean is your topic, students who heed the poet's invitation to "Push away from the stillness of the nut-brown land" ("Song of the Boat"), will experience the sea and its creatures through the poems in Kate Coombs's *Water Sings Blue: Ocean Poems* (2012) These poems, as the collection's title suggests, sing in dazzling images of ocean life. Many of the poem titles themselves are metaphors. The poet goes "shopping" in a tide pool, confident that "They carry everything there—" ("Tide Pool Shopping"). The jellyfish is a "prim bell jar / with ruffled rim" ("Jellyfish Kitchen"), "free-floating noodles / escaped from a dish" ("Not Really Jelly"), and a "kimono trailing" ("Jellyfish"). The octopus is an author who "autographs the water / with a single word—/ good-bye" ("Octopus Ink"). The shark "circles and stares / with a broken-glass grin" ("Shark"), while the hermit crab ("Frank Hermit") is a realtor who presents readers with his card as he describes the various shell homes in his listings ("Ocean Realty"). Both books offer so much to savor, enjoy, and think about as students encounter life in the water in these unique ways.

Young and older students as well will enjoy the poems in Amy Sklansky's *Out of This World: Poems and Facts about Space* (2012) since the easy-to-understand poems suitable for the young are supplemented by more detailed information to satisfy curious older students. The poems begin with a blast off into space, reveal what space travel is like, and what can be seen in the heavens. In the striking poem, "After Blastoff," the poet describes Earth from the space travelers' window as the rocket moves further and further away: a "basketball / baseball / golfball / marble." The Big Dipper is a "Great water sipper, / Scooping up / The night" ("Stargazing"), and the moon is described at various stages of hunger. When it is but a sliver, it is hungry, while the full moon is well fed ("Hungry Moon"). The text invites students to consider their own space travel as well. After describing what some astronauts brought into space, the poem "Packing for the Moon" asks, "What / would you pack?" Finally, the poem "What If" asks readers to imagine what kinds of things aliens living on a newly discovered planet would do.

The poems in Janet S. Wong's *Twist: Yoga Poems* (2007) do much more than describe sixteen yoga poses. Using metaphor and imagery, the poet helps readers understand the spirit and feeling of each pose in addition to how it should be performed. "Breath is a broom / sweeping your insides." For the "Triangle" pose, she writes, "My body is a puzzle of triangles. / The lines are invisible / but straight and strong." "Cobra . . . lifts herself higher, / to dry out her heart." The children pictured doing the poses represent different ethnic groups, and all of them are wearing Indian clothing. This is an excellent book to use when some calming is in order, and it will help children see their bodies in creative ways.

Tracie Vaughn Zimmer's *Steady Hands: Poems about Work* (2009) features poems about such occupations as entrepreneur, park ranger, dog walker, programmer, surgeon, librarian, and many more. It is the perfect book to use with older students considering different careers, and will provide them with some interesting images. In the poem "Fisherman" (9), the tackle box is "a false candy store / for foolish fish." The "Welder" (16) is a "knight preparing for battle," and the "Florist" (36) studies the "rainbow of blooms" in her refrigerator, among them "elegant iris in purple gowns." As she arranges her flowers, "Hope bursts / from the palms / of her hands." A funnier celebration of different professions that will appeal to younger students is J. Patrick Lewis's *The Underwear Salesman and Other Jobs for Better or Verse* (2009), which begins by telling readers there are many jobs "at the occupation salad bar!" The butcher describes himself in both word and picture as pieces of meat: "I'm a guy / Named Sloppy Joe / In my prime / Rib (as you know). / My eye is round, / My butt is lean, / I operate a / Guillotine." The "Poet" exercises words "til they learn / A song to sing, a phrase to turn." But what happens when these various professionals die? Well, they need a tombstone, of course, and the poems in J. Patrick Lewis's *Once upon a Tomb* (2006) provide some hilarious inspiration. Filled with word play and puns, these poems will cause children to consider the humor in some professions and ponder how to express that creatively in verse. In a poem entitled "Fortune Teller," Lewis simply writes: "Here lies." It would be fun for students to research professions or jobs that they've never heard of before and then to write tombstone sayings for each.

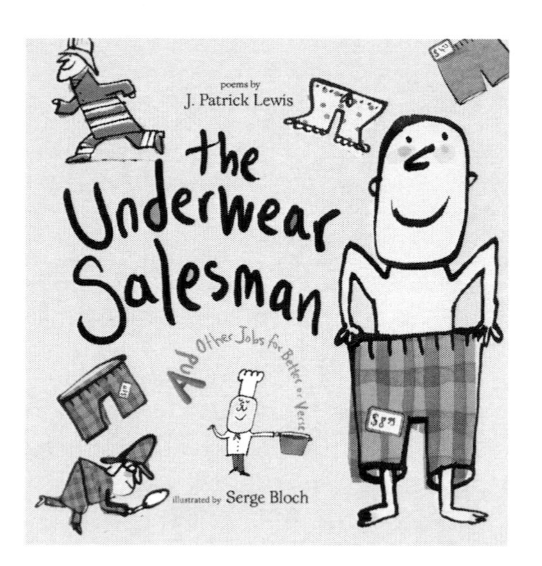

Older children who feel poetry is not for them may well change their minds when they hear some of the poems in *Hip Hop Speaks to Children: A Celebration of Poetry with a Beat* (Giovanni, 2008). They may even want to get up and move to the beat of some of these delightful poems, especially when they hear the thirty powerful performances by some very famous poets on the accompanying CD. In Jacqueline Woodson's "Hip Hop Rules the World" (2), a young person rejoices because Ms. Marcus said, "of course rap is poetry! / One of the most creative forms." In "Aloneness" (4–5), Gwendolyn Brooks writes about two kinds of aloneness: one that means loneliness, which "never has a bright color" and aloneness that is "delicious," "Almost like a red small apple that is cold." After enjoying the poem, form the students into small groups and ask them to discuss times when being alone feels good and times when it feels bad. After they have made lists that include both kinds of aloneness, bring them together to share their work. Next, as a class, select one kind of aloneness from each list, create a metaphor for each one and write them on the board. For example, if they describe a lonely situation as coming home from school alone to an empty house, they might create a metaphor such as, "loneliness is the key to an empty house." If they consider reading by themselves a good kind of aloneness, they might create a metaphor such as, "aloneness is a good book on a rainy day." When the class has a clear understanding of how these metaphors are created, return the students to their groups so they can come up with metaphors for other situations on their lists. An extension of this activity might be for the groups to write a rap poem for one of their metaphors. They could also work with the music teacher to create music to go with it or choose music they feel is appropriate for their poem. Would they like to perform it as a rap?

Written supposedly by Mrs. Mertz's sixth grade class (but really by Joyce Sidman), *This Is Just to Say* (2007), the title a play on the William Carlos Williams poem about purloined plums, is a poignant collection of apology poems to various people and animals both at home and in school and response poems from the recipients of those apologies. There is so much that is wonderful about this collection, not just because of the language and images the poems contain, but also because of their powerful emotional content. Students will surely be able to identify with many of the situations, which range from taking things without permission, to accidentally breaking treasured objects, to speaking unkindly to someone. In "The Black Spot" (15), Carrie says that a

"nugget of darkness" within her made her stab her sister with a pencil. In "Ode to Slow-Hand" (45), a poem of pardon to the classmate who inadvertently caused the class lizard's death, the lizard's skin is "rough green cloth," its tongue "lightning's flicker." Bao Vang reaches across "the river of forgiveness" to open her forgiving arms to her friend Mai Lee ("River of Forgiveness," 42). Savoring these poems, written in a variety of poetic forms, might readily spark a similar project with some students writing apologies while others write responses of forgiveness. Are there staff members in the school who deserve apologies? Friends? Even the neighborhood for littering its streets or the planet for not caring sufficiently for its resources?

A Unit on Birds (Or Any Other Member of the Animal Kingdom)

Most curricula require extended study of different kinds of animals as students move through the grades. In this section, we feature "birds" as an example and provide descriptions of several poetry books about birds along with an activity that illustrates how poetry can help students think deeply and creatively about these creatures. But whether your students are researching mammals, fish, insects, reptiles, or any other member of the animal kingdom, you can find a variety of stand-alone collections as well as relevant poems in recent anthologies you can use in a similar way. See the separate bibliography at the end of the chapter for a listing of a variety of animal poetry books too numerous to discuss at length here, but that are, nevertheless, highly recommended.

In her lovely poem, "Oystercatchers on Parade," Jane Yolen (In *Birds of a Feather*, 2011, 21) compares these wading birds to "windup toys." She continues,

> All we see is orange bill, orange bill, orange bill
> A signal lamp, a traffic cone,
> A poster for a chemical spill,

Her *An Egret's Day* (2010) contains fourteen poems, most of them filled with simile and metaphor, about this regal bird. "The Great Egret's wings / are like fresh sheets / hung out upon a line" ("Great Egret," 9). The egret is "an arrow" ("Egret in Flight," 12), "his own Laundromat" ("Preening Egret," 15), and has "plumes of Belgian lace" ("Plumes," 16).

Douglas Florian calls the hummingbird a "helicopter of a bird" ("The Hummingbird," 14) and, in another poem, provides us with an unusual view of an egret: "On morning tide / An egret sat / And gave the beach / A feathered hat." ("The Egret," 6) in his book of poems about birds entitled *On the Wing* (2000).

What is so wonderful about Michael J. Rosen's *The Cuckoo's Haiku and Other Birding Poems* (2009) is that he manages to create such powerful images in just three lines of poetry for the different birds he sees during each of the four seasons. In writing about the American goldfinch perched in a tree overlooking yellow flowers, for example, he writes:

> above gold jonquils
> feeding finches stacked like coins
> April's alchemy

The collection is taken from the author's field notebook, and his cursive jottings appear along with the poems and Stan Fellows's stunning watercolor illustrations. The appearance of this notebook conveys an important message for students: Carry a small pad with you (or jot notes on Evernotes on your smartphone) at all times. You never know when a sight you capture in brief jottings can turn into a powerful piece of writing.

Deborah Ruddell combines humor and fantasy in her poems featuring twenty-two different birds in *Today at the Bird Café*. She calls cardinals "stoplights," "a flame from a dragon," and even "a Brazilian sunset" ("The Cardinal") and describes the hummingbird as "covered all in sequins" ("Hummingbird Search").

Older students will be fascinated by the poems that comprise a continuous journal about an extraordinary event: a hummingbird builds a nest in the potted ficus tree on poet Kristine O'Connell George's back patio. She and her family watch the process of building, laying and hatching eggs, and teaching the young to fly over two months. George recounts every step of the process in lyrical poems that are enhanced by Barry Moser's beautiful watercolor illustrations (*Hummingbird Nest: A Journal of Poems*, 2004). The mother bird, a "pixie tidbit" ("Visitor") sits patiently, a "gentle captain / of [her] cobweb ship" ("Rainy Evening") waiting for her eggs to hatch. When, finally, the babies are airborne along with their mother, all three dazzle the family with their "magicking all day long" ("New Visitors"). An extensive author's note provides more information about hummingbirds and a bibliography of books for both younger and older readers. George's close observation of these birds over many weeks and writing about what she saw and heard, a project if you will, is a fine catalyst for students' engagement in a lengthy learning project. It is only when they live with a subject over time that students can examine it from all sides, think about their learning, discover unique ways to talk and write about it, and even move beyond to new ideas that this learning may engender.

The Florida Everglades is the lavish habitat Sue Van Wassenhove has chosen to describe through poems paired with her lovely quilts in *The Seldom-Ever-Shady Glades* (2008), focusing mainly on its diverse bird population. In "Standoff" (11), Wassenhove describes the quick-witted heron that views other birds as a "too handy buffet" for the alligator, betrayed by the "surfaced periscopes" that reveal his gray form beneath the water. And so, rather than stay and fish, he "spreads his wings and flies away." In "Professor Heron" (12) she dresses the great blue heron in the garb of a university scholar, complete with "slicked-back hairpiece," and "mottled cravat" that hides his "bony neck," and a "gray tweed jacket / with rusty academic shoulders and elbows." "Night Cousins" (32) calls the black-crowned heron a "strutting butler, black and white" and his cousin, the yellow-crowned heron as "spruced up in his best / flamboyant feather cloak and vest." The poet provides additional information on each of the animals and urges readers to be alert to the sky above and the waters and grasses below so as to catch sight of the wondrous creatures she describes, for "If you don't attend their thronging, / know the world will turn without you" ("Bird Watching," 30–31). Discuss how the quilt illustrations in the book complement the poems. What symbols or metaphors do the students see in the quilts? Obtain some books about well-known quilts, or better still, visit a museum that has quilts on display, and study them. Before reading explanations of the quilters' intent, what do the students see in the symbols and figures on the quilts? Is it possible to collect scraps and make a class quilt related to the study of a particular animal species? Is there a local quilter who might be available to offer advice and expertise? Divide the students into small groups, each group being responsible for a particular square. The groups should make a list of the particular animal features they wish to represent in their square and then discuss how they will do so. Such discussions guarantee that the group will have to consider its subject far more closely than they might have by simply writing a report. Display the finished quilt in the school lobby or library—possibly along with some original poems the students have written to accompany it.

Judy Sierra's *Antarctic Antics: A Book of Penguin Poems* (2003) is a collection of humorous poems about emperor penguins that provide a good deal of information about the lives and feeding habits of these birds. They "slurp squadrons of fish" ("Mother Penguin's Vacation"), try to steer clear of the "Suka Bird," a "two-legged pest," and live among "skyscraping icebergs" in their frozen land.

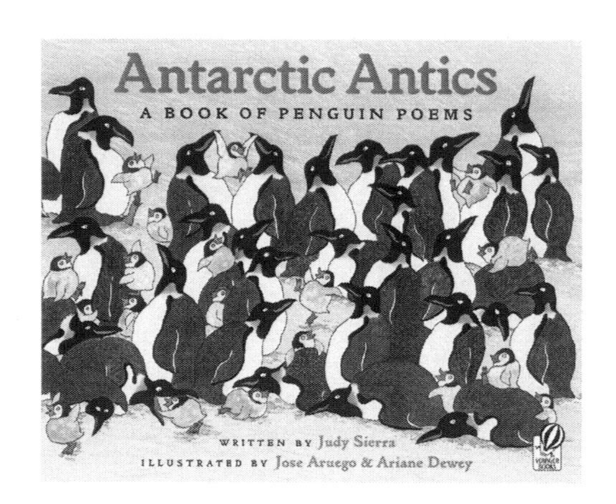

While it is currently out of print, Eileen Spinelli's *Feathers: Poems about Birds* (2004) is readily available in libraries and well worth finding. There are poems about twenty-seven different birds and back matter containing additional facts about them. Spinelli calls the woodpecker a "feathered alarm" ("Wake Up," 4), and the goldfinch a "roller-coaster bird" ("Goldfinch," 15). "penguins fly / through / watersky" ("Water-Wings," 11) and the nighthawk soars in the night sky, "its wings a flight of / lullabies" ("Nighty-Night," 37).

While not poetry, two fine books would make wonderful additions to a poetry unit on birds. (In fact, combining other texts with poetry during a unit of study is always a good idea.) Rita Gray's *Have You Heard the Nesting Bird?* (2014) is a poem story featuring different bird calls in contrast to the silent robin, who suppresses her call while she sits on her nest. An interview with the mother robin enables readers to learn much about birds' nesting habits, and the book itself introduces them to many different birds. Melissa Stewart's *Feathers: Not Just for Flying* (2014) describes all the different ways birds use their feathers. While students might have considered them very ordinary parts of a bird's anatomy, they will learn that feathers are quite amazing indeed.

After enjoying several of these books about birds for some time, pick out particular images / metaphors and talk about how the poets created them. Be certain students understand that a metaphor connects two objects that are not literally alike and creates a meaningful new image or idea—as the "feathered alarm" example earlier represents the woodpecker as an alarm clock because of the noise its beak makes rapidly tapping tree bark early in the morning. Then return to the particular birds students have been studying. Review the characteristics of these birds: they have feathers, are hatched from eggs, and so on. What do they eat? How do they build their nests? What do adults and young look like? What are their most prominent features—a special beak, vibrant colors, elaborate tail, and so on? Either orally or in groups, create metaphors for different phases of the birds' life cycles: hatching, appearance, gathering materials for a nest, how they fly or obtain food, where they live, and so on. Students will have to take what they know and apply it so that the connections they make result in a new image that truly reflects what the bird is like or how it lives. Different groups or pairs might write about the same bird and then compare their work. Or each group or pair can read its metaphor aloud and have the class decide which bird is being described. Students might wish to combine the work of the different groups into an illustrated book of metaphors.

Dare to Dream . . . Change the World (Title of a Poetry Book Edited by Jill Corcoran): Poems that Tell a Story

There are several books of poetry for children that tell the story of an important event, a life, a relationship. These collections are powerful accompaniments to history or social studies units, biography study, or even creating characters for a story. Many of these story poems feature people who took risks and kept pushing on even when those around them said it was useless. One such collection bears the title of this section: *Dare to Dream . . . Change the World* (2012), edited by Jill Corcoran. The poems, their accompanying biographical information, and related poetry focus on "people who invented something, stood for something, said something, who defied the naysayers and not only changed their own lives, but the lives of people all over the world" (Jacket flap). David L. Harrison's "Nicholas Cobb" tells how the four-year-old, disturbed by the sight of people living under a bridge, was so distressed that ten years later, he was able to convince people to donate enough money to buy coats for those in need. In "Jonas Salk Poem," Elaine Magliaro puts these words in the famous doctor's mouth: "I would be a problem solver, / Find a way / To vanquish the unseen foe—/ A virus crippling many." There are poems about Christa McAuliffe, Temple Grandin, and so many other world-changers. Corcoran's poem, "Dare to Dream" opens the book. "Dreams whisper / Crystalize / Grow, cell by cell / Thought by thought / Transforming / Transfixing." Students can take Corcoran's challenge to heart by daring to confront a local problem in their school or neighborhood or to make life better for a person or group and grow a solution "thought by thought." Brainstorm ideas together as a class or ask students to work in groups. Make a list of issues or problems and prioritize it so that one issue stands out as something the students would like to work on. Research what is currently being done about the issue, if anything. Can the students add something to make the solution more effective? Subtract something to make it more efficient? How will they put their plan into action?

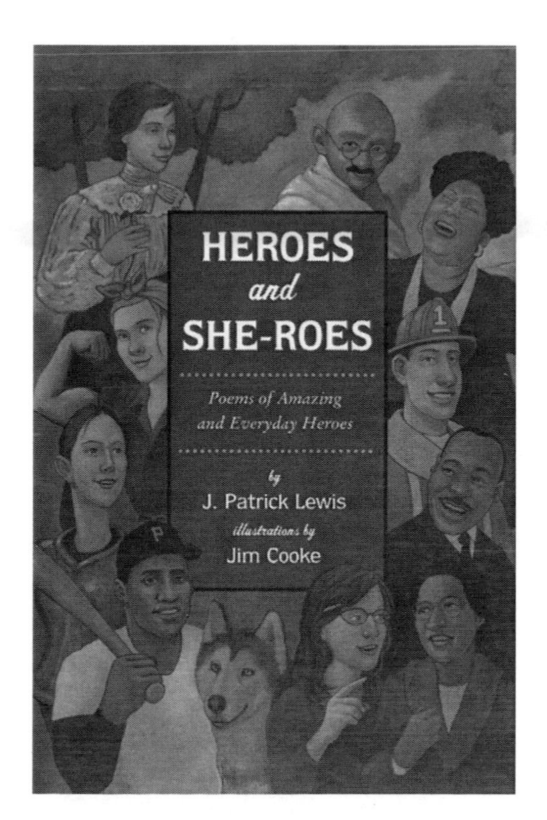

J. Patrick Lewis's *Heroes and She-Roes: Poems of Amazing and Everyday Heroes* (2005) is a collection of poems written in a similar vein. Of the unknown person who stood before the Chinese tank in Tiananmen

Square, Lewis writes, "Suppose we call him Courage, / Defiance-to-the-Bone," ("The Unknown Rebel"). He calls baseball great, Roberto Clemente "Unofficial Ambassador to Home Plate" and "Emperor of Extra Bases, Owner of the Rifle Arm." Students will surely be inspired by these poems. As an extension, they might research other people in similar fields, or even child heroes and she-roes.

For older students studying civil rights, the Civil War, the Klu Klux Klan, and the abolition movement, Elizabeth Alexander's and Marilyn Nelson's *Miss Crandall's School for Young Ladies & Little Misses of Color* (2007) is a fine extension. In twenty-one sonnets, the poets tell the heroic story of Prudence Crandall who opened a school for African American girls in Canterbury, CT, in 1833. The townspeople were enraged and engaged in many acts of vandalism including poisoning the school's well water and setting fire to the place to drive Crandall and her pupils out. The poets call Crandall's mother's illiteracy a "death" ("Family," 14) and "an uneducated mind . . . a clenched fist / that can open, like a bud, into a flower" ("Fire from the Gods," 19). Another excellent book is Ntozake Shange's *We Troubled the Waters* (2009), a collection of poems about the indignities and persecution suffered by African Americans in the segregated South and the people who went against the tide to right these wrongs. In "Where I Live," the poet calls the homes inhabited by the poor "shotgun houses" because there were so many drafts "you could shoot straight / through them." "Roadkill" is the title of a poem in which she describes how African Americans were viewed: "we aint people / we animals / roadkill." She calls the "venom & hatred" a "stench" that accompanies the aromas of food served at the lunch counters where "WHITES ONLY" were served in "Sittin Down Is Standin Up." J. Patrick Lewis's *When Thunder Comes: Poems for Civil Rights Leaders* (2013) contains poems that celebrate seventeen people who fought for equal rights for all people, who saw the wrongs described in Shange's verses, and worked to right them. In "The Slugger," Josh Gibson, who was later entered into the Baseball Hall of Fame, is called "A tower in the tarnished game" that had refused to hire him. Mohandas Gandhi is called "The Voice of the Voiceless" in a poem of that name. In "The Journalist," Chinese American activist Helen Zia's pen is a "fine and fearless sword" that opens doors "for which there are no keys."

J. Patrick Lewis's *The Brothers' War: Civil War Voices in Verse* (2007) is a moving collection of poems that tells the story of the Civil War from the differing points of view of those involved. It is illustrated with archival photographs. There are author notes on each of the poems as well. "White Nightmare" (21) is a poem in the voice of a runaway slave, who describes the corn fields through which he is making his flight to freedom: "Cracked jackets of field corn bake . . . Tallboys." Sherman's march was "a nail in the coffin of / Surrender" (I Can make Georgia Howl," 25). The powerful images in these poems and the accompanying photographs will bring home to students studying this period the human cost of war.

Two exquisite poetry books tell musical stories, and what makes them so exceptional is that the beat of the poems convey the message the poems express. The poems in Marilyn Nelson's *Sweethearts of Rhythm* (2009) are about the interracial all-girl swing band that toured the United States from 1937 to 1946. Each of the poems is about a member of the band, and it is written in the voice of the instrument that musician played, while the accompanying watercolor and collage art depicts aspects of the time: Rosie the Riveter, Japanese internment camps, among others. The author and illustrator both provide

lengthy notes, and students can go to http://www.youtube.com/watch?v=94fcqEkPmSk and http://www.youtube.com/watch?v=tpNjAmQmq90 to see and hear the band play. Arnold Adoff's *Roots and Blues: A Celebration* (2011) recounts the history of the blues from its roots in slavery to famous blues performers. In the rhythms of Adoff's poems we can hear the whip's lash, the cries of street peddlers, and the soulful voices of the blues singers. For example, in the poem "Kansas City" (70), about Big Joe Turner, Adoff places his words to emphasize the wailing notes of the Blues. He introduces spaces to slow us down to a slow moan:

> Wailing when
> it goes:
> so
> so sad,

Both books exemplify for older students ways to tell a story they might never have considered: write in the voice of an instrument? Allow your spacing to become part of the story? Perhaps they can take up the challenge to write poetry in the voices of whatever persons/things they are studying and craft their poems to express the characteristics of their subjects.

What is the area around it like on the day a volcano erupts? How do the creatures living there react? Lisa Peters's poems in *Volcano Wakes Up!* (2010), tell the story of just such a day in an innovative way: from five alternating viewpoints: ferns, a road, a lava cricket, the sun, the moon, and the volcano itself. The ferns uncurl in the early morning "when / Fire-maker / sleeps / late" ("Ferns"). The road "Buckle[s] up / For safety" ("Small Black Road").

All of the poems in Kristine O'Connell George's *Emma Dilemma: Big Sister Poems* (2011) are written in the voice of an older sister and tell the story of her sometimes exasperating, always interesting, and once even scary relationship with her younger sister. Emma's antics turn her sister's sneaker into "a sports-shoe car / loaded with rock people" ("Late for School," 13); cause secrets to come out "in one enormous / Tattletale Explosion" ("Snooping," 25), and turn dinner time into "Silverware clink time" ("Telling Time," 33). These funny yet poignant poems could be models for young middle grade students who wish to write about siblings or friends.

Joyce Carol Thomas tells the story of her family's move from Oklahoma to California in 1948 in her collection entitled *In the Land of Milk and Honey* (2012). The title itself is a metaphor for California, the family's destination as they set off on a train in the first poem and look over their new land at the edge of the Pacific in the last one. The strawberries in the land of milk and honey are "heaven in your mouth."

The desert snake they see from the train window "is a pen / writing calligraphy / on the paper-dry earth." Talk about this picture book poem with the students and the unusual ways in which Thomas writes about the sights and sounds she and her family experience on their journey. Can they think of different ways to describe what they see on the walk to school or from the windows of the school bus?

Poems That Stretch Thinking

In "Mouse?" (In *Rhymes for Annie Rose*, 2006) Shirley Hughes asks youngsters to ponder something that they may never have considered before, though they may have heard and recited "Hickory, Dickory, Dock" many times:

Tick, tock, dickory dock,
Where is the mouse
Who ran down the clock?

The rest of the poem suggests several places the mouse might have gone. Do the students have other suggestions for where that mouse went? Why do they think their suggestions are possible? Just as Shirley Hughes asked questions in her poem, encourage the children to do the same. Creative, divergent thinkers go through life wondering about what they see and hear and learn. Share other familiar rhymes with the class and model some questions these rhymes might elicit. For example, "Why did the spider sit down beside Little Miss Muffet? "or "Why did Jack jump over the candlestick?" What questions do the children have about these or other rhymes?

Mary Ann Hoberman's poem "I Like Old Clothes" first appeared in 1976. Thankfully, it has resurfaced as a picture book (2012) with new illustrations featuring a young girl and her little brother gleefully trying on and playing with old clothes. The poem is bouncy and alliterative and will surely tickle young listeners, but it will also afford them an opportunity to enlarge their thinking. Speaking in the voice of the little clothes lover in the poem, the poet muses, "Clothes, / I wonder who wore you before you were mine? / Was she light-haired or dark-haired, seven or nine? / Did you make her look awful or make her look fine?" Share the poem and the illustrations with the children and ask them to answer the little girl's questions about who might have previously worn the clothes. What activities might they have engaged in while wearing them? Have their own parents ever given away their clothes when they became too small? Who do they think will use those clothes next?

Avis Harley's *Sea Stars: Saltwater Poems* (2006) is a model of creative thinking. In an unusual twist, the pictures came first rather than the reverse, and inspired Harley's ingenious poems. Not only did she form an idea of what to write about by viewing these beautiful photographs, but her thinking also went even deeper to consider what particular poetic form would be most suited to the images. The poet explains,

"Looking at the photograph of a couple of starfish, I immediately saw two sumo wrestlers locked in combat. Sumo wrestling is an ancient Japanese sport, and haiku is a very old Japanese poetic form, so it seemed a natural partnership to combine these two in the poem "Two sumo wrestlers" (Introduction, 5). To accompany a picture of a beluga whale and her calf swimming together, Harley writes "Side by Side" (7) as a list poem consisting of several questions the calf might ask its mother: "How big will I be? / Will you always be here / swimming with me?" Filled as well with striking metaphors and images, the poems in this collection can become the underpinning of an interesting and thought-provoking activity for older students. Enjoy the poems together. Talk about the different poetic forms the poet employs: rhyming couplets, haiku, list poems, acrostics, concrete poems, and so on. Are there rules to follow for each form? With the students' help, collect photographs relevant to a topic the class is studying. The Internet can be a rich source of such photographs, especially for historical periods. After choosing the most interesting pictures from those gathered, distribute one or two to students working in pairs or groups. Ask them to proceed with these steps:

1. View each photograph carefully. If there are people in the picture, what might they be saying or thinking? If creatures, what are they doing? What is happening in the scene?
2. After a good deal of conversation, write a paragraph about each picture. The paragraph should tell what is happening as well as describe the people, creatures, objects, and scene. This information will eventually be incorporated into their final poem.
3. Discuss what images or metaphors they might use to express the information they have gleaned from each picture. For example, in the picture of a Pacific spiny lumpsucker, the fish is looking at the viewer face-on with its big, round eyes. Harley writes, "Dinner-Plate Eyes, good morning to you" ("The Shy One," 9).
4. Discuss what poetic form best suits the picture and what they have written about it. Why is that form particularly suitable?
5. Finally, incorporate their writing and ideas into a poem.
6. Share the poems, form them into a book, and add it to the other books the class is using for its topic or unit study. Present them to another class studying the same topic via slides or invite that class to visit a wiki. Go to http://wikispot.org/Create_a_wiki for help in creating a wiki.
7. As an additional step that will enrich their learning, the students can research more information about the subject of their picture, incorporate it into the paragraph they have previously written, and add it as additional back page information in their book, as Harley provided more information on the sea creatures in her poems. They might also wish to design an innovative cover.

Poems That Stretch Imagination: Making the Impossible Possible

"[O]nly the poet / With wings to his brain" can ride the majestic Pegasus, "stallion of heaven" writes Eleanor Farjeon ("Pegasus" in Morris's *The Barefoot Book of Classic Poems*, 2006, 60–61). Enjoying the following poems and others like them may give wings to children's imaginations so that they, too, can create fanciful worlds or even develop ideas that will result in better lives for many in previously undreamed of ways.

A Children's Treasury of Poems (2008) discussed earlier for the wonderful metaphors it contains, also has many poems that usher children into a fanciful world. "The Man in the Moon" tries to take a drink of milk from the Big Dipper. An elf uproots a toadstool and uses it as an umbrella, much to the consternation of the Dormouse asleep under it ("The Elf and the Dormouse"). A young girl hosts some cats for tea ("The Cats Have Come to Tea"); a special dream fairy waves her silver wand over the heads of sleeping children to bring them dreams filled with fountains of "fairy fish" and "talking birds with gifted tongues"

("The Dream Fairy"); and children turn a flight of stairs into a ship upon which they "sail along for days and days" ("A Good Play").

When the narrator of George Shannon's poem, "Dancing in the Breeze" (in *Busy in the Garden*, 2006, 18–19), goes into the garden to pick peas, he discovers a cast of dancing vegetables: peppers polka, beans boogie, squash square dances, chard does the cha-cha, and the watermelon waltzes.

The Golden Books, treasures of children's literature, came on the scene in the 1940s and have delighted generations of children. Now, a collection of five of these books and some selections from the *Golden Song Book*, all illustrated by Mary Blair, have been compiled in a beautiful edition entitled *Mary Blair Treasury of Golden Books* (2012). One of the books, *The Golden Book of Little Verses*, offers poems that accompany young children into the delicious world of make-believe where all things impossible surely exist for those who see with the eyes of the imagination. In this world, there is a "little Rabbit-Town, / With rabbits marching up and down" ("Town," 78); where "A little worm went down to see / His cousins, underground. . . . And passed dirt cakes around." ("Worm," 81); where a Froggie likes to bathe in a bathtub, not in a brook ("Frog," 85); and where a blanket "is a den / And we are bears." or "a cave / All made of ice." or "a hole / And we are mice" ("Game, 88). What objects in the classroom can become something else in the children's imaginations? What are some things the pencils in a box, the toys on a shelf, could say to each other?

Would an owl really marry a pussycat? In Edward Lear's world of nonsense, such a union is definitely possible. Anne Mortimer (2006) has created a beautifully illustrated version of Lear's *The Owl and the Pussycat* featuring lush vegetation, lovely borders, and a realistically depicted owl and pussycat sailing away over rolling waves to be married by an accommodating turkey, followed by celebratory dancing by the light of an observant moon. If you can obtain a copy of James Marshall's (1998) more humorous illustrations of the poem, youngsters might enjoy comparing the merits of both interpretations. Older children can revel in more of Lear's imaginary world in a compilation of his work "masterminded" by Daniel Pinkwater (*His Shoes Were Far Too Tight*, 2011). The poems feature a Pobble minus his toes; Jumblies who go to sea in a sieve, a Quangle Wangle with a hat "a hundred and two feet wide," and much more. "Come inside this book and find poetry to feed your mind, a place to see the world anew. Let your imagination stretch" invites its creators.

The title of Jeff Foxworthy's collection, *Silly Street* (2010), says it all. Young children who walk down this street via his poems will find imaginary sights galore. On "Silly Street" they will see "the flying squirrel circus / And pink elephant races." "The Odds and Ends Market" has "a big pony / That eats fried baloney" and "Phil ['s] "Fluffy and Light" restaurant has made only one pancake that "took four hundred people / A whole year to eat it." Can the students create an imaginary school where all sorts of strange things happen? An imaginary airport? A park?

From its very title, readers know that Lenny Hort's *Tie Your Socks and Clap Your Feet* (2000) contains poems about a topsy-turvy world in which anything is possible. In Hort's poems, the basement is upstairs while one must go "downstairs to the attic ("Our New House," 4–5), "five's an even letter" ("Five Hats," 11), "desert . . . days are green and wet" ("Down in the Desert," 12), snowy days are hot ("Broccoli Pie," 20), and oranges are purple ("A Pair of Purple Oranges," 13).

Paul Janeczko entitles the introduction to the collection of poems he selected for *Hey, You! Poems to Skyscrapers, Mosquitoes, and Other Fun Things* (2007) "Imagination on the Loose" (3) for it surely takes quite an imagination to write poems to things like pens, paper, a maggot, hat hair, and so many other objects and places addressed in this book. Sometimes two poems to the same or related creature or environment appear opposite each other. But whatever their position in the collection, all of them are fun and guaranteed to spark imaginations as well as present some poignant images. In "Little Blanco River" (12), Naomi Shihab Nye tells the river it has a "smooth shale skull" and that it "square dance[s] with boulders." Norman MacCaig tells "Toad" (13) it looks "like a purse" that squeezes under the door and into his house. "I love you for . . . / crawling like a Japanese wrestler," he continues, and, carrying the toad outside in his "purse hand," thanks it for being a "tiny radiance in a dark place." Marjorie Maddox ("Warning to a Fork,"21) warns her fork to "steer clear of the electric disposal, / . . . mortuary of soup spoons and knives." And in "Hat Hair" 925), Joan Bransfield Graham scolds her hat for giving her hair "a sweat band, / a halo-bent,". Ask your students to follow Janeczko's advice: "As you read these poems, let your imagination go. You might even want to get out your pencil and paper and write a poem of your own. Give it a try!" (3).

Since there are some poems about birds in the collection, Jack Prelutsky's hilarious *Behold the Bold Umbrellaphant and Other Poems* (2006) could readily have been discussed in the bird section earlier. But it appears here because of the outlandish and unique ways in which the poet views these animals. Although the names he gives the creatures about which he writes are pure fantasy, they somehow aptly fit the physical characteristics of each creature. There are "Ballpoint Penguins" (9), an "Eggbeaturkey," and "Hatchickens" among the birds. The octopus is a "Clocktopus" (18), while the tortoise is a "Circular Sawtoise" (16). More impossible animals and happenings appear in the poems in Prelutsky's *I've Lost My Hippopotamus* (2012). There are poems about such fantastical creatures as "The Thopp" (75), "The Insufferable Asparagoose" (93), "The Spotted Pittapotamus" (113), and "The Alpacalculator. Readers can travel "On the Road to Undiscovered" (64), or perform such feats as "turn a butterfly / Into a loaf of bread. / . . . catch a kangaroo / With nothing but a spoon" or "sing a song so loud / You'd hear it on the moon" ("I Can Juggle Bowling Balls," 36). If you can obtain more than one copy of either or both of these books, have the students enjoy the poems in groups as they discuss the title choices the poet has made. Poems and illustrations go hand-in-hand in helping students discover the relationship between the animal and Prelutsky's titles. Can they think of different fantastical names and state why their choices are similarly appropriate? Coming up with unique names that fit particular creatures would be a great activity for the bird unit discussed earlier

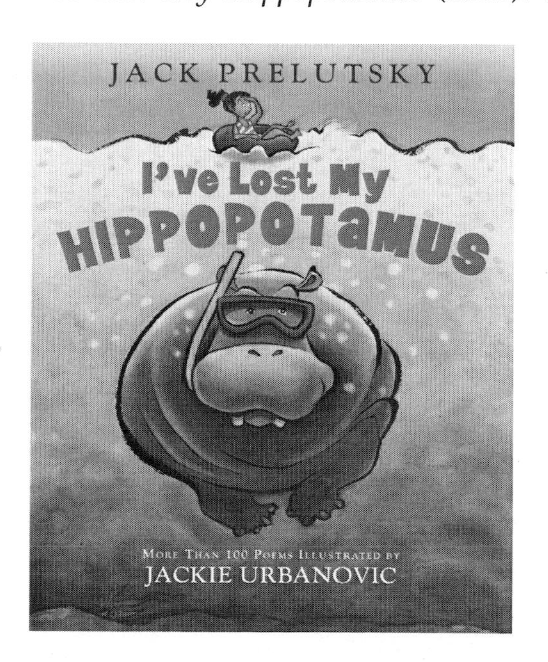

or for any animal study in the curriculum. Another Prelutsky collection whose name announces preposterous fun is *The Frogs Wore Red Suspenders* (2005). The poet has people and animals engaging in shenanigans that stretch credulity in different locales. In Indianapolis (25), for example, "An elephant perched on a sycamore tree, / sipping warm milk through an oversize straw . . . / In Indianapolis, what did we do? / We danced on the green with a blue kangaroo." In his *Stardines Swim High Across the Sky and Other Poems* (2012), Prelutsky again combines an animal name with another object to create a poem about creatures that while preposterous, do most often exhibit some of the attributes of that animal. For example, in the poem "Stardines" (8) from which the collection's title comes, the creatures "brightly shine as they glide by. / In giant schools." In an activity a bit different from the one suggested earlier, ask the children to create two lists: one with animal names and one with object names. Then match each animal to an object that best captures the characteristics of the animal. This is a good group activity.

In *Poem-Mobiles* (2014), J. Patrick Lewis and Douglas Florian have teamed up to create a book of poems about vehicles different from any students have ever seen. There is a "Fish Car" with scale seats (10); a "Paper Car (14); a High-Heel Car" (16–17); a "Hot Dog Car" (27); and many more. After enjoying these poems, ask students to create an advertising brochure for a car company featuring their latest line of fantastical cars. Each page of the brochure should feature a car name along with an illustration and description.

The poems in Francisco X. Alarcón's *Poems to Dream Together Poemas Para Soñar Juntos* (2011) not only celebrate the dreams he had growing up in California and Mexico, but also encourage children to dream their own dreams, "to dream on and on / and never stop dreaming" ("Dreaming Up the Future"). So much of the content of these poems is what divergent thinking is all about: "daydreaming—another way / of brainstorming ("Daydreaming"); "real questions / have no answers / just more questions" ("Questions"). In his "Family Garden" everyone in the family "take[s] time to tend / each other's dreams . . . even [the] puppy knows how / to grow bones . . . in this garden the sun shines green smiles." What are the students' dreams for themselves, their country, the planet? Do they have any suggestions, however improbable they might seem at first, for making these dreams a reality? Can they tweak each other's suggestions to make them work? Can they combine dreams to form a possible reality? Might they be interested in writing about their dreams for a better community/world to an appropriate agency or legislator to obtain some results?

Experimenting with Forms

Writing concrete poems, that is, poems in which the text takes the shape of the poem's subject or emotional content instead of being placed vertically down the page, is hardly a new idea. However, after viewing several examples of concrete poems, students may be able to come up with unique layouts for their poems in ways that fit their content. Betsy

Franco has two simple books of concrete poetry for young children: *A Curious Collection of Cats* (2009) and *A Dazzling Display of Dogs* (2011). In "Fast Al, The Retired Greyhound," for example, the text is written in a circle to resemble a circular race track, while in "Apollo at the Beach," a poem about a dog harassed by seagulls, many seagulls appear on the page, each containing parts of the text in its body (both examples from *A Dazzling Display of Dogs*). In "Tabitha's Tail" from *A Curious Collection of Cats*, the text curls within a spiraling cat's tail. John Bransfield Graham's short, simple concrete poems in *Flicker Flash* (1999, 2003) are just right for very young children. Ask them to decide why the poet has arranged the words for "Light" in a cone shape that stretches down the page, and why some words for "Days and Years" appear in the shape of an orbit. Another collection of concrete poetry for young children, Joyce Sidman's *Meow Ruff: A Story in Concrete Poetry* (2006), tells the story of a dog that leaves its house and an abandoned cat and how they meet in a park to wait out a storm. In addition to the examples of concrete poetry, the language is simply delicious. J. Patrick Lewis's *Doodle Dandies: Poems that Take Shape* (2002) will also appeal to younger children. Not only is the text in the poem "Giraffe" shaped like its subject, but Lewis also offers this wonderful image: "Tree-tall giraffe up to his neck in brown and yellow patchwork quilts."

Christy Hale's *Dreaming Up: A Celebration of Building* (2012) contains concrete poems, but it is so very much more. The book begins with a quote from Madhu Thangavelu: "If they can dream it, they can build it." And surely, after reading this book, any parent or teacher will certainly realize the value of giving children time to play, to create structures out of their imaginations using a variety of materials. Children, too, may see in their creations the foundations of even greater dreams to come. An equally powerful incentive for sharing this book and engaging students in the suggested activity that follows its description, is a study highlighted by Douglas Quenqua in his article, "Study Finds Spatial Skill Is Early Sign of Creativity" (*New York Times*, July 16, 2013, A12). Researchers from Vanderbilt University in Nashville followed 563 adults who had scored high as thirteen-year-olds, not only on the SAT, but also on the differential aptitude test, which "measures spatial relations skills, the ability to visualize and manipulate two-and-three-dimensional objects." As adults, these formerly gifted students were highly successful in the STEM fields of science, technology, engineering, and math. Because of these findings, the researchers urge that spatial ability (described by them as the "'orphan ability' for its tendency to go undetected"), as well as proficiency in math and literacy, be cultivated and tested in our schools. In *Dreaming Up: A Celebration of Building*, spatial skills are given the attention they deserve. Concrete poems in the shape of the different structures accompany illustrations of children from around the world shown building with materials such as blocks, containers, plastic rings, mud, cardboard boxes, sticks, and so on. Opposite each illustration is a photograph of an actual 20th- or 21st-century building that resembles the shape and characteristics of the children's creations. For example, this poem, printed in the shape of soft pillows leaning against each other appears below an illustration of two children whispering secrets in a cozy fort they have made by stacking and leaning sofa cushions against each other: "Soft forms / tumble / making / ever-changing / caverns, secret spaces, pillow forts." The opposite page contains a photograph of the Guggenheim Museum in Bilbao, Spain, that contains many of the leaning, curving elements of the children's construction. All the architects and buildings are identified at the end of the book. A natural extension of this incredible book for older as well as younger children is a building session using all the materials you can collect, from popsicle sticks to playing cards, to blocks.

Older students will readily relate to the opinions and trying situations expressed by the narrator of John Grandits's concrete poem collection entitled *Blue Lipstick* (2007). The words in the poem "Bad Hair Day" appear as squiggly lines emanating from a semicircular head depicted at the bottom of the page. In "Pep Rally" some of the words appear in cheerleaders' bodies. Text appears in sprays of water in "All My Important Thinking Gets Done in the Shower." What's especially interesting about these poems is that the illustrations formed by the ways in which the words are arranged are themselves metaphors. For example, in the poem "Missing," Jessie is called to task because she seems to be "totally out of it" one morning. Part of the poem is printed on a "Stupor Farms" milk container containing "2% awake" milk. All of the concrete poems in Paul Janeczko's *A Poke in the I* (2005) are very enjoyable, but one in particular will especially appeal to older students. The poem appears without a title (15), but two diagonal lines of partial words come together to look like this: >——After looking at it for a few moments, they will realize it says "merging traffic." Pair this poem with Zoran Milich's *City Signs* (2002; while meant for younger children, it is appropriate for this activity) or a similar title, divide the students into groups, and offer this challenge: study the different signs in the book and write a concrete poem to go with one or more of them. The poems should form a shape that conveys the idea of the sign. For example, a concrete poem to go with a sign for a fire extinguisher might not just form the shape of a fire extinguisher as it appears on the sign, but might express the idea of fire. After sharing the results of their work, the students may wish to make large posters of their signs and display them in the hall.

Linda Sue Park's *Tap Dancing on the Roof* (2007) is a collection of *sijo* poems, a special poetic form that originated in Korea. *Sijo* has a fixed number of syllables and usually three or six lines. But what is especially interesting for our study is that the last line always has an unexpected twist that forces the reader to look and think again. For example, in the poem "Breakfast" Park writes:

> For this meal, people like what they like, the same every morning.
> Toast and coffee. Bagel and juice. Cornflakes and milk in a white bowl.
> Or—warm, soft, and delicious—a few extra minutes in bed.

Park provides the history of the form and a bibliography for further information. And if students follow her tips for writing their own *sijo* poems, they will have to think about the subjects of their poems in ways that are surprising and different.

Anna Grossnickle Hines has combined her quilt-making skills with her talent as a poet to create three unusual and striking poetry collections. In *Pieces: A Year in Poems and Quilts* (2003), Hines pairs her quilts and poems seamlessly so that one reflects the other. For example, in her poem, "Do You Know Green?" she describes the slow awakening of color in early spring after a long winter: "Green comes . . . / tickling the tips / of twiggy tree fingers / *Psst! / Psst! Psst!*" and the accompanying quilt shows sprays of light scattering through the trees. In addition to the back pages in which Hines describes her quilting process, students will enjoy her web page, http://www.aghines.com/anna_html_pages/Quilt/piecestory.htm, in which she shows her work on this book in detail and provides follow-up activities for quilting and poetry writing. Hines uses several different poetic forms for the poems in *Peaceful Pieces: Poems and Quilts about Peace* (2011). There are poems about peace between siblings, peace in the school yard, among countries, and even the peace experienced in calming nature or in a pause on a busy day. A stunning quilt containing interconnected black and white pieces in various patterns including musical notes accompanies the poem "Dominoes" in which the poet declares "we are / connected / one to / another / to another / to another." In *Winter Lights: A Season in Poems & Quilts* (2005), Hines not only celebrates the lights of winter holidays such as Hanukkah, Christmas, Santa Lucia, and Chinese New Year, but also the lights that brighten dark winter days. She calls icicles "Star catcher[s]" ("Star Catcher") and the aurora borealis "a billowing curtain / of swirling, / swooping light" ("A Sight to See"). Enjoying the poems in any or all of these books will enable students to see and think about the seasons, peace, and light in original and exciting ways and may spark their own poetry writing. As in a previously discussed activity, quilt-making in fabric or colored paper is an excellent extension after enjoying Hines's poetry.

Cynthia Grady's beautiful poems about slavery in the United States in *I Lay My Stitches Down: Poems of American Slavery* (2012) are themselves metaphors for the many different circumstances and events that make up the story of that sad period of U.S. history just as the many squares patched together make up the story told in a quilt. She writes:

> Each poem . . . is named for a traditional quilt block and reflects a metaphorical patchwork of circumstances encountered by enslaved people in America.
>
> The poems are written in unrhymed verse, ten lines of ten syllables, to mimic the square shape of a quilt block. To reflect the three layers of a quilt, I've engaged three references in each poem: a biblical or spiritual reference, a musical reference, and a sewing or fiber reference. (Author's note)

There are fourteen poems in this collection, each one beautifully illustrated in a full page acrylic painting. Any class studying slavery or the Civil War period should experience the poems in this book.

Bob Raczka's *Lemonade and Other Poems Squeezed from a Single Word* (2011) presents students with a special challenge. Can they create poems using only the letters in the single word of their title? That's exactly what Raczka does, and this book is a fascinating foray into the word puzzles he has turned into poetry. For those who have trouble unlocking these puzzles at first, the poet provides the same poem, written conventionally, after a page turn. For "bleachers," here's what he writes:

b a

l

l

r

e

ache s

her

e

b a s

e s

c

lea r

che

ers

Conventional form: ball reaches here bases clear cheers (3–4). Students who undertake the challenge of writing these puzzle poems will not only have to become skilled at making words with a given set of letters, but they will also have to think of unique ways to describe familiar things. In the poem "bleachers" cited earlier, the poet doesn't write about what we might expect when we think of bleachers: hard benches, far above the field, and so on. He writes about bases clearing when a ball is hit that far—and then the reaction of the crowd.

In her poem, "A Valentine for Ernest Mann" (read at a poetry event), Naomi Shihab Nye writes,

> Maybe if we reinvent whatever our lives give us
> we find poems. Check your garage, the odd sock
> in your drawer, the person you almost like, but not quite.
> And let me know.

Georgia Heard has done exactly that in putting together a book of poetry written by poets who have reinvented their lives, finding poems where, at first glance, no poems could possibly exist: teacher's notes to parents, drop-down computer menus, lawn signs, calendars, titles of Van Gogh paintings, and much more. Heard's *The Arrow Finds Its Mark: A Book of Found Poems* (2012) is, indeed, a find, especially for older students. It demonstrates that we can uncover poems anywhere, and it won't take much convincing to have students scour the school, their neighborhoods, their computers, iPads, and smartphones for words they can refashion into poems of their own. In doing so, they will be seeing words that become beautiful in different and pleasing ways when they are transformed into poetry.

Can those dreaded vocabulary words be turned into poems? Absolutely in Michael Salinger's highly original collection entitled *Well Defined: Vocabulary in Rhyme* (2009). In it, he creates a poem that actually defines the meaning of vocabulary words beginning with most letters of the alphabet. A brief dictionary definition appears below each poem. "Incessant," for example, is "that dog barking at all hours of the night / that friend who always borrows money." Can older students create poems from the vocabulary connected to a unit of study or the words they are currently learning in language arts classes?

Although it is currently out of print, *Birds on a Wire* (2008) by J. Patrick Lewis and Paul B. Janeczko is readily available in libraries and well worth obtaining because it introduces a poetic form called *renga,* which can spark an enjoyable activity. The poets explain that

> A traditional **renga** is written by two or more poets. The first poet writes three lines (similar to a haiku), the second poet follows that with two lines, the first poet comes back with another three lines, then two, three, two, and so on. (Introduction)

The second poet must link his or her work in some way to the lines written by the first poet. And the poem can be just five lines written by two people, be many stanzas of five lines by the same two poets, or go on and on linking many poets. After enjoying these poems, the students might like to try their hand at writing *renga.* They can work in pairs to create a three-line / two-line poem or several five-line stanzas; or the class can work in groups of six on a single poem, each student connecting his or her lines to the preceding student's work in a three-line, two-line pattern. To take the idea even further, the students could create a wiki so that students in other classes or schools or even students in other countries can add to their *renga*.

Poetry and Art Link to Help Students See Details

In an online article entitled "Art appreciation class improves student doctors' diagnosis" (2001), Helen Pearson describes a surprising project undertaken by Irwin Braverman of Yale University. Realizing that medical students often missed the details they needed to make an accurate diagnosis, that they came to patients with preconceived notions rather than an ability to "think outside the box," he partnered with the Yale Center for British Art to provide a fine arts class for his medical students. After spending just two hours viewing and discussing a painting, the students were able to pick up clues in patient photos far more frequently than students who simply had an additional anatomy lecture. Fine arts classes are now required of all Yale medical students.

Seeing with fresh eyes, seeing details others miss, often leads to new thinking, even to innovative products. Many poets and anthologists who write for children have linked their deep observations of fine art works to poems that best express the mood or content of these works. Share some of these poetry books with your students and discuss why the authors have made these pairings. Do the students see any of the paintings or art works differently? If so, why?

Young children will enjoy the art selections Justine Rowden made when she visited the National Gallery in Washington, D.C., and the poems she wrote to accompany them for her book, *Paint Me a Poem: Poems Inspired by Masterpieces of Art* (2005). In one particularly creative poem, "So Close" written to accompany "Flowers in a Vase" by André Derain, the blossoms and stems of the flowers engage in an argument, each accusing the other of taking up too much space in the vase. In "Don't I Know You?" the poem written in response to the anonymous work, "Cat and Kittens," a mother cat asks questions of those who view the painting. Choose some art works for viewing that would enable young children to use Rowden's poetical responses as models for group poems written on a chart.

Words with Wings: A Treasury of African-American Poetry and Art (Rochelle, 2001) pairs twenty works of art by African American artists with twenty poems by African American poets. These works celebrate ordinary moments, the humiliation of prejudice, triumphs, and famous African American men and women. Carole Boston Weatherford traces 400 years of African American history by pairing period photographs and engravings with her poems in *Remember the Bridge: Poems of a People* (2002). The "bridge" to which she refers is the multitude of African American men and women who paved the way toward their People's freedom. There are bridge-builders in many fields: politics, sports, music, explorers, cowboys, quilters, and more.

Jan Greenberg (*Heart to Heart*, 2001) invited forty-three poets to write a poem in response to a work of modern art of their choice. This award-winning collection features well-known poets such as Jane Yolen, J. Patrick Lewis, X.J. Kennedy, and Kristine O'Connell George, and such famous artists as Georgia O'Keeffe, Frank Stella, Alexander Calder, Grandma Moses, and Andy Warhol. Even beyond the beauty of the poetry and art, the works prod readers to think. Gary Gildner ("A Word," 19) wants a "round word" or perhaps a square one, for "square maybe / will lead us to round." Jane Yolen urges readers to look beyond the brooch and fork owned by the couple in Grant Wood's "American Gothic" (39) to see what they could become. In "Pantoum for These Eyes" (43), Kristine O'Connell George wonders what stories the eyes in the accompanying print tell. "Look deeply, don't look away, / find their truth, discover their lies," she urges. "How would you paint a poem?" Bobbi Katz asks ("Lessons from a Painting" by Rothko, 55), while Tony Johnston ("The Bison Returns," 11) speculates, "What will I say to keep [the bison] here? / What song will I sing?" In addition to making their own discoveries in the poems and art, older students may wish to consider the questions posed by these poets. In *Side by Side: New Poems Inspired by Art from Around the World* (2008) Greenberg extends the scope of the offerings in *Heart to Heart*, and thus enlarges students' horizons, by including art and poetry from different parts of the world. The poems appear both in their original language and in English translation. Both of these books are wonderful treasures that will spark discussion and projects.

After spending considerable time with these books, it would be ideal for students to visit a museum or gallery, notebooks or smartphones in hand, to study, discuss, and write their impressions of the art they see. But since this may not be possible, it is very fortunate that museums have made their collections beautifully available to us online. In fact, viewing art works online may enable students to linger longer over the art pieces they enjoy. They can even focus on specific parts of paintings by clicking to zoom in for a closer look. Here are just a few sites, but a search of any of the museums in your area, around the country and even around the world will surely result in a site that will engage your students. The New York Metropolitan Museum of Art site, http://www.metmuseum.org, has links for children of all ages, including some videos and interactive activities. A link on the Louvre site, http://www.louvre.fr/en/oal, brings visitors to "A Closer Look" section in which several works of art are described in great detail. It's an art lesson in the classroom. If students go to http://www.mfa.org/collections/mfa-images, a link on the Museum of Fine Arts Boston website, they can zoom in on 160,000 images for detailed study. At the Art Institute of Chicago site, this link, http://www.artic.edu/aic/collections/citi/themes, enables visitors to select paintings by themes such as African art, Chicago artists, among others, and zoom in on individual pieces. The National Gallery of Art, www.nga.gov, has an interactive section for young people, a section for teachers, and much more. A natural extension of discussing the art and poetry in the books described earlier and viewing art works in other books or online, is for students to choose particular works they especially enjoy and write poems or short narratives to accompany them. If the class is studying a particular art period in art class or in the classroom, they might choose works from that period. Or they might choose works by artists who lived during a historical period they are studying. This is a fine small group activity since collaboration will help students see things they might not discover on their own. The group might wish to present their work to another class in a slide or movie presentation. Would they like to choose an appropriate piece of music as well to accompany each art work?

The poems discussed and referenced here, in keeping with the scope of this book, have been those that encourage students to look at objects and their world in new ways so that, as the poet Ralph Fletcher suggests (in *Poetry Matters: Writing a Poem from the Inside Out*, 2002) they can "get in the habit of observing the world so [they] can create [their] own pictures using words" (21); to make unlikely connections; to think imaginatively and divergently; to take risks and experiment with new forms But there is so much more to poetry for children to enjoy: delicious words bursting with alliteration and assonance; emotions and situations that perfectly express what young people are thinking and feeling. So, even while you share poems and activities that spark your students' creativity, be sure to offer them all kinds of poetry, both joyful and somber; poems that connect to what they are studying, what they are feeling, what they are wondering about. Offer them your favorite poems, those that "hold a wooden spoon of words / and whisper: / Taste" (Tracie Vaughn Zimmer, "The Poems I Like Best" in Janeczko, 2009, 13):

References

Adoff, Arnold. 2011. *Roots and Blues: A Celebration.* Illustrated by R. Gregory Christie. New York: Clarion/ Houghton Mifflin Harcourt. ISBN 978-0-547-23554-7. Adoff's poems trace the history of the Blues from its slave roots to the instrumentalists who made the music known.

Alarcón, Francisco X. 2011. *Poems to Dream Together Poemas Para Soñar Juntos.* Illustrated by Paula Barragán. New York: Lee & Low. ISBN 978-1600606571. These poems celebrate the poet's dreams growing up in California and Mexico and encourage readers to dream as well.

Alexander, Elizabeth, and Marilyn Nelson. 2007. *Miss Crandall's School for Young Ladies & Little Misses of Color.* Illustrated by Floyd Cooper. Honesdale, PA: Wordsong. ISBN 078-1-59078-456-3. In twenty-one sonnets, Alexander and Nelson tell the story of Prudence Crandall who was forced to shut down her school for African American girls in Canterbury, CT, in 1834.

Blair, Mary. 2012. Forward by John Canemaker. *Mary Blair Treasury of Golden Books.* New York: Random House. ISBN 978-0-375-87044-6. Five Golden Books and several selections from the *New Golden Song Book*, all illustrated beautifully by Mary Blair, are gathered in this new edition.

Bleck, Linda (Illus.). 2008. *A Children's Treasury of Poems.* New York: Sterling. ISBN 978-1-4027-4498-3. This illustrated collection of well-known poems by a variety of poets is printed on large board book stock and very suitable for young children.

Brown, Margaret Wise. 2012. Forward by Leonard S. Marcus. *Give Yourself to the Rain: Poems for the Very Young.* Illustrated by Teri L. Weidner. New York: Margaret K. McElderry. ISBN 978-1442460638. pb These twenty-four poems touch on things in the world of the young child.

Coombs, Kate. 2012. *Water Sings Blue: Ocean Poems.* Illustrated by Meilo So. San Francisco: Chronicle. ISBN 9788-0-8118-7284-3. This collection contains exquisite poems about the ocean and its many life forms.

Corcoran, Jill, ed. 2012. *Dare to Dream . . . Change the World*. Illustrated by J. Beth Jepson. Tulsa, OK: Kane Miller/Edc Publishing. ISBN 978-1-61067-065-4. Corcoran has paired the poems of several famous poets with biographical information to celebrate the accomplishments of brave individuals who changed the world in some way by their lives.

Davies, Nicola. 2012. *Outside Your Window: A First Book of Nature*. Illustrated by Mark Hearld. Somerville, MA: Candlewick. ISBN 978-0-7636-5549-5. This stunning book of poetry, suitable for the very young, has poems that celebrate all four seasons.

Field, Eugene W. 2008. *Wynken, Blynken, and Nod*. Illustrated by Giselle Potter. New York: Schwartz & Wade/ Random House. ISBN 978-0375841965. Potter beautifully illustrates Field's famous poem in picture book format.

Field, Eugene W. 2009. *Wynken, Blynken, and Nod*. Illustrated by David McPhail. New York: Cartwheel/ Scholastic. ISBN 978-0439921442. bb McPhail depicts the three fishermen as bunnies sailing off into the sky in this lovely book.

Fletcher, Ralph. 2002. *Poetry Matters: Writing a Poem from the Inside Out*. New York: HarperCollins. ISBN 0-06-623599-5. In very readable text, Fletcher guides students through the many phases of writing a poem.

Florian, Douglas. 2000. *On the Wing*. Boston: Sandpiper/Houghton Mifflin. ISBN 978-0152023669. Florian writes about twenty-one different birds and accompanies the poems with innovative paintings.

Florian, Douglas. 2010. *Poetrees*. New York: Beach Lane/Simon & Schuster. ISBN 978-1-4169-8672-0. Florian's poems, filled with word play and metaphor, describe many trees. He provides additional information in a "Glossatree."

Foxworthy, Jeff. 2010. *Silly Street*. Illustrated by Steve Björkman. New York: HarperCollins. ISBN 978-0-06-17652855. Paper I Can Read edition. Anything youngsters' imaginations can conjure up can be found on the extremely silly street that is the subject of these zany poems.

Franco, Betsy. 2009. *A Curious Collection of Cats*. Illustrated by Michael Wertz. Berkeley, CA: Tricycle Press. ISBN 978-1-58246-248-6. Franco's thirty-four poems capture the characteristics of their subject by the way in which they appear on the page.

Franco, Betsy. 2011. *A Dazzling Display of Dogs*. Illustrated by Michael Wertz. Berkeley, CA: Tricycle Press. ISBN 978-1-58246-343-8. Franco captures the characteristics of the dogs she writes about in the way her poems appear on the page.

George, Kristine O'Connell. 2011. *Emma Dilemma: Big Sister Poems*. Illustrated by Nancy Carpenter. New York: Clarion/Houghton Mifflin. ISBN 978-0-618-42842-7. A big sister describes the joys and trials of living with her little sister in these poems.

George, Kristine O'Connell. 2004. *Hummingbird Nest: A Journal of Poems*. Illustrated by Barry Moser. New York: Harcourt, Inc. ISBN 0-15-202325-9. The author writes a journal of poems about a hummingbird that builds a nest and tends her young on her patio.

Giovanni, Nikki, ed. 2008. *Hip Hop Speaks to Children: A Celebration of Poetry with a Beat*. Naperville, IL: Sourcebooks/Jabberwocky. ISBN 978-1-4022-1048-8. This wonderful collection of poems with a hip hop beat comes with a CD of thirty performances by well-known poets.

Grady, Cynthia. 2012. *I Lay My Stitches Down: Poems of American Slavery*. Illustrated by Michele Wood. Grand Rapids, MI: Eerdmans. ISBN 978-0-8028-5386-8. Fourteen poems contain many of the elements involved in quilt making and tell the story of slavery in the United States.

Graham, Joan Bransfield. 2003. *Flicker Flash*. Illustrated by Nancy Davis. New York: Houghton Mifflin. ISBN 0-395-90501-X. Also available in paperback from Sandpiper. ISBN 978-0618311026. These short, simple concrete poems are very suitable for young children.

Grandits, John. 2007. *Blue Lipstick: Concrete Poems*. Boston: Sandpiper/Houghton Mifflin. ISBN 978-0618851 324. pb. This collection of concrete poems features concerns and situations that will resonate with older students.

Gray, Rita. 2014. *Have You Heard the Nesting Bird?* Illustrated by Kenard Pak. New York: Houghton Mifflin Harcourt. ISBN 978-0-544105805. This poem story introduces students to many different birds and helps them learn about birds' nesting habits.

Greenberg, Jan, ed. 2001. *Heart to Heart: New Poems Inspired by Twentieth-Century American Art*. New York: Harry N. Abrams. ISBN 0-8109-4386-7. Forty-three U.S. poets contribute poems to accompany twentieth-century American Art in this beautiful Printz Honor award book.

Greenberg, Jan, ed. 2008. *Side by Side: New Poems Inspired by Art from Around the World*. New York: Harry N. Abrams. ISBN 978-0-8109-9471-3. Poems written in their original language along with the English translation accompany art works from around the world.

Hale, Christy. 2012. *Dreaming Up: A Celebration of Building*. New York: Lee & Low. ISBN 978-1-60060-651-9. Concrete poems resemble children's constructions and the constructions appear opposite photos of actual buildings that resemble the shapes and forms the children have built.

Harley, Avis. 2006. *Sea Stars: Saltwater Poems*. Photographs by Margaret Butschler. Honesdale, PA: Wordsong. ISBN 978-1-59078-429-7. Harley's twenty-seven poems, written in different poetic forms, accompany colored photographs of sea creatures. The poet provides additional information on the creatures in back pages.

Heard, Georgia, ed. 2012. *The Arrow Finds Its Mark: A Book of Found Poems*. Illustrated by Antoine Guilloppé. New York: Roaring Brook. ISBN 978-1-59643-665-7. Famous poets craft forty poems from found pieces of writing: signs, detergent boxes, memos, among others. A gem.

Hines, Anna Grossnickle. 2011. *Peaceful Pieces: Poems and Quilts about Peace*. New York: Henry Holt. ISBN 978-0-8050-8996-7. Hines's poems about making peace among siblings, friends, even countries are accompanied by beautiful quilts.

Hines, Anna Grossnickle. 2003. *Pieces: A Year in Poems & Quilts*. New York: Greenwillow. ISBN 978-0-0605-5960-1. Hines celebrates the four seasons in her poems and quilts.

Hines, Anna Grossnickle. 2005. *Winter Lights: A Season in Poems & Quilts*. New York: Greenwillow. ISBN 978-0-06-00818-5. Hines writes poems about the lights of winter holidays as well as other lights that brighten a dark winter. Her lovely quilts accompany the poems.

Hoberman, Mary Ann. (sel.) 2012. *Forget-Me-Nots: Poems to Learn by Heart*. Illustrated by Michael Emberley. Boston: Megan Tingley Books/Little Brown and Company. ISBN 978-0-316-12947-3. Hoberman has collected 120 poems from classic and contemporary poets that she believes children should memorize.

Hoberman, Mary Ann. 2012. *I Like Old Clothes*. Illustrated by Patrice Barton. New York: Knopf. ISBN 978-0-375-86951-8. This picture book version of a single poem features two youngsters who delight in old clothes. The rhyming text is bouncy, alliterative and perfect for young children.

Hopkins, Lee Bennett. 2009. *City I Love*. Illustrated by Marcellus Hall. New York: Abrams. ISBN 978-0-8109-8327-4. Hopkins's poems celebrate various aspects of city life.

Hopkins, Lee Bennett (sel.). 2010. *Sharing the Seasons: A Book of Poems*. Illustrated by David Diaz. New York: Margaret K. McElderry. ISBN 978-1-4169-0210-2. Many famous poets write about the four seasons in this collection brilliantly illustrated by Diaz.

Hort, Lenny. 2000. *Tie Your Socks and Clap Your Feet: Mixed-up Poems*. Illustrated by Stephen Kroninger. New York: Anne Schwartz/Atheneum. ISBN 978-0689831959. op. In this collection of nonsense poems, anything is possible.

Hughes, Shirley. 2006. *Rhymes for Annie Rose*. Cambridge, MA: Candlewick Press. ISBN 978-0763629403. Hughes writes twenty-seven poems about the everyday lives of very young children.

Janeczko, Paul B. (sel.). *Firefly July: A Year of Very Short Poems*. Illustrated by Melissa Sweet. Somerville, MA: Candlewick. ISBN 978-0-7636-4842-8. Many different poets describe in unusual ways the various joys in each of the four seasons.

Janeczko, Paul B. (sel.). 2009. *A Foot in the Mouth: Poems to Speak, Sing, and Shout*. Illustrated by Chris Raschka. Somerville, MA: Candlewick. ISBN 978-0-7636-0663-3. This collection of poems, several written in two voices, are perfect for reading aloud and performing.

Janeczko, Paul B. (sel.). 2007. *Hey, You! Poems to Skyscrapers, Mosquitoes, and Other Fun Things*. New York: HarperCollins. ISN 978-0-06-052347-3. The authors of the thirty poems in this collection write directly to such unlikely objects as maggots, dust, mailboxes, and sneakers.

Janeczko, Paul B. 2005. *A Poke in the Eye: A Collection of Concrete Poems*. Illustrated by Chris Raschka. Somerville, MA: Candlewick. ISBN 978-0-7636-2376-0. pb. The thirty concrete poems in this collection are great fun and cover a wide range of topics.

Katz, Bobbi. 2006. *Once Around the Sun*. Illustrated by LeUyen Pham. San Diego: Harcourt. ISBN 0-15-216397-2. Katz's twelve poems capture the special characteristics of each month of the year.

Lear, Edward. 1998. Afterword by Maurice Sendak. *The Owl and the Pussycat*. Illustrated by James Marshall. New York: Michael diCapua Books/HarperCollins. ISBN 0-06-205010-9. op. Marshall's illustration of this poem is hilarious and sure to be enjoyed by readers of all ages.

Lear, Edward. 2011. "Masterminded" by Daniel Pinkwater. *His Shoes Were Far Too Tight.* Illustrated by Calef Brown. San Francisco: Chronicle. ISBN 978-0-8118-6792-4. Following a brief account of Edward Lear's life, this collection contains several of the poet's nonsense poems, humorously illustrated by Brown.

Lear, Edward. 2006. *The Owl and the Pussycat.* Illustrated by Anne Mortimer. New York: HarperCollins/Katherine Tegen. ISBN 978-0-06-027228-9. Mortimer depicts the famous wedding of the Owl and his Pussycat.

Lewis, J. Patrick. 2007. *The Brothers' War: Civil War Voices in Verse.* Photographs by Civil War photographers. Washington, DC: National Geographic. ISBN 978-1-4263-0036-3. The poems in this moving collection adopt the voices of those different groups who fought in or were involved in some way in the Civil War.

Lewis, J. Patrick. 2002. *Doodle Dandies: Poems that Take Shape.* Illustrated by Lisa Desimini. New York: Atheneum. ISBN 978-0-689-84889-6. Brief poems are written in the shape or emotional content of their subjects.

Lewis, J. Patrick. 2013. *Face Bugs.* Photographs by Frederic B. Siskind. Illustrations by Kelly Murphy. Honesdale, PA: WordSong/Highlights. ISBN 978-1-59078-925-4. Poems and photographs combine in this incredible book to help students see bugs as they have never seen them before.

Lewis, J. Patrick. 2005. *Heroes and She-Roes: Poems of Amazing and Everyday Heroes.* Illustrated by Jim Cooke. New York: Dial/Penguin. ISBN 0-8037-2925-1. Lewis celebrates both famous and unknown heroes in the twenty-one poems in this collection.

Lewis, J. Patrick. 2006. *Once upon a Tomb: Gravely Humorous Verses.* Illustrated by Simon Bartram. Cambridge, MA: Candlewick. ISBN 076361837-3. Lewis's twenty-two poems tell of the untimely demise of their subjects. Very funny.

Lewis, J. Patrick. 2009. *The Underwear Salesman and Other Jobs for Better or Verse.* Illustrations by Serge Bloch. New York: GineeSeo Books/Atheneum. ISBN 978-0-689-85325-8. Humorous poems and illustrations celebrate professions as diverse as map makers and dog trainers.

Lewis, J. Patrick. 2013. *When Thunder Comes: Poems for Civil Rights Leaders.* Illustrated by Jim Burke, et al. San Francisco: Chronicle Books. ISBN 978-1-4521-0119-4. Lewis's poems celebrate seventeen activists from around the world who fought for equal rights for all people.

Lewis, J. Patrick, and Douglas Florian. 2014. *Poem-Mobiles: Crazy Car Poems.* Illustrated by Jeremy Holmes. New York: Schwartz & Wade/Random House. ISBN 978-0-375-86690-6. The poets offer twenty-one poems about preposterous cars. The illustrations are priceless.

Lewis, J. Patrick, and Paul B. Janeczko. 2008. *Birds on a Wire.* Illustrated by Gary Lippincott. Honesdale, PA: Wordsong. ISBN 978-1-59078-383-2. These poems describe a day in an American village and employ a poetic form called renga.

Milich, Zoran. 2002. *City Signs.* Tonawanda, NY: Kids Can Press. ISBN 978-1553370031. Milich has photographed thirty signs that commonly appear in city environments.

Moore, Lilian. 2005. *Mural on Second Avenue and Other City Poems.* Illustrated by Roma Karas. Somerville, MA: Candlewick. ISBN 978-0-7636-1987-9. Moore captures the small moments in city life in these seventeen poems.

Mora, Pat. 2009. *Yum! ¡ MmMm! ¡ Qué Rico! Americas' Sproutings.* Illustrated by Rafael López. New York: Lee & Low. ISBN 978-1600602689. pb. The haiku poems in this collection celebrate foods that originated in the Americas.

Mordhorst, Heidi. 2009. *Pumpkin Butterfly: Poems from the Other Side of Nature.* Illustrated by Jenny Reynish. Honesdale, PA: Wordsong. ISBN 978-1-59078-620-8. This collection of exquisite poems about nature will help children see their world in new ways.

Morris, Jacke (compil.). 2006. Introduced by Carol Ann Dufy. *The Barefoot Book of Classic Poems.* Illustrated by Jackie Morris. Cambridge, MA: Barefoot Books. ISBN 1-905236-56-5. This lovely collection contains well-known poems that encompass all of life from birth to death.

Nelson, Marilyn. 2009. *Sweethearts of Rhythm: The Story of the Greatest All-Girl Swing Band in the World.* Illustrated by Jerry Pinkney. New York: Dial. ISBN 978-0-8037-3187-5. Poet and artist tell the story of a female swing band and the time in which they lived.

Paolilli, Paul, and Dan Brewer. 2003. *Silver Seeds.* Illustrated by Steve Johnson and Lou Francher. New York: Viking. ISBN 0-670-88941-5. pb. Simple acrostic riddle poems help children see familiar things in ways they may never have considered before.

Park, Linda Sue. 2007. *Tap Dancing on the Roof: Sijo (Poems).* Illustrated by Istvan Banyai. New York: Clarion. ISBN 978-0-618-23483-7. The twenty-seven poems in this collection are written in a special Korean poetic form called sijo.

Pearson, Helen. 2001. *Nature.* "Art Appreciation Class Improves Student Doctors' Diagnosis." http://www.nature.com/news/1998/010913/full/news010913-11.html (accessed April 11, 2014). Pearson relates how studying fine art pieces helps medical students improve their diagnostic abilities.

Peters, Lisa Westberg. 2010. *Volcano Wakes Up!* Illustrated by Steve Jenkins. New York: Henry Holt. ISBN 978-0-8060-8287-6. The poems in this collection encompass one day on which a volcano erupts.

Prelutsky, Jack. 2006. *Behold the Bold Umbrellaphant and Other Poems.* Illustrated by Carin Berger. New York: Greenwillow/HarperCollins. ISBN 978-0-06-054317-4. Prelutsky's funny titles of these poems about animals capture some physical characteristic of each creature.

Prelutsky, Jack. 2005. *The Frogs Wore Red Suspenders.* Illustrated by Petra Mathers. New York: Greenwillow/HarperCollins. ISBN 978-0-06-073-776-4. pb. These twenty-eight poems take readers on a nonsensical journey to see fantastical creatures.

Prelutsky, Jack. 2012. *I've Lost My Hippopotamus.* Illustrated by Jackie Urbanovic. New York: Greenwillow. ISBN 976-0-06-201457-3. In over 100 poems Prelutsky presents fantastical animals and happenings.

Prelutsky, Jack. 2012. *Stardines Swim High Across the Sky and Other Poems.* Illustrated by Carin Berger. New York: Greenwillow/HarperCollins. ISBN 978-0-06-201464-1. Prelutsky combines animal names with object to write the funny poems in this collection.

Quenqua, Douglas. July 16, 2013. "Study Finds Spatial Skill Is Early Sign of Creativity." *The New York Times.* CLXII (56,199). The author describes a study in which adults who scored high in spatial ability as thirteen-year-olds became exceptionally successful in the STEM fields of science, technology, engineering, and math.

Raczka, Bob. 2011. *Lemonade and Other Poems Squeezed from a Single Word.* Illustrated by Nancy Doniger. New York: Roaring Brook. ISBN 978-1-59643-541-4. Raczka creates poems using only the letters in each poem title and scrambles those letters to form a puzzle.

Rochelle, Belinda (sel.). 2001. *Words with Wings: A Treasury of African-American Poetry and Art.* New York: Amistad/HarperCollins. ISBN 0-688-16415-3. African American poets contribute poems that celebrate the lives and contributions of their people to accompany art works by African American artists.

Rosen, Michael J. 2009. *The Cuckoo's Haiku and Other Birding Poems.* Illustrated by Stan Fellows. Somerville, MA: Candlewick Press. ISBN 978-0-7636-3049-2. Rosen accompanies his lovely haiku poems about more than twenty North American birds with field notebook entries about their characteristics.

Rowden, Justine. 2005. *Paint Me a Poem.* Honesdale, PA: Wordsong. ISBN 978-1-59078289-7. Rowden writes a poem for each of fourteen paintings at the National Gallery of Art.

Ruddell, Deborah. 2007. *Today at the Bluebird Café.* Illustrated by Joan Rankin. New York: Margaret K. McElderry. ISBN 978-0-689-87-153-5. Ruddell's twenty-two poems highlight the characteristics of twenty-two different birds.

Salinger, Michael. 2009. *Well Defined: Vocabulary in Rhyme.* Illustrated by Sam Henderson. Honesdale, PA: Wordsong. ISBN 978-1-59078-615-4. All the rhyming poems in this collection actually define sophisticated vocabulary words.

Shange, Ntozake. 2009. *We Troubled the Water.* Illustrated by Rod Brown. New York: Amistad Collins/HarperCollins. ISBN 978-0-06-133735-2. This poetry collection recounts the suffering and prejudice African Americans endured in the segregated South.

Shannon, George. 2006. *Busy in the Garden.* Illustrated by Sam Williams. New York: Greenwillow/HarperCollins. ISBN 978-0060004644. Shannon's collection of twenty-four poems about gardening is perfect for very young children.

Sidman, Joyce. 2006. *Meow Ruff: A Story in Concrete Poetry.* Illustrated by Michelle Berg. New York: Houghton Mifflin. ISBN 978-0-6184-4894-4. Two lonely animals wait out a storm together.

Sidman, Joyce. 2005. *Song of the Water Boatman & Other Pond Poems.* Illustrated by Beckie Prange. Boston: Houghton Mifflin. ISBN 978-0-6181-3547-9. Sidman writes poems about the animal and plant life in a pond. Accompanied by additional scientific information and beautiful illustrations.

Sidman, Joyce. 2007. *This Is Just to Say: Poems of Apology and Forgiveness.* Illustrated by Pamela Zagarenski. Boston: Houghton Mifflin. ISBN 978-0-618-61680-0. This is a collection of poems of apology and responses from those who received the apologies.

Sidman, Joyce. 2012. "Why I Write Poetry." *School Library Journal* 55(4): 32–34. Sidman illustrates with stories from her own life and work why she writes poetry.

Sierra, Judy. 2003. *Antarctic Antics: A Book of Penguin Poems.* Illustrated by Jose Aruego and Ariane Dewey. Boston: Sandpiper/Houghton Mifflin. ISBN 978-0152046026. pb. Poems provide a glimpse into the lives and antics of emperor penguins in the Antarctic.

Singer, Marilyn. 2012. *A Stick Is an Excellent Thing: Poems Celebrating Outdoor Play.* Illustrated by LeUyen Pham. Boston: Clarion/Houghton Mifflin Harcourt. ISBN 978-0-547-12493-3. The poems in this book capture children's excitement and joy as they engage in imaginative play.

Sklansky, Amy E. 2012. *Out of This World: Poems and Facts about Space.* Illustrated by Stacey Schuett. New York: Knopf/Random House. ISBN 978-0-375-86459-9. These poems about space are accompanied by additional facts and explanations.

Spinelli, Eileen. 2004. *Feathers: Poems about Birds.* Illustrated by Lisa McCue. New York: Henry Holt. ISBN 0-8050-6713-2. op. This is a collection of poems about twenty-seven different kinds of birds.

Starko, Alane Jordan. 2010. *Creativity in the Classroom: Schools of Curious Delight.* 4th ed. New York: Rutledge Publishers. ISBN 978-0-415-99707-2. Starko links research in creativity with classroom practice.

Stevenson, Robert Louis. 2011. *A Child's Garden of Verses.* Illustrated by Barbara McClintock. New York: Harper/HarperCollins. ISBN 978-06-028228-8. McClintock's beautiful illustrations adorn the many famous Stevenson poems contained in this collection.

Stewart, Melissa. 2014. Feathers: Not Just for Flying. Illustrated by Sarah S. Brannen. Watertown, MA: Charlesbridge. ISBN 978-1-580894302. Readers learn about the many ways birds use their feathers.

Thomas, Joyce Carol. 2012. *In the Land of Milk and Honey.* Illustrated by Floyd Cooper. New York: Amistad/HarperCollins. ISBN 978-0-06-025383-7. This picture book poem, beautifully illustrated by Cooper, tells the story of Thomas's family's journey from Oklahoma to California in 1948.

Van Wassenhove, Sue. 2008. *The Seldom-Ever-Shady Glades.* Quilts by Sue Van Wassenhove. Honesdale, PA: Wordsong. ISBN 978-1-59078-352-8. Van Wassenhove combines poems and quilts to describe the animals of the Everglades.

Weatherford, Carole Boston. 2002. *Remember the Bridge: Poems of a People.* Designed by Semadar Megged. New York: Philomel. ISBN 0-399-23726-7. The poet's poems about African Americans who bridged the way to freedom accompany period photographs and engravings.

Weisburd, Stefi. 2008. *Barefoot: Poems for Naked Feet.* Illustrated by Lori McElrath-Eslick. Honesdale, PA: Wordsong/Boyds Mills. ISBN 978-1-59078-306-1. Weisburd celebrates all the things feet can do and the joys we experience through our feet.

Wong, Janet S. 2007. *Twist: Yoga Poems.* Illustrated by Julie Paschkis. New York: Margaret K. McElderry/Simon & Schuster. ISBN 978-0-689-37394-2. In these sixteen poems, Wong uses imagery to help readers understand the spirit of the different yoga poses and how to perform them.

Yolen, Jane. 2010. *An Egret's Day.* Photographs by Jason Stemple. Honesdale, PA: WordSong/Boyds Mills. ISBN 978-1-59078-650-5. Yolen's fourteen poems about egrets are accompanied by beautiful photographs and additional information about each bird.

Yolen, Jane. 2011. Foreword by Donald Kroodsma, Ph.D. *Birds of a Feather.* Photographs by Jason Stemple. Honesdale, PA: WordSong/Boyds Mills. ISBN 978-1-59078-830-1. Yolen's poems about fourteen different birds are accompanied by beautiful photographs and additional information about each bird.

Yolen, Jane. 2007. *Shape Me a Rhyme: Nature's Forms in Poetry.* Photographs by Jason Stemple. Honesdale, PA: Wordsong. ISBN 978-1-59078-450-1. The twelve poems in the collection are about shapes found in nature and appear along with great photographs and synonyms for the shape names.

Zimmer, Tracie Vaughn. 2009. *Steady Hands: Poems about Work.* Illustrated by Megan Halsey and Sean Addy. New York: Clarion. ISBN 978-0-618-90351-1. The poems in this great collection capture what different workers do during their work days.

Poetry Books Featuring Animals

Cyrus, Kurt. 2005. *Hotel Deep: Light Verse from Dark Water.* New York: Harcourt. ISBN 0-15-216771-4. The title itself is a metaphor in this collection of twenty-one poems about animals that live in the sea.

Elliott, David. 2012. *In the Sea.* Illustrated by Holly Meade. Somerville, MA: Candlewick. ISBN 978-0-7636-4498-7. Like Elliott's books, *In the Wild* and *On the Farm,* these poems are about animals—this time those that live in the sea. Elliott calls the "Dolphin . . . the jester / of the briny deep, / an acrobat with fins." "The Moray Eel [is] a sword without its sheath."

Elliott, David. 2012 (reprint ed.). *On the Farm*. Illustrated by Holly Meade. Somerville, MA: Candlewick. ISBN 978-0-7636-5591-4. This collection of very short poems about farm animals is beautifully illustrated with woodcuts and suitable for young children.

Florian, Douglas. 2003. *Bow Wow Meow Meow: It's Rhyming Cats and Dogs*. San Diego: Harcourt. ISBN 0-15-216395-6. In "The Dachshund," (26), this elongated dog declares that fleas ride in his "stretch limousine."

Florian, Douglas. 2009. *Dinothesaurus*. New York: Atheneum/ Simon & Schuster. ISBN 978-1-4169-7978-4. Florian's dinosaur poems reveal the characteristics of these creatures. In "Stegoceras" (27), he plays with descriptions of the animal's head: "Brick head . . . Mound head . . . tone head."

Florian, Douglas. 2001. *In the Swim*. Boston: Sandpiper/Houghton Mifflin Harcourt. ISBN 978-0152024376. pb. Among his poems about sea creatures, Florian, in "The Whale" (18) describes this mammal as "A wall with a tail. / A ship."

Florian, Douglas. 1998. *Insectlopedia*. San Diego: Harcourt. ISBN 0-15-201306-7. These poems are perfect for a unit on insects. In "The Dragonfly" (9), Florian calls the insect a "demon of skies."

Florian, Douglas. 2005. *Lizards, Frogs, and Polliwogs*. Boston: Sandpiper/Houghton Mifflin Harcourt. ISBN 978-0152052485. Among these twenty-one poems about reptiles and amphibians are "The Tortoise" (9) who wears a helmet on its back and "The Wood Frog" (38)" a "frozen frogsicle."

Florian, Douglas. 2004. *Mammalabilia*. Boston: Sandpiper/Houghton Mifflin Harcourt. ISBN 978-0152050245. pb. Among this collection of poems about mammals is one on "The Beaver" (17), a "tree-dropper," and "stream-stopper."

Florian, Douglas. 2004. *Omnibeasts*. San Diego: Harcourt. ISBN 0-15-205038-8. If you cannot obtain some of Florian's individual books of animal poems, this collection of the best ones culled from the set will be invaluable.

Florian, Douglas. 2012. *UnBEElievable*. New York: Beach Lane/Simon & Schuster. ISBN 978-1442426528. The poems and information in this collection are wonderful additions to any unit on bees, their life cycle, contributions, and endangered status. The bees engage in various descriptions of themselves such as "summer hummer" and "pollen nation."

Florian, Douglas. 2005. *Zoo's Who*. San Diego: Harcourt. ISBN 0-15-204639-9. All kinds of animals are the subjects of these poems. In "The Owl" (45), the creature describes itself as "the eyes / And ears of night."

Grimes, Nikki. 2007. *When Gorilla Goes Walking*. Illustrated by Shane Evans. New York: Orchard/Scholastic. ISBN 978-0-439-31770-2. Cecilia, the narrator of these poems, tells us her cat, Gorilla, is "rain-cloud gray" ("Gorilla"), "a huff of fur" (Telephone"), and a "feline nurse" ("Sick Day").

Harley, Avis. 2008. *The Monarch's Progress: Poems with Wings*. Honesdale, PA: Wordsong. ISBN 978-1-59078-558-4. The beautiful poems in this collection are a perfect addition to a study of the monarch butterfly. They are filled with metaphors too numerous to include here.

Hauth, Katherine B. 2011. *What's for Dinner? Quirky, Squirmy Poems from the Animal World*. Illustrated by David Clark. Watertown, MA: Charlesbridge. ISBN 978-1-57091-471-3. These thirty

poems feature many different animals, including several kinds of insects.

Kumin, Maxine. 2006. *Mites to Mastodons*. Illustrated by Pamela Zagarenski. Boston: Houghton Mifflin. ISBN 978-0618-507 53-5. Mites, octopi, ancient mastodons—all manner of creatures are featured in this collection.

Lewis, J. Patrick. 2012. *National Geographic Book of Animal Poetry: 200 Poems with Photographs that Squeak, Soar, and Roar!* Washington, DC: National Geographic. ISBN 978-1-4263-1009-6. The marvelous collection consists of classic poems as well as those written by contemporary poets. The interesting juxtapositions, great photos, and everything else about this collection make it a must for every home and classroom.

Lewis, J. Patrick, and Jane Yolen. 2012. *Last Laughs: Animal Epitaphs*. Illustrated by Jeffrey Stewart Timmins. Watertown, MA: Charlesbridge. ISBN 978-1-58089-260-5. The thirty poems in this collection are written as humorous epitaphs for different animals, each one fitting the characteristics of the animal buried within. These poems will inspire students to create epitaphs for their own favorite animals.

MacLachlan, Patricia, and Emily MacLachlan Charest. 2013. *Cat Talk*. Illustrated by Barry Moser. New York: Katherine Tegen Books/HarperCollins. ISBN 978-0-06-027978-3. Cats speak for themselves in each of fourteen poems that are beautifully illustrated in two-page spreads. The black cat in "Minnie" says, "I am a shadow," and in "Peony," the cat says of herself, "I am a flower. / My face blooms / Big / Fluffy / Full."

Plomer, William. Nature notes by Richard Fitter. 2009. *The Butterfly Ball and the Grasshopper's Feast*. Illustrated by Alan Aldridge. Somerville, MA: Templar/Candlewick. ISBN 978-0-7636-4422-2. Creatures that walk, hop, crawl, or fly deck themselves out for the butterfly ball in this stunning collection of poems that is beautifully illustrated. In his poem about caterpillars, "Eseralda, Seraphina and Camilla" (18), he says they are "Each a glad and glorious Caterpillar, / A live mosaic of orange, green and gold."

Prelutsky, Jack. 2004. *If Not for the Cat*. Illustrated by Ted Rand. New York: Greenwillow/HarperCollins. ISBN 0-06-059678-3. In these haiku poems about different animals, the hummingbird is a "hoverer," elephants are "wrinkled hulks," and a kangaroo calls her joey "the future of my kind."

Ruddell, Deborah. 2009. *A Whiff of Pine, a Hint of Skunk: A Forest of Poems*. Illustrated by Joan Rankin. New York: Margaret McElderry. ISBN 978-1-4169-4211-5. In this forest birds sit in trees where "A million arms in woody sleeves / wave a zillion brand new leaves" ("Spring Welcome"), beavers are "Bucktoothed Cleaver[s] / Tree Retriever[s]" and "Building Conceiver[s]" ("Biography of a Beaver").

Ryder, Joanne. 2007. *Toad by the Road: A Year in the Life of These Amazing Amphibians*. Illustrations by Maggie Kneen. New York: Henry Holt. ISBN 0-8050-7354-X. Ryder describes the toad's hatching and activities over four seasons in these delightful poems.

Sidman, Joyce. 2010. *Dark Emperor & Other Poems of the Night*. Illustrated by Rick Allen. Boston: Houghton Mifflin. ISBN 978-0-547-15228-8. This award-winning book illustrated with stunning linoleum prints features poems about nocturnal animals and insects. Filled with metaphor throughout, Sidman ushers readers into the book as she describes the night as "a sea of dappled dark" ("Welcome to the Night," 6).

Sidman, Joyce. 2012. *In the Sea*. Illustrated by Holly Meade. Somerville, MA: Candlewick. ISBN 978-0-7636-4498-7. Sidman's poems about animals that live in water are filled with powerful images. The "Moray Eel" is "a sword without its sheath," "The Orca" is "an elegant torpedo." "The Chambered Nautilus" is "a staircase with no end / a question with no answer."

Singer, Marilyn. 2003. *Fireflies at Midnight*. Illustrated by Ken Robbins. New York: Atheneum. ISBN 0-689-82492-0. The rhythms in these poems about different animals, including insects, fit the actions and habits of the creatures. Highly recommended.

Singer, Marilyn. 2012. *A Strange Place to Call Home: The World's Most Dangerous Habitats & the Animals that Call Them Home*. Illustrated by Ed Young. San Francisco: Chronicle. ISBN 978-1-4521-0120-0. Singer's poems feature fourteen animals that live in the harshest environments on the planet, from intense heat, biting cold, and even the depths of the ocean. She uses several different poetic forms to tell their stories. She writes that a mountain goat is "king of cliffs" ("Top of the World"), and dippers are birds that are "bathtub-toy small" ("A Bird in the Water").

Worth, Valerie. 2007. *Animal Poems*. Illustrated by Steve Jenkins. New York: Farrar Straus Giroux. ISBN 978-0-374-38057-1. This collection of twenty-three poems about different animals is beautifully illustrated with cut paper collages.

Worth, Valerie. 2013. *Pug: And Other Animal Poems*. Illustrated by Steve Jenkins. New York: Farrar Straus Giroux. ISBN 978-0-374-35024-6. In these poems, Worth portrays a wide range of animals and their behavior.

Zimmer, Tracie Vaughn. 2011. *Cousins of Clouds: Elephant Poems*. Illustrated by Megan Halsey and Sean Addy. New York: Clarion/Houghton Mifflin. ISBN 978-0-618-90349-8. These poems feature the wonder and majesty of elephants present, past, and future, and there is a considerable amount of text that provides additional information. An elephant's legs are "great pillars"; its tail, an "accessory, a fancy tassel"; its feet "giant padded slippers"; and its ears "tattered sails." The poet writes that the "Trunk" is "finger, fork, arm, nose, straw, megaphone, telescope, rope."

2

Finding the Extraordinary in the Ordinary World of Fiction

Fiction is to the grown man what play is to the child;
it is there that he changes the atmosphere and tenor of his life.

—Robert Louis Stevenson

Fiction, and here we include picture books that contain both realistic and fantastical content, encompasses topics limited only by the interests and concerns of the young people for whom it is intended. Regardless of their day-to-day experiences, the emotions that consume them, their problems, trials, and joys, young people from birth through high school can find topics and characters in fiction that resonate with them. The variety and number of books in all formats from picture books, through novels, graphic novels, and eBooks, are seemingly endless. From this wealth, we discuss here some of those books that offer readers new ways to look at their world and the lives of others; new approaches to solving problems; characters who pursue their dreams despite the risks involved, who dare to do the unpopular, the unexpected; and even books that are written using surprising and unconventional formats. By giving youngsters the opportunity to see the world through the eyes of these bold and resourceful characters and gain insights into the imaginative ways authors have created them, we provide them with models for facing their own challenges—and, ultimately, the challenges of our world—as divergent thinkers.

Picture Books

Picture books are our most accessible classroom literary resources. Their brevity makes it possible for a group of students to read or listen to a picture book and discuss it satisfactorily in a single session. In addition, there is such a variety of picture books that many are suitable for use with middle and even high school students. While not having the luxury of length to develop characters in depth, the best of these books do offer characters and situations that can help our students become more alive to the world around them and envision new ways to interact with it.

The young heroine of Michael Ian Black's hilarious *I'm Bored* (2012) is, well, bored. When she meets a potato who also announces he's bored, she asks him if he wants to do something. The potato, who only likes flamingos and thinks kids are boring, refuses to have anything to do with her. "Kids are **boring**," he states. Incensed, the girl sets out to prove that kids are really fun. She turns cartwheels, skips, spins in circles, plays games, does ninja kicks, walks on her hands, and finally imagines all kinds of stuff like being a ballerina or a princess with dragons and unicorns, or taming lions. No matter what imaginary scenarios the girl creates, the potato's response is always the same: "boring . . . boring . . . boring." Utterly frustrated, she screams, "How can you possibly think kids are boring when we can do ALL this COOL stuff and think ALL these AMAZING thoughts and be ANYTHING we want to be!" Taking their cue from this protagonist who has clearly changed her mind about her own capacity for amusing herself, ask the students to come up with creative ideas for things to do when they feel bored—things they may, perhaps, never have tried or that seem outlandish at first, but might actually be enjoyable. Each child or groups of children can contribute ideas, which can then be illustrated and collected into a book for the library shelf. This would be a fine book to promote when school vacations loom.

"My name is Marisol McDonald and I don't match because . . . I don't want to!" says the young protagonist of Monica Brown's bilingual *Marisol McDonald and the Clash Bash* (2013). So it's no surprise that when she sends out invitations to her birthday party, each one describes a different theme. The result is a group of attendees all dressed in different kinds of costumes. In the end, everyone becomes infected with the spirit of this girl who refuses to conform, and they have a grand time at her "Clash Bash." Another unconventional dresser is Zoe, who gets ready for a Saturday outing with her mother and little brother in Bethanie Deeney Murguia's *Zoe Gets Ready* (2012). She is trying to choose the appropriate outfit, but she just can't decide what kind of a day she would like to have. Perhaps she will go collecting treasures, or do cartwheels so that her toes "tickle the clouds." Then again, Zoe might initiate "an exploring day," and "lead the way to secret places." In the end, this creative youngster dons all the outfits she had previously discarded in one grand ensemble, complete with wings. Clearly, she is planning to soar the heights. After enjoying these stories together, create a chart with the children and write down their ideas as you encourage them to mention how they would spend a free Saturday if they had the power to do

anything they wished. Read over their ideas together. Then extend the conversation by asking what might be the result if they were to pursue some of the activities. What might they see, discover, and so on, that they might not have seen or discovered had they just stayed home? Would they also like to design never-before-seen outfits that would be appropriate for their chosen activities? To spur youngsters on to the challenge of inventive clothing design, share Seymour Chwast's *Get Dressed!* (2012). This book has a sturdy cover shaped like a suit jacket with many gate folds within, and follows easily on Zoe's outfit-selection quandary. Unlike conventional books about getting dressed, Chwast presents unlikely articles along with recognizable pieces of clothing for each spread. What are readers supposed to make of a page that offers a pot, a garbage can cover, a funnel, and a feather along with a belt and sweat shirt? Well, a dragon peeks out of the opposite page. What kind of hint is that? Open the flap and a boy appears wearing strange head gear made with the pot, funnel, and feather and holding the cover as a shield. The text reads, "Get dressed to read about dragons." Rubber gloves, a towel, kerchief, boots, and boxer shorts appear opposite a piano. When readers lift the flap, they see a masked, cape-clad lad, booted feet behind, gloved hands stretched in front as the boy flies through the air. "Get dressed to make believe," reads the text. This is a creative book that begs children to continue the fun. Ask one group of students to create a short list containing objects as well as articles of clothing. They hand the list to another group charged with creating an outfit from the items along with the words, "Get dressed to. . . ."

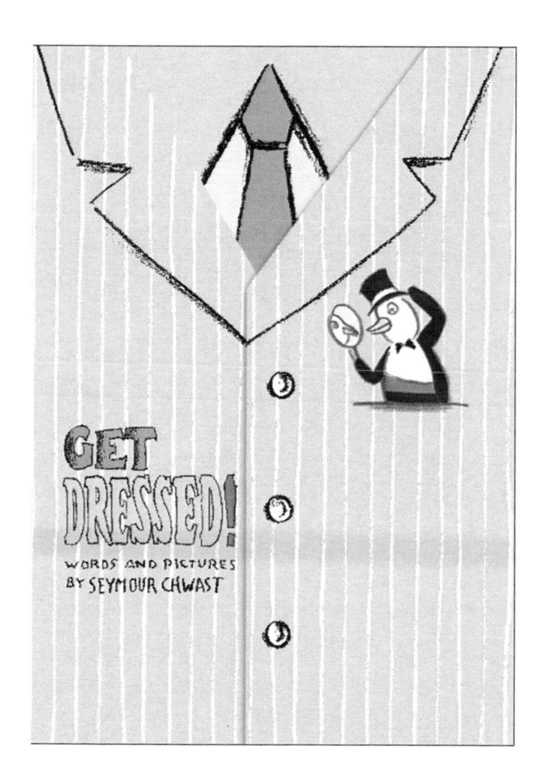

We can start fostering our children's imaginations from their very earliest years. Emily Winfield Martin's gorgeous *Dream Animals* (2013) is the perfect bedtime book for a young child or for a read-aloud to encourage imaginative dreams before children in daycare or preschool settle down for their afternoon nap. Different dream land animals carry their young charges to special imaginative lands such as an "elfin hollow hidden underground" or "beneath the seven seas," or to a circus where animals perform daring feats. To what imaginary land would the children like to travel as they fall off to sleep? An individual child or group of children could work on creating an imaginary land on a large sheet of paper or mural.

In a follow-up book to *Dream Animals* for slightly older children, the narrator of Dallas Clayton's *An Awesome Book!* (2008) laments, "Yes, there are places in the world / where people dream up dreams / so simply un-fantastical / and practical / they seem . . . / to lose all possibility / of thinking super things." Their dreams are ho-hum, like dreams of silverware or furniture. "Sometimes they even dream / of dreams that aren't / even their own." But the

readers of this book are urged to dream the biggest dreams possible, and then one "ten times as big" as that, and then "a million dreams that roar . . . scream . . . sing and shout!" What's the most elaborate dream the children can create? Perhaps drawing their dream will help them attend to its details so that it moves from an abstract image to a more concrete plan or idea. Will the dream benefit anyone besides themselves?

When his new teacher questions why Billy has arrived at school with a soiled shirt in Al Yankovic's *My New Teacher and Me!* (2013), the boy relates a story about digging to China and finding a dinosaur skull. He follows that with stories about the two-headed cow on his cousin's farm, his grandfather's ukulele playing on the moon, and others—all declared outlandish by Mr. Booth who demands, "Admit that your stories are simply absurd! / I just do not believe them—not one single word!" Billy counters, "I'll bet every great thinker and leader we've got / Could see *all* kinds of things other people could not! / So then why get upset if somebody like me / Tries to look at the world just a bit *differently?*" Why, indeed! Thinking and imagining differently is what divergent thinking is all about. It is what the gifted writers we so admire do all the time. Following on Billy's stories, ask the students to make up the most imaginative stories they can. They may need a few prompts such as "Make up a story about where you went last weekend," or "Make up a story about what you saw on the way home from school yesterday." Give the students some time to gather their thoughts, divide them into groups, and ask them to tell their stories to one another. They may wish to write them down and illustrate them at another time.

In addition to the prompt in Nina Laden's *Once Upon a Memory* (2013) that encourages young children to consider some of their "favorite things to remember," the story also provides a unique opportunity for them to look at the ordinary objects around them and think about what those objects might have been before the moment in which the children first see them. Some of the responses that complete each query in the book are expected, but others are examples of divergent thinking at its best. For instance, the unseen narrator asks, "Does a chair remember it once was" "a tree?" completes the question on the opposite page. Far more intriguing is a picture of a young boy raking leaves. Above the illustration is the question, "Does work remember it once was." The illustration opposite depicts three raccoons leaping in a pile of leaves, with the answer to the question beneath: "play?" Share the paired questions and illustrations with the children. Can they think of a logical completion for each question that is different from the one in the book? Can they provide an illustration for the way in which they answered the question? Follow this with other questions such as "does a shoe . . . a flower . . . an ice cream cone . . . a window . . . and so on remember it once was." Ask children to supply as many completions as they can. They might wish to recite the questions and their completions antiphonally—a fine way for them to see patterned text in action as well.

Paul Schmid's *Perfectly Percy* (2013) is the story of a young porcupine who loves balloons: "Red balloons. / Blue balloons. Round balloons. / Curly balloons." Of course, as soon as he clutches a balloon in his eager hand and runs with it, his quills pop it. Percy does "not want to give up," so he goes for help. Since his sister's solution doesn't work, and his mom is too busy to listen, Percy decides to think through the problem, even when no ideas come to him at first. He thinks through the day and even during the night until he makes an interesting connection when he looks at his breakfast cereal bowl. Percy turns the bowl into a helmet which, when worn on his head, keeps his quills from popping his balloons. Can the children think of other ordinary household objects and ways Percy might have used them to solve his problem? Making connections is an effective way to solve problems and one that divergent thinkers employ frequently. Help young children see how this is so in their everyday lives. They are cold. A sweater is a heavy, warm garment. Connecting the characteristics of a sweater with the feeling of being cold enables them to solve the problem by putting on the sweater. This is an easy connection, but calling attention to more subtle ones as they arise will enable students to become more proficient at making connections to form new ideas or solve problems by themselves.

Children will find another innovative problem solver in Mark Pett's *The Boy and the Airplane* (2013), an unusual wordless book about a boy who receives an airplane as a gift. He gleefully runs outside to fly it and has a grand time—until the plane lands on the roof. The first thing he does is climb a ladder, but he is still too short to reach it. Then, donning different head gear to match his efforts, he, in turn, tries to lasso it, knock it down with a baseball, bounce up on a pogo stick, and turn a hose on it. Nothing works, so he sits down to think. When a seed falls from the tree under which he is sitting, he connects the seed to his problem and devises a solution by planting it near the roof. Subsequent pages show the tree's growth through seasons and years until it becomes a huge tree and he becomes a bearded old man. He then happily climbs the tree and retrieves his plane. As he is about to fly it, he has another idea. Before a page turn reveals what he does with the toy, ask the students what they think he should do and why. How else do they think he could have gotten his plane down? What role do they think the tiny bird plays in almost every picture? What are the students' opinions of the boy's willingness to wait so long to get his plane back? Do they think it is a believable solution? Why or why not?

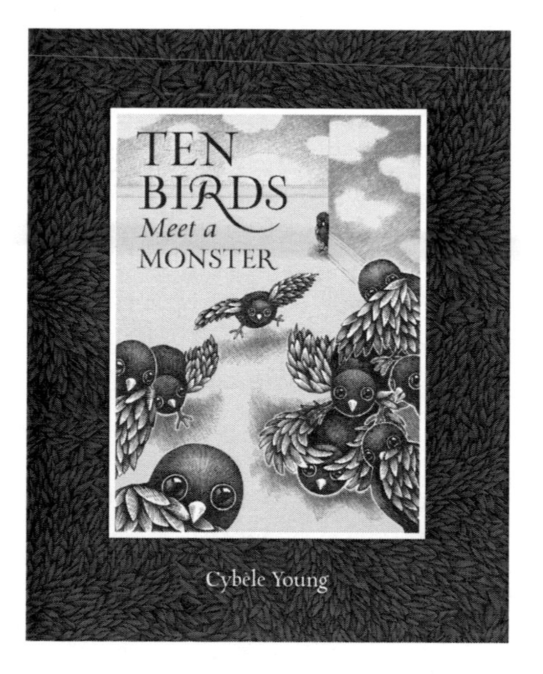

The ten birds featured in Cybèle Young's *Ten Birds Meet a Monster* (2013) have a terrible problem. Peeking out of a doorway is a hideous monster, mouth agape, horns at the ready. Making use of a pile of materials heaped in the room in which they are gathered, the birds try to frighten the monster by creating a scary disguise. Donning polka-dot material, the first bird becomes a *"Vicious Polka-dactyl,"* but the monster stays put. The second bird joins the first by adding additional materials and "Together they [become] *"Gnashing Grapplesaurus."* The effect on the monster: nada. Birds continue to join in the effort, adding more and more materials to the disguise until nine birds become a *"Hideous Whiptail Gangle Raptor."* The monster, though, stands firm. Students will love these ingenious disguises, especially the giant one formed by all nine birds. Stop the story at this point and ask students for more ideas the birds can use to scare away the monster. What materials would they use? Involve them in creating a list of additional disguise names, aiming for the most amusing and original ones the children can devise. Discuss the various descriptors for the birds: "inventive," "resourceful," "hard-worker," "attentive," "diligent," "creative," "eager to participate," "team player," and "imaginative," and how having these characteristics would help a person (or creature) come up with great ideas. What do the children think the tenth bird is going to do? What would they do in this situation? Do they have any idea what the monster is? Continue with the story and enjoy the surprise.

Cindy Moo (Mortensen, *Cindy Moo,* 2012) just can't get that nursery rhyme about the cow jumping over the moon out of her head. "If that cow could jump the moon, / by golly, I can too," is her conviction. The other farm animals beg to differ, though, and when her heroic leaps result in painful landings, their "Told you so . . . too bad . . . cows weren't meant to jump the moon . . . why don't you just give up?" is less than encouraging. But Cindy Moo refuses to quit. She tries and fails again, and then, on a rain-swept night, the moon disappears altogether. How can she jump over the moon when there is no moon in sight? However, she notices the moon reflected in a rain puddle and "with a happy moo" jumps over it, to accolades all around. Repeated efforts and patience here bring success to a determined bovine. Grahame Baker-Smith's lovely book, *Farther* (2013), another story of extraordinary patience, is narrated by a man, now grown, as he tells of his father's obsession with building a successful flying machine. "Day and night, he sewed and stitched and sawed and hammered and trimmed the feathers of a thousand hopeful wings." But "nothing he did could claim the sky." When father goes off to war and never returns, his dream of flight dies with him—or so it seems. But then his son takes up the task and not only succeeds, but also wonders if his own son will yearn for the sky as well. All of these books can engage students of different ages in conversations about the role of patience in developing new products, new drugs, and new ideas. Often these projects require repeated tests in the lab, controlled trials, discarding what doesn't work and starting over, among other efforts. Older students might want to research several innovative products or medicines. When did people start working on a particular idea? What was the process involved? How long did it take? In sobering press conferences, almost all the 2013 Nobel Prize recipients in science and medicine in the United States related that their work took decades, and that in today's culture that demands instant results, none of their projects would probably be funded. What do students make of these comments? What repercussions do they see for future advances in science and medicine? What are their ideas for combating this "instant gratification" attitude?

While Cindy Moo wants to jump *over* the moon, the young lad in Mordicai Gerstein's *How to Bicycle to the Moon to Plant Sunflowers* (2013) wants to go *to* the moon to cheer it up by planting sunflowers because he feels "the full moon always [looks] . . . like a big, sad clown face." He has a plan to get there, too, and it only involves twenty-four easy steps. The only problem is that what with "homework, soccer, violin, and all the other stuff" he has to do, he doesn't have time to execute the plan himself. But he does provide the reader with simple-to-follow steps to get there. It only requires a bicycle, 2,000 used inner tubes, a very long rubber band, a pole twenty-five feet long, a ship's anchor, 238,900 miles of garden hose, and a space suit, which NASA will happily supply. The youngster provides all the necessary instructions, so of course, the mission is successful. This is a fantastical plan dreamed up by a boy with a vivid imagination to solve what he perceives to be a problem. In a project that is sure to be fun, ask students to come up with a detailed, equally outlandish plan to solve a school or community problem. While it would not be possible to execute the plan in the real world, it should, nevertheless, follow logical steps just as the boy's plan in this hilarious book does.

Jack complains about the family's house in Chris Van Dusen's *If I Built a House* (2012). "This house is OK, but it's like any other. / It's boxy and boring and basically bland." So he proceeds to design his own imaginary house. The kitchen has a robotic machine with lots of hands to do all the cooking and dish washing. The bathroom has an automatic "Scrub-a-Dub-Dub" machine so he can sit and relax in the tub while the machine washes him thoroughly. All the rooms in his house, in fact, are specially designed to be fun and help its inhabitants with chores. If the students could design their own house, what would it look like? What kind of furniture would it have? Appliances? What kind of machinery would it contain and what would the machines do? Set the students to work on such a project, asking them to create their ideal home. What chore do they least enjoy doing and how would that chore be handled in their dream house? Make certain the students understand that no idea is too preposterous. Another book that might spark children's ingenuity as they plan is Frank Viva's *Young Frank, Architect* (2013). Young Frank, an architect, lives with old Frank, also an architect. But each time the boy designs something: a chair made of toilet paper rolls; a book skyscraper; a whole city laid out on a large roll; old Frank objects that real architects don't make such things. They proceed to the Museum of Modern Art where old Frank learns that indeed, architects *do* make such things, and no idea is too outrageous. From that time on, both architects work together on creative projects. After the children's creations are completed, discuss whether any of the elements they have included in their houses have a real chance of being developed. Why or why not? Consider including a trip to a modern art museum in reality or virtually (see the architecture and design exhibit of the Museum of Modern Art in New York at http://www.moma.org/search/collection?query=architecture+and+design for inspiration.)

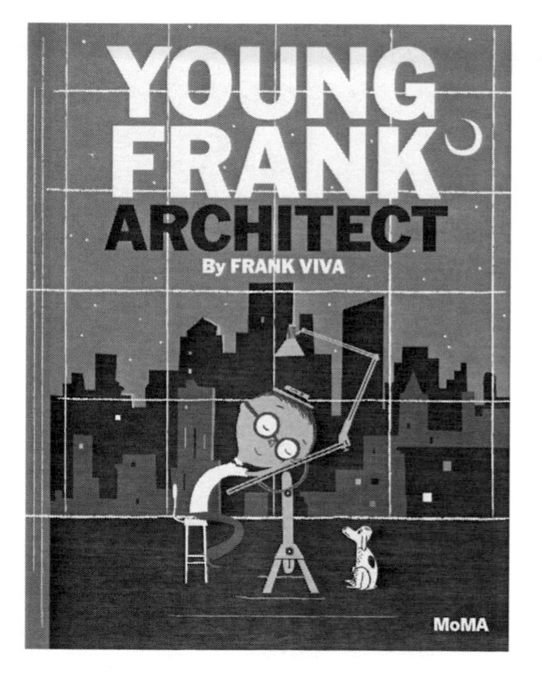

Ever since he was very little, Dawson has been inventing new things from broken toys and discarded objects in Chris Gall's *Awesome Dawson* (2013). Empty soup cans and a baby bottle nipple become a crawling insect toy. An old shoe becomes the head and bill of a rolling duck. A camera and old telephone become a robot. But when he creates a giant machine to do his chores, the thing gets out of control and threatens to destroy the entire town. Dawson has to figure out a way to stop it. Pause the story and ask for student suggestions before continuing to discover Dawson's solution. Would the students' suggestions work? Why or why not? The story concludes with the words, "everything can be used again!" Rosie, star of Andrea Beaty's *Rosie Revere, Engineer* (2013) is a reuser par excellence. Young though she is, Rosie dreams of being an engineer. "Where some people see rubbish, Rosie sees inspiration," and her room is filled with all kinds of gizmos she has built from the odds and ends she finds. But Rosie keeps her creations secret, especially after being ridiculed by her classmates. It is only when her aunt encourages Rosie, even when a flying machine she makes fails, that she continues making things. From this wise older woman Rosie learns that flops are opportunities to learn and improve, and that note-taking helps generate ideas. Another builder who makes things from found objects is the heroine of Ashley Spires's *The Most Magnificent Thing* (2014). One day she decides to build "the most MAGNIFICENT thing," and after collecting a variety of materials, proceeds to draw up plans. Her faithful canine assistant looks on, occasionally growling, tugging, or nudging. When she completes her work, however, she discovers to her surprise that it is not magnificent. She starts again, wrench[ing] and fiddl[ing]. Still wrong. In the end, she has a collection of attempts, all unsatisfactory. "She gets MAD." She even "EXPLODES!" But after a cooling-off walk, she looks at all her objects again and notices that "there are some parts of the WRONG things that are really quite RIGHT." By making connections, using what works in each creation, she finally figures out how to make what she has in mind. It's not quite magnificent and still needs improvements, but it works. And readers will be surprised at what it turns out to be. After enjoying these three books, ask students to begin collecting safe (no sharp edges, etc.) used objects. When the class has a good number of objects at its disposal, as well as tools, glue, pipe cleaners, craft sticks, and other helpful items, divide the students into groups and challenge them to create something completely new and *useful* from the old objects—a toy, a decorative piece, among others. While the children work, talk about the role of failure and how flops can often be springboards to new ideas. Prepare a display of the new creations for the school lobby as an incentive for the student body to both renew their recycling efforts and to develop spatial skills as well. Students of all ages will love watching an incredible builder at work by going to http://www.youtube.com/watch?v=faIFNkdq96U to see Caine's arcade. (Also see chapter 1 for a description of Quenqua's article describing the importance of spatial skills and chapters 4 and 5 for discussions of tinkerers and inventors—and new opportunities to actually turn a design into a 3D object.)

In Paul Fleischman's *The Matchbox Diary* (2013), a young girl visits her great-grandfather and discovers a collection of match boxes. They are actually a diary kept by her grandparent chronicling his life in Italy, his journey to America, and his first years in his new country. "I had a lot I wanted to remember," he says," but I couldn't read or write. So I started this." Opening the boxes one by one enables the girl to learn about her grandfather's life: an olive pit symbolizing the beloved trees of his native land; a piece of macaroni symbolizing the drought that caused such hunger the family had to leave for America; the typeset letters symbolizing his job as a printer; and so on. After reading the book, invite the students to think of ways to keep a diary other than writing events in a book or on an electronic device. Make a list of their ideas. Would any of them like to keep a diary for a week, a month, or longer using one of listed methods? Those who do so might want to share them with the group. The class might also use one of these methods as a class learning journal about a topic they are studying.

A delightful story that illustrates how thoughtful, creative people can honor their traditions while still allowing modern progress in a way that benefits everyone is Uma Krishnaswami's *Out of the Way! Out of the Way!* (2010). A boy in a village, possibly in India, finds a tree sapling on a path. He builds a protective ring of stones around it and the villagers wear a path around it as they scurry to and fro carrying on their busy lives. The tree eventually grows into a giant providing a home for animals and a meeting place for people beneath its branches. A city grows beyond the village, the dirt path becomes a paved road for cars and trucks, and the boy becomes a man with his own children. Through the years, people learn to carry on their activities "out of the way" of the *tree* rather than sacrificing it to make way for themselves. They even take time, occasionally, to sit under the tree and listen to the old stories. So often progress comes at the expense of established neighborhoods, buildings, traditions. Only those who can think divergently can devise ways to keep what is valuable while still providing for modern conveniences and economic growth. Discuss this charming story with the class. In what ways did the villagers benefit from the tree? What would their lives have been like without it? Would it have been a better idea to remove the tree and widen the road to allow for more commerce? Why or why not?

"Are you ever perplexed? / Completely vexed? / Do you have questions? / Queries? / Odd theories?" asks the narrator of Calef Brown's zany *Boy Wonders* (2011). He certainly does, and his questions fill every page. Most are jokes like "Do bees get hives?" but there are some ingenious word plays as well: "Is water scared of waterfalls?" and "If I'm too tired, am I a bike?" The boy's mind is "always wandering" and his thirst to know so many things is the point of the book—to foster in children a deep sense of curiosity about their world and to encourage them to ask questions. Oliver in Judith Rossell's book of that title (2012) is another curious chap who "[likes] finding things out." His questions are nonstop: "How do planes stay up in the sky?" "How does the fridge work?" Oliver's attempt to find out what lives in the bathtub drain leads him to build a submarine out of a cardboard box and this starts him on an imaginary journey to the sea. There he cavorts with penguins until he decides his mother will miss him, and returns home. Solutions to even the stickiest problems often begin by asking questions, even ones that seem foolish at first. After enjoying either or both of these books with the children, make a list with them of things they are wondering about. Their list might be questions about a topic they are currently studying. How might they find answers to some of these wonderings? Is the classroom a place where asking questions is safe and encouraged? Set out as a class to find answers to one or two of their questions and encourage students to work on their own

or in groups to research others. If they wish to use the Internet as a source of information, what steps can they take to assure that the sites they are using provide accurate information? Another possible activity is to present the class with a group of related stand-alone objects and ask them to formulate questions about them.

Vasya Kandinsky is often credited with founding the abstract art movement. Brought up in 19th-century Russia in a formal, constrained household, his life changed when he received a box of paints and began hearing the colors make sounds "like an orchestra tuning up." Barb Rosenstock tells the story of this painter and his groundbreaking works of swirling colors in *The Noisy Paint Box* (2014). "It took a long time for people to understand" Kandinsky's work, but the painter insisted on painting in his own way, unafraid to paint pictures that made people "feel" rather than just see. Several picture book characters follow Kandinsky's lead in daring to create art in their own way. In *Mousterpiece* (2012) by Jane Zalben, Janson, a mouse, lives in a museum and loves to explore at night when visitors have gone. One evening she arrives at the modern art section and is awestruck. There are dots, squares, squiggles, stripes, all dazzling to the little mouse. She immediately begins making her own art in the different styles she sees on the walls. She cuts shapes, splatters paint, makes swirls, and even tries sculpture. Her work is so good that when the museum director discovers it, he gives Janson her own show. Many people admire her art, but Janson's very favorite piece is the one she created all on her own, "in her own style. / Unlike anyone else's. / And that is when / Janson knew she / had become a true artist." All the art works Janson sees and their creators are identified at the end of the book, making *Mousterpiece* a fine introduction to modern art for young children. Equally important, though, is the message that observing art closely, even imitating it for a time, fuels one's own creative juices and enables one to move from imitation to original work. Another museum visitor, a young girl this time, in Susan Verde's *The Museum* (2013), states, "When I see / a work of art, / something / happens in / my heart." Her body as well as her mind reacts to what she sees. She slumps in sadness before sad paintings, feels hungry before food-filled still lifes and makes faces in imitation of the strange visages she sees. When she comes upon a huge blank canvas, though, she's puzzled at first: "Is this a joke?" Soon, however, all she has experienced at the museum fills her with joy and she declares, "It's mine to fill / the way I choose, / . . . It's my creation . . . I am feeling such elation!" Marisol, the enthusiastic young artist in Peter Reynolds's *Sky Color* (2012), doesn't hesitate to share her art "with the world"—on the refrigerator, through the mail, even on posters. So when the class prepares to paint a mural for the library, she is right there shouting, "I'll paint the sky!" But she is flummoxed when she can't find blue paint. The problem gnaws at her until she watches a sunset. That night she dreams she is flying "through a sky swirling with colors," and next day at school, mixes paints into "an all-together new [sky] color." The final spread reveals the mural with Marisol's dazzling sky as backdrop for the multicolored fish leaping from the water, testament to her daring creativity. This story, along with Reynolds's *The Dot* (2003) and *Ish* (2004) carry the important message that there is an artist inside everyone and that sometimes finding that creative spark means doing the unexpected. In these days of filling in circles on tests, it's an important message to share with youngsters.

As discussed in the first chapter, viewing art work closely enables us to notice more about the people and world around us and can awaken our own creativity. Bob Raczka's *The Vermeer Interviews* (2009) offers an interesting way to help students notice details in works of art. In it, he conducts interviews with the different subjects of Jan Vermeer's beautiful paintings.

A reproduction of each painting appears in color on a full page opposite each interview so readers can refer to it as the interview progresses. When the author interviewer tells the milkmaid "there is something beautiful and even heroic about you," the maid answers that Vermeer used visual tricks to make her seem more than just a milkmaid. To Bob's query, "Like what?" the maid calls attention to different parts of the picture to show viewers how the play of light makes her seem important. Raczka follows this process with the seven Vermeer paintings in the book. Gregory Rogers's *The Hero of Little Street* (2012) is a wordless book about art that unleashes readers' creative imaginations. What would happen if a person suddenly entered into a famous painting? That's exactly what happens when a young boy, chased by three bullies, hides in the National Gallery. There a dog leaps out of a painting by Jan van Eyck and leads the boy into another by Jan Vermeer. Together they roam Vermeer's city of Delft, and the boy manages to save a big group of dogs from a butcher's knife. All of these books, and so many more children's books about art and artists (see Saccardi, *Art in Story*, 2007, for extensive bibliographies and ideas), lend themselves to many activities in the classroom or in collaboration with the art teacher. Encourage students to create their art works in the spirit of Janson who paints "in her own style"; the young museum visitor who fills a blank canvas "the way [she[choose[s]"; Marisol who devises "an altogether-new [sky] color"; Vashti who, in Reynolds's *The Dot* is brave enough to create her art by allowing a dot on the page to lead her wherever it will; or, finally, Raymond in Reynolds's *Ish*, who comes to realize that his paintings don't have to resemble any specific objects or places. Allow them the freedom to create their own art using any media (paints, crayons, pastels, etc.) they wish. Or they may wish to experiment with what would happen if they cut apart a piece of art they have created and rearrange the pieces in an entirely new way. Do they like the result? Why or why not? Visit a museum and/or view art works on the Web and study some paintings closely, asking students to notice different parts of each work. Provide art books for children to peruse at their leisure to see how artists use color and shape in their work. (See Bob Raczka's *Speaking of Art*, 2010 to hear quotes from the artists themselves about their work) Ask the children to imagine themselves inside a favorite painting and write a story about their adventures there. Older students might choose an artist they enjoy and write interviews for subjects in several of his or her paintings. Collect the interviews into a book for use by another class. *A World of Food: Discover Magical Lands Made of Things You Can Eat!* (2012) by Carl Warner can launch an especially creative art project. In it Warner creates pages of unique worlds, each world formed by foods of a particular color. For example, "If all the world were yellow, / A desert it would be / Of couscous, rice, and yellow beans." The scene depicts cheese pyramids, dunes made of grains, a pasta ship beneath a corn-shaped hot air balloon, and much more. A brown world features a chocolate train with chocolate-covered-pretzel wheels traveling on chocolate bar rails amid chocolate-covered raisin pebbles and cocoa powder hills. What kinds of worlds would the students like to create through their art? Might they use pictures of household objects or foods or clothing cut from magazines? Clay sculptures? Cut shapes?

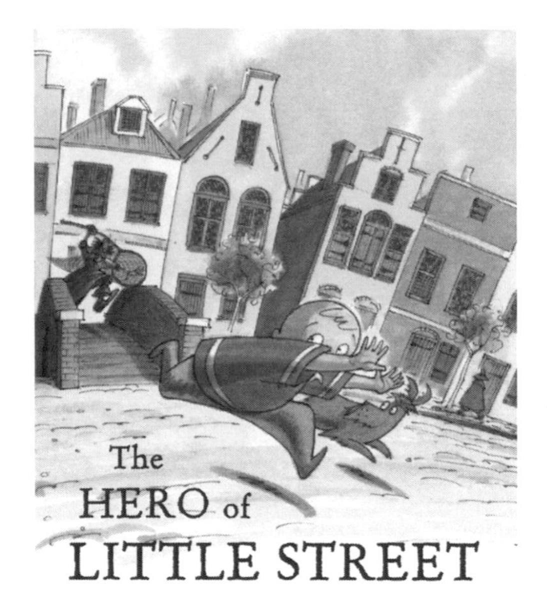

Two robots, each formed by shapes such as circles, squares, rectangles, and so on, try to outdo each other in Annette Simon's *Robot Zombie FRANKENSTEIN!* (2012). When one transforms himself into "Robot Zombie Frankenstein," the other leaves the scene and returns as "Robot zombie Frankenstein PIRATE!" This prompts the first robot to become "Robot zombie Frankenstein pirate SUPERHERO!" The one-upmanship continues to escalate until one of them transforms into a chef and produces a cherry pie, which they both enjoy. In addition to being great fun, this story game provides an opportunity for children to identify shapes and, ultimately, to create their own outlandish robots with cut-out shapes in various colors.

Another story about a robot, *Doug Unplugged* by Dan Yaccarino (2013), contains in one simple picture book the central message of this text. Because they want their son to be the smartest robot ever, his parents plug him in every morning so he can download all kinds of information. One morning they announce that the day's download would provide him with lots of information about the city. And he does learn many facts like how much trash people in the city discard each day and that 500 million pigeons live there. But when a pigeon lands on his window sill and coos, Doug realizes that there is much more involved in knowing than learning facts. So he unplugs himself and goes out to explore the city first-hand. He discovers, among many things, that pigeons scatter when you move among them, subway cars screech, skyscrapers provide excellent views of the city, "garbage cans are smelly," and "cool water in a park fountain feels good on a hot day." Best of all, he learns how much fun it is to have a friend when he plays with a boy in the park. To be creative, to become, as we advocate here, a divergent thinker and problem solver, we need more than facts. As Professor David L. Kirp states in his insightful article, "The Secret to Fixing Bad Schools" (*New York Times*, February 10, 2013, 5), "To succeed, students must become thinkers, not just test-takers." We need to dig deeper, notice the world around us, experience it with all our senses. After enjoying this important story, ask the children to use all their senses to notice their surroundings on the way home—even if they simply view the route from a bus or car window. If that is the case, perhaps they can imagine how something might feel if they were to touch it or smell if they were to get near it. The next day, discuss what they have discovered. Did they notice anything they had never focused on before? (If there are woods near the school, this activity would be even more meaningful if the class could go out and explore this outdoor environment—hear the crunch of leaves or birdsong, experience the feel

of dirt or mud in their hands, see the beauty of flowers and smell their perfume, etc.) In his book *Birthright: People and Nature in the Modern World* (2012), Stephen R. Kellert writes "dependence on nature has shaped and continues to shape our capacities to feel, reason, think, master complexity, discover, create, heal, and be healthy" (Introduction: Biofilia, x). It is a clarion call for us to enable our students to leave their classrooms and experience the natural world first-hand.

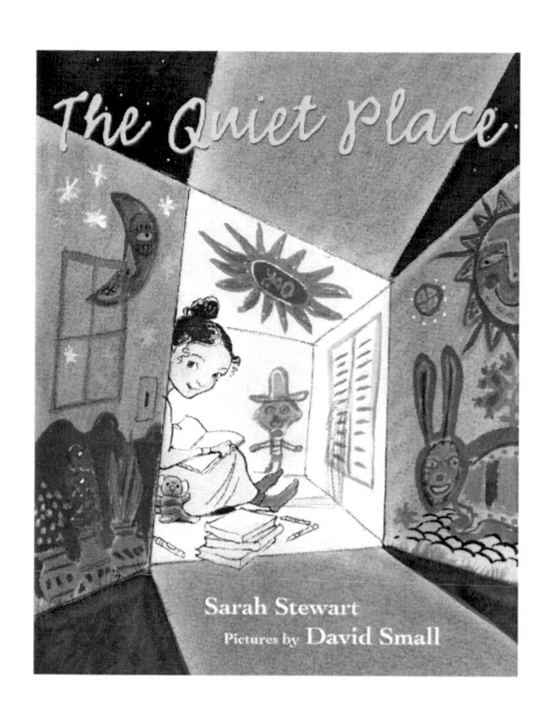

It is 1957 and Isobel and her family are traveling from Mexico to make a new life in the United States in Sarah Stewart's lovely *The Quiet Place* (2012). Experiencing snow for the first time, trying to learn a new language, getting along in school—all these things are scary. Isobel is able to live with the challenges of her new environment by creating a safe, quiet place out of a big box her father gives her after unpacking their new refrigerator. Then she continues to enlarge her space with new boxes her mother obtains from the birthday parties she caters. Here Isobel can shut out some of the disquieting things in her new world—at least for a while. She has devised, all on her own, a creative way to help herself cope. A beautiful fold-out in the book reveals Isobel's quiet place with all its decorated rooms. Are there times when the children feel uneasy or fearful—perhaps when trying to make a new friend or when undertaking a new activity? What creative plans can they think of to help themselves through these uncomfortable times? Older students can research a local shelter where the children might feel strange or afraid. Can they work with those children to create a safe, quiet place that might provide some comfort?

Two other books feature protagonists who make creative use of boxes. Chloe, the middle bunny of twenty siblings (McCarthy, *Chloe*, 2012), loves family fun time each evening. But when father brings home a television, her brothers and sisters gather motionless around the set, leaving Chloe to declare, "This is the worst family fun time EVER!" She then proceeds to pop the bubble wrap in the box the TV came in and the sounds become so enticing her siblings leave their program and join her. Next, she turns the large box into a TV set and puts on a show, again joined by her siblings. In Suzanne Bloom's *A Mighty Fine Time Machine* (2009), Samantha tells her friends Grant and Antoine, that they've been "bamboozled" because they've traded some yummy goodies for a very plain time machine box. "It has no . . . rocket-blaster boosters, and no thingamabobs!" she declares. Nevertheless, she gets to work with them on improvements. They load the box, inside and out, with all kinds of household objects and toys. They try again, making some adjustments. Nothing. Not even a "map-o-meter" helps it do much more than wobble and then tumble over. But when her friends become intrigued with the books in Samantha's wagon, she thinks of a whole new, quite wonderful use for the box. Boxes, bubble wrap, kitchen utensils can all become objects of imaginary play, so important for arriving at innovative ideas. Being willing to use them in many different ways to achieve desired results puts children on the road to divergent thinking. Make a "fun family time" list of activities with your students that includes household objects they can use for pretend play. Circulate this list among parents and caregivers to encourage time away from the tube and other electronic devices.

In her book of "wordles," which she defines as "groups of words that sound exactly the same but mean different things," Amy Krouse Rosenthal (*I Scream Ice Cream!*, 2013) pushes the idea of homonyms beyond what we ordinarily see in picture books. As in the title, she doesn't hesitate to split words or move letters around to create her different meanings. And her text rhymes besides—a double challenge. A page turn transforms the text, "Me, cloud." that appears above an illustration of a self-satisfied cloud into "Meek," then "Loud," with each word depicting in turn a shy child and a boisterous one. A Funnel Cakes cart proprietor tells disappointed customers, "Sorry, no more funnel cakes." On the following pages, we see two elks who did get some of those funnel cakes holding their stomachs as the text reads, "Sorry, no more fun . . . elk aches." In another book, *Wumbers* (2012, Rosenthal has some fun combining words and numbers. Accompanying a girl learning to play the tuba are the words, "She's learning a 2ne on the 2ba." Her teacher gives the girl these instructions, "Tigh 10 your mouth . . . then 4ce out the air." From the beginning endpapers to its conclusion, this book is just plain fun and demonstrates an innovative way to think about both words and numbers. These two books offer children opportunities to surprise their classmates and families with their creative word and number play and to add to their creative enjoyment by drawing humorous cartoons to illustrate their writing. Make one or both books available to the students as models and then encourage them to produce their own "wordles" or "wumbers" working alone or in groups. Younger children will likely find *Wumbers* an easier model.

Several picture books invite readers to imagine the impossible, the improbable, the absolutely ridiculous. After all, isn't that what divergent thinkers do all the time? Consider the present state of our world if no one had ever imagined being able to fly; imagined a machine that could wash dishes; imagined a medicine that could cure the plague. All of these thinkers imagined and attempted the impossible, and they succeeded, in spite of the often discouraging comments, or even ridicule of those around them. "Imagine a ladder without steps" (6), "a padlock without a keyhole" (7), "a world where things are not quite what they seem" (18), invites Norman Messenger in his book entitled *Imagine* (2005). In addition to his fantastical illustrations, he uses foldouts and rotating wheels to fashion outrageous animals and absurd-looking people. In little squares at the corners of the pages, he presents several challenges for children to do outside the book as well. Three exquisite books by Sarah Thomson, *Imagine a Night* (2003), *Imagine a Day* (2005), and *Imagine a Place* (2008), invite older children to stretch the boundaries of their world. Luscious paintings accompany each summons to consider the impossible, and it is essential to share them if children are to experience the full impact of the books. For example, the illustration opposite "Imagine a night . . . / . . . when you might find / that gravity / doesn't work / quite as you expected." depicts children riding bikes up a flight of stairs. "Imagine a day . . . / . . . when grace and daring / are all we need / to build a bridge." shows myriads of people standing on each others' shoulders to form a human bridge. People carrying lanterns as they skate across a river onto which snow banks mirror the clouds accompanies the injunction, "Imagine a place . . . / . . . / where water is solid, / light is liquid, / sky a frozen river / flowing under your feet." Another champion of the imagination was the artist René Magritte who, in the words of D. B. Johnson who captures the artist's imaginative spirit wonderfully in his picture book, *Magritte's Marvelous Hat* (2012), created worlds in which "ordinary things appear in unlikely places, and the familiar is suddenly very strange" (D. B. Johnson, author's note). In Johnson's fictional account, the artist appears as a dog who purchases a hat that floats above his head. The hat inspires him to paint a surrealist world that both surprises and delights those who view his paintings. Expose the class to more Magritte works through Susan Goldman Rubin's board book, *Magritte's Imagination* (2009). In it trains fly out of a fireplace, a horseback rider rides through trees, and trees grow eyes and noses. All the paintings in this small book are identified in the end pages. A most unusual book celebrating the imagination is Richard Lewis's *The Bird of Imagining* (2001), in which his poem about the imagination, personified as a bird, is illustrated with a series of drawings by school children. The flyleaf of the book declares that "there lives, perhaps in each of us, a bird of imagining," and "this book opens . . . the life of the imagination to all its winged possibilities." Once this bird is allowed to fly freely in our minds, "nothing / and no one, / [is] ever the same afterwards." Do students think a bird is an apt metaphor for the imagination? Why or why not? Are there other creatures that would be equally suitable? Challenge the students, working alone or in groups, to create an illustration for such a creature—real or imaginary—and then, as the children in Lewis's project have done, write a piece or statement about what the creature can do.

In addition to the activity for Lewis's book, you might also stage a grand finale after sharing one or more of these books on the imagination with older students. Declare a "Celebration of Our Imaginations Day" during which they will be free to stretch their imaginations as far as they can. Perhaps they would like to work in groups to share their ideas. They might wish to create fantastical foldout creatures such as those in Messenger's book and bring their creations to students in another class to unfold and savor. They might want to turn their school yard, via drawings, into a place where impossible and wonderful things can happen, or draw night scenes beyond what anyone has ever seen or contemplated. They may even wish to create surrealist paintings like Magritte and display them in the hall or in a school art show. The possibilities are limited only by their imaginations!

Sunny Acres was always a happy, friendly place—until a grumpy goat arrives on the scene (Helquist, *Grumpy Goat*, 2013). The goat wants no part of the other animals who try to befriend him, and instead, eats and sulks alone—until he notices a small yellow flower blooming atop a hill. Tenderly he waters it, crops the grass around it, and nestles nearby to bask in its beauty. Slowly other animals approach and the goat actually looks forward to seeing them. But one day a breeze blows the flower's seeds everywhere, and the flower disappears. The goat, with his friends close by for support, remains on the hill in sorrow all winter until, when warm weather returns, that hill becomes a sea of bright yellow flowers. This story is striking, not only for the beautiful oil and acrylic illustrations that enrich it, but also for the transformation it chronicles. When the goat "never [looks] up at the blooming flowers or the green leaves or the bright sky," he remains trapped in his own gloominess. But

when he stops to notice the natural world around him, even though the object of his admiration is a lowly dandelion, it changes him profoundly. The ability to notice even small things can bring joy into otherwise "ho-hum" days, and the habit of noticing can awaken students to their peers and community. Take the class on a walk around the neighborhood or school yard, ask them to notice something that gives them joy—even something they have noticed before but now see with new eyes—and then return to the classroom and write about it.

"A is for apple," right? Of course it is, according to Zebra who, in Erin Cabatingan's *A Is for Musk Ox* (2012), is trying to create a normal, conventional alphabet book. But musk ox has other ideas. "Every other alphabet book starts with A is for apple. That's sooo boring. I think you should do something different. How about this: A is for musk ox." Zebra is outraged because everyone knows musk ox doesn't begin with A. But the clever musk ox proceeds to explain how such a statement would work because, after all, a musk ox is **a**wesome and lives in the **A**rctic, which includes **A**laska. Mollified, the zebra grants him his A for musk ox, but soon has to concede that every letter of the alphabet can stand for musk ox once he hears the beast's surprising explanations. After exposure to this zany alphabet book, students will be itching to create unusual alphabet books of their own. Another option would be to design creative alphabet letters. How many different designs can students devise for each letter?

In Jon Agee's wacky *The Other Side of Town* (2012), a New York cabbie picks up a strange-looking guy dressed in a green body suit topped with a pink pompom. The fare wants to go to "Schmeeker Street" on the other side of town. To get there, they must go through the "Finkon Tunnel," skirt "spotholes," and turn on their "nog lights" when the streets get dark. When they finally arrive, they are surrounded by people in green body suits topped with pink pompoms who drive pink cars and create the most crowded "mush hour" ever. Once the guy in the green suit pays his fare, he assures the cabbie all he has to do to return home is drive across the "Snooklyn Bridge." Sure enough, there is Times Square in all its bright familiarity, and he can hardly wait to tell everyone about the strange goings on, on the other side of town. But much to his surprise, his wife and children greet him dressed in green body suits topped with pink pompoms, and "tweet loaf with bravy" is being served for dinner. Children from New York will likely recognize famous landmarks despite Agee's fun wordplay, but it won't take much figuring for children in any locale to see how the author is having fun by rearranging letters. He presents this preposterous trip in a very matter-of-fact way, and it is up to readers to get the joke. Get it they will, and they will savor the illustrations in all their pink and green hilarity. When the laughter subsides, ask the children to write their own creative stories about the other side of their towns. Spend some time talking about possibilities before they begin. What might the buildings look like? The pets, vegetation, food? How will the people be dressed? How will they speak? What are their occupations? The possibilities for creativity and divergent thinking are endless here. As an alternative, the students might wish to work together to create "the other side of town," and make a model of that alternate city to go with their written story, complete with people, buildings, and so on. (For much more zaniness and out-of-the-ordinary thinking, be sure to check out Agee's many other unusual picture books.)

Ruby, in Matthew Harvey's *Cecil the Pet Glacier* (2012) is a normal little girl whose eccentric parents constantly embarrass her. Her father has a topiary business and her mother makes tiaras, and both of them tango on the front lawn in front of their yellow and pink striped house. So when it comes to wanting a pet, a nice conventional dog would suit Ruby just fine. But, much to her chagrin, a family trip to Norway nets her a pet glacier, Cecil, which follows her everywhere. Ruby doesn't want to be different, and surely, a pet glacier would make her stand out in a crowd. So she ignores Cecil. When the glacier risks its life to find her beloved doll, however, Ruby changes her mind and cares for him tenderly ever after. Children often fear being different from their peers. They want to dress the same way, engage in the same activities, even share the same likes and dislikes. But divergent thinking by its very nature requires being different—thinking differently, taking new risks, challenging the old way of doing things. The new clothing style, the different building, the unusual symphony—all were created by people who were able to think and see and hear differently.

Risk-Taking, Divergent-Thinking Characters

Often creativity springs from doing the unexpected, and doing the unexpected usually involves risk. On a live radio broadcast, host Joe Frank invited an actor friend to make a mock appearance as a mime on tour in the United States. After engaging with the actor in a discussion of his work and the history of mime, Frank asked him to perform a piece from his upcoming show for his radio audience. What followed was thirty seconds of absolute silence—on the radio! While some listeners complained, many "thought it was one of the funniest things they ever heard" (Gross, 2012, 25). Like Joe Frank who dared to do the unthinkable—broadcast extended silence on radio—the characters in the following picture books solve problems or demonstrate divergent thinking by using their mental and physical resources in ways that go beyond the expected.

When a hungry fox meets a goose on the street in Mo Willems's *That Is NOT a Good Idea!* (2013), he invites her for a stroll. She agrees, but a page turn reveals that two of her goslings think "That is NOT a good idea!" Fox and Goose proceed on their way nevertheless, into the dark woods and even into the fox's kitchen. With each milestone in their trip, more and more goslings warn, "That is REALLY NOT a good idea!" and finally, when the soup pot appears and the fox invites the goose to look inside for the missing ingredient, the goslings scream while jumping up and down in extreme agitation, "That is REALLY, / REALLY, / REALLY, / REALLY, / NOT a good idea! At this point, children will assume the goose "is cooked," but a page turn reveals it is the fox who lands in the soup while the goose provides a tasty meal for her children who, spoons in hand, tell readers, "Well, / we DID try / to warn him." This surprise will delight and relieve youngsters but more importantly, it gives them the message that risks undertaken with a definite plan in mind often result in very good outcomes. Discuss the story with the children emphasizing that while the goose would have been eaten if she had been careless and let down her guard, she did risk going off with the fox confident that she had the skills she needed to fool him. In Linda Bailey's humorous *Toads on Toast* (2012), a fox, disgusted and bored with his daily diet of big fat boiled toads, heads for the book store to look for tastier toad recipes. Surrounded by cookbooks, he discovers that he should have been looking for young, tender, small toads that are far tastier. Back to the pond he goes, and he captures a net full of the little creatures. Just as he settles on a feast of toad legs, mamma toad jumps through his kitchen window and convinces him to make "toad in the hole" instead—which, it turns out, is made with toast, butter, and eggs—and NOT toads. Fox is so delighted with his meal he makes some for everyone. Bonus: the illustrations depicting toadlet shenanigans while mom is dealing with the fox are hilarious. Still another fox gets tricked out of a meal in Mike Twohy's *Outfoxed* (2013). This time, a resourceful duck is whisked out of the hen house by a fox anticipating a delicious chicken dinner. When he pulls a duck out of his pocket, he's disappointed but resigned. The duck, on the other hand, isn't. To avoid being a meal he pretends to be a dog, slobbering all over the fox, eating his socks, and peeing on the carpet. It's just laugh-out-loud funny.

Mimi lives with her family in a village in Western Kenya in Katie Smith Milway's *Mimi's Village and How Basic Health Care Transformed It* (2012). When her little sister becomes very ill after drinking contaminated water, the family has to walk all the way to a clinic in a neighboring village to save her. The nurse there is able to provide the care and advice little Nakkissi needs, but now mosquito season is coming, and Mimi's village has no readily accessible health care. Mimi can't rest knowing the very real threat to her family and neighbors, and she finally comes up with an idea: "Pa, you and our uncles built our house, didn't you?" Could you build a clinic, too? Maybe then a nurse would come." Her father dismisses the idea as a big dream and nothing more. But later, he agrees to approach the elders and the other families. With donations, hard work, and their own savings, the community does succeed in building a clinic and hiring a part time nurse to staff it. Mimi's conviction that the seemingly impossible would not be so impossible with community effort had life-saving results. Her story is one in the Citizen Kid series published by Kids Can Press. All of them "inform children about the world and inspire them to be better global citizens," (Jacket cover) and they all contain suggestions for action.

Laura Vaccaro Seeger (*Bully*, 2013) uses art work to great effect in showing how bullies loom ever larger and become ever more powerful when we allow them to continue their bullying. "Wanna play?" asks a rabbit, chicken, and turtle, in turn, of a bull they encounter in a field. The bull answers with a resounding "NO!" and proceeds to call each animal an insulting name. As he does so, he becomes larger and larger across each spread so that finally, all that fits is one gigantic hoof. But then a goat comes along and confronts him, calling out,

"Bully!" refusing to be intimated even though the bull tries to scare him off. Eventually the bull realizes what being a bully means, is reduced to normal size, and apologizes. Now the bull asks the rabbit, chicken, and turtle, "Wanna play?" and they, along with the goat, go off together. Discuss how the goat's willingness to take a risk and confront the bully resulted in a change in the bully's behavior. While it may not always be wise to take such a risk alone in dealing with a bully, what other things can the children do that, while they may be risky, could prove helpful? (Offer friendship, tell a parent, school administrator or teacher, for example.) In Lana Button's *Willow Finds a Way* (2013), Willow and her classmates must deal with a manipulative "bully." Kristabelle doesn't physically harm other children, but she is, nevertheless, "the boss." She tells kids where to sit, "what to play, and who to play with." One day Kristabelle announces that she is having "a *fantastic* birthday party" and anyone who is on her list can attend. Of course, to remain on her list, the children have to do everything Kristabelle says: drop what they are doing on the playground and clap for her tricks on the climber, give up first place on line, and so on. Those who defy her have their names crossed off in front of everybody. Willow wants to tell Kristabelle what she is doing is wrong, but she can't find the words—until she can't take the bossy girl's behavior any longer and crosses her *own* name off the list. This gives everyone else the courage to do the same, and they are finally free to make their own decisions. But what about Kristabelle? Is she to remain friendless? Willow has a solution for that, too—one that effects change not only in her classmates, but in Kristabelle as well.

Kendi loves going to her little village school room in Cameroon (Rockliff, *My Heart Will Not Sit Down*, 2012). But one day her American teacher brings the sad news that there is a Depression in the United States, there is no work, and "people were starving because they did not have money to buy food." Kendi becomes so upset "her heart [will] not sit down." She asks her mother and neighbors for money for the people across the "great salt river," but everyone is so poor. Nevertheless, the next day, though she hasn't enough to pay the "head tax," Kedi's mother gives her a single coin. She's embarrassed to give so little to her teacher until the other villagers arrive with their coins as well—a total of $3.77. It took great courage for Kendi to approach her family and neighbors for money—all of them so poor that their collected resources added up to less than five dollars. Nevertheless, she saw a need and had to act. The author tells us that this story was "inspired by a true event. In 1931, the city of New York received a gift of $3.77 to feed the hungry. It came from the African country of Cameroon." Her lengthy author's note also describes other poor communities around the world that found ways to help others. Camen Agra Deedy's *14 Cows for America* (2009) tells a similar story based on a true event. When a Maasai village hears about the attacks in New York City on 9/11, they send their most precious possessions—cattle—to comfort the grieving. Perhaps after reading either or both of these beautiful books, the students can find a way to help someone in need in their own community.

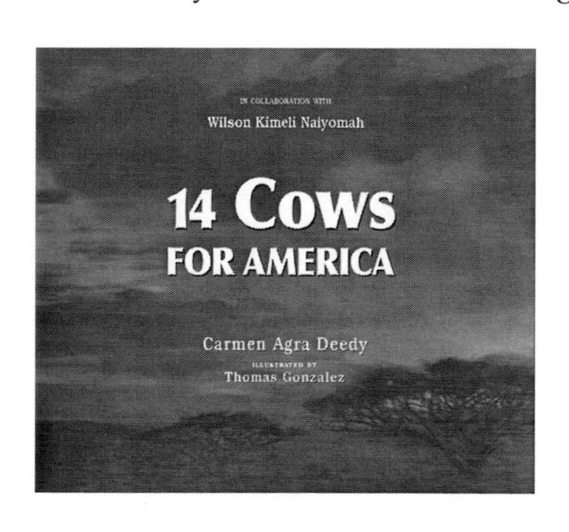

John Fardell's *The Day Louis Got Eaten* (2012) is a cumulative tale featuring Louis who, while out in the woods with his sister Sarah, is eaten by a "Gulper." This creature is eaten by another and that one by another, and so on, each monster bigger than the last.

Beginning readers will love chiming in on the predictable text, and the creatures are much more humorous than scary. But more importantly, they will meet two siblings who are very capable creative problem solvers. When her brother is first eaten by the Gulper, "Sarah [doesn't] panic." She might have run to save herself, or run to get help, or stood rooted to the spot sensing a hopeless situation. Instead, Sarah, in an unusual move for one so young, carefully considers the Gulper's eating habits, feels her brother will be safe if she acts quickly, and even has the clear thinking to collect what she might need to save him. Even when she encounters ever larger monsters, she remains resolute until her plan achieves Louis's rescue. But Louis is no wimp either, as he proves in the story's surprise ending.

Monsters destroy things, scare people, and create general chaos. Right? That's what Grouch, Grump, and Gloom 'n' Doom are hoping the huge monster they create will do since they can't agree on who among themselves is the "biggest, baddest monster" (McDonnell, 2012). But contrary to expectations, the first thing their monster does is say "Dank you!" and proceed to greet the creatures around him with great gentleness. He's just so grateful to be alive. Grouch, Grump, and Gloom 'n' Doom are aghast but take comfort when Monster crashes through a wall and enters a bakery. Gleefully they look through the window waiting for the "howls and yowls" to begin. Instead, Monster emerges with a bag of donuts that he shares with them. This unexpected, totally "unmonsterly" behavior brings about a sea change in the three formerly miserable, complaining, tantrum-prone monsters. Now they are content to watch the sunrise and enjoy the seashore with their new friend, and "no one [is] thinking about being a monster."

A group of toys are left outside in Mini Grey's *Toys in Space* (2012). As the sky darkens and the toys become frightened, Wonder Doll makes up a story to distract them. "Once upon a time," she begins, a space ship carrying a space creature named Hoctopize comes to Earth and beams seven toys left in the garden into its space vehicle. It is looking for its lost toy, Cuddles, and has been collecting thousands of toys in the hope of finding it. They encourage Hoctopize to return the toys since their owners miss them, and eventually the little creature does find his Cuddles. Throughout Wonder Doll's story, the listening toys offer comments in speech balloons, making it easy for readers to separate the tale about Hoctopize from the story of the animals left in the yard overnight. This wonderfully imaginative yarn is a fine launch for students' original stories featuring lost objects. What happens to keys, or gloves, or socks, and other such items while they are missing and where might they be found?

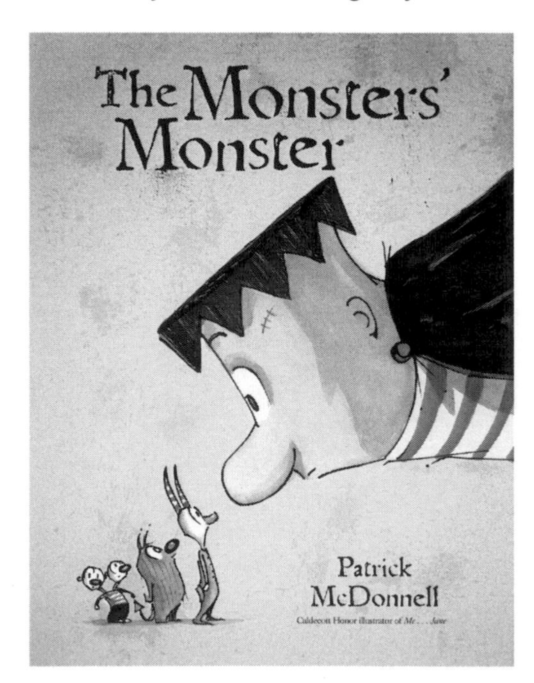

Most slave masters don't allow their slaves to learn how to read and write, but that doesn't stop Rosa, her momma, and some of their neighbors from sneaking out in the dead of night and "walk[ing] till [Rosa's] legs feel like they can't walk anymore," to attend classes in a deep hole in the ground in Lesa Cline-Ransome's poignant *Light in the Darkness* (2013). They risk beatings, being sold away, and even death to learn from Morris, a slave from another plantation whose mistress taught him to read the bible when he was young. Every noise and hoof beat above their hiding place fills them with dread, and still they come to learn, "taking in learning like it's their last breath." The beautiful illustrations, most shrouded in the dark cover of night, reveal a determined people willing to risk all to read and write. Although this is a story about conditions among slaves long ago, many people today are deprived of the ability to attend school because of poverty or the restrictive laws of their governments. A picture book that helps young readers understand the restrictions placed on girls and women by the Taliban regime is Jeanette Winter's *Nasreen's Secret School: A True Story from Afghanistan* (2009). Nasreen stops speaking after her parents disappear, and it is only when her grandmother risks everything to enroll her in a secret school that the girl is able to overcome her sadness. After researching some modern-day situations—children in Africa who stay home because their families cannot afford the school uniform required for school attendance; or young girls deprived of an education in many countries, for example; ask the children to write a pamphlet about their findings and to design a cover for it that is so inviting it will spur their school mates to action such as collecting money to send to a relief organization.

Many African Americans escaped slavery by fleeing under cover of night and following the North Star to freedom. Throughout this journey they were under constant threat of being tracked by dogs and captured, and depended upon the kindness of people in houses on the Underground Railroad for food and safe passage. But Henry Brown, thereafter known as Henry "Box" Brown, came up with an idea no one else had ever tried—a dangerous idea that almost cost him his life. Sally M. Walker tells Henry's remarkable story in *Freedom Song!* (2012). After his beloved wife and children were sold away to another plantation, Henry, whose master hired him out to work in a tobacco factory, deliberately injured his hand so he would be excused from work until it healed. But instead of resting at home, he had friends seal him into a box and mail him from the plantation in Richmond, Virginia, to James McKim in Philadelphia. The arduous journey via wagon and steamboat was horrific. Twice the box was placed upside down and caused the veins in his temple to become as thick as a finger. But he survived and later moved to England to avoid recapture under the Fugitive Slave Act. Older students can read about Henry's life and journey in his own words and see the actual dimensions of the relatively small box into which he squeezed his five-foot-eight inch, 200-pound body by going to http://docsouth.unc.edu/neh/boxbrown/boxbrown.html.

Taro and his little brother Jimmy have a good life in California where their parents emigrated from Japan and where they now own a vegetable market with two friends. But early in December 1941, after the bombing of Pearl Harbor, three FBI agents come to their door and take their father away. Shortly after that, the rest of the family is ordered to pack, leave their home and business, and board a bus along with other Japanese-Americans. The bus brings them to an internment camp where they must live in stark barracks surrounded by barbed wire and guards. Life is strange and difficult for all of them, but Jimmy fares worst of all, refusing to eat or play with the other children, and becomes ill. Taro, who promised his father he would look after the family, feels he must do something. Remembering his brother's fascination with fish, Taro sneaks out during the night carrying his mother's scarf and garden shears, and creeps along the shadows to the fence, hoping to escape the guards' notice. After cutting a hole in the fence, he races to a distant mountain where he finds a pool of water, catches a fish and carries it back in the scarf. Taro does this each week, and by eating the fish their mother cooks in their barrack, Jimmy thrives. The story of *Fish for Jimmy* (2013) by Katie Yamasaki is based on a true incident from her family's history and exhibits amazing bravery and risk taking from one so young.

Picture Book Creators Help Readers Reimagine Their World

Noted children's literature historian, Leonard Marcus, writes that there are picture books that enable us to see "that the world we find ourselves in can be re-imagined" (2012, 47). Creators of these works, through their use of color, how they tell their stories, the ways in which words are arranged on the page, even the very format of the books themselves, shake our preconceived notions and take us to places we might never have gone on our own. Here are some of the ways in which they do this:

A. Extraordinarily Creative Storytelling

Lemony Snicket's *The Dark* (2013) is one of the most stunning and unusual depictions of a common childhood anxiety—fear of the dark and all those things a child's imagination pictures lurking there. Instead of simply telling readers that his protagonist is afraid of the dark and ways he or his parents try to assuage his fear (as many authors of picture books on this topic do), Snicket actually makes "dark" a character who visits Laszlo, a young pajama-clad boy in his suddenly dark bedroom to show him something. But that something is not in the boy's dark closet, or behind the shower curtain. That would be scary enough. It's in his most dreaded place—dark's special room down the basement stairs. "Come closer," says the Dark. Now Laszlo "had never dared come to the dark's room at night," but this time he is able to swallow his fear and risk the scary trip down those creaky stairs. And his risk taking is rewarded with a remedy for his dark room. Follow the reading of this special book with a discussion of the times the children have taken a risk and tried something they were afraid to do. What was the result?

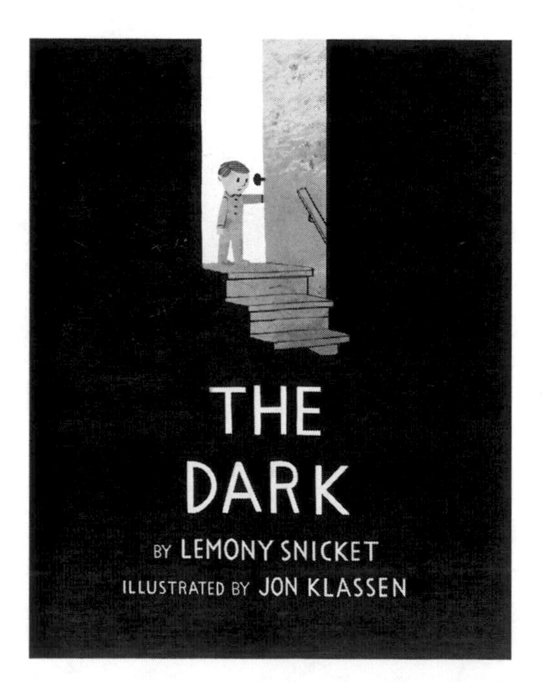

The Bear in the Book (2012) by Kate Banks is a book within a book. A boy takes his favorite book down from the shelf and sits on his bed while his mother reads it to him. It's about a bear that goes to sleep for the winter and all the activity that goes on outside his cave: "Rabbits hopped through the snowdrifts. / The trees shivered. / And the wind blew its icy breath across the fields." As she reads, mother and boy encourage the bear to continue sleeping. "Shh." "Sleep, big black bear." Throughout the story, viewers see pages from the book the mother is reading as well as images of child and mother enjoying it together—until finally, the bear wakes in spring just as the boy falls off to sleep. "Sleep, little boy, sleep." Banks could have written a book about what animals do in winter or how bears hibernate. There are plenty. She could have written about a boy reading a book with his mother before getting into bed. There are plenty of those, too. Instead, she's written a unique bedtime book that is actually contained within another book, while enlarging children's knowledge of animal behavior in winter. This book, in addition to being beautiful, is absolute genius.

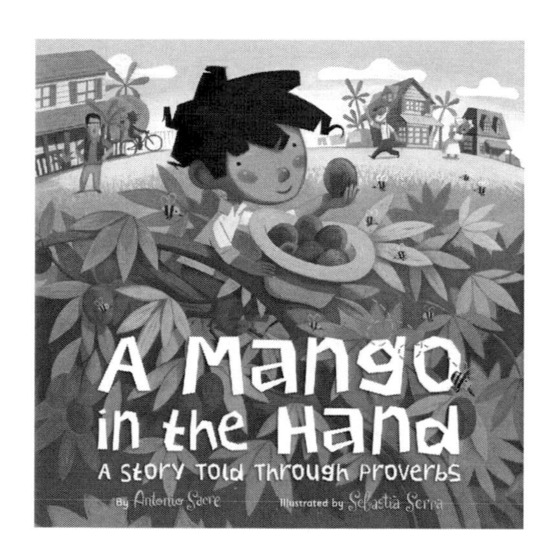

In Antonio Sacre's *A Mango in the Hand* (2011), young Francisco, who lives with his parents in Cuba, sets out to get fruit from a mango tree for a feast to celebrate his saint day. His father insists the boy is old enough to accomplish this mission on his own, but in his first attempt, bees frighten Francisco away. On his second trip, he puts so many mangos in the hat he is using to carry them that they smash to the ground on his way down the tree. Finally, having learned his lesson, he collects one mango at a time until the hat is full, but gives all the mangos away to relatives, even crabby Tia Clara, and friends on the way home. But they have a special surprise in store for him as well, and his saint day celebration is a special feast after all. What makes this story so extraordinary is that it is told through proverbs such as "Better one mango in the hand than a hundred in the tree"; "Nothing bad happens that good doesn't come of it"; "Where there's a will, there's a way." These and many other expressions appear in both English and Spanish. Reading this enjoyable story can be a catalyst for a creative project that would be especially enticing to students of different ethnicities. Divide the students into groups, either by country of origin or mixed groups so that students can learn about the literary heritages of their classmates. Provide copies of Sacre's book as well as other books featuring proverbs such as *The Night Has Ears: African Proverbs* (Bryan, 1999), *My First Book of Proverbs* (Gonzalez, 2003), and *Facts on File: Dictionary of Proverbs* (Manser et al., 2007), and invite each group to create its own story centered around proverbs they select. Children might wish to canvas their parents and other relatives for proverbs particular to their culture or family traditions. The stories the students write can be set in a particular country using only proverbs from that culture, or they might wish to use a mix of proverbs. When the stories are completed and edited, the students can illustrate them and form them into picture books for the class or school library. They might also like to read them aloud in a special gathering of families and other relatives. Extend the project beyond the classroom by putting the stories up on a wiki (or in a blog) and invite another class, especially one from another country, to share its proverb stories as well. Students can even create and share podcasts of their stories. Go to http://www.youtube.com/watch?v=-hrBbczS9I0 for a tutorial on how to do this.

Are two books involving dots, *Press Here* (2011) by Hervé Tullet, and *Dot* (2011) by Patricia Intriago examples of creative storytelling or innovative formats? No matter. Neither are really stories, but both are exceptional models of design breakthroughs and inventive use of

graphics that result from thinking about dots in divergent ways. *Press Here* begins with a single yellow dot that readers are instructed to "press . . . and turn the page." The dot then becomes two yellow dots on the following spread. Subsequent presses result in more dots, dots that change colors, dots that line up in vertical or horizontal formations. When readers shake the book as instructed, the dots spread over the pages, or tilt to top or bottom or side to side. Hard presses and soft presses bring different results: a dot that covers an entire double page spread, and then, finally, the single, original yellow dot. "Bravo!" says the invisible instructor. "Want to do it all over again?" Of course we do! Intriago uses dots to help readers understand the concept of opposites. A red dot is stop while a green one is go. A black dot with a large packman-like slice out of it is loud, and one with a tiny slice missing is quiet. A hungry dot is a white one outlined in black; a full dot is a huge black dot that covers the page. Enjoying either or both of these books may lead students to think about other shapes in divergent ways. What messages can they convey by manipulating triangles, squares, and other shapes?

Christie Matheson invites readers to interact with her as she tells the story of how trees change with each new season in *Tap the Magic Tree* (2013). A bare brown tree, its branches spread out and reaching to the sky, appears on empty white ground. "There's magic in this bare brown tree. / Tap it once. / Turn the page to see." After the child presumably taps the tree, a page turn reveals a single green leaf. More taps result in more leaves. When the reader rubs the tree as instructed, small pink buds appear in the next illustration. Jiggles make the buds fall. The tree is filled with green leaves when the petals are brushed away; apples appear and then hit the ground when the tree trunk is knocked; leaves change color and fall when the child "blow[s] a whooshing breeze"; and snowflakes fall at a hand clap. Then the bare brown tree appears again, but when the reader counts to ten and turns the page, "Magic! / It begins again," with the first green leaves of spring.

A boy recounts his great-grandfather's life in Lane Smith's extraordinary *Grandpa Green* (2011). Smith accompanies his young narrator's story with topiaries that reflect great-grandpa's life and profession: horticulture. A large topiary carrot and a hen with chick just breaking out of an egg accompany "He grew up on a farm with / pigs and corn and carrots . . . / and eggs." A berry-filled bush reflects grandpa's chicken pox and a topiary maiden depicts his future wife, first glimpsed at a café. Since grandfather is a horticulturalist, this green topiary-filled book is the perfect way to tell his story. Use the book with any age student and give them many opportunities for rereading. They will make more and more connections with each viewing. This

extraordinary storytelling can also serve as a model for older students who might want to tell a parent's or grandparent's story or for a project involving writing the story of someone in a nursing home or senior residence. The students should conduct an initial interview with the person to determine what is unique about him or her. Perhaps it is a profession or a hobby or a philanthropic work. Then they can figure out how to tell that person's story in a way that incorporates that unique feature just as the narrator of *Grandpa Green* used topiaries to tell the story of a horticulturalist. Future interviews will provide the information they need to write the story. Presenting the life story in its unique form to the person would be a logical and meaningful conclusion to this creative project.

Though not a picture book, the creative storytelling done by Jessica Anthony and Rodrigo Corral, authors of *Chopsticks* (2012) must be included here. Older teens will be absolutely fascinated by this novel. Using photos, e-mail conversations, and artifacts including advertisements, songs, theater tickets, newspaper articles, and so on, Anthony and Corral tell the story of two teens, one a piano prodigy (Glory) and the other an artist (Frank), who fall in love. There is also an interactive app and website that extend the novel. As the story opens, Glory is missing. Cut to eighteen months earlier when Glory and Frank meet. They are separated when Glory's father forces her to go on a European concert tour, but instead of playing her advertised pieces at each venue, she begins playing variations of Chopsticks and can't stop. Meanwhile, Frank is expelled from his private school for unacceptable behavior. Additional pictures and clues pop up and readers have to decide whether the relationship actually took place or is a figment of Glory's imagination as mental illness begins to take over. The authors state,

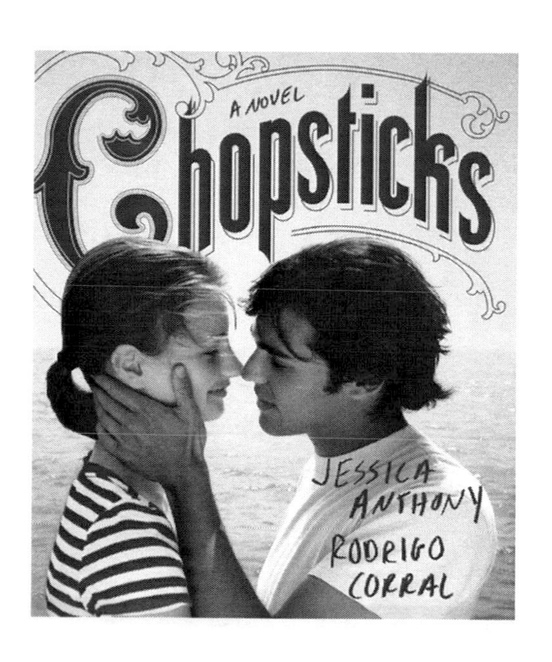

> However you choose to read *Chopsticks*, whether in hand, on a digital tablet or through both book and website, your reading experience will change. Every platform offers readers different ways of encountering the lives of Frank and Glory. (Authors' note.)

This innovative storytelling will have readers talking and rereading as they try to fit the pieces of the tale together. See the website at http://chopsticksnovel.tumblr.com/ and the demo app at http://www.youtube.com/watch?v=I_EZZKziXQs.

Another novel that falls into this category of innovative storytelling is Brian Selznick's masterful *Wonder Struck* (2011). After his mother's death in a car accident, Ben, who is twelve in 1977, goes to live with his aunt and uncle in Minnesota. Rose's story begins when she is also twelve—but fifty years earlier. Her movie star mother has remarried, and Rose is living with her father in New Jersey. Both children are hearing impaired, and both are convinced they can find their longed-for parent—Ben his father and Rose her mother—if they go to New York. Using text and hundreds of pages of black-and-white drawings, Selznick eventually brings these two together in their search, which leads both of them to New York's Museum of Natural History. As readers move through this novel, they will notice that the illustrations provide full scenes and then close-ups on succeeding pages, much like the zoom lens on a camera. The publisher has provided a website that contains activities related to *Wonder Struck*: http://www.scholastic.com/wonderstruck/ and another site that contains several wonderful essays based on the world readers encounter in reading the book: http://wonderstruckthebook.com/essays.htm. After looking at the topics of these essays and reading several of them, can the students think of other places, times, events in the book they might research and write about? Where might they publish their work? (Also see Selznick's *The Invention of Hugo Cabret*, 2007.)

B. Innovative Formats

Search and find books for children have been around for a long time. Most children will have encountered and enjoyed the *Where's Waldo* books, and Walter Wick continues to amaze with the searches for specific objects he devises for young readers as they peruse the multitude of items in his *I Spy* books. But Bob Staake takes readers a step further in *Look! A Book!* (2011) and *Look! Another Book!* (2012). In both books, Staake provides themed displays of dizzying amounts of wacky objects and antics. In between these displays are die-cut images for children to find in those same displays. At the end of each book, Staake sends children back to hunt for even more things. The rhymed hints are fun but the focus is on the images in the die-cuts that force children to focus on objects and actions they might surely miss when viewing the entire display. This attention to detail, on the unexpected, is precisely how we want children to live their lives. Provide time for the children to pour through one or both books. Then ask them to create a hunt for one another. Working alone or in groups, ask them to look carefully at their classroom, pretending they are seeing it for the first time. Can they find things, large or small, they never noticed before? Encourage them to write a sentence, possibly even in rhyme, that will send their classmates on a hunt for the object. Groups might create hunts for several objects.

Lizi Boyd's wordless *Inside Outside* (2013) also utilizes die-cuts to follow a young boy through the seasons, beginning and ending with winter. Die-cut windows show what is going on outside during each season while a spread reveals what the boy is doing inside the house. Die-cuts isolate relevant drawings displayed on the walls and refrigerator. Careful scrutiny uncovers more and more connections not only within a particular season but from season to season as well.

Justine Fontes makes brilliant use of die-cuts and flaps to show what happens when black and white intersect in *Black Meets White* (2005). "First there was black"—the black of night. But then twinkling stars and moon and clouds usher in white, "bright, clean, / plain as day." When they spatter onto each other, they become polka dots, the dots become a checkerboard, which, when elongated, become stripes. Black then laughs and the stripes become intersecting wiggles and create gray, "soft as dawn . . . lovely as a sleeping cat" that stares out at the reader and then closes its eyes with the pull of a tab. A mouse follows the action throughout, but youngsters will be happy to note that the cat has no evil intentions! This is such an inventive way to show the use of black and white to form patterns and what happens when these colors mix. Use it as a catalyst to challenge older students to create novelty books for a younger class. Can they build a story around other colors, shapes? Younger students can create original colors by mixing different paints or crayons.

The die-cuts in Laura Vaccaro Seeger's exceptional book, *Green* (2012), actually forecast what readers can expect in the next spread as they explore the author/illustrator's unusual presentation of the color green. For example, on the spread for "forest green," two die-cut leaves sprout from the trunk of a tall tree. Turn the page for a view of "sea green," and the die-cut leaves become fish in the sea, complete with eyes. Die-cut peas for "pea green" become the eyes of a tiger on the next spread for "jungle green." Astonishingly, even some of the titles for the different kinds of green are hidden in the die-cut illustration. The word "jungle" in the lush spread depicting a tiger hidden among long blades of grasses is formed in the background environment in which a salamander dwells, and the word "khaki," which describes the green of the salamander, is formed by those blades of grass in the preceding jungle scene. A huge stop sign indicates that it is "never green" while a final spread suffused with grass and trees bears the hopeful caption, "forever green." This view of a single color in all its different shades and dimensions can serve as a model for students' exploration of color as well. How many shades of a particular color can they create by mixing paints or crayons? What distinctive names can they devise for each variation?

Nicholas Blechman's *Night Light* (2013) is a counting book that makes use of a number of die-cut lights that correspond to the number being counted. These are arranged on black backgrounds in the order in which they appear on a vehicle, and readers must turn the page to discover the vehicle to which the lights belong. A number and question appear opposite each arrangement of die-cut lights. For example, "6 lights, / visiting many / sights? precedes an arrangement of six die-cut circles: two pairs of red and orange circles on top and two widely spaced white circles on the bottom. A page turn reveals a school bus with its four top lights and two headlights parked in front of a zoo. Children will have fun trying to guess which vehicle

they will find when they turn the page, and this format will help them notice where lights are placed on different kinds of vehicles as well, thus sharpening their observation skills. Something else to consider: what does the title have to do with the content of the book?

Different kinds of vehicles are also featured in Chiêu Urban's clever board book, *Away We Go!* (2013). Each left-hand page begins with a question regarding a specific shape. The query on the first page is, "Do you see a square?" Next to the question is a small square that children can use as reference. The truck below appears with a die-cut square carved out behind the cab. That square is carved out of the train opposite and a red square as well as other shapes also form parts of the train. The book continues with different shapes forming a spaceship, an airplane, a sailboat, an ice cream truck, a bicycle, and more. This inventive book is a delightful demonstration of the ways in which shapes can relate to each other and be placed strategically to form both common and not-so-ordinary modes of transportation. Encourage children to play with arranging shapes to form objects in connection with a current topic of study: community helpers, mammals, insects, among others. Preschools may also have sets of trucks and cars with interchangeable parts so that children can create new vehicles by combining different pieces.

Frank Viva's *A Long Way Away* (2013) is beautifully designed to be read vertically and consists of twenty-six feet of continuous art. Read one way, a creature from a distant planet bids loving parents farewell and descends through space moving through and around heavenly bodies and objects down, down to the depths of the ocean. Turn the book around and read up, and the creature travels from the ocean floor up, up to its home planet and a happy reunion. Besides following the continuous trail of this journey from page to page, youngsters will meet plenty of prepositions in such an enjoyable way that the learning will be fun. Of course this is a book for young students, but older children might use it as inspiration for creating a book involving prepositions to present to a younger class.

Barney Saltzberg's *Andrew Drew and Drew* (2012) might easily have been located among the books about creative young artists discussed earlier, but its innovative format makes it at home here. Barney can't resist a pencil. He doodles, he draws, and he "never knew what would happen when he began." When youngsters flip the flaps, they see how a simple zigzag line becomes a dinosaur's tail; how diagonal lines become a kite that becomes a rocket for blasting into space; and how a small sketched hat produces a host of rabbits. Barney draws things he both sees and imagines. "A drawing is simply a line going for a walk," says Paul Klee (In Tan's *The Bird King*, 2013, unpaged). Where can a simple line take the readers of this book? Invite them to take out their pencils and see.

In an unusual wordless picture book suitable for readers from preschool through adult, Staake has created a story of friendship set in New York City called *Bluebird* (2013). Working only in shades of blue and gray and using images contained within squares and rectangles that bleed to the ends of every page (most extraordinary), he tells the story of a lonely boy who is befriended by a small blue bird. The bird looks in on the boy as he sits in his classroom, accompanies him on his walk home after school, and follows him into Central Park where disaster eventually leads to joy. There is so much to consider with this unique story. Show the book to the class without comment, turning the pages slowly so the children can take in as much as possible. Or, even better, try to obtain several copies so that groups can look at it closely. What do the children think the story is about? Why is it laid out in the geometric shapes of squares and rectangles? Why are shades of only two colors used through most of the story? What do they think the ending means and why are many colors introduced at the end? Come together and discuss the book as a class. The students will likely see this as a story about friendship and bullying. Why did the author choose to tell a friendship story in this way? What is he saying about the ways in which friends should act toward one another? At the end of the discussion, go to http://www.bobstaake.com/bluebirdbook/1.shtml and read with the class the ten-year process involved in the creation of this story. Finally, challenge the children to tell their own friendship stories in whatever form they feel suits what they wish to say. The goal is to lead them to the most innovative and unexpected ways to convey their message. Perhaps they would like to use drama, puppets, art work. It would be especially effective if the students could present their stories at the culmination of a school-wide discussion of bullying. As an extension activity, older students might like to study Bob Staake's other works. They can begin by going to http://blaine.org/sevenimpossiblethings/?p=2268 where they can read about the artist. Perhaps they might like to obtain some of his other books from the library.

Another picture book suitable for older readers is Germano Zullo's *Line 135*. A young girl who lives in the city boards a train for the long journey to the country where her grandmother lives. The book's long narrow shape is the perfect format for this train trip, and the illustrator makes excellent use of its horizontal length to depict in thin black pencil lines the tall buildings and shops of the city and their gradual transformation into the quieter country landscape. The only color used is for the sleek train with its dark green windows, red doors, and chartreuse exterior. The young traveler has ample time to muse along the way. Some day she wants to "travel everywhere" and "know the entire world." But both her mother and grandmother assure her this is impossible, countering that it is "difficult enough to know yourself." Undaunted, however, the child asserts that she "*will* go this way and . . . that way. [She] will know the entire world . . . because [her] mother and . . . grandmother have forgotten what [she has] always known: It *is* possible." As students look at the book closely, they will notice that the line drawings not only change from city to country scenes, they become more fanciful as the journey progresses. What seems to be a rock is really a large animal. Small bridges are suspended from trees in a forest. Tall castle-like spires appear in a field, and mansions totter crookedly on piles of stones—all before a more realistic country landscape appears and grandmother arrives to meet her grandchild. What is the artist saying through these unusual illustrations? Why is the child convinced she can know the world while her elders are sure she cannot? What connections do they see between the adults' belief that the child's goal is impossible with the nay saying often faced by those with innovative ideas? What does knowing the "entire world" mean? Ask the students to write their own responses to some of these questions or other issues the book raises. Divide them into groups so that they can discuss their responses with one another. Finally, what can they do now to know the world? How will knowing the world around them as well as the world in distant places equip them to become the divergent thinkers who will make the world a better place? What do they know about themselves—their talents and character traits—that will help them choose the life journey that will suit them best?

Open This Little Book (Klausmeier, 2013) is the invitation on the cover of the picture book that bears this name. However, the book is quite tall and not so little—until readers do open it and see a small red polka-dotted book about a ladybug within. The ladybug opens a smaller green book about a frog, the frog opens a little orange book about a rabbit and the rabbit opens a still smaller blue book about a monster. But the blue book is too little for the monster's huge fingers to open, so the new animal friends do it for her. They then close all the books one by one with a final invitation for readers. The flyleaf of the book describes it as "a book of startling imagination" and "a stunning showcase of design," and these are not exaggerations. What an unusual way to design a story about friendship. Older students would enjoy working in groups to, first, decide on a story it would be fun to tell, and then, to settle on an interesting design for the book they create to tell it. They must decide on a design that will suit the content of their story. Perhaps they will need the help of the art teacher to execute their plans. This website: http://mystudio3d.tripod.com/handbook.htm, may provide some ideas, but the students' final design should be solely their own and a meaningful match for their story.

Illustrations as Metaphor

Pictures are the crowning glory of picture books, and they are instrumental in telling the story. One of the standards in the Common Core states: "Explain how specific aspects of a text's illustrations contribute to what is conveyed by the words in a story (e.g., create mood, emphasize aspects of a character or setting)" (CCSS.ELA-Literacy.RL.3.7). Here we ask students to go even further, to move beyond what is actually seen on the page and determine how illustrators sometime use their pictures to stand for something else, that is, as metaphors for an idea or a message they wish to convey. In his book *The Bird King: An Artist's Notebook* (2013), Shaun Tan shares work from twelve years of his sketch books, replete with the drawings, doodles, enlarged images of tiny creatures that might appear within a larger framework—all grist for what may or may not be incorporated into his films, books, and other art works. He states that from viewing these images, "interesting or profound ideas can emerge of their own accord, not so much in the form of a 'message', but rather as a strangely articulated question. A scene or character seems to look back from the page and ask, 'What do you make of this'?" If you can obtain several copies of this fascinating book, distribute one to each of several groups of older students and provide ample time for them to peruse the scenes and figures. Encourage the groups to write down the questions they have about the different drawings; the stories these drawings seem to be telling. They might engage in a similar exercise with Tan's wordless book, *The Arrival* (2006). The more time they spend with this book, the more they will see in the tiny figures that abound on the pages as metaphor for the confusion and fear experienced by a newly arrived immigrant who does not speak the language of his adopted country and is not sure what is happening. Why has the author chosen these shapes? What is he saying through them? Why is the entire book done in sepia shades? With either or both books, it may help for students to make two columns with their own renderings of the shapes on one side and what the students feel they mean on the other. As a follow-up, they can create some symbols that might explain an event or topic they are currently studying.

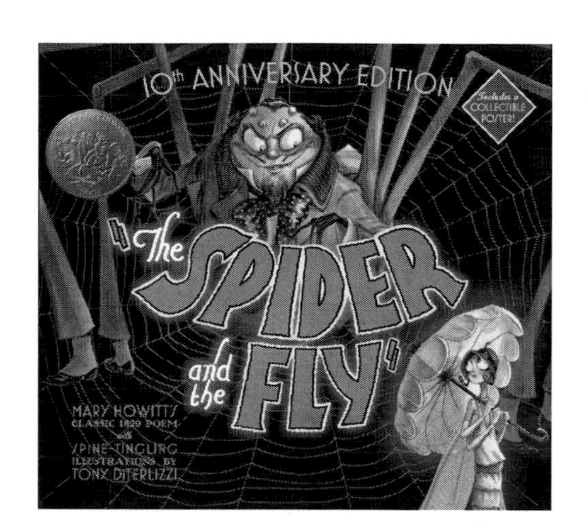

Mary Howitt's cautionary poem, *The Spider and the Fly*, has been around for over a hundred years, but in Tony DiTerlizzi's (2002) talented hands, it becomes a brilliant piece of metaphorical storytelling well deserving of the Caldecott Honor it received over a decade ago. The design of the book, with its images rendered in black-and-white gouache and pencil and reproduced in silver-and-black duotone, and much of its text printed in white on black ground framed in silver with insects at the corners, already portend a dire outcome. The story unfolds like a silent black-and-white horror movie, and indeed, the delicate fly is attired in 1920s flapper garb. Silvery insect ghosts (probably victims of a previous capture), one even holding a book entitled "The Joy of Cooking Bugs," try to warn the heedless fly, to no avail. The spider, appearing first in an ornate chair in a quilt-trimmed smoking jacket, and later in a tux proffering insets under glass, in aspic, on platters and trays to entice the fly to stay for dinner, is deliciously scary. Bugs serve as candelabra, curtains, and wall decorations. But does the fly pay attention to these metaphors for her own death? No, the lure of that luxurious gothic parlor is just too strong. Provide sufficient time for students to study the illustrations. How many metaphors for the fly's death can they discover? Do they notice that the web the spider is spinning becomes larger with each subsequent page of framed text? Do they have other ideas for ways to warn the fly, via illustrations, of her impending doom?

Students will likely have heard and perhaps even discussed ideas swirling around in newspapers, on the Internet, and in news broadcasts about the sharp dichotomy between the extreme wealth of a few as opposed to the resources of the majority and even the poverty of many persons in the United States. It may even be the topic of dinnertime conversation. Students may have heard of employers who have elaborate salaries and yet deny workers benefits or a fair wage. Children's book author I. C. Springman obviously believes in a fair distribution of wealth, but rather than hammering this message home in a book that might have veered into the didactic, she uses only forty-five words along with Brian Lies's exquisite metaphorical pictures in her book *More* (2012) to convey her ideas even more powerfully. A magpie who has nothing receives a colorful marble from a mouse and deposits it in her newly constructed nest. This sets her on a collecting spree as she flies about looking for treasures and adds more and more to the nest. Now she has so much one nest is insufficient and she builds several others. Eventually the weight of her many objects proves too much, the tree branch breaks, and the bird's treasures scatter to the ground. She and her mice friends then dispose of almost everything until the magpie has just enough to decorate a new nest. The story concludes, "Yes, enough. "*More* is a warning about greed. Ask students to consider what other things it might be important to warn people about. Choose one or more from a list of ideas. How might these warnings be conveyed metaphorically—in the form of posters, billboards, and so on? Provide time for students, alone or in groups, to design their messages using as few words as possible.

In Paul Fleischman's *Sidewalk Circus* (2007), a theater marquee announces, "Coming soon . . . World-renowned Garibaldi Circus!!!!" and a young girl watches life unfold on a city street while she waits for her bus. As an elderly man starts putting up posters for that circus, the sidewalk itself turns into a procession of circus acts. A construction worker balances on a steel beam above a poster that advertises "The Great Tebaldi Prince of Tight Rope Walkers." A cook inside a restaurant flips pancakes while a sign outside forecasts "Fantastic Feats of Juggling." Next to the marquee that praises "Daring Sword Swallowers!!" is a view inside a dentist's office and the dentist inserting an instrument into a man's wide open mouth. Juxtapositions like these abound throughout this wordless story (except for the signs and posters) in which one scene suggests another. The shadows are not to be ignored, either. Readers who pour over this masterful book will be prompted to see their own world anew. Are there objects in the school yard or that they see on their way to and from school that might suggest something else?

Duncan Tonatiuh's *Pancho Rabbit and the Coyote* (2013) is a metaphor in both story and illustration. Because of a drought in their homeland, Papá Rabbit has to head north to earn money to send to his family. When he doesn't return at the appointed time, Pancho Rabbit, his eldest son, sets off to find him. On the way he meets Señor Coyote, who offers to help. At each stage of the journey, he forces Pancho to give him some of the food meant for his father until he is left with nothing. At that point, instead of leading Pancho to his father as promised, Coyote imprisons him saying, "I will roast you in the fire and eat you." Eventually, though, father and son are reunited. Metaphor for the immigrants who come north seeking a better life and the coyotes who cheat and otherwise take advantage of them, this is a moving story that will surely spark discussion from all sides of the issue about the treatment of immigrants.

Novels

Tom Jacobs, in an article in *Pacific Standard* entitled "Study: Reading Novels Makes Us Better Thinkers" and reprinted on the website Salon (http://www.salon.com/2013/06/15/book_nerds_make_better_decisions_partner/?utm_source=Publishers+Weekly&

utm_campaign=a753e561aa-UA-15906914-1&utm_medium=email&utm_term=0_0bb2959cbb-a753e561aa-304481097), provides us with an important reason to share novels with our students. He cites a study conducted by three University of Toronto scholars led by Maja Djikic. For those uncomfortable with ambiguity (recall as cited in the Introduction to this text (p. xiii) that Starko lists "tolerance for ambiguity" as a characteristic of the divergent thinker)—a condition, according to Jacobs, that "can inspire snap judgments, *rigid thinking*, and bad decision-making"—reading novels can be a way to open their minds by enabling them to see how different characters in the stories—even characters they dislike—think. They can think and feel along with these characters in ways very different from their own thinking processes. They can move away from an either/or outcome that might be the result of their own rigid ideas and accept a more open-ended conclusion.

Unlike brief picture books, both contemporary and historical fiction novels enable readers to live inside a story for a considerable period of time so that they can watch characters develop: see how events, settings, and other people influence them; watch them make both good and bad, difficult and easy decisions and try to figure out what prompted them to do so; see how they solve problems; witness risk taking that brings about change or influences others; empathize with them and gain insight into how those around them or even in distant parts of the world might be feeling in similar circumstances; and ultimately, learn how to live their own lives more creatively, more bravely, and with greater empathy toward others. In describing the characteristics that make books deserving of the Newbery Medal, the highest award for books for children up to age fourteen (excluding picture books), editor Patricia Lee Gauch writes, "At the heart of every Newbery is a remarkable character . . . Not just a character who carries the weight of story, but a character original in voice, in spirit, in ideas, perhaps even in looks! Certainly original in imagination" (July/August, 2011, 52). While not named Newbery medalists at this writing, the novels discussed here offer readers just such characters—characters whose unique ways of moving through the world live on in our minds and hearts long after the books return to the shelf.

A. Realistic Contemporary Fiction

Violet Mackerel's Brilliant Plot (2012) by Anna Branford is an early chapter book young readers will enjoy. Violet accompanies her mother and older siblings to a flea market every Saturday where they sell things to support the family. While perusing the merchandise on other venders' tables, Violet comes across a blue China bird and from that moment on, she is obsessed with a desire to own it. The bird, however, costs ten dollars, a sum the little girl simply does not have. But Violet, armed with the small red button she found on the ground just that morning—a sure sign that a brilliant idea is within sight—decides to follow her mother's advice: "Mama sometimes says that it is quite helpful, when you are trying to solve a difficult problem, to think *outside the box*" (19). That's how her mama got the outside-the-box idea of knitting and selling her wares instead of doing inside-the-box things like taking a class when her father left them. Violet draws a big box and begins by putting ordinary ideas, like asking her mother for the money, inside it. Then she writes extraordinary ideas on the outside, but none of them add up to a brilliant plot until she finally decides that if she goes on a dig like archeologists do, she will likely find a treasure worth so much that she will have enough money to buy the China bird. The only problem is that she chooses the back yard for her dig and her mother is not pleased with the destruction of her lawn. Well, not all out-of-the-box ideas bear fruit! Young readers need not fear, though, since all turns out fine in the end. Draw a box on the board and, just as Violet worked on coming up with a good idea, ask the children to do the same regarding a school-wide or class issue they are grappling with. Divide them into groups and ask them to share ideas and write the results either inside or outside the box as the different groups report. Ask the children to figure out why an idea is ordinary or extraordinary and why each might or might not work.

Brendan Buckley, hero of Sundee T. Frazier's *Brendan Buckley's Sixth-Grade Experiment* (2012) has many interests. He wants to become a world class scientist, earn a black belt in Tae Kwon Do, and hang out with his friends. He also wants to cooperate with his parents in their efforts to adopt a baby. But his life becomes complicated when he meets Morgan, another science enthusiast, and she wants to be his friend—and maybe even more. Morgan and Brendan are paired by their teacher in a project for a science competition, and Brendan suggests they work on whether cow patties might be a viable source of alternative energy. Their project requires that they work together a good deal, though, making Brendan the butt of his friends' teasing. To make matters worse, all that time spent on his first love, science, means he's not spending time practicing his Tae Kwon Do moves, and this displeases his father who doesn't seem to value Brendan's scientific bent. Can Brendan help his father understand how important science is to him and that it's actually OK for him to like school? Can he begin to think of Morgan as a possible girl friend and still keep the boy friends he has? Readers will enjoy reading to discover how Brendan manages the challenges of being a sixth grader. But even more, they'll meet a boy whose notebook is filled with questions and observations. He says,

> Some people never ask questions. Maybe they're afraid they'll look dumb . . . But not me, It's like my brain is one big bowl of Rice Krispies and all my questions are the milk. It's a constant *snap*, *crackle*, and *pop* up there. (2)

Brendan can count on his grandfather for support. "You go on and be a scientist . . . You'd be joining a long line of our people who made life-changing discoveries. Made this world a better place, they did . . . you'll make it better yet" (56–57). Discuss students' feelings about asking questions in class. Are they afraid to do so, ashamed? Do they see any benefits to be gained by asking questions? Are they afraid of being considered "nerds?" Why do they think some classmates ridicule those who take their studies seriously? How can such attitudes be changed?

Ellis Weiner's *The Templeton Twins Have an Idea* (2012) features twins Abigail and John, children of Professor Elton Templeton, a very brilliant but very absent-minded inventor. When adult twins, Dean D. Dean and Dan D. Dean, kidnap John and Abigail along with their not-so-ordinary dog in order to force their father to surrender his latest "genius" invention, the children have to figure out a way to save themselves and their father. This is an uproarious romp in which the author constantly addresses the reader with funny quips at the end of each chapter such as

1. The author has succeeded in writing an actual Prologue. Aren't you proud of him?
2. What do you mean, "no"? (19)

But while readers will enjoy the nonstop humor and quirky illustrations, the book is invaluable for the ways in which the twins demonstrate divergent thinking throughout. To begin with, John approaches life with an inquiring attitude. "John was extremely clever when it came to . . . devising plans and putting them into action. His favorite thing to say was "LET'S DO IT AND VIEW IT!" For example, "On a hot summer's day, could you really fry an egg on the sidewalk? 'Let's . . .'" (33, 34). When Abigail and John are kidnapped and held prisoner in a basement, Abigail knows they cannot solve their problem by escaping. "We'll never get anywhere because we can't do it ourselves. So let's not think about escaping" (145). In other words, she cautions her brother not to waste time thinking of the obvious. This is a problem that must be solved by thinking divergently. So the twins set to work examining the materials they have at hand and how they might be used to their advantage. This kind of thinking and problem solving is exhibited throughout the book and is excellent material for discussion.

Ten-year-old Auggie Pullman (Palacio, *Wonder*, 2012) was born with such extreme facial abnormalities that his parents have tried to protect him from the world and the ridicule of others by home schooling him. But when he reaches fifth grade, they decide to send him to a private school in Manhattan where Mr. Tushman, the director of the middle school, is sympathetic to Auggie's needs. Of course Auggie is apprehensive about this. He says,

> when I was little, I never minded meeting new kids because all the kids I met were really little, too. What's cool about really little kids is that they don't say stuff to try to hurt your feelings, even though sometimes they do say stuff that hurts your feelings . . . they don't actually know what they're saying. Big kids, though: they know what they're saying. And that is definitely not fun for me. (20–21)

The director asks three students to show Auggie around before the actual start of the school year to help him adjust. But not all of them turn out to be real friends and even go along when kids shun Auggie and make his life miserable. Even his older sister, who has always championed and protected him, is now ashamed to have her friends see him. But one classmate bucks the crowd and befriends Auggie at considerable cost to his own social life until, eventually, Auggie's charming and quirky personality wins over his peers. At the beginning of the school year, Auggie's English teacher announces he will give the students a precept or "rule about really important things" (46). His precept for September is "When given the choice between being right or being kind, choose kind." During his middle school graduation address at the end of the year, Mr. Tushman urges his students to go even further—to "always try to be a little kinder than is necessary" (299). This is a fine story of courage, of warm family love, and the support of teachers, and peers. But it can be a catalyst for even more. At a special website, choosekind@randomhouse.com, Random House, the publisher of *Wonder*, offers a pledge to choose kindness that willing readers can sign. At this printing there are over 1,000 signatures. There are also resources and other ideas on the site. This is an opportunity for students to devise an original kindness campaign—something that will motivate their peers to engage in "even more kindness than is necessary." If students come up with a plan and execute it, they can contact Random House via the website, so that their idea can reach even more people. Also recounted in *Wonder* is the English teacher's request that the students write a precept of their own. If a class decides to do this as well, they can publish a book of precepts to share with other classes. They can even write and dramatize scenes in which characters exhibit more kindness than is necessary. A picture book to pair with this novel, and one that might also inspire students to promote a kindness campaign, is Jacqueline Woodson's *Each Kindness* (2012). In it, a new girl, Maya, enters the class. But since her clothing indicates she is poor, the girls shun her, refusing all her invitations to play. Even Chloe, who is forced to sit next to Maya, turns away instead of befriending her. But when Maya no longer comes to school and the teacher talks about how each act of kindness has a ripple effect on the world, Chloe regrets her behavior toward Maya and thinks about all the kind things she should have said to her. (To provide even more motivation, go to: http://www.yeehee.com/2013/10/31/football-team-rallies-to-give-an-unpopular-kid-a-touchdown-but-hes-not-the-one-that-will-make-you-cry-that-comes-at-230-in-the-video/#chitika_close_button to see how a young group of football players, without telling their coach, conspired to enable a learning disabled player to score a touchdown and how one player was profoundly changed by the experience.)

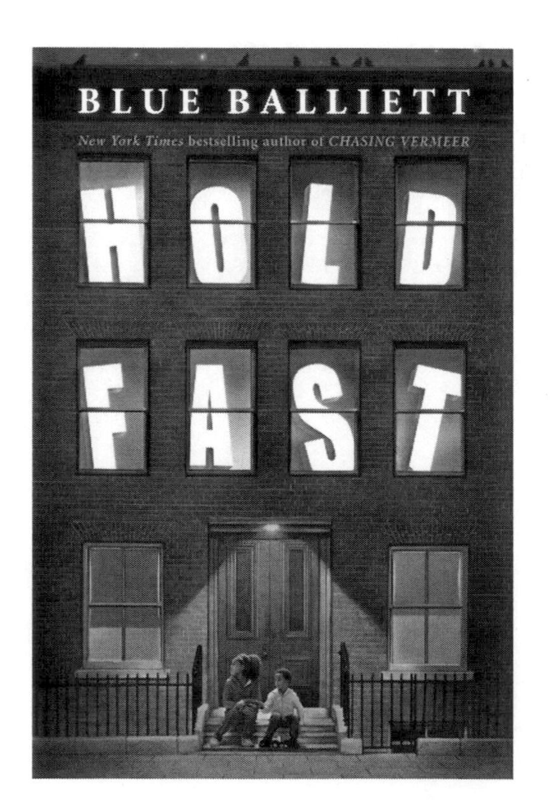

The Pearl family, the subjects of Blue Balliett's *Hold Fast* (2013), lives in a tiny apartment, but, inspired by their hero, Langston Hughes, they dream of one day having a home of their own. That dream seems far away since Mr. Pearl earns a meager living as a library page, and Mrs. Pearl must remain home to care for their young son. To earn much-needed extra savings, Dashel Pearl agrees to catalog used books and things are fine until he suddenly disappears. Even worse, a gang breaks down the door of their apartment and ransacks it, forcing Early, her mother, and young brother to flee to a shelter. Now, the police suspect Dashel of wrongdoing, though the family is convinced of his innocence. With her mother sunk in ineffective grief, it is up to Early to follow clues and solve the mystery of her father's disappearance—which she eventually does. But even more, her sudden homelessness makes her aware of the many other homeless families living in Chicago. When she sees boarded up homes as she gazes out a train window, she asks her mother, "How come there are so many homes standing empty in Chicago and so many people like us who don't have a home? How come those empty homes aren't being fixed up and filled with people who need a place to live" (171)? Early then comes up with a daring plan involving children in shelters throughout the city. She has to convince adults that it's a good idea and then see her plan through to completion, but she faces these tasks with courage and determination. This is a wonderful story of dreams combined with risk taking and daring action. It is about noticing one's environment and the needs of others and making connections. This would be an excellent novel to read in conjunction with *An Awesome Book* and *If I Built a House*, picture books discussed earlier. In addition to talking about their own dreams, encourage students to look closely at their community. What dream might benefit their community, neighborhood, school? How might they go about making that dream a reality? Can they, as Early did, "Spin [their idea] around, look at it from all sides, try to find the weak spot, if there [is] one" (199), and then get busy translating their idea into action?

In Patrick Ness's *A Monster Calls* (2011), thirteen-year-old Conor wakes at midnight to find a monster in the shape of a yew tree outside his window. It is not the monster of his nightmares, though. This is another monster and he has come to get Conor. Strangely, this doesn't frighten the boy, and he ignores the monster's earth-shattering screams. The monster tells Conor three stories and insists the boy tell one himself. In the telling, Conor calls on his inner resources and learns to face himself and his fears. This fascinating novel for older middle-grade readers is filled with metaphor. Who is this monster and what does it have to do with Conor's fear as he faces his mother's inevitable death? The pen and ink art illustrations throughout adds to the power of the story. This not-to-be-missed novel will spark deep discussion.

Raphael, Gordo, and Rat, three young teens, live in a dump in an unnamed developing country in Andy Mulligan's moving novel, *Trash* (2010). Every day they pick through the trash looking for things they might recycle or sell to sustain themselves. One day, Raphael finds a small leather zipped bag containing a wallet, a map, a key, and 1,100 pesos. When the police come asking if anyone has found the bag, Rafe's aunt arouses their suspicion, and from that moment on, Rafe is on the run from the law. He, Gardo, and Rat try to uncover the meaning behind the mysterious objects in the bag, cracking secret codes (which the reader can try as well) along the way. What door does the key unlock? Where does the map lead? They take unbelievable risks to discover the truth, always running from those who are trying to kill them. While faced with the temptation of easy gain, these desperately poor boys have a keen sense of morality and consistently choose the right path. In doing so, they uncover deep-seated government corruption and ultimately achieve a better life, helped in no small part by adult aid workers. Students will love this page-turning story as they follow the boys on their courageous journey. And they will encounter a world that, hopefully, they will never have to face themselves as they confront the dire poverty and difficult lives experienced by these dump dwellers. This book is ripe for creative extensions that require divergent thinking. Random House has an extensive website dedicated to the novel: http://www.randomhouse.com/catalog/teachers_guides/9780385752145.pdf with discussion questions, lists of organizations that help the poor around the world, and opportunities for classroom projects and research. Students can obtain a free subscription to Prezi at prezi.com for creative ways to present what they have learned in their research. *Waste Land*, about the largest dump in the world located in Brazil and the people who live there, is an Academy Award–nominated documentary well worth watching. It tells the story of Vik Muniz, an artist living in Brooklyn, New York, who travels to Brazil and helps the people create beautiful art works using materials found at the dump. These pieces are then sold to benefit its creators. A trailer for the film is available at wastelandmovie.com. This example of using what is surely a terrible environment—a dump in which people spend their working days—to actually lift them out of poverty is divergent thinking par excellence. Related to this subject is the whole idea of trash itself and why there are mountains of it throughout the planet. There are recycling efforts in many communities, and yet we still have incredible amounts of trash—much of it quite toxic. Can the students come up with ideas to encourage greater recycling efforts in their own community? Might they be interested in researching and possibly contacting companies that use toxic materials in their products?

B. Historical Fiction

In *P.S. Be Eleven* (2013), her sequel to *One Crazy Summer* (2011), in which the three Gaither sisters travel to Oakland, California, to reunite with their activist mother, Rita Williams-Garcia takes up the story of Delphine, Vonetta, and Fern as they return home to Brooklyn, New York. Their uncle returns from serving in Vietnam, and the joy of seeing him with all his limbs intact is soon dampened when it becomes obvious that he is not the same. He's withdrawn, moody, can't find a job, and seems to have a perpetual cold. Then there are those pictures of Vietnamese children "shot up dead . . . and bony Vietnamese people . . . pointing to clouds of smoke and helicopters" (86) shown on the news. Add to that, the girls' struggle, after seeing their mother's involvement in the fight for equal rights and learning of the work of the Black Panthers, to live with a strict grandmother who believes in obeying the rules, unjust though they are, and minding one's own business. Delphine, the oldest, is especially resentful of her grandmother's continual put-downs and sexist statements such as "they ought to stick to teaching arithmetic in schools . . . not all this jaw-jerking about women running for president. A woman running for president. When pigs fly over Alabama" (185). With the support of her father's new progressive wife, Delphine takes part in a group project about women in politics at school, despite her grandmother's objections. This account of three African American girls coming of age in the 1960s, a time of great unrest and change in the United States, offers readers a feisty character in Delphine, who is not afraid to think differently and voice her views to a grandparent who might likely respond with punishment. Is there a prevailing opinion in the students' school or neighborhood community, their state, or even in the country? Whether they agree with this opinion or not, challenge them to consider an alternate point of view. What would the consequences of this different view be? Can they uncover documentation to back up an alternate opinion? Once students have considered their contradictory opinion, gleaning as much information as possible, help them set up an interview talk show, with different interviewees expressing alternate views on the chosen issue. Being able to see a situation from different angles is an important characteristic of the divergent thinker.

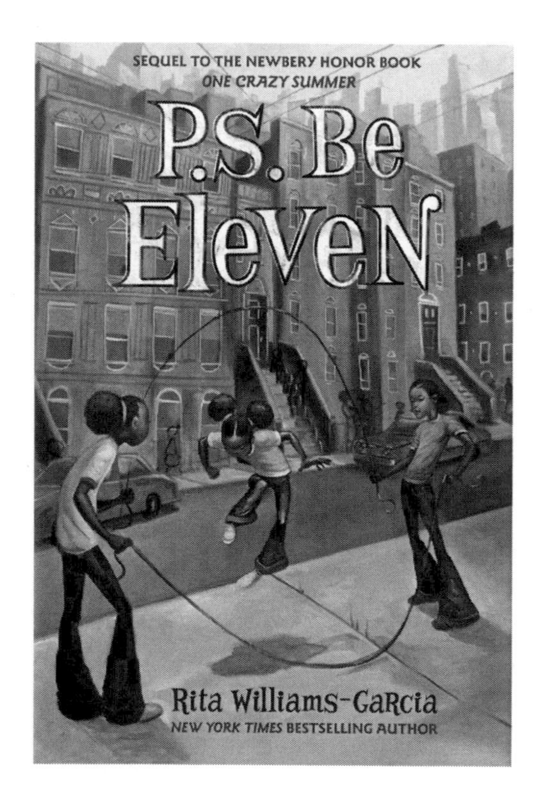

As Katherine Rundell's *Rooftoppers* (2013) begins, scholar Charlex Maxim lifts an infant floating in a cello case in the English Channel into his rescue boat, determines to keep her, and names her Sophie. Together they live an unconventional life in which schooling for Sophie consists of voluminous reading, for "Books crowbar the world open for you" (34); excursions; learning most of Shakespeare by heart; playing the cello; and digesting all the wisdom Charles imparts. This, along with their unconventional housekeeping, dress, and eating habits, doesn't sit well with the social worker who visits weekly. When Sophie turns twelve, the woman succeeds in obtaining a decision to remove her to St. Catherine's Orphanage. But before the order is carried out, Sophie discovers an address in the cello case in which she was found, and she and Charles escape to France to seek Sophie's mother who, the girl insists against all odds, is alive. Thus begins a search that brings Sophie into contact with Matteo, an orphan who makes his home on the rooftops of Paris, and his friends. Sophie follows Matteo on the dangerous journey from rooftop to rooftop listening for her mother's unique cello rendition of Fauré's *Requiem* played double time—all the while ignoring bloodied knees and the opinion of everyone, including Charles, that her mother could not have survived the shipwreck. "That is almost impossible . . . so profoundly improbable that it's not worth building a life on. It would be like trying to build a house on the back of a dragonfly," he tells her—to which she replies, "*Almost* impossible means still possible . . . You always say, 'Never ignore a possible'" (16). In creating Sophie and Charles, Katherine Rundell provides readers with characters who exemplify several characteristics of divergent thinkers. Provide students with a list of those characteristics listed in the Introduction (p. xiii) and ask them which ones they feel Sophie and Charles possess. How do these characteristics make it possible for a person to think in unusual ways and to pursue a goal? Do students feel Sophie should have acted as she did? Why or why not? Would they have any other suggestions as to how she might have undertaken her search for her mother? Sophie and Charles know there is something strange about the shipwreck of the Queen Mary, the ocean liner from which Sophie escaped, and surely that mystery will unfold in an exciting sequel.

Readers meet "Verity" in *Code Name Verity* (2012), Elizabeth Wein's unforgettable novel for older students, in a Nazi prison cell where she is writing a "confession" as a reprieve from torture and execution. This confession reveals her friendship with Maddie, the woman who piloted her into France where she was captured, the British war effort during World War II, and what life was like for women in the service at that time. But Verity's confession is not what it seems, nor is Verity even her real name. Readers will be gripped by her account, and it is only when they reach the end of the novel that they will realize what Verity was actually doing. They will surely want to start over again to see anew how all the pieces fit together in this tour de force. Verity and Maddie are women of incredible courage and cunning who will inspire students to think of unconventional ways to solve their problems, which, hopefully, will never be as severe as what these heroines had to surmount. (Also see Wein's *Rose under Fire* (2013), about Rose Justice, who, while transporting a fighter plane from Paris to England during World War II, tries to knock down an unmanned German bomb before it can do any damage, is taken prisoner and sent to Ravensbrück concentration camp. There she endures horrific conditions and witnesses the effects of the German medical experiments until she escapes with a few companions.)

It is 1944 in Florence and Paolo and his sister Costanza are living in the midst of Nazi occupation in Shirley Hughes's fine novel, *Hero on a Bicycle* (2013). Their father has disappeared, presumably helping the Partisans in their defiance of the German enemy, and that, along with being children of a British mother, means the family is under great scrutiny by the occupiers. The Partisans involve Paolo's mother, Rosemary, in housing prisoners of war until they can be returned to the Allies, but Paolo wants to help the Italian resistance as well. Each night he breaks curfew, seeking adventure by riding his bicycle around the city. He gets his chance to be a hero when he is enlisted to escort prisoners to their next place of safety en route back to their units. The story is told from all three characters' points of view. Rosemary fears for her husband, being discovered for harboring Allied prisoners, and for her son who risks being discovered in his evening forays. Costanza is aware of the danger the family is in as they defy the rules. Paolo, while wanting to be a hero, knows the risks. And there are plenty—even a search of the family's cellar by a member of the Gestapo. Hughes does a splendid job of presenting the terrible aspects of war while at the same time not painting any group as all good or all evil. The Partisans have their faults, and there is that Gestapo soldier who conveniently did not find anything amiss in the cellar. This is a story of courage and risk taking against what often seems like insurmountable odds. What traits helped these characters and what obstacles within themselves as well as outside challenges did they have to overcome?

A hero of another war, Sarah Emma Edmonds, is the subject of Marissa Moss's novel, *A Soldier's Secret* (2012). Based on Sarah's own writings, it is the exciting story of a young girl who disguises herself as a man and serves in the Civil War as Frank Thompson. Serving under different generals, she faces battles with the

Confederates as a Union Army soldier, works as a nurse tending wounded soldiers on the battlefield, and even infiltrates enemy lines as a spy. She must struggle daily to hide her identity and act like a man to avoid detection and expulsion from the army. She says,

> I've become a master of relieving myself in hidden places, expert at changing my clothes beneath blankets, skilled at using and disposing of bandages for my monthlies. I've proven my bravery many times over. Not just as a soldier but as a postmaster, orderly, nurse, and spy. No one could suspect a woman of having such abilities. (279)

Men in Sarah's time considered women capable of very little, but her desire to serve and the unusual transformation she underwent to accomplish her goal proved them wrong. While she was not the only woman disguised as a man in the Union Army, Marissa Moss writes in an author's note, "Sarah was the only woman to be recognized by acts of Congress as an honorably discharged soldier, with rights to back pay and a pension, and the only woman allowed to join the Grand Army of the Republic, the association for Civil War veterans" (366). Students can see a documentary prepared by a student about this remarkable woman on YouTube by going to: http://www.youtube.com/watch?v=t1lCqkgTxkw.

Bird McGill (real name Belinda, but don't tell anyone) in Michael Ferrari's *Born to Fly* (2011) is not like other girls. Her father has taught her everything he knows about planes, and her dream is to fly a P-40 fighter plane. She can do it since she knows the plane inside and out, but it's common knowledge that even when she's grown, she'll never get the chance since women will still not be allowed to join the air force. Her life becomes especially difficult when her beloved father goes off to war and she must endure the taunts of the school bully without his comforting words. When Kenji, a Japanese-American boy enters her school, he becomes a bully target as well. Joined in friendship, both children see a submarine in the water and determine to find a way to make people believe them. Before they're able to accomplish their mission, however, a factory blows up, the bully's father is found murdered, and suspicion immediately falls on Kenji's uncle. But Bird has seen the real culprit who warns her to keep quiet—or else. Will Bird have the courage to tell the truth? She wants to save Kenji's uncle, but what will happen to her family if she comes forward? Readers will learn about the Japanese internment camps, victory gardens, and more about life on the home front during World War II. But facts don't stand in the way of this exciting story. Talk with the students about difficult or risky decisions they have had to make. How did they find the courage to do the right thing?

Terry Pratchett's novel, *Dodger* (2012), plunges older readers into Victorian London where, in addition to the extraordinary protagonist, Dodger (so called because he can dodge in and out of any situation), they will meet the likes of Charles Dickens, Benjamin Disraeli, and the infamous Sweeny Todd. Dodger makes his living as a tosher, one who hunts the London sewers for money and other valuables that find their way down there. He knows these subterranean waterways like the back of his hand, and he knows the streets and alleys and the characters who inhabit the poor section of the city where he lives with a kind Jewish jeweler. When he hears the screech of carriage wheels and screams overhead on a rain-soaked night, he leaps out of the sewer and rescues a mysterious woman who is being beaten as she tries to escape her captors. This rescue brings Dodger into contact with Dickens, Disraeli, the wealthy Angela Burdett-Coutts, Sir Robert Peel, head of the London police force, Henry Mayhew, who actually documented a great deal about the lives of the poor during this era, and even Queen Victoria herself. Poor and of little account, Dodger takes on the politicians of two governments as he plots to save the woman, eventually the love of his life, from being returned to Germany and a husband who is unspeakably cruel to her. To do this, he invents disguises, enlists the help of friends throughout the city, and hatches a daring plot that saves the day, all the while respecting even the most downtrodden of those he meets along the way—even an unclaimed dead girl whom he sees to a decent burial—and sharing his newfound wealth generously with them. A telling passage in the book sums up Dodger's adventurous spirit: "If [life] was a game, then were you the player or were you the pawn? It seeped into his mind that maybe Dodger could be more than just Dodger, if he cared to put some effort into it. It was a call to arms" (47). Dodger is a risk taker par excellence, and readers will cheer for him every step of the way. Moreover, they will be steeped in metaphor as used by a master writer. Permeating the novel is the mention of fog—of course the fog that bathed London so intensely at the time that it was often difficult to see a few feet ahead. But does fog have other meanings here as well?

Max, the delightfully spunky and resourceful character in Cynthia Voigt's *Mister Max: The Book of Lost Things* (2013), is a younger version of Dodger discussed earlier, and his exploits are perfect fodder for younger readers to explore. One day in the early 1900s, presumably in England, Max's parents, both actors and theater owners, sail off to India in answer to a mysterious summons to found a theater there. Max is supposed to join them at sailing time, but when he gets to the dock, no one has seen a trace of them. Alone, except for his librarian Grammie, Max must try to find out what happened to his parents and, meanwhile, figure out a way to support himself. Not one to sit around feeling sorry for himself, Max gets right to it. Fortunately, after he finds a missing child, his reputation as a finder spreads, and others come to him for help. Wearing various disguises from his parents' costume trunk, Max finds a stray dog, a very precious spoon, and even a couple who have lost each other. His sometime assistant, Pia, talks incessantly, asking questions while not bothering to listen for the answers. It's annoying but "some of them [are] just what Max need[s] to hear in order to discover his own ideas" (259). Students will be intrigued by those ideas and the clever ways in which Max and Pia solve difficult problems and their striving to make life better for several people they encounter. "Problems have solutions. That's what I do," says Max. "I'm a solutioneer. What do you think of that for a job" (286)? After they have read or listened to the novel, make a list with students of the things Max did throughout the story to show he is an independent risk taker and a list of the strengths that make him a good "solutioneer." What are Pia's strengths and weaknesses? Reading detective stories is an excellent way for students to sharpen their observation skills. Were they able to unearth any clues before Max does? So much of Max's successes result from his ability to connect the things he has observed. Were students able to make these connections as well? Can they suggest any different ways to cope with the situations facing Max from the ones he chose? Max seems to be able to solve everyone's problems but the big one facing himself: what happened to his parents? Are they safe? Will they ever return? What do the students think about their fate? Unfortunately, or fortunately, the novel provides no answers to the mystery of their disappearance—so sequels are definitely on the horizon.

Clare Vanderpool's masterful *Navigating Early* (2013) is set just as World War II is coming to a close. After his mother's sudden death from a brain aneurism, Jack Baker's father, a navy captain, uproots him from his Kansas home and brings him to a boys' boarding school in Maine. There he meets a strange boy, Early Auden, who seldom attends class and disputes some widely held beliefs: that pi is NOT a never-ending number; that there are no timber rattlesnakes in Maine; and especially that his brother, Fisher, is not really dead even though the army has declared him so and returned his dog tags. During school break Jack and Early embark on a trip along the Appalachian Trail to track down an enormous black bear, but ultimately, in Early's plan, to find his lost brother. Early is an autistic savant who sees numbers in stories and colors. He tells Jack stories about Pi's trials and adventures as Pi follows the stars to discover the answers to all the "whys" that have consumed him from his earliest days. Pi becomes lost on his journey and endures incredible hardships as do Jack and Early, whose adventures and the people they meet seem to mirror Pi's dangers and encounters. This is a story of loss and of finding oneself again by becoming alert to connections. Jack, who is trying to navigate his way through life without his mother, nevertheless lives with her words ringing in his head: "Jackie, if you don't like the bed you're in, take it apart and make it right" (9). And,

> Maybe you should focus on the beauty of those stars up there apart from their function. Just take them in, admire them, stand in awe of them, before you expect them to lead the way. Besides, who's to say that one group of stars belongs together and only together? Those stars up there are drawn to each other in lots of different ways. They're connected in unexpected ways, just like people. (36)

Divergent thinkers see connections others miss and use those connections to effect change. The needs and problems of society cause an itch inside them, cause them to become dissatisfied "with the bed they're in" and prompt them to "take it apart and make it right." Surely this is a story to share and discuss with students if we want them to think in new ways. Some discussion options: What is the significance of the title? Describe the various losses both boys are suffering. How do the students interpret Pi's story and how does it connect to Jack's and Early's stories? How was Early able to make connections that eluded Jack until the very end? Were students able to suspend their disbelief and go along with the magical realism in this story, or did it put them off? Why or why not? How does Jack's relationship with his father begin to change, and why? Have the students ever met anyone who sees things as differently as Early does? How can they celebrate and benefit from this difference instead of excluding the person as being strange?

Whether it's a simple picture book about a robot who discovers that real knowledge requires being immersed in the world around him, or a complex novel that follows characters as they find the courage to make connections, engage with their surroundings, and take the risks involved in making difficult decisions, any or all of the books in this chapter, and so many more that could not be discussed here, will lead readers to think differently about their lives, their challenges, and their goals. These fictional works offer them characters with whom they can identify and from whom they can learn.

References

Agee, Jon. 2012. *The Other Side of Town*. New York: Michael Di Capua/Scholastic. ISBN 978-0-545-16204-3. When a New York cabbie picks up a guy dressed in a green body suit topped with a pink pompom, he discovers the strange things that are happening on the other side of town.

Anthony, Jessica, and Rodrigo Corral. 2012. *Chopsticks: A Novel Experience*. New York: Razorbill/Penguin Group. ISBN 978-1-59514-435-5. Using pictures, apps, a website, songs, e-mail conversations, and artifacts such as concert programs and newspaper articles, the authors tell the story of a missing girl and teenage love.

Bailey, Linda. 2012. *Toads on Toast*. Illustrated by Colin Jack. Toronto: Kids Can Press. ISBN 978-1-55453-662-7. Mamma toad convinces a fox to make toad in the hole using toast, butter, and eggs instead of her baby toads. Recipe included.

Baker-Smith, Grahame. 2013. *Farther*. Somerville, MA: Templar/Candlewick. ISBN 978-0-7636-6370-4. A man describes how his father tried unsuccessfully to build a flying machine and how he himself eventually built one to fulfill his father's dream.

Balliett, Blue. 2013. *Hold Fast*. New York: Scholastic Press. ISBN 978-0-545-29988-6. Inspired by the poetry of Langston Hughes, the Pearl family hold fast to the dream of having their own home one day, but when Mr. Pearl mysteriously disappears one day and their apartment is destroyed, they are forced to flee to a shelter. Only young Early's determination to solve this mystery can save them.

Banks, Kate. 2012. *The Bear in the Book*. Illustrated by Georg Hallensleben. New York: Frances Foster/Farrar Straus Giroux. ISBN 978-0-374-30501-8. A boy listens to his favorite book about a hibernating bear as he gets ready for bed.

Beaty, Andrea. 2013. *Rosie Revere, Engineer*. Illustrated by David Roberts. New York: Abrams Books for Young Readers. ISBN 978-1-41970845-9. Rosie, who longs to be an engineer, learns that flops are a means to learn and improve on her creations.

Black, Michael Ian. 2012. *I'm Bored*. Illustrated by Debbie Ridpath Ohi. New York: Simon & Schuster. ISBN 978-1-4424-1403-7. A young girl changes her mind about being bored when a potato declares that all kids are boring.

Blechman, Nicholas. 2013. *Night Light*. New York: Orchard/Scholastic. ISBN 978-0-545-46263-1. Numbers of die-cut shapes correspond to the number of lights on various vehicles in this counting book.

Bloom, Suzanne. 2009. *A Mighty Fine Time Machine*. Honesdale, PA: Boyds Mills Press. ISBN 978-1-59078-527-0. Three friends turn an ordinary box into something wonderful.

Boyd, Lizi. 2013. *Inside Outside*. San Francisco: Chronicle Books. ISBN 978-1-4521-0644-1. In this wordless book, Boyd uses die-cuts to reveal special aspects of each season both inside and outside the house.

Branford, Anna. 2012. *Violet Mackerel's Brilliant Plot*. Illustrated by Elanna Allen. New York: Atheneum/Simon & Schuster. ISBN 978-1-4424-3585-8. Violet tries to arrive at an outside-the-box idea that will earn her enough money to buy the China bird she desires.

Brown, Calef. 2011. *Boy Wonders*. New York: Atheneum/Simon & Schuster. ISBN 978-1-4169-7877-0. A young boy has many questions.

Brown, Monica. Spanish translation by Adriana Dominguez. 2013. *Marisol McDonald and the Clash Bash*. Illustrated by Sara Placios. New York: Children's Book Press/Lee & Low. ISBN 978-0-89239-273-5. A bilingual story about a Peruvian-American girl who arranges for an unconventional birthday party.

Bryan, Ashley. 1999. *The Night Has Ears: African Proverbs*. New York: Atheneum/Simon & Schuster. ISBN 0-689-82427-0. This is a beautifully illustrated collection of twenty-six proverbs from different African cultures.

Button, Lana. 2013. *Willow Finds a Way*. Illustrated by Tania Howells. Toronto: Kids Can Press. ISBN 978-1-55453-842-3. When Kristabelle manipulates her classmates into doing her bidding so they can come to her birthday party, Willow finds a way to change the girl's behavior.

Cabatingan, Erin. 2012. *A Is for Musk Ox*. Illustrated by Matthew Myers. New York: Roaring Brook/Holtzbrinck. ISBN 978-1-59643-676-3. A musk ox convinces a zebra that every letter of his alphabet book can stand for musk ox.

Chiêu, Anh Urban. 2013. *Away We Go!* New York: Scholastic. ISBN 978-0-545-46179-5. Different shapes form various kinds of vehicles.

Chwast, Seymour. 2012. *Get Dressed!* New York: Abrams/Appleseed. ISBN 978-1-4197-0107-8. Readers see a page of clothing and articles and are encouraged to use what they see to create an outfit. Children appear under each flap dressed in the articles for different activities.

Clayton, Dallas. 2008. *An Awesome Book!* New York: Harper/HarperCollins. ISBN 978-0-06-211468-6. The author urges readers to dream big dreams.

Cline-Ransome, Lesa. 2013. *Light in the Darkness: A Story about How Slaves Learned in Secret*. Illustrated by James E. Ransome. New York: Disney/Jump at the Sun. ISBN 978-142313495-4. Slaves who are forbidden to learn to read and write gather in the cover of darkness to learn their letters, at the risk of their lives.

Deedy, Carmen Agra. 2009. *14 Cows for America*. Illustrated by Thomas Gonzalez. Atlanta: Peachtree. ISBN 978-1561454907. People in a Maasai village send their precious cows to America to comfort those grieving after 9/11.

Fardell, John. 2011. *The Day Louis Got Eaten*. London: Andersen Press USA/Random House. ISBN 978-1-4677-0315-4. While out in the woods with his sister, Louis is eaten by a monster, and this sets off a comical chain of ever-larger monsters dining on one another.

Ferrari, Michael. 2011. *Born to Fly*. New York: Yearling/Random House. ISBN 978-0-375-84607-6. In 1942, an eleven-year-old girl who longs to be a pilot and her family try to manage their lives in Rhode Island when father goes off to war.

Fleischman, Paul. 2013. *The Matchbox Diary*. Illustrated by Bagram Ibatoulline. Somerville, MA: Candlewick. ISBN 978-0-7636-4601-1. A young girl views the matchboxes that hold mementos of her great-grandfather's journey from Italy and first years in America, a unique diary he kept in objects because he could not read or write.

Fleischman, Paul. 2007. *Sidewalk Circus*. Illustrated by Kevin Hawkes. Cambridge, MA: Candlewick. ISBN 978-0-7636-2795-9. A busy sidewalk becomes a circus as its inhabitants seem to mimic circus acts in this wordless book.

Fontes, Justine. 2005. *Black Meets White*. Illustrated by Geoff Waring. Cambridge, MA: Candlewick. ISBN 978-0-7636-61933-6. Die-cuts and flaps reveal what happens when black and white meet.

Frazier, Sundee T. 2012. *Brendan Buckley's Sixth-Grade Experiment*. New York: Delacorte/Random House. ISBN 978-0-385-74050-0. Brendan tries to balance his love of science with his father's wishes that he engage in more macho activities and learns a great deal about himself and his father during his sixth-grade year.

Gall, Chris. 2013. *Awesome Dawson*. New York: Little Brown/Hachette Book Group. ISBN 978-0-316-21330-1. Dawson believes everything can be reused, so he collects things that others throw away and creates both fantastical and usable objects.

Gauch, Patricia Lee. 2012. "What Makes a Good Newbery Novel?" *The Horn Book* 87(4): 52–58. Gauch discusses the characteristics of a good Newbery-winning novel.

Gerstain, Mordicai. 2013. *How to Bicycle to the Moon to Plant Sunflowers*. New York: Roaring Brook/Holtzbrinck Publishing. ISBN 978-1-59643-512-4. A boy who feels the full moon looks sad has a plan that will enable someone to cheer him up by bicycling there and planting sunflowers.

Gonzalez, Ralfka. 2002. Introduction by Sandra Cisneros. *My First Book of Proverbs/Mi primer libro de dichos*. Illustrated by Ana Ruiz. New York: Lee & Low. ISBN 978-0-892392001. pb Each of the Mexican proverbs in this book appears in English and Spanish and is beautifully illustrated in brilliant colors particular to the culture.

Grey, Mini. 2012. *Toys in Space*. New York: Knopf/ Borzoi/Random House. ISBN 978-0-307-97812-7. Wonder Doll makes up a story about toys beamed into space by a space creature who is looking for his toy, Cuddles.

Gross, Jesica. September 30, 2012. "Great Moments in Inspiration." *The New York Times Magazine*. 25. The author interviews six creative people to discover how a particularly inspirational moment came about.

Harvey, Matthew. 2012. *Cecil the Pet Glacier*. Illustrated by Giselle Potter. New York: Schwartz & Wade/Random House. ISBN 978-0-375-86773-6. On a family trip to Norway, a glacier becomes Ruby's pet—much to her consternation.

Helquist, Brett. 2013. *Grumpy Goat*. New York: HarperCollins. ISBN 978-0-06-113953-6. A grumpy goat is transformed into a friendly fellow when he notices the beauty of a small flower.

Howitt, Mary. 2002. *The Spider and the Fly*. Illustrated by Tony DiTerlizzi. New York: Simon & Schuster. ISBN 978-0-689-85289-3. Howitt's cautionary poem is brilliantly illustrated in gothic style and filled with metaphor.

Hughes, Shirley. 2013. *Hero on a Bicycle*. Somerville, MA: Candlewick. ISBN 978-0-7636-6037-6. In Florence, Italy, in 1944, the Crivelli family defies the Nazi occupiers to help the Allied cause.

Intriago, Patricia. 2011. *Dot*. New York: Margaret Ferguson/Farrar Straus Giroux. ISBN 978-0-374-31835-2. Intriago uses dots to convey the concept of opposites.

Jacobs, Tom. June 15, 2013. "Pacific Standard. Study: Reading Novels Makes Us Better Thinkers." Printed on the website Salon. http://www.salon.com/2013/06/15/book_nerds_make_better_decisions_partner/?utm_source=Publishers+Weekly&utm_campaign=a753e561aa-UA-15906914-1&utm_medium=email&utm_term=0_0bb2959cbb-a753e561aa-304481097 (accessed April 12, 2014). Jacobs cites research that finds readers of novels can open their minds to more ways of thinking and be better able to cope with ambiguity.

Johnson, D. B. 2012. *Magritte's Marvelous Hat*. New York: Houghton Mifflin. ISBN 978-0-547-55864-6. The artist René Magritte, appearing as a dog, purchases a hat that floats above his head. This inspires him to create his surrealistic paintings in which other strange things happen.

Kellert, Stephan R. 2012. *Birthright: People and Nature in the Modern World*. New Haven, CT: Yale University Press. ISBN 978-00300176544. Kellert argues that it is vital for humans to experience nature if they are to live creative, healthy lives.

Kirp, David L. February 10, 2013. "The Secret to Fixing Bad Schools." *New York Times*, Sunday Review, 5. Kirp describes the extraordinary improvement in Union City, NJ, schools due to excellent teaching, student engagement, and a vigorous curriculum.

Klausmeier, Jesse. 2013. *Open This Little Book*. Illustrated by Suzy Lee. San Francisco: Chronicle Books. ISBN 978-0-8118-6783-2. When readers open this book, they see ever smaller books, each one revealing a new animal friend for the creature that came before it.

Krishnaswami, Uma. 2010. *Out of the Way! Out of the Way!* Illustrated by Uma Krishnaswamy. Toronto: Groundwood/House of Anansi Press. ISBN 978-1-55498-130-4. Villagers find a way to live with a tree on the path while at the same time allowing for a modern paved road.

Laden, Nina. 2013. *Once upon a Memory*. Illustrated by Renata Liwska. New York: Little Brown. ISBN 978-0-316-20826-1. A series of questions enable children to look creatively at the "before" and "after" of objects in their world.

Lewis, Richard. 2001. *The Bird of Imagining*. Drawings by Children from New York City Public Schools. New York: Touchstone Center Publications. ISBN 1-929299-01-X. A poem about the power of the imagination, personified as a bird, is illustrated by school children.

Manser, Martin H. 2007. Edited by Rosalind Fergusson and David Pickering. *Facts on File: Dictionary of Proverbs*. 2nd ed. New York: Checkmark Books. ISBN 978-0-81606674-2. pb This book contains over 1,500 sayings from ancient times to the present day arranged alphabetically.

Marcus, Leonard S. May/June 2012. "Good Vibrations: Picture Books and Color." *The Horn Book Magazine*. LXXXV 111 (3): 44–48. Marcus discusses how picture book illustrators use color to convey meaning.

Martin, Emily Winfield. 2013. *Dream Animals: A Bedtime Journey*. New York: Random House. ISBN 978-0-449-81080-4. Different animals carry young children to imaginary lands in their dreams.

Matheson, Christie. 2013. *Tap the Magic Tree*. New York: Greenwillow/HarperCollins. ISBN 978-0-06-227445-8. As the seasons change, a tree changes in response to different actions performed by readers.

McCarthy, Peter. 2012. *Chloe*. New York: Balzer + Bray/HarperCollins. ISBN 978-0-06-114291-8. Chloe lures her siblings away from the TV by playing with packing materials and a box.

McDonnell, Patrick. 2012. *The Monsters' Monster*. New York: Little Brown. ISBN 978-0-316-04547-6. Three monsters create one huge monster hoping he will be the "baddest" monster of all.

Messenger, Norman. 2005. *Imagine*. Somerville, MA: Candlewick. ISBN 978-0-76362757-7. Messenger invites readers to imagine the impossible in this interactive book.

Milway, Katie Smith. 2012. *Mimi's Village and How Basic Health Care Transformed It*. Illustrated by Eugenie Fernandes. Tonawanda, NY: Kids Can Press. ISBN 978-1-55453-722-8. Mimi takes a risk and is instrumental in having a clinic built for the people in her Western Kenyan village.

Mortensen, Lori. 2012. *Cindy Moo*. Illustrated by Jeff Mack. New York: Harper/HarperCollins. ISBN 978-0-06-204393-1. Inspired by the cow in the nursery rhyme, Cindy Moo tries repeatedly to jump over the moon until she finally succeeds.

Moss, Marissa. 2012. *A Soldier's Secret: The Incredible True Story of Sarah Edmonds, a Civil War Hero.* New York: Abrams. ISBN 978-1-4197-0427-7. Based on Edmonds's writings, the author of this novel tells the story of a woman who disguised herself as a man and served as a soldier, spy, and nurse during the Civil War.

Mulligan, Andrew. 2010. *Trash.* New York: Ember/Random House Children's Books. ISBN 978-0-385-75216-9. When Rafe finds a bag containing a wallet, a map, and a key in the dump where he and his friends Rat and Gardo eke out a living, they try to discover what the objects mean and end up running for their lives and uncovering widespread government corruption.

Murguia, Bethanie Deeney. 2012. *Zoe Gets Ready.* New York: Arthur A. Levine/Scholastic. ISBN 978-0-545-34215-5. Zoe tries to select an outfit suited to each of the activities in which she might engage on a Saturday outing.

Ness, Patrick. Based on an idea by Siobhan Dowd. 2011. *A Monster Calls.* Illustrated by Jim Kay. Somerville, MA: Candlewick. ISBN 978-0-7636-5559-4. In this metaphorical tale, a monster comes in the middle of the night and calls Conor to face his fears.

Palacio, R. J. 2012. *Wonder.* New York: Alfred A. Knopf/Random House. ISBN 978-0-375-86902-0. Ten-year-old Auggie Pullman, who was born with extreme facial abnormalities, goes from being home-schooled to entering fifth grade in a private school in Manhattan, which entails enduring the taunting and fear of his classmates.

Pett, Mark. 2013. *The Boy and the Airplane.* New York: Simon & Schuster. ISBN 978-1-44245123-0. A boy's plane lands on a roof, and when several attempts to reach it fail, he grows a tree and waits until it is tall enough to climb.

Pratchett, Terry. 2013. Reprint edition. *Dodger.* New York: HarperCollins. ISBN 978-0-06-200951-7. pb Dodger, who forages in the sewers of Victorian London, uses his wits to save a girl and helps many others along the way.

Raczka, Bob. 2010. *Speaking of Art.* Minneapolis: Millbrook Press/Lerner. ISBN 978-0-7613-5054-5. Raczka includes quotes from fifteen famous artists along with an example of each artist's work printed in full color.

Raczka, Bob. 2009. *The Vermeer Interviews: Conversations with Seven Works of Art.* Minneapolis: Millbrook Press. ISBN 978-8225-9402-4. The author imagines conversations with the subjects in seven of Vermeer's paintings to help readers look at them more closely.

Reynolds, Peter H. 2003. *The Dot.* Cambridge, MA: Candlewick. ISBN 978-0-76361961-9. Vashti follows a dot wherever it leads to create her art.

Reynolds, Peter H. 2004. *Ish.* Cambridge, MA: Candlewick. ISBN 978-0-76362344-9. Raymond learns that his art doesn't have to resemble any specific objects or places.

Reynolds, Peter H. 2012. *Sky Color.* Somerville, MA: Candlewick. ISBN 978-0-76362345-6. Marisol creates a completely new sky color for a class mural.

Rockliff, Mara. 2012. *My Heart Will Not Sit Down.* Illustrated by Ann Tanksley. New York: Alfred A. Knopf/Random House. ISBN 978-0-375-84569-7. A young girl in Cameroon presses her family and neighbors, poor as they are, to offer money to help the hungry in New York City during the Depression.

Rogers, Gregory. 2012. *The Hero of Little Street.* New York: Neal Porter/Roaring Brook. ISBN 978-1-59643-729-6. A young boy runs into the National Gallery to escape bullies and has adventures with a dog inside a Jan Vermeer painting.

Rosenstock, Barb. 2014. *The Noisy Paint Box.* Illustrated by Mary Grandpré. New York: Knopf/Random House. ISBN 978-0-307-97848-6. Kandinsky's ability to experience colors as sounds enabled him to paint the splashes and swirls that became known as abstract art.

Rosenthal, Amy. 2013. *I Scream Ice Cream!* Illustrated by Serge Block. San Francisco: Chronicle Books. ISBN 978-1-4521-0004-3. Rosenthal rearranges words to create entirely new meanings in this funny demonstration of word play.

Rosenthal, Amy. 2012. *Wumbers.* Illustrated by Tom Lichtenheld. San Francisco: Chronicle Books. ISBN 978-1-4521-1022-6. Rosenthal combines words and numbers to describe the activities going on in humorous illustrations.

Rossell, Judith. 2012. *Oliver.* New York: Harper/HarperCollins. ISBN 978-0-06-202210-3. Oliver's curiosity and countless questions lead him on an imaginary journey down the bathtub drain.

Rubin, Susan Goldman. 2009. *Magritte's Imagination.* San Francisco: Chronicle, 2009. ISBN 978-08-1186583-8. bb Brief rhyming text introduces readers to eleven of the artist's paintings.

Rundell, Katherine. 2013. *Rooftoppers*. Illustrated by Terry Fan. New York: Simon & Schuster. ISBN 978-1-4424-9058-1. Sophie and her guardian Charles race to Paris in search of her mother before Sophie can be sent to an orphanage.

Saccardi, Marianne. 2007. *Art in Story: Teaching Art History to Elementary School Children*. Westport, CT: Teacher Ideas Press/Libraries Unlimited. ISBN 1-59158-359-4. Saccardi provides background information, stories about the artists, curriculum connections, and extensive children's book bibliographies for many different art periods on various continents.

Sacre, Antonio. 2011. *A Mango in the Hand: A Story Told through Proverbs*. Illustrated by Sebastia Serra. New York: Abrams. ISBN 978-0-8109-9734-9. In this story told through proverbs, Francisco sets out to gather fruit from a mango tree for his saint day feast and encounters obstacles on the way.

Saltzberg, Barney. 2012. *Andrew Drew and Drew*. New York: Abrams. ISBN 978-1-41970377-5. Readers follow Andrew and his pencil through flaps and gate folds to see how the story unfolds.

Schmid, Paul. 2013. *Perfectly Percy*. New York: Harper. ISBN 978-0-06-180436-6. Percy, a porcupine, tries to think of a way to prevent his quills from popping his balloons.

Seeger, Laura Vaccaro. 2013. *Bully*. New York: Neal Porter/Roaring Brook. ISBN 978-1-59643-630-5. A rabbit, chicken, and turtle are intimidated by a bull until a goat has the courage to confront him.

Seeger, Laura Vaccaro. 2012. *Green*. New York: Neal Porter/Roaring Brook. ISBN 978-1-59643-397-7. Seeger explores the color green in its varying shades using creative die-cuts.

Selznick, Brian. 2007. *The Invention of Hugo Cabret*. New York: Scholastic. ISBN 978-0-439813785. An orphan who lives within the walls of a Paris train station encounters a girl and an old man and solves a mystery.

Selznick, Brian. 2011. *Wonder Struck*. New York: Scholastic Press. ISBN 978-0-545-02789-2. Ben and Rose, though living fifty years apart, have stories that ultimately intertwine in this masterful novel that unfolds in both words and pictures.

Simon, Annette. 2012. *Robot Zombie FRANKENSTEIN!* Somerville, MA: Candlewick. ISBN 978-0-7636-5124-4. Two robots, formed by shapes such as squares, rectangles, circles, among others, try to outdo each other by transforming into ever-grander characters.

Smith, Lane. 2011. *Grandpa Green*. New York: Roaring Brook/Macmillan. ISBN 978-1-59643-607-7. Through the use of topiaries a young boy tells his great grandfather's story.

Snicket, Lemony. 2013. *The Dark*. New York: Little Brown. Illustrated by Jon Klassen. New York: Little Brown/Hachette. ISBN 978-0-316-18748-0. A young boy is afraid of the dark, especially the dark in the basement. So when the dark invites him down there, what is he to do?

Spires, Ashley. 2014. *The Most Magnificent Thing*. Toronto: Kids Can Press. ISBN 978-1-55453-704-4. A young girl makes repeated attempts to build the most magnificent thing she has in mind until she finally creates something that works.

Springman, I.C. 2012. *More*. Illustrated by Brian Lies. Boston: Houghton Mifflin. ISBN 978-0-547-61083-2. A magpie collects so many treasures for her nest that the branch upon which it rests breaks and she must eliminate most of her possessions.

Staake, Bob. 2013. *Bluebird*. New York: Schwartz & Wade/Random House. ISBN 978-0-375-87037-8. This wordless book tells the story of a lonely boy who is befriended by a small blue bird.

Staake, Bob. 2011. *Look! A Book!* New York: Little Brown. ISBN 978-0-316-11862-0. In rhymed text, Staake sends readers on a hunt for objects among the many displayed in each themed spread as well as objects that appear in die-cuts.

Staake, Bob. 2012. *Look! Another Book!* New York: Little Brown. ISBN 978-0-316-20459-0. In rhymed text, Staake sends readers on a hunt for objects among the many displayed in each themed spread as well as objects that appear in die-cuts.

Stewart, Sarah. 2012. *The Quiet Place*. Illustrated by David Small. New York: Margaret Ferguson/Farrar Straus Giroux/Macmillan. ISBN 978-0-374-32565-7. Isobel, a Mexican immigrant, creates a quiet space out of boxes where she can retreat to assuage the anxieties she experiences in her new country.

Tan, Shaun. 2006. *The Arrival*. New York: Arthur A. Levine/Scholastic. ISBN 978-0-439-89529-3. Tan's illustrations in this wordless book convey the fear and confusion experienced by a new immigrant.

Tan, Shaun. 2013. *The Bird King: An Artist's Notebook*. New York: Arthur A. Levine/Scholastic. ISBN 978-0-545-46513-7. Tan shares the drawings, doodles and scenes from real life he has done over twelve years in preparation for his books, films, and other art works.

Thomson, Sarah L. 2005. *Imagine a Day*. Illustrated by Rob Gonsalves. New York: Atheneum/Simon & Schuster. ISBN 0-689-85219-3. The author invites readers to imagine fantastic happenings that could take place during the day.

Thomson, Sarah L. 2003. *Imagine a Night*. Illustrated by Rob Gonsalves. New York: Atheneum/Simon & Schuster. ISBN 0-689-85218-5. The author invites readers to imagine fantastic happenings that could take place at night.

Thomson, Sarah L. 2008. *Imagine a Place*. Illustrated by Rob Gonsalves. New York: Atheneum/Simon & Schuster. ISBN 978-1-416968-02-3. The author invites readers to imagine fantastic happenings in various places.

Tonatiuh, Duncan. 2013. *Pancho Rabbit and the Coyote: A Migrant's Tale*. New York: Abrams. ISBN 978-1-4197-0583-0. Pancho Rabbit goes looking for his father who has gone north for work, but is tricked by a coyote.

Tullet, Hervé. 2011. *Press Here*. San Francisco: Handprint Books/Chronicle. ISBN 978-0-8118-7954-5. An invisible instructor asks readers to press dots or shake pages, with surprising results.

Twohy, Mike. 2013. *Outfoxed*. New York: Paula Wiseman/Simon & Schuster. ISBN 978-1-4424-7392-8. To avoid being eaten by a fox, a duck pretends to be a dog.

Vanderpool, Claire. 2013. *Navigating Early*. New York: Delacorte/Random House. ISBN 978-0-38574209-2. Two boarding school boys set out to find the Great Appalachian Bear and find much more during their arduous journey.

Van Dusen, Chris. 2012. *If I Built a House*. New York: Dial/Penguin. ISBN 978-0-8037-3751-8. Because his family's house seems so ordinary and boring, Jack decides to build his own fantastical dream house.

Verde, Susan. 2013. *The Museum*. Illustrated by Peter H. Reynolds. New York: Abrams. ISBN 978-1-4197-0594-6. A young girl creates her own art after viewing the art in a museum.

Viva, Frank. 2013. *A Long Way Away*. New York: Little Brown/Hachette. ISBN 978-0-316-22196-2. Readers can follow a creature's journey from a distant planet to the ocean floor or from the ocean floor to the planet by reading the book vertically up or down.

Viva, Frank. 2013. *Young Frank, Architect*. New York: The Museum of Modern Art/Abrams. ISBN 978-0-87070-893-0. An old architect criticizes young Frank's work until they discover by visiting a museum that the boy's ideas are not so outlandish.

Voigt, Cynthia. 2013. *Mister Max: The Book of Lost Things*. Illustrated by Jacopo Bruno. New York: Knopf. ISBN 978-0-375-97123-5. After his parents mysteriously disappear, Max makes a living for himself finding lost things and solving problems.

Walker, Sally M. 2012. *Freedom Song!* Illustrated by Sean Qualls. New York: Harper. ISBN 978-0-06-058310-1. Henry Brown has friends seal him in a box and mail him to freedom in the north. His journey in the box took him from Virginia to Philadelphia.

Warner, Carl. 2012. *A World of Food: Discover Magical Lands Made of Things You Can Eat!* New York: Abrams. ISBN 978-1-4197-0162-7. Warner creates incredibly beautiful worlds, each formed by foods of a specific color.

Wein, Elizabeth. 2012. *Code Name Verity*. New York: Hyperion. ISBN 978-142315219-4. Captured by the Nazis during World War II, Verity writes a "confession" to earn a reprieve from torture and execution. Her account reveals her role, that of her friend Maddie, and British pilots during the war.

Wein, Elizabeth. 2013. *Rose under Fire*. New York: Hyperion. ISBN 978-1423183099. While Rose Justice is transporting a fighter plane from Paris to England during World War II, she is captured and sent to Ravensbrück concentration camp.

Weiner, Ellis. 2012. *The Templeton Twins Have an Idea*. Illustrated by Jeremy Holmes. San Francisco: Chronicle Books. ISBN 978-0-8118-6679-8. Twins Abigail and John have to devise a plan to escape kidnappers and save their father and his invention from thieves.

Willems, Mo. 2013. *That Is NOT a Good Idea!* New York: Balzer + Bray/HarperCollins. ISBN 978-0-06-220309-0. A fox invites a goose for a walk intending to eat her for dinner but the goose has other plans.

Williams-Garcia, Rita. 2013. *P.S. Be Eleven*. New York: Amistad/HarperCollins. ISBN 978-0-193862-7. The Gaither sisters confront the radical changes facing African Americans in the turbulent 1960s.

Winter, Jeanette. 2009. *Nasreen's Secret School: A True Story of Afghanistan*. New York: Beach Lane/Simon & Schuster. ISBN 978-1-416994374. Nasreen, a young girl living in Afghanistan, stops speaking when her parents disappear until her participation in a secret school helps her overcome her sadness.

Woodson, Jacqueline. 2012. *Each Kindness*. Illustrated by E. B. Lewis. New York: Nancy Paulsen Books/Penguin Group. ISBN 978-0-399-24652-4. After Maya, a girl who is obviously poor, leaves the class, Chloe regrets not having befriended her.

Yaccarino, Dan. 2013. *Doug Unplugged*. New York: Knopf/Random House. ISBN 978-0-375-86643-2. Doug, a robot, learns more about the city when he explores it first-hand than when he learns downloaded facts.

Yamasaki, Katie. 2013. *Fish for Jimmy*. New York: Holiday House. ISBN 978-0-8234-2375-0. Taro risks capture in an internment camp for Japanese when he escapes every week to secure a fish for his ailing brother.

Yankovic, Al. 2013. *My New Teacher and Me!* Illustrated by Wes Hargis. New York: Harper/HarperCollins. ISBN 978-0-06-219203-5. When Billy tells outlandish stories, his teacher asks him to admit they are not true.

Young, Cybéle. 2013. *Ten Birds Meet a Monster*. Toronto: Kids Can Press. ISBN 978-1-55453-955-0. Ten birds don creative disguises to scare away a monster.

Zalben, Jan Breskin. 2012. *Mousterpiece: A Mouse-Sized Guide to Modern Art*. New York: Neal Porter/Roaring Brook. ISBN 978-1-59643-549-0. A mouse creates her own art after viewing modern art in a museum. All art works and their creators are identified at the end of the book.

Zullo, Germano. 2013. *Line 135*. Illustrated by Albertine. San Francisco: Chronicle Books. ISBN 978-1-4521-1934-2. A young girl travels to the country by train to stay with her grandmother and muses along the way about her ability to know the world. Most unusual illustrations and format.

3

Folklore, Fantasy—The Tale Is a Lie; What It Tells Is the Truth (Traditional folktale ending)

> If you want your children to be intelligent, read them fairy tales. If you want them to be more intelligent, read them more fairy tales.
>
> —Albert Einstein

In his brilliant essay entitled, "On Fairy Stories," J.R.R. Tolkien wrote,

> The realm of fairy-story is wide and deep and high and filled with many things: all manner of beasts and birds are found there; shoreless seas and stars uncounted; beauty that is an enchantment, and an ever-present peril; both joy and sorrow as sharp as swords. (1)

In fantasy literature with its wide sweep of subgenres, including myth and legends,[1] folk and fairy tales, readers enter fantastic worlds inhabited by extraordinary creatures, both human and beast, who use magic and other means to both save and destroy. Because they can have no experience of fantasy situations in the world in which they live, it is essential, if readers are to make sense of and learn from these stories, that they read for more than plot; that they learn to read beneath the words to hear what the protagonists of fairy stories have to tell them about the reality of their 21st-century lives. We have talked about metaphor and its importance in poetry and in illustration. When readers meet metaphor in words, poems, and pictures, they have an opportunity to look with fresh eyes, to see beneath and beyond the page to a new world of meaning, a new awareness. But perhaps nowhere is metaphor more powerfully met than in the literature of folklore and fantasy. Metaphor IS the language of folklore. Folk and fairytales and the high fantasy and science fiction novels of today's literature for children abound in archetypes for good and evil, wisdom and foolishness, kindness and selfishness, and so on. Begun orally most likely among cave dwellers sitting before their fires, elders passed on their values and cautions to each succeeding generation through these metaphorical stories. Tolkien, in the essay quoted earlier, says "Speaking of the history of stories and especially of fairy-stories we may say that the Pot of

Soup, the Cauldron of Story, has always been boiling, and to it have continually been added new bits, dainty and undainty" (9).

The stories eventually spread on ships and trade routes until peoples around the world embraced them, adding their own customs, values, and twists to the tales, becoming more fixed once they were captured and written down by collectors such as Perrault and the Brothers Grimm. Today, modern storytellers write their own tales, keeping ever in mind the motifs and metaphors used by the ancients so that the lessons of the past become fused with the cultural mores in which our students live to provide a new summons to a life of the imagination; a new summons to read beneath the words to the truths they signify; a new summons to answer the needs of the community. Jane Yolen (2000) writes, "The best of the old stories spoke to the listener because they spoke not just to the ears but to the heart as well" (24).

Nursery Rhymes

Nursery rhymes are among the first poem-like fantasy literature we share with young children, and their value in youngsters' development is enormous. These brief pieces contain all the patterns and sounds of language so essential for children to hear and internalize as they learn to speak and eventually to read. And where else would they meet such wonderful words so early in their lives as "fetch," "contrary," "tuffet," "tumbling," "tarry," and so many more. In *Nursery Rhyme Comics* (2011), edited by Chris Duffy, children's literature historian Leonard S. Marcus writes:

> Everything about the rhymes lines up to make them memorable: their pulsing, beat-the-drum rhythms, close-knit rhyme schemes, and nutshell narratives featuring quirky, vivid characters with quirky, vivid names: Hector Protector! Georgie Porgie! Little Bo Peep! (1)

Once the children have become familiar with a number of rhymes, ask individuals or groups to devise original motions and/or dance steps; or rhythmic beats with instruments such as drums, triangles, tambourines, xylophones, among others, the class can enjoy while reciting them. They might also create a booklet in which they print the rhymes along with directions for accompanying gestures and steps and present it to another class. A list of excellent nursery rhyme books appears at the end of this chapter. At least a few of them deserve a place in every home and classroom.

Nursery rhymes provide many opportunities for older students to develop innovative projects, and there are several books we can offer them to spark their thinking. In addition to enjoying the rhymes themselves, students can do what divergent thinkers do all the time: ask questions. In her article, "Reinventing Education to Teach Creativity and Entrepreneurship," Jennifer Medbery (2012) writes, "Imagine a world where the math textbook was replaced with open-ended, thought-provoking opportunities to question the world around us. In these classrooms, students would learn how to think, how to find problems, not just plug in numbers to solve them. What if quizzes measured kids' ability to question, not answer?" Encourage students to ask such questions as "Where did these rhymes come from?" "Do they represent real characters or real events in history as many believe?" "How old are they?" Iona and Peter Opie, recognized authorities on nursery rhymes, updated their 1951 classic, *The Oxford Dictionary of Nursery Rhymes* in 1997. While not strictly a book for children, older students can learn much from the wealth of information it contains about the more than 500 rhymes within. Among many other things, they will learn who Mother Goose was, see some very early illustrations of the rhymes, and how the wording of some rhymes has changed over the years. It would be a fine book to have on hand for students to examine whenever they wish and as a resource for such projects as comparing the different wording of individual rhymes, deciding which they enjoy more and why; deciding what different illustrators have added to the rhymes by their pictures; and so on. Ask students to choose a rhyme and change its wording to reflect today's political scene or events in the community in which they live.

Randolph Caldecott was one of the most popular and beloved illustrators of children's books in the late 1800s. His pictures are so beautiful that the prestigious Caldecott medal, the highest award an illustrator of children's books can receive in the United States, was named after him. Fortunately, The Huntington Library Press has published a collection of nine of Caldecott's most popular books in *Randolph Caldecott's Picture Books* (2008). These nursery rhyme books are a perfect source for investigating the ways in which authors and illustrators invent new interpretations of works that we may already know so that we see them in a new light. In some instances, Caldecott used words to give the rhymes a new spin, as when he added another blackbird to replace the poor maid's snipped off nose in *Sing a Song for Sixpence* so that it doesn't end harshly. He made additions with pictures as well, as in *The Queen of Hearts* in which there are four royal children and four kings and queens. In Caldecott's version, told only through an illustration, it is a cat that reveals who stole those tarts. If you are fortunate enough to own this collection or can obtain it from a library, set the class to work scrutinizing Caldecott's words and pictures. They can begin by examining his extensions in illustration only, such as the pig in *The Farmer's Boy* who is putting together a puzzle, or the child king and queen in *Sing a Song for Sixpence*. In *The Milkmaid*, the words tell of a young squire whose mother sends him off to "seek a Wife with a Fortune!" He meets a pretty milkmaid, accompanies her as she goes "a-milking," proposes marriage but then reneges when he discovers she has no fortune. The text simply concludes, "Nobody asked you, Sir!" But in the marvelous pictures, three young women have been watching this exchange, and they chase the young man, catch him, sit him atop a bucking bull, and then dance with glee at his exit. But beyond seeing these extensions that so enrich the stories, students can explore the pictures even more deeply to uncover their hidden metaphors—metaphors that add even more depth, perhaps even a dark note, to these simple rhymes. To cite just a few examples: what is the meaning behind what the two dogs are doing as they witness the exchange between Milkmaid and Squire? In *Hey Diddle Diddle*, what is behind the incident depicted in the last illustration? In *Baby Bunting*, why are the baby's eyes riveted on the cluster of rabbits on the hill? Divide the students into nine groups, each group being responsible for studying one of the books. Ask the groups to select pictures in a given rhyme in which they see metaphors, write their understanding of the pictures, then present the pictures to another group or the entire class for comments. Compare the group's comments with those of the class or another group.

Nursery Rhyme Comics, mentioned earlier, contains fifty well-known rhymes illustrated in comic form by fifty famous contemporary cartoonists. What is fascinating about this book is that each illustrator has added his or her take on the rhyme. For example, in "Hickory, Dickory, Dock" (8–9), we see that the mouse runs up the clock because it is he, wielding a huge mallet, who strikes the one o'clock chime. In "Pussycat, Pussycat, Where Have You Been?" (72–73), the cat who frightens the little mouse under the chair in turn receives a surprising fright herself. After enjoying the book, ask the students to work alone or in groups to select a rhyme not included in it and illustrate it as a comic. What additional elements will their comics include? Students might wish to upload their comics to a wiki (see http://wikispot.org/Create_a_wiki), invite another class to view the wiki and contribute their own ideas as well. Both classes should discuss each other's contributions and add or subtract ideas to arrive at the best depictions of the rhymes.

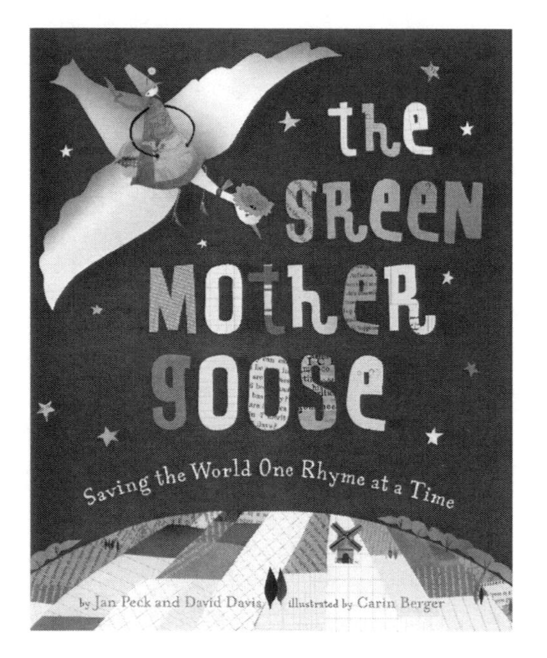

In *The Green Mother Goose* (2011) by David Davis and Jan Peck, the authors rewrite thirty rhymes and children's songs to reflect ecological themes. For example, Old Mother Hubbard buys only local food to provide for her dog. As Humpty Dumpty sits on his wall, he's clearly "on the fence" about the reality of global warming. Heckety Peckety is a free range hen in this iteration. The little piggies recycle on the way home. In addition, the illustrations utilize recycled materials such as newspapers and ticket stubs, and the book is printed on recycled paper. The illustrations depict Mother Hubbard carrying a canvas bag, and laundry that is dried outside on a clothes line. Ask students to rewrite other rhymes to reflect a theme—a topic they are studying, for example.

Nursery rhymes are unique in that they can tell an entire story in four brief lines. Writing briefly and effectively is a skill worth cultivating. Challenge students to create an original story, or tell about an event at school in four rhymed lines.

Folktales

Folktales, except for those that originate much later in written form such as those penned by Hans Christian Andersen and other contemporary writers, are anonymous and have their origin in the oral tradition. They have a large umbrella that includes, fables, tall tales, and pourquoi tales (stories that helped people come to terms with unusual happenings in nature or animal behaviors they did not understand). Fables always have a moral that listeners discover through the actions of animals standing in for humans. Often ordinary folk or animals inhabit folktales, the plots are simple and repetitious (three being a common number as in three tasks or three characters such as "Three Little Pigs," or "Three

Billy Goats Gruff," etc.) to facilitate memory, and the endings are usually sure and swift, meting out reward or punishment as deserved. Descriptions are brief, characters often generic (e.g., Jack, an everyman like our common "John Smith.") The stories come from countries throughout the world, often with different variations of the same tale (over 500 variants of Cinderella). Some stories feature trickster characters who try to achieve their goals by devious means. Brer Rabbit is a trickster who originated in African American stories; African nations tell of the trickster spider Anansi; coyote and raven inhabit Native American trickster tales; wolf exhibits his wiles in European tales; and badger is a trickster found in Japanese stories. Fairytales are often included under this umbrella and will be discussed separately later.

Trickster Tales

Folktales from many different countries and regions are retold in picture book form, making them very accessible to our younger students. These books also provide opportunities for students of all ages to engage in creative projects and divergent thinking. In looking at tricksters, for example, they might consider why certain animals were selected by different cultures to represent these wily characters. Why is it that sometimes tricksters are wise and clever and sometimes foolish—often within the same story? Apart from the obvious entertainment they provide, what lessons or cultural beliefs do these tales impart? Perhaps a study of a particular culture, in conjunction with a social studies unit, for instance, would enable students to see aspects of that culture in a tale. It might be interesting to consider a particular trickster's actions across several tales. Students could study Anansi the Spider, beginning with Kojo's *The Parade: A Stampede of Stories about Ananse the Trickster Spider* (2011). It includes seven tales, and the opening story, *The Parade*, tells why Ananse (a spelling variation) became a trickster. Kimmel's *Anansi and the Magic Stick* (2001) and *Anansi's Party Time* (2009 are stand-alone stories that can also help students consider Anansi's actions and the lessons they convey. In Lucine Kasbarian's Armenian folktale entitled *The Greedy Sparrow* (2011), a trickster sparrow learns a hard lesson. When he gets a thorn in his foot, a baker kindly removes it and throws it into the fire. Later, the sparrow asks for the thorn, and when the woman can't produce it, he demands a loaf of bread. The sparrow leaves the bread with a shepherd and after the shepherd eats it, sparrow demands a sheep. This trade continues with the sparrow escalating his demands at each encounter until he is left as he began—with a thorn in his foot. A variation on this trickster tale is Jessica Souhami's *Foxy* (2013). A fox carrying a bag containing a bee warns a woman not to look into it. Of course she does, and when the bee escapes, the fox demands a rooster in exchange. He continues to demand ever-grander treasures from the gullible folks he meets until trickster Foxy, like Sparrow, meets his comeuppance. After reading Anansi stories as well as tales involving other tricksters, students could devise a trickster character of their own. What animal might they choose and why? What lessons do they want their tale to demonstrate? Will their trickster be wise or foolish or both? (See "Brer Rabbit and the Tar Baby" in Lester, 2006, for an example of how the trickster uses his wits to undo the trouble he initially gets himself into through his foolish behavior.) Will they illustrate their story? Photograph their illustrations for the tale and turn them into an iMovie? Dramatize it? Would they like to create a three-dimensional trickster figure using papier-mâché, clay, or other materials? Do the students wish to work as a class or create several stories by working in groups? Another option is for students to put their own trickster character or a trickster from a tale they have read on trial for his actions. They will need a judge, jury, and lawyers for the trickster as well as the plaintiffs who have been wronged by him or her.

Creative Problem Solving and Life Lessons

Chitra Benerjee Divakaruni retells a Bengali folktale, *Grandma and the Great Gourd* (2013). Grandma lives alone at the edge of a little village in India. When she receives an invitation from her daughter, who lives on the other side of the jungle, to come for a visit, the woman is understandably apprehensive about "traveling through the jungle where so many fierce animals live[d]." But she decides to go anyway, and sure enough, is confronted, in turn, by a fox, a black bear, and a tiger—all hungry, and all planning to eat her on the spot. Surely an old woman is no match for these powerful animals, so she uses her ingenuity instead, convincing each of them that she will be much fatter on her way home after eating all her daughter's fine cooking. Her trick works, but she knows she will not be able to fool the animals with words on her return. So together she and her daughter come up with a clever plan that, with the help of her dogs, wins the day. Another picture book in which a character uses ingenuity to overcome difficulty is Ann Redisch Stampler's *The Wooden Sword: A Jewish Folktale from Afghanistan* (2012). When an Afghani shah leaves his palace to learn more about his people, he encounters a Jewish shoemaker who, while not wealthy, is very happy. To test his subject, the shah enacts a series of laws that make it impossible for the shoemaker to continue his trade. Still the man remains content and continually finds new work. When he is named royal executioner and has to behead a thief, however, the man even then finds a clever way out of doing so. These two folktales as well as some familiar *Brer Rabbit* tales, *The Three Billy Goats Gruff*, *The Three Little Pigs*, and many others, demonstrate how weaker or smaller characters can outwit those much more powerful by thinking rather than fighting. Reading several similar tales with students can lead them to thinking their way through a difficult problem facing the class. Perhaps they might turn the problem into the plot of a folktale with a character solving the problem through clever thought.

While Janice N. Harrington's *Busy-Busy Little Chick* (2013), a tale based on a fable told by the Nkundo people of Central Africa, doesn't involve problem solving via trickery, it does offer an industrious little problem solver who helps his family through determined industry. Mama Nsoso and her five chicks live in a much-too-small home. Each evening the chicks complain, "Peo-peo, Mama, Peo-peo. We're chilly-cold. Our tummies are chilly-cold. Our feet are chilly-cold. We're chilly-cold *all* over." And each evening mama promises that on the morrow, she will build them a new home so sturdy and cozy that "rain will not drip in, and the dark night will not bother [them]." But each day, she is distracted by tempting food to eat and the house-building is deferred. The chicks continue to complain—all but busy chick who works tirelessly in secret on a new house and collapses exhausted each evening. Finally he's able to invite his family into their new home. A glossary of Nkundo words and author's note are included.

Margaret Read MacDonald's and Nadia Jameel Taibah's *How Many Donkeys? An Arabic Counting Tale* (2009), serves as both a counting book and a folktale. Jouha is leading his caravan of donkeys loaded with dates to sell in the market. He knows he has packed ten donkeys with dates, but every time he mounts one on the journey and looks behind him, he counts only nine. When he walks alongside the donkeys, however, he counts ten again. Youngsters will soon see how very foolish Jouha is and why the number of donkeys keeps changing. An added bonus is the appearance of cardinal numbers one to ten in Arabic and English transliteration on the bottom of the pages. Slightly older students will meet tricksters and other characters in the seven tales in Elizabeth Laird's *Pea Boy and Other Stories from Iran* (2010). Not all the stories end happily, and sometimes foolish characters, as often happens in Aesop's fables, gain hard-earned wisdom. Such is the case with the lazy cockroach, in "Miss Cockroach and Mrs. Mouse," who makes such a ridiculous demand of her devoted mouse husband who is trying desperately to save her life that it costs him his life instead.

Leah Sharpe retells an Italian folktale, *The Goat-Faced Girl* (2009) to signal the folly of laziness. A foundling raised by a sorceress turns into a beautiful but lazy young woman. Still, her beauty captivates an equally lazy prince who proposes marriage. When the prince later views his intended bride, now sporting the head of a goat inflicted upon her by the sorceress as punishment for her laziness, he devises three tasks for her to perform to forestall the marriage. The girl actually accomplishes them and discovers that she likes being industrious and independent. She also realizes that the prince only valued her for her beauty, and even after her pretty face is restored, spurns him. The illustrations are lovely, filled with touches of the Italian renaissance period.

Folktales about Nasreddine, a person who might have actually lived in Turkey during the Middle Ages, are popular in the Middle East. In *Nasreddine*, Odile Weulersse (2013) recounts several trips the protagonist makes to market with his father Mustafa. In one trip Mustafa rides their donkey while Nasreddine walks, and on lookers criticize the man for making the young boy walk. On the next trip, they reverse positions and still they are criticized, this time for a strong youngster allowing his father to walk. When they both ride the donkey, onlookers express pity for the animal who must carry such a load. Each time Nasreddine is saddened by the criticism until his father tells him, "You have to decide if what you hear from others is wise or silly and hurtful," an important lesson that, while being mindful of the feelings of others, it is not wise to be overly concerned about their opinions. Peer pressure to act in ways with which they might not always be comfortable is a situation often faced by older students. Yet "independence in judgment" (Introduction, p. xiii) is an important characteristic of the divergent thinker. Divide the class into groups and ask each group to discuss instances in which they or others they know have faced this kind of pressure. Then challenge them to devise an innovative way for students to extricate themselves from such situations while still maintaining friendships. Compile their ideas into an illustrated brochure that might be distributed to other classes in the school. Select an attractive title for the brochure.

Judy Goldman retells animal folktales from five indigenous peoples of Mexico—the Tarahumara, Seri, Huichol, Triqui, and Tseltal in *Whiskers, Tails & Wings* (2013). Everything about this collection is wonderful: the language (Hant Caai, the creation god, "sing[s] the earth into being"), the vivid illustrations, and the glossary and discussion of each culture that follows every story. There is also an extensive bibliography at the end. Goldman concludes:

> where else in the world will you find a clever cricket who defeats a puma, a patient turtle who helps to create the world, a brave opossum who gives mankind a wonderful gift, a flea who saves humanity, and a frog who . . . keeps his heart in his chest? Only in Mexico! (46)

All the stories discussed here are fine examples of the multilayered role of the folktale: to teach life lessons; to show the weak how they can overcome difficulties by using their wit and talents; or simply to laugh at our own foibles. All of them can inspire students, as Goldman urges in her conclusion, to create original tales of their own.

Fables

Jerry Pinkney (2000), Eric Carle (2008), Beverly Naidoo (2011), and Charles Santore (2012) have created illustrated collections of Aesop's fables. What is unique about the sixteen fables in Naidoo's collection is that all of them are set in Africa with some words in Afrikaansas as well. Mary Ann Hoberman's *You Read to Me, I'll Read to You: Very Short Fables to Read Together* (2010) contains thirteen short fables meant to be read by a child and adult taking turns. The different colors for the adult and child parts make it easy to know when to read. Teachers and children can read these tales alternately as well, or perhaps pairs of children might like to take turns. There are also several stand-alone picture book versions children can delve into. Jerry Pinkney has two almost wordless versions of an Aesop Fable, *The Lion & the Mouse* (2009), winner of the Caldecott Medal, and *The Tortoise & the Hare* (2013). Both books are breathtakingly beautiful and enable very young readers to tell the story from the pictures. In addition, the illustrations are filled with metaphors to explore: the mouse lost in enormous lion paw prints and the owl hoots, among others, in the former; the animals' clothing in the latter. (Hint: see author's note.)

After students have become familiar with the original Aesop fable of "The Ant and the Grasshopper" in which the ant refuses to help the cold starving grasshopper when winter sets in because the grasshopper wasted his summer days singing while the ant worked, they can compare it to retellings of the same fable by two contemporary authors. Rebecca and Ed Emberley give the fable a Cajun flavor in their version of *The Ant and the Grasshopper* (2012), a beautiful book illustrated with vibrantly colored graphics. An ant struggling to carry some picnic bits back to the nest is enchanted by the music being played by a grasshopper and his band. "Hey there, baby, why don't you put down that big sticky thing and come groove with us?" asks the grasshopper. Not only does the ant accept his invitation, she also invites the entire band down to her cool nest underground to play for the entire ant colony. In *Ant and Grasshopper* (2011), Luli Gray gives the two insects added dialogue and personality. In addition, she brings the fable to a new level by giving the ant a troubled conscience as he contemplates the plight of the poor grasshopper and invites him into his cozy home. Thus the ant, while convinced that hard work has its rewards, now comes to realize that music has its place as well and that we have an obligation to be concerned for one another. Students can use these two recent retellings as models for rewriting some original fables. What if some of Aesop's animals not only learn a bitter lesson but also extend that lesson to make some changes in their lives as ant did in caring for the grasshopper?

As a follow-up to their enjoyment of fables, engage in either or both of the following projects:

1. Ask the students to identify a problem plaguing a particular part of the world today. It could be a problem in their community, state, another country, or other such entities. Identify the causes of that problem and then write a fable that incorporates both the problem and at least one of its causes.
2. Change the animal characters into human ones and place them in a contemporary setting. How does the human behave and what lesson can he or she learn from that behavior?

Tall Tales

Tall tales originated in the American West during the 1800s, the period of the westward movement. It was a time when wide open spaces beckoned easterners with the lure of cheap land and freedom from the restraints of city life. Their horizons loomed large and so did their stories—tales featuring larger-than-life heroes who accomplished incredible feats with seemingly superhuman physical strength and resources. Many of the heroes in these stories actually lived (Davey Crockett, for example), but their deeds were greatly and amusingly exaggerated. Impossible rescues, jobs that required amazing strength and endurance, taming of the elements—nothing was too much for the heroes of these tales to undertake. Fortunately, many of the old stories, as well as recently written tall tales, are available for today's children. The following are a few excellent ones to share with them.

Many traditional heroes of tall tales are male, but in recent years, authors have created stories about several larger-than-life women as well. Doña Flor in Pat Mora's *Doña Flor: A Tall Tale about a Giant Woman with a Great Big Heart* (2005), is so tall she can snatch stars from the sky and reach for snow on the mountain tops to wash herself with each morning. She can also speak the language of every animal and plant. But instead of being a scary giant Doña Flor is actually a helpful member of her little village community where she makes huge tortillas for her neighbors to use as roofs and their children to float on in the river. So when the roars of a seemingly gigantic animal threatens the village, she sets out, with the help of her animal friends, to locate the culprit, who doesn't seem so menacing after all. This story, beautifully illustrated in the warm shades of the southwestern landscape, offers an added bonus in the Spanish words sprinkled throughout. Bobbi Miller's *Miss Sally Ann and the Panther* (2012) features Miss Sally Ann Thunder Whirlwind Crockett and her encounter with a red-eyed panther. Sally is wearing her very best fur coat and the panther wants it, so they engage in a fight so fierce that they create a gorge and even curdle the Milky Way. When they assess the situation the next morning, they discover that they really admire each other's great fighting skills and become good friends. One of the delights of this story is the author's marvelous use of words, specially coined exaggerations, that make this preposterous fight even funnier: thunderific, swaggerous, terrifiacious, and more. If students are curious about how Sally Ann Thunder ended up marrying Davey Crockett, offer them Miller's exaggerated account of their meeting: *Davey Crockett Gets Hitched* (2009). On his way to a dance in Sally's honor, Davey gets a burr stuck in his pants. His jumping about to get free of the irritating burr is seen by Sally as mighty fine dancing so she joins him on the dance floor. They not only outlast all the other dancers, but their leaping and stomping also results in making the mashed potatoes and applesauce served later during the feast. Angelica Longrider, hero of Anne Isaacs's *Swamp Angel* (2000), was hardly an extraordinary child. In fact, she didn't build her first log cabin until she was two. Yet she does grow up to be the most famous Tennessee woods woman ever, able to lasso a tornado and drink an entire lake dry. At age twelve, she earns the nickname Swamp Angel by rescuing a wagon train stuck in the mud and later defeats the huge, fearsome bear known as Thundering Tarnation and tosses him into the sky. You can still see that Great Bear among the stars if you look closely enough. The gorgeous folk art paintings are done on wood, so appropriate for the story's context, and won a Caldecott honor for the illustrator. Angelina's adventures continue in Isaacs's *Dust Devil* (2010). Because Tennessee has become too small for her, she moves to the wide open spaces of Montana where she wrestles a bucking bronco and forms the Grand Canyon (though other tall tale heroes claim this feat as well). Angelina also has to face a nasty bandit named Backwards Bart, so ugly at birth that his mother wheeled his carriage backward to avoid the prying eyes of the neighbors. Now Bart even speaks backward when he threatens the unfortunates he tries to rob. This is one hilarious romp from beginning to end. Fortunately for tall tale lovers,

Anne Isaacs gives us a new larger-than-life heroine in *Meanwhile, Back at the Ranch* (2014). In 1870, the widow Tulip Jones of England inherits 35,000,000 dollars and buys a ranch in By-Gully, Texas where she discovers it's "so hot that chickens [lay] hard-boiled eggs," and tomatoes are so big you need to climb ladders to pick them. She also discovers that 1,000 unmarried cowboys, including Sheriff Arroyo and his brother Spit, leaders of the Hole in the Pants Gang, show up at the ranch daily seeking her hand and her fortune. How Tulip and her ranch hands outsmart them and actually capture the gang make for entertaining reading.

In tribute to the African Americans who ventured into the vast spaces of the West after the Civil War, Jerdine Nolen created an original tall tale featuring Rose MacGruder, "first child born free to Jackson and Millicent MacGruder," in *Thunder Rose* (2003). On the day she was born, Rose astonished her parents by gathering the lightning flashing outside into a ball, giving herself her own name, and announcing that she would do great things. It became obvious that this child was full of lightning and thunder, but she also has within herself a "melody so real and sweet and true" that it can calm an angry bull leading a stampede. She makes alphabet letters of iron to help neighbor children learn to read and brings thieves to justice. But when "the cataclysmic efforts of a windstorm bent on her disaster" faces Rose, she stops to think about her situation. And then summoning the song deep inside her, she lets it ring out "like a healing river in the breathing air around her." Clearly, Rose is a woman of action who knows how to slow down and do the unusual to solve a serious problem.

"Paul Bunyan was the largest, smartest, and strongest baby ever born in the state of Maine," begins Steven Kellogg's (2004) tall tale bearing his name. Why, as a baby he could even lift a cow over his head. Paul's interest in trees eventually leads him to a career as a powerfully strong lumberjack whose adventures with his constant companion, Blue Ox, form the Great Lakes and the Grand Canyon, among other geographic wonders. Kellogg's book reveals many of Paul's exploits through enjoyable text accompanied by illustrations that are full of action. Teresa Baleman tells another story about the great lumberjack in *Paul Bunyan vs. Hals Halson: The Giant Lumberjack Challenge!* (2011). When Hals, another very big man, comes into lumber camp, Paul offers him friendship, but Hals is intent upon proving he is the greater lumberjack and tries to wrestle Bunyan. His moves only tickle the hero, though, and Hals ends up hurting himself instead—though the two do eventually become friends. The author provides additional stories in her end notes about this big-hearted Maine hero.

Pecos Bill was tossed from a wagon when he was a baby and raised by coyotes. As an adult he could wrestle anything that moved, tame wild mares, and even ride a mountain lion. Sean Hamann Tulien recounts several of the Texas cowboy's extraordinary feats in *Pecos Bill, Colossal Cowboy: The Graphic Novel* (2010) Pecos, named for the river in which he crawled as a baby, becomes the no-nonsense sheriff of No Man's Land, but his greatest challenge is trying to tame a fierce cyclone that threatens to destroy the entire western frontier. How he does this and performs so many other amazing feats is entertainingly told and depicted in this graphic novel that will keep comic lovers turning the pages.

John Henry is the subject of many tall tales, and there is speculation about whether he actually lived. The stories surrounding him have to do with the railroad tracks being laid across the country in the mid-1800s. Companies hired scores of men to clear the land and rid it of obstacles. One such obstacle was a mountain in West Virginia. Using huge hammers and stakes, steel-driving men like John Henry had to drive holes in the rock so that explosives could be placed in them to blast the Big Bend Tunnel through that mountain for the Chesapeake & Ohio Railroad. To speed up the process, the company began using steam-driven drills to get into the rock, but John Henry claimed he was faster. A contest ensued between the man with his hammer and the drill, and the story goes that although John won, he died of exhaustion. Many writers have told John's story for young people. In an easy reader version, Stephen Krensky (*John Henry*, 2007) begins, "Nobody ever said for sure that John Henry was born with a hammer in his hand. But nobody ever said he wasn't, either. He always seemed to be holding one" (6). Speaking of John Henry in the gorgeous picture book (*John Henry*, 1999) that won illustrator Jerry Pinkney a Caldecott honor, Julius Lester writes, "the wind was out of breath trying to keep up with him." Share any or all of these fine books with students and, if possible, enrich the experience by viewing a YouTube film of Harry Belafonte's singing of *The Ballad of John Henry* at http://www.youtube.com/watch?v=g6vcvYJCkic.

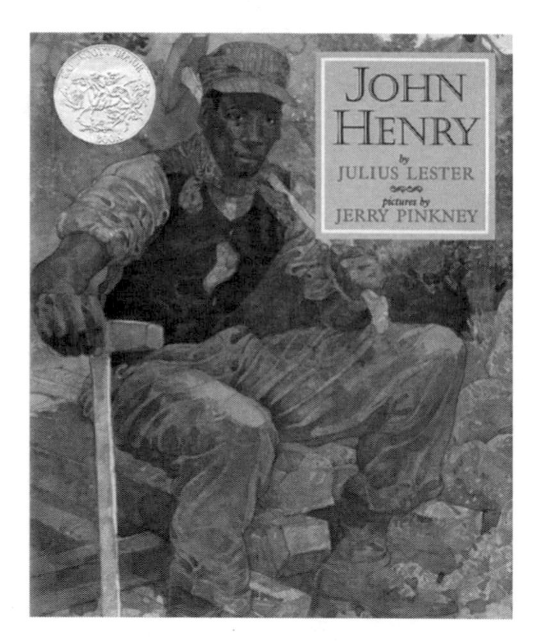

After spending time with some of the tall tales described earlier or others of your choosing, involve the students in some activities that will require them to think about these stories; their origins; what their tellers were trying to accomplish; whether tall tales have a place in today's society; and how tall tales might be created and told in innovative ways. Some suggestions:

1. Some subjects of tall tales actually lived and some did not. Research the hero of a favorite tale to find out as much as possible about him or her. Compare actual facts of the person's life with feats presented in stories and legends. In what ways, if any, did tellers and writers take actual events and stretch them into exaggerations? Older students might begin by reading or listening to *Ain't Nothing but a Man: My Quest to Find the Real John Henry* (2007) by Scott Reynolds Nelson and Marc Aronson. In this marvelous book, Nelson, a historian, explains how he works to uncover mysteries and how he used the *Ballad of John Henry* as a jumping-off point to discover the real man behind the words. The authors also talk about what was happening in the country during Henry's time—especially the dramatic expansion of cross-country railroads, labor songs, and so much more.
2. Worker versus machine has been a continuing conflict, as evidenced by John Henry's challenge that his manual labor was better than a machine any day. Workers today

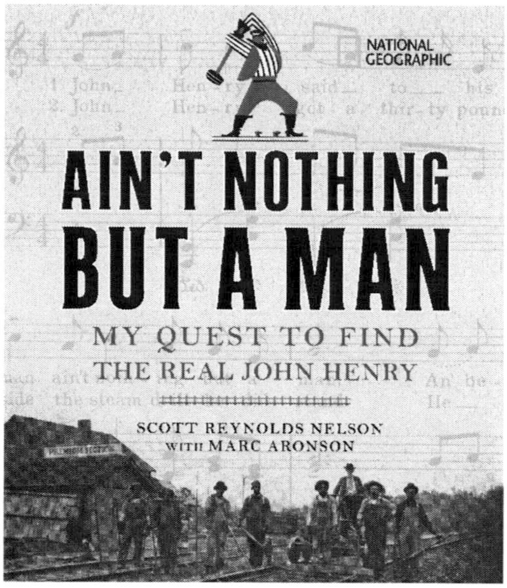

face the same issues as robots in factories replace people on the assembly line and computers replace them just about anywhere. What are students' opinions about this dilemma? What ground-breaking ideas can they come up with that will enable people to have work while still advancing progress through technological developments?

3. Compile a list of some of the humorous expressions encountered in the tall tales students have read. Did the expressions add to or detract from the story? How and why? Make up some exaggerated expressions to describe the characters and/or their exploits in favorite tales. Research the role of humor in literature and its effect on the reader.
4. Compare this *Ballad of Davey Crockett* at http://www.youtube.com/watch?v=W1KYpizprfI with the one at http://www.youtube.com/watch?v=bff8NCdTl-A. What do the students notice about stereotypes and prejudice? Discuss how songs often reflect the beliefs and mores of the time in which they were written. The ballads about Davey Crocket, along with the one about John Henry, might inspire some students to write an original ballad about a tall tale character of their choice. What are some characteristics of ballads the students have discovered after listening to several? How can they incorporate these characteristics into their original ballad? How would they like to go about writing a ballad—as a whole class activity, divided into groups with each group writing a stanza? Can they put their ballad to music with the help of the music teacher?
5. Discuss the characteristics of tall tales after the students have experienced several. Invite them to incorporate these characteristics into the creation of an original tall tale. Will they choose an actual person—a political figure, the principal, each other, for example—or make up one. How will they create the tale? It need not be in written or book form. For example, students can create an audio slideshow of their tale (see animoto.com) and imbed it into a blog. What other inventive ways can students devise? Can they represent their hero artistically to accompany their tale or solely as an artistic representation that exemplifies the exaggerated powers and feats of that person?

NATIONAL GEOGRAPHIC
AIN'T NOTHING BUT A MAN
MY QUEST TO FIND THE REAL JOHN HENRY
SCOTT REYNOLDS NELSON WITH MARC ARONSON

Pourquoi Tales

Thousands of years ago, the Yorta-Yorta, one of Australia's aboriginal tribes, told pourquoi tales that helped them explain natural phenomena. James Vance Marshall has assembled ten of them in *Stories from the Billabong* (2008). The stories explain how the world was created, various characteristics of some Australian animals, and universal questions that have puzzled humans through the ages. Each story is brief and ends with additional information. The illustrations feature aboriginal colors and symbols, and there is a glossary of terms and several pages that explain the symbols.

Any students who have had to endure teasing or bragging will savor Joseph and James Bruchac's *How Chipmunk Got His Stripes* (2001), an East Coast Native American

pourquoi tale. A little squirrel hears Big Bear walking along bragging: "I am the biggest . . . I am the strongest . . . I am the loudest . . . I can do anything, yes I can!" So the small fellow challenges the bear to command the sun not to rise in the morning. Of course, the bear fails at the task and when the little squirrel, not content just to have bested the large animal, teases him: "Bear is foolish, the sun came up. Bear is silly, the sun came up," the bear becomes so enraged that he claws the squirrel's back, leaving stripes. From that time on, the animal is known as a chipmunk.

After students have enjoyed the stories in these two books or any others available, ask them to brainstorm a list of things about life, their relationships with others, and/or their environment that they are wondering about. Why does a particular plant grow in a certain way, why does an animal or insect look a certain way or behave in a certain way? From this list, students can select one or more questions that particularly interest them and write original pourquoi tales that answer them. Their stories should have at least three elements: (1) A beginning that describes a time that existed before the thing their tale is meant to explain. For example, the creation story, "The Rainbow Serpent and the Story of Creation," a tale in *Stories from the Billabong*, begins, "In the beginning there was no life on the surface of the earth"; (2) A problem along with its solution; and (3) A just and fair ending. (See http://www.ehow.com/info_8475556_three-elements-pourquoi-tale.html for a more detailed explanation of these elements.)

Fairy Tales

Fairytales often involve royalty and magical transformations. Like folktales, they feature generic characters, both good and evil—kings and queens, princes and princesses, sons and daughters—often without names, or names that denote their duties, as Cinderella, who spends her time among the cinders. Usually the original stories took place "a long time ago" and have familiar language patterns that bring listeners into and out of the tale such as "Once upon a time" and "They lived happily ever after."

It is important that students have a grounding in fairy tales. Besides being crucial in helping them recognize and understand fairy tale elements and motifs in modern stories, they will be able to grasp the meanings behind the myriad of fairy tale references used in the media and in the communities in which they live. There are several collections that make it easy and enjoyable to steep students in this important literature. These collections are perfect for read-aloud sessions and for introducing stories youngsters might not know. One of the most comprehensive and information-packed collections is Philip Pullman's *Fairy Tales from the Brothers Grimm: A New English Version* (2012). This thick volume contains fifty stories, each told in an engaging and clear way, and each followed by Pullman's own commentary, sources, and list of similar tales. Younger students who simply listen to the stories read aloud will love the snappy dialogue and humorous retellings. For older students, the book is a treasure trove of information for research as they compare tales with common themes or learn where different stories originated. *The Fairy Tale Book: Classic Tales from Childhood* (2010) contains retellings of twenty stories by Liz Scoggins. Both Grimm and Hans Christian Andersen are represented in this collection. Each story is illustrated with line art and enclosed in decorative borders. An *Illustrated Treasury of Scottish Folk and Fairy Tales* (2012), retold by Theresa Breslin, is a collection of eleven tales. Students will recognize that some of them are variants of those with which they are familiar. "The Wee Bannock" will remind them of "The Gingerbread Boy" as he calls out, "I'm the wee bannock who / jumped out of a pan / To run away as fast as I can" (12), and they can compare the people the Bannock runs away from with those chasing the Gingerbread Man. What other stories in the collection do they recognize? These retellings are beautifully illustrated and contain many Scottish words that also appear in a glossary at the end. As he did with nursery rhymes (mentioned earlier), Chris Duffy has edited a collection of fairy tales in comic format entitled *Fairy Tale Comics: Classics Told by Extraordinary Cartoonists* (2013). There are seventeen tales in this collection, and since most of them will be familiar to students, it will be especially interesting for them to discuss how the different cartoonists add to each story through their illustrations and the comic-book-type dialogue. See the earlier discussion of *Nursery Rhyme Comics* for a suggested activity.

A. Picture Book Retellings

As with folktales, a fine and accessible way to introduce children to fairy tales or to revisit familiar ones, is through picture books. Before looking at any of the hundreds of fairy tales offered in picture book format, it might be fun to share Adele Enersen's lovely *When My Baby Dreams of Fairy Tales* (2013), to celebrate the imagination and to determine beforehand what fairy tales the children already know and love. "Once upon a time," begins the text, "there was a baby girl named Mila . . . Far, far away in dreamland . . . live Mila and her fairy-tale friends. These are Mila's dreams." The following pages depict the little baby asleep wearing different outfits surrounded by articles that indicate what fairy tale dream she is having. One picture shows her asleep on a bed covered in green material, a fabric pond, water lilies, and rocks alongside her, with a stuffed frog placed near her lips. The text reads, "[she] escapes to the garden . . . then gives a kiss to the frog prince! Smack!" How many fairy tales depicted so creatively in the book can the

children name? What suggestions do they have for more outfits and surrounding artifacts should the author wish to continue the project with another book? Would they like to write to the author with their suggestions? Or perhaps they would like to work in groups to create original scenes out of cut paper, fabric, or other materials for tales not in the book and then display their creations for another class that must name the fairy tales depicted.

Rachel Isadora, while being faithful to the content of the original stories, has set some fairy tales in Africa. Her lovely collage illustrations depict details of clothing and jewelry and lush jungle settings. Among those she has retold are *The Fisherman and His Wife* (2008), *Rapunzel* (complete with the girl's pregnancy) (2008), *Hansel and Gretel* (2009), and *The Princess and the Pea* (2007)). Students can compare one or more of Isadora's versions with regard to text and illustrations with the same tales set in European or other countries.

Among several gorgeous fairy tales rendered in picture book form by Jerry Pinkney are the more recent *Puss in Boots* (2012) and *Little Red Riding Hood* (2007). As befits a classic French tale, *Puss in Boots* is set in 18th-century France, and Pinkney's illustrations dazzle with their period clothing and court scenes. Students will be struck by the king's fancy high-heeled shoes and curly wig and the women's elaborate hairdos. Pinkney has a lengthy note on the research he did to recreate this fairytale. His *Little Red Riding Hood* features a brown-skinned protagonist. While his text is substantially similar to that with which students are likely familiar, he provides ample opportunities for them to uncover even greater depth of meaning through the metaphors hidden in his illustrations. Red Riding Hood stands out in the snowy landscape in which Pinkney places her. What do students see in the shapes and lines in the background, in the wolf's postures, in the red bird that appears outside grandmother's cottage?

Jan Brett's beautifully illustrated retelling of *Beauty and the Beast* (2011) is a perfect choice for helping students see the power of metaphor. This, of course, is a fairy tale that cautions against being seduced by appearances alone, and the illustrations are filled with depictions of peacock feathers and peacocks—birds whose striking appearance with their feathers displayed certainly invoke thoughts of beauty. Read the story while showing the pictures without comment. Do the students notice the unusual number of peacocks throughout the pages? If so, why do they think this is so? Why are peacocks present in some illustrations and not in others? Ask the students what symbols they would use to signify the main themes of the other fairy tales they know. Make a chart giving the name of the fairy tale, its main message or theme, and the symbol the students create to carry the message of that theme. Pat Cummings's illustrations for H. Chuku Lee's picture book retelling of *Beauty and the Beast* (2014) draw "inspiration from the cultural imagery of West Africa and the architecture of the Dogon of Mali" (jacket flap). This is a beautiful version with close-up views of Beauty and her Beast in their elaborate setting. Students can compare the

art in this book with the work of Jan Brett discussed earlier. What does each artist bring to the tale?

Sleeping Beauty (2012) is retold with all the traditional elements and beautifully illustrated by Maja Dusíková. A turreted castle, winding stairways, elaborately dressed royals, and a princess and her rescuing prince charmingly usher youngsters into the setting of this familiar fairy tale.

The Bearskinner is one of the lesser-known Grimm fairy tales, and its retelling by Laura Amy Schlitz (2007) is a fine version to use with older students. A soldier who has just returned from the war has no home, no family, and no hope. Sensing an opportunity to win over another soul, the devil makes a bargain with the soldier: wear a rotting bear skin, never bathe or cut his hair or pray for seven years, and he will always have gold in his pockets. If he fails, the devil will own him forever. The seven years are a dreadful ordeal for the young man as evidenced in the somber illustrations, but he uses his gold to help others and they, in turn, help him. This is a powerful lesson in the rewards of perseverance, of independent judgment regardless of the opinions of others (characteristics of the divergent thinker) and of being mindful of the needs of others.

Uma Krishnaswami's *The Girl of the Wish Garden* (2013) is based on Hans Christian Andersen's *Thumbelina*, but with an important difference. Like little Thumbelina, Lina's mother finds her in a flower "in a garden of wishes." She is fearful for the girl's safety since she is no bigger than a thumb, but, unlike her namesake, Lina is not powerless. When a frog traps her, she teaches a fish to chew so that the leaf she is on is cut free and floats away. When insects trap her floating leaf, Lina "paddle[s] with all her might" to release it. This book is simply beautiful and a great example of a tale that, while faithful to the idea of the original, is reworked to feature a resourceful female.

The stories in the collection of *The Arabian Nights* (or *A Thousand and One Nights*) are gleaned from India, Persia, and Arabic-speaking countries and date from the Middle Ages. There are many collections of these tales, and an excellent one to use with older students (available in paperback as of this writing) is that of Lebanese writer Wafa Tarnowska entitled *The Arabian Nights* (2010). There are eight stories in this collection, based on a 14th-century Syrian manuscript, and while students may think they know nothing of these tales when they are first introduced, they will soon discover that they actually know at least one: "Aladdin and His Wonderful Lamp." In addition to the beautiful illustrations with their magical images, this collection is particularly valuable in that it wraps the tales in the frame story of the shah Shahriyar and Shahrazade. Previously, the shah had discovered that his wife had been unfaithful and, in retaliation, vowed to marry a new wife every day and then have her put to death. (Hence the recommendation for older students.) After he beheads women for three years, Shahrazade offers herself in an attempt to save the remaining maidens in the kingdom. She tells the shah a story through the night, ending at such an exciting part that he keeps her alive another day to hear the rest. This continues for a thousand and one nights until the shah's opinion of women mellows and he makes Shahrazade his queen.

Read the eight stories in this collection. Any or all of the following activities might help students dig deeper into the tales:

1. Talk about the feminist aspect of these tales: a woman takes action at the risk of her own life to save other women in the kingdom. What do the students think of the shah's original mind-set to judge all women by the actions of his unfaithful wife? Do they know of modern-day instances of the stereotyping of women? In their school community? Their country? Other countries? If so, what are their ideas for combating this attitude? What examples of the stereotyping or mistreatment of women can they find in other fairy tales?
2. Discuss the story of Aladdin, included in this collection. Given what they know about the uses of magic in fairy tales or fantasy novels, discuss the pros and cons of being granted wishes by a genie. If they could have one or more wishes granted by such a genie, what would those wishes be? Ask students to visualize themselves as the recipients of a particular wish of their choosing. What would their life be like—better or worse? Why? What would the effect be on their families and others around them?
3. Rimsky-Korsakov has written a symphonic suite entitled "Scheherazade." Listen to all or parts of it. Students can actually see the work performed on YouTube. A particularly beautiful violin solo by a young violinist in the Nordic Youth Orchestra is available at http://www.youtube.com/watch?v=KMKTaLaYBB8. Discuss the music. What elements make it suitable for the story? Why? Can they select other classical or contemporary music that might accompany the other seven tales in the collection?
4. Shahrazade stops her stories at an enticing part to keep the shah interested in hearing the rest. Students can begin telling an original fairy tale, stop at an interesting part and have the tale continued by another student or group. Each section might be written and handed off to another group or told aloud and continued from student to student.

B. Original Fairy Tales Written by Contemporary Authors

Using many fairy tale elements and themes such as royalty, magic, the rewarding of good and punishment for evil, some contemporary writers have created original tales in picture book form to delight young readers. Jane Ray offers a few examples of original fairy tales based on ancient themes. In *Ahmed and the Feather Girl* (2010), Ahmed works in cruel Madame Saleem's traveling circus. He finds an egg, brings it back to the circus, and when it hatches into a beautiful feathered girl with a lovely voice, Madame Saleem cages her as a money-making circus exhibit. In time the feathers become wings, and Ahmed unlocks her cage to allow her to fly to freedom. This makes his life even harder than before, but the girl eventually finds a way to free him as well.

A happy kingdom full of laughter and birdsong becomes a quiet, sad place after the queen dies in Ray's *The Apple-Pip Princess* (2008). Before her death, the queen had asked each of her three daughters to choose something of hers as keepsakes. The eldest chooses sparkly shoes. The middle daughter chooses a lovely mirror. But the youngest, Serenity, chooses a box of things her mother had collected in her childhood. When the king asks each of the girls to perform a task that will determine who will next rule the kingdom, both of the older girls build a soaring structure. Serenity, however, simply selects a single apple pip from her treasure box and plants it. This planting leads to others until the kingdom is abloom and happy again, and the youngest daughter is deemed worthy to be its next ruler.

Mac Barnett's contemporary picture book *Extra Yarn* (2012) has all the trappings of a traditional fairy tale: magic, royalty, and an unassuming girl who transforms a town with her kind deeds and her refusal to give in to evil. Annabelle lives in a town bereft of color. There is just endless snow and blackened soot from chimneys—until she finds a box of colored yarn. She knits herself a sweater and, finding that she has yarn left over, knits one for her dog. The yarn never seems to give out, and soon she is knitting for her family, classmates, and neighbors, and she even knits lovely covers for the drab buildings in town. But things change when a clothes-hungry archduke comes along and, unable to convince Annabelle to accept his money in exchange for her knitting, steals the box of yarn. Students will find the end of this modern fairy tale satisfying as evil is punished and goodness rewarded. Encourage them to pour over the illustrations that fit the story so perfectly since they are created in part by using skeins of yarn.

Another modern story that emphasizes the folly of greed is Michael Catchpool's *The Cloud Spinner* (2012). A young boy can spin cloth from the clouds: gold in the morning, white in the afternoon, crimson at sunset. He makes himself a scarf as protection from the heat of the day and one to warm himself at night. When the king sees the beautiful scarves, he wants one, too, and even though he knows the king doesn't need a scarf, the boy complies. This only creates more demands as the king orders clothing for his wife and daughter as well. Soon there are no more clouds and hence, no more rain. It is the young princess who finds a way to fix this calamity. The lovely illustrations are filled with metaphors that students will discover through repeated readings.

After enjoying these and/or other modern tales, ask students to discuss their main elements and themes. What traditional tales can they find that are either similar in content or in message or theme? Can they rewrite any or all of these four tales or others by changing some of the elements yet conveying the same message? For example, how else might the clouds be restored in *The Cloud Spinner*? What other artifact might Serenity have selected from her box of treasures and how might it have affected the kingdom?

C. Cinderella around the World

Variations of the Cinderella tale have crossed the globe over the centuries, keeping the original story of punishment for cruelty and injustice and reward for goodness and hard work, but adding cultural trappings as well. Examining some of these variants is an excellent way to put into practice a Common Core standard that asks students to "compare and contrast two or more versions of the same story (e.g., Cinderella stories) by different authors or from different cultures" (2.RL.9). A fascinating way to begin looking at some of these Cinderella variants is with Paul Fleischman's amazing *Glass Slipper, Gold Sandal* (2007). In it he combines many versions from around the globe into one fascinating Cinderella tale. Often each page or spread features elements from a specific country, but just as frequently, the elements from several countries are combined. In describing the new garments and accessories provided for the girl, for example, she wears "a sarong made of gold . . . (Indonesia) a cloak sewn of king fisher feathers . . . (China) and . . . a kimono red as sunset" (Japan). The illustrations are done in fabric patterns from the different countries as well. This book is a tour de force and should be part of any discussion of the Cinderella tale.

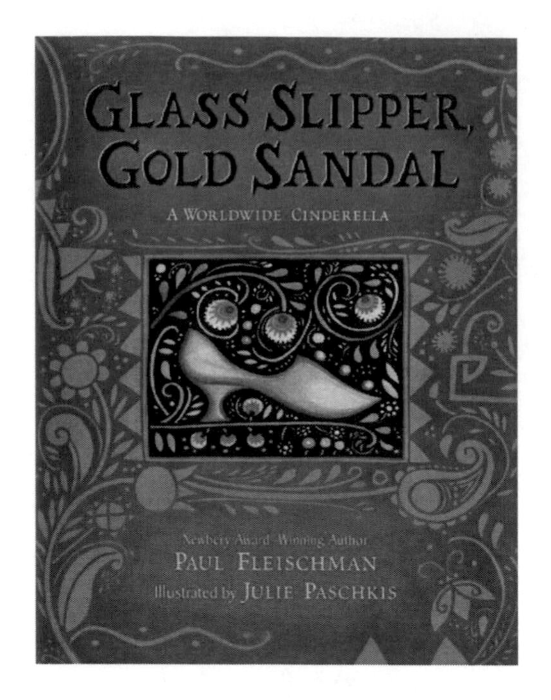

After examining Fleischman's book, look at tales from several different countries and discuss the cultural elements that are included in each. How are the stories alike? Different? In Dan Jolley's *Pigling: A Cinderella Story* (2009), a Korean tale, the girl's name is Pear Blossom. When her mother dies, her father remarries. Her stepmother and stepsisters are cruel to her and name her Pigling, Little Pig. Magical creatures come to the girl's aid, and a handsome magistrate instead of a prince features prominently in her future. In Shirley Climo's *The Persian Cinderella* (2001) the girl's name is Settareh, and she buys a jug instead of fabric for a gown to wear to the prince's celebration. But the jug contains a magic creature who does get her to the ball. When her stepsisters find out about the jug, they order its inhabitant to destroy Settareh. Instead, a magical transformation takes place and eventually, girl and prince are reunited. Judy Sierra sets her *The Gift of the Crocodile: A Cinderella Story* (2000) in the Spice Islands. When Damura loses her sarong in the river, a crocodile answers her calls for help. Damura treats the creature politely and is rewarded with a new silver sarong. When her greedy stepsister goes to the river and pretends to need a new sarong as well, she receives a leech-covered rag instead. The crocodile plays a key part in providing a sarong for Damura's trip to a dance at the palace where she wins the prince's heart. Read these and some other variants in the selective bibliography provided later. Compare them to the original Perrault fairy tale. A fine picture book retelling of Perrault's tale is Sarah L. Thomson's *Cinderella* (2012), a beautiful book with illustrations that depict the elegance and luxury of King Louis XIV's court. Would the class be interested in writing a Cinderella tale that reflects their or their community's lives in the 21st century? Who would their Cinderella be and what difficulties might she have? She would not likely want to attend a prince's ball, but perhaps she would be looking for a job, trying to get into college, or have some other goal. What is holding her back? How is she going to overcome her difficulties? Since they are writing a fairy tale, magic and/or transformations should be part of the plot. What role will the magic play? Will their Cinderella sit by and wait for it to happen, or will she take charge and go after it? Make a list of plot possibilities with the class, then divide the students into groups, making each group responsible for writing a different part of the tale. Then ask the students to work the parts into a single tale. Students can illustrate their Cinderella, bind it into a book, and place it alongside other Cinderella stories in the school or class library or dramatize it for another class.

D. Fractured Tales in Picture Book Format

Some contemporary authors retell ancient tales in unique ways. For example, in Mo Willems's extremely talented hands, Goldilocks visits dinosaurs, not bears (*Goldilocks and the Three Dinosaurs*, 2013). And in a hilarious twist, it is the two dinosaurs plus one "who happened to be visiting from Norway" who deliberately set out to entice a visitor. In a loud voice, Mama Dinosaur says, "I sure hope no innocent little succulent child happens

by our unlocked home while we are . . . uhhh . . . someplace else!" Of course, Goldilocks leaps across the welcome mat, stuffs herself on chocolate pudding, investigates the huge furniture, and comes to a conclusion that causes her to think things over—very uncharacteristic behavior for her. Children will revel in the many jokes in both text and illustration. Allan Ahlberg goes even further in his retelling, actually many retellings, of the Goldilocks tale in his innovative *The Goldilocks Variations* (2012). This attractive book, with its pull tabs and pop-ups, tells several different stories, all featuring a "cheeky" girl named Goldilocks. The first story most closely resembles the one with which we are most familiar, in which Goldilocks, when discovered, races home to her own breakfast of Choco Pops, and the small wee bear is given many consolation breakfast courses, especially "a lovely little bun." In the next story, the girl visits a huge cottage housing thirty-three bears. The third tale is set in 2076, and Goldilocks climbs into a spaceship in the woods—home of the Three Bliim. A picture dictionary inserted into the book provides readers with the meanings of the Bliim words scattered throughout the story. Next Goldilocks encounters talking furniture belonging to a baby bear living in cottage Number 12. Then a booklet inserted into the larger book contains the script of a play in which the audience interacts with the actors and, as the play ends, receives "delicious buns." In a grand finale, many different fairy tale characters, including Red Riding Hood, Snow White, the three pigs, and at least one prince charming, gather in the cottage until it is completely full. When Goldilocks finally returns home after an exhausting day of adventuring and settles down to sleep, she discovers everyone she has visited now in her bed, and they all sleep 'til morning. In Steve Guarnaccia's *Goldilocks and the Three Bears: A Tale Moderne* (2010), three hip bears dine on chili, not porridge, and decorate their split level home with furnishings created by some top international designers. Students will enjoy some of the bears' expressions such as "Oh, fur and honey!" and "Buzz fuzz!" and matching the labeled furnishings on the end papers with those in the illustrations. All three of these authors were able to envision Goldilocks's story in completely different ways. Willems changed the story from a home invasion to a trap set by dinosaurs to entice a tasty meal. Ahlberg not only saw different characters inhabiting that cottage, but even turned the cottage into a space ship in a future time, and created a play with audience and actor interaction. Guarnaccia emphasized the bears' furnishings as a way to call attention to famous designers. Challenge

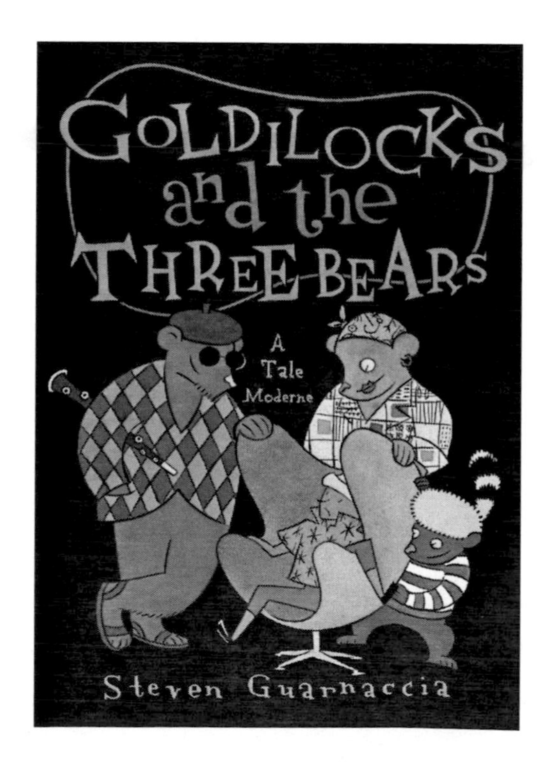

students who have enjoyed these different variations to envision the Goldilocks story in still another original and innovative way. Who is Goldilocks? What is her life like before that adventure in the woods? What are her intentions? Will she meet anyone along the way? Who will be in the house (or whatever structure the students decide upon) and what will Goldilocks do there? What will become of Goldilocks after this incident? Picture her in ten, twenty years. How will students tell their story? A book is not the only vehicle they might choose. What other ideas do they have for presentation? Would they like to share their story with another class?

Corey Rosen Schwartz's *The Three Ninja Pigs* (2012) features a clever, resourceful female. Three pigs are fed up with a wolf, who continues to persist in blowing down people's houses. So they enroll in Ninja School to develop the skills they need to take the wolf on once and for all. But the first pig drops out and later is no match for the wolf. The second pig also fails to defeat the villain. But their sister, the third pig, practices karate long and hard, and when the wolf appears at her door, she is able to send him running. Obviously, this fine fractured tale is set in Japan, complete with Japanese scenery and architecture depicted through manga-style illustrations. In contrast to her porcine brothers who, after the farmer sells the farm on which they had been living, build their houses out of cheap straw and sticks so they can spend their money on junk food, their sister builds her house of brick and plants a vegetable garden in Mark Teague's *The Three Little Pigs and the Somewhat Bad Wolf* (2013). When a very hungry wolf comes to town and is refused food by every eatery, he's drawn to the sweet smell of pig. "I can't believe that worked!" he exclaims after he's blown down the first pig's house, evidence that he's not really all that bad. When he faints from hunger and exhaustion, the pigs revive him and they all enjoy a dip in the third pig's pool. Steven Guarnaccia designs each of the Three Pigs' houses, the first made from scraps, the second from glass, the third of stone and concrete, to reflect the work of three famous architects: Frank Gehry, Phillip Johnson, and Frank Lloyd Wright in his *The Three Little Pigs: An Architectural Tale* (2010). Each house is filled with clever details, including furnishings by the architects and their contemporaries. Students can match the labeled buildings and furnishings (including the Philippe Starck motorcycle driven by the boot-and-leather-clad biker wolf) on the endpapers with their depictions within the book. When the wolf in David Wiesner's brilliant, Caldecott-winning *The Three Pigs* (2001) blows each of the pigs' houses down, he actually blows the pigs outside the confines of the illustrations and into the book's margins where they engage in adventures of their own—including the rescue of a dragon who later returns the favor. There is so much to see and investigate in the illustrations of this fractured story, including the fact that all the newspaper text in the paper airplanes matches perfectly. In a radical twist on the tale of the Three Little Pigs, Liz Pichon offers *The Three Horrid Pigs* (2008). In this version, the pigs behave so badly their mother sends them away. Indeed they are so lazy that all three build shoddy houses, and they even refuse kind handyman Wolf's offer to make improvements. Eventually the pigs lose their houses to straw-eating cows, birds who need sticks for their nests, and a rooster who reclaims the third pig's hen house. But all ends well as pigs and wolf, amazingly enough, live happily ever after together.

In another of Steven Guarnaccia's fractured tales, *Cinderella: A Fashionable Tale* (2014), Cinderella and her stepsisters are clothed in garments and accessories designed by some famous fashion designers of the 20th and 21st centuries. Even Cinderella's rags are patched together with swatches of fabric from designer patterns. There are Prada-inspired crystal

slippers as well. All the fashion designers are referenced in the back of the book, and students can match them to the illustrations in the story. *Seriously, Cinderella Is SO Annoying!: The Story of Cinderella as Told by the Wicked Stepmother!* (2011) by Trisha Speed Shaskan gives readers a completely different view of the person they have come to view as a downtrodden heroine. According to her stepmother, the girl tells crazy stories about talking animals, does her chores so fast that, of course, she needs more work just to keep occupied. And you think the stepmother kept Cinderella home from the ball out of meanness? Certainly not! The poor girl was sick and had to be nursed at home to keep her sore throat from getting even worse. When Cinderella does finally go off with the prince, stepmother and sisters are delightedto have the pest out of the house and live happily ever after without her.

The Three Billy Goats Gruff appear as *The Three Cabritos* in Eric Kimmel's (2007) rendition. As the Cabritos head across the Rio Grande to play their instruments at a fiesta in Mexico, each encounters a Chupacabra living under the bridge and manages to escape being eaten using cunning and instruments to fool him.

Mary Pope Osborne and Will Osborne have turned the story of Sleeping Beauty around, titling it to become *Sleeping Bobby* (2005) who, at age eighteen, climbs a mysterious staircase, pricks his finger on a spinning wheel, and promptly falls asleep along with everyone in the castle for 100 years. This time it is "a kind, clever, modest, and very lovely princess" who sets out to find him, breaks the spell with a kiss, and becomes his bride. In similar fashion, Kate Osborne creates a feisty female in *Kate and the Beanstalk* (2005). Lazy Jack is now resourceful Kate who climbs the beanstalk, retrieves the items previously stolen from her father by a giant who lives at its top, and then chops the beanstalk down, causing the giant to fall dead at her feet.

Honestly, Red Riding Hood Was Rotten! The Story of Little Red Riding Hood as Told by the Wolf (2011), Trisha Speed Shaskan's fractured tale, gives readers new insight into the girl and her grandmother. The wolf is actually a vegetarian who happens to love apples. In fact, he can name all the different varieties. But it's not apple season and he hasn't eaten in a very long time. So when he meets Red Riding Hood as she's admiring herself in a puddle, his mind wanders to thoughts of food. Of her cape she says to the wolf, "Isn't it pretty? followed by "Aren't I pretty?" Well, what's a hungry wolf to do? She looks so much like a juicy red apple, and while he really doesn't want to eat meat, he just can't resist racing her to grandmother's for not one, but two tasty tidbits. There he finds an equally vain grandmother so busy admiring herself in the mirror that she doesn't notice the wolf. After his meal, the wolf congratulates himself in ridding the world of two people so hung up on themselves.

Older students will be treated to not just one alternative viewpoint in John Warren Stewig's *Nobody Asked the Pea* (2013), but ten, all expressed in monologues. Even members of the palace staff have a say. The Pea is proud of his robust physique. The Queen is a constant nag who pressures her lazy son to find a wife. A few princesses show up to claim the prince and are sent away. But when Princess Lucy arrives, rain-drenched and bedraggled, she proves to be the opposite of a delicate female with sensitive skin. Turns out she's just the kind of outdoor girl after Prince Harold's own heart. And their marriage gives Queen Mildred the opportunity to plan the wedding of the century. The illustrations are humorous caricatures of this zany cast of characters. After reading this version of *The Princess and the Pea*, students can write monologues for other fairy tale characters, or draw them in caricature.

These and so many more fractured fairy tales readily available in picture books lend themselves to several activities that require looking anew at what was originally familiar—a key ingredient of divergent thought. These are just a few suggestions:

1. Students will be familiar with the points of view expressed in the fairy tales they know. But what if a different character tells the story—a character who reveals a completely different scenario as in some of the fractured tales described here. Students can:
   a. Completely rewrite a tale from a different character's point of view—one they have never encountered in a book. For example, how might the first pig justify his house of straw or explain his encounter with the wolf?
   b. Interview several characters from a story for a newspaper article.
   c. Enact a courtroom drama in which a fairy tale character is put on trial for his or her deeds. Write a script for the lawyers, the judge, and the defendant, among others.
2. Rewrite a fairy tale so that the ending is completely different—different characters "live happily ever after" or are punished, or other such different endings.
3. Change a fairy tale so that female protagonists become male and vice versa. Will their actions differ and if so, how?
4. Rewrite a familiar tale so that the magical intervention is completely different. How does Cinderella get to the ball if there is no fairy godmother, for example?

E. Fractured Fairy Tale Novels or Novels Based Directly on Fairy Tales

Often contemporary writers for young people work directly with a fairy tale and turn it into a modern novel with a plot twist, added characters, fairy tale characters who act in unexpected ways, and so on. These fractured fairy tales are great fun to read and discuss, especially when students are familiar with the original tale from which they spring. Here are just a few that will initiate thought and discussion:

a) Novels for Younger Readers

Rumpelstiltskin springs from out of nowhere into the room in which a miller's daughter is locked with mounds of straw she is expected to spin into gold in the fairy tale *Rumpelstiltskin*. Ever wonder where he came from and who he really is? Author Liesl Shurtliff supplies some fascinating answers in *Rump: The True Story of Rumpelstiltskin* (2013). Rump, an orphan, has never known his full name and is teased mercilessly about it and his small size by the bullies in his village at the foot of The Mountain. All the villagers must dig incessantly on The Mountain for gold that they trade with a dishonest miller for the food that sustains them. But that gold is in ever shorter supply and the miller makes greater and greater demands since he must continually give King Barf the gold that monarch craves.

When Rump accidentally discovers he has enough magic to spin straw into gold, he disregards his friend, Red's, warning: "All magic has consequences, Rump. Even small magic can have big consequences" (34), and bargains with the miller to trade his spun gold for food. This is the beginning of a spiraling web from which Rump can't seem to extricate himself, and it leads him to the miller's daughter, the king, trolls, into other fairy tales, and other dangerous misadventures as he tries to untangle himself and discover his true name. Along with a fascinating look at the background and youth of a well-known fairy tale character, Shurtiff raises interesting questions about the use of magic as an easy way out of difficulties rather than the power of hard work and careful thought; about the weakness of human nature: "The humans take one look at any living creature and think only of how they can use it" (142), a troll tells Rump; and about the importance of one's name. Do humans use one another for their own gain? Can students think of instances where this is so—or not? How might they conquer this flaw as humans interact in their environment, in industry, in their dealings with one another? Have they ever experienced times in which taking the easy way out of a difficult situation resulted in even greater difficulties? How might they rewrite that situation to reflect a different decision even if that decision involves more unpleasantness or effort on their part? The importance of one's name is a central theme of this novel. Divide the students into groups and ask each group to create a sheet with two columns labeled attribute and related name. Have each group devise a list of attributes or characteristics in the first column and then create a name that expresses that attribute in the second. For example: extraordinary power/Superman.

In Sage Blackwood's *Jinx* (2013), readers catch glimmers of such fairytales as Little Red Riding Hood and Hansel and Gretel. Jinx is an orphan whose stepfather means to abandon him in the woods until Simon, a wizard, finds and adopts him. Jinx works for Simon for many years, learning bits of magic and being treated kindly, if not politely. As in *Rump*, this fantasy is replete with references to the dangers of magic. "Magic corrupts people" (132) says Sophie, Simon's wife. In fact, in Samara where Sophie lives, magic is forbidden under pain of death! Jinx will learn only too soon magic's hazards as he undergoes a dangerous spell and encounters Bone Man, who obtains his magic in a dastardly manner. There is much to discuss here, including a dangerous journey undertaken by Jinx and two friends and continual references to the "Terror" facing the trees.

In her "Whatever After" series, consisting of five books at this writing, Sarah Mlynowski catapults ten-year-old Abby and her younger brother Jonah into fairy tales where their adventures change the outcome of the original story. In the first book, *Fairest of All* (2012), Jonah finds an old mirror in the basement that leads the children into Snow White's kingdom where they foil the evil queen's plan to poison her stepdaughter with an apple. Now Snow White doesn't need rescuing, but can she live "happily ever after" just the same? In the second, *If the Shoe Fits* (2013), they encounter Cinderella whose foot is swollen because the glass slipper has fallen on it. Her fairy godmother refuses to use magic to heal her foot and insists the girl use her own ingenuity to solve her problem instead of relying on outside intervention. Here readers meet a new Cinderella who is not the passive recipient of her fairy godmother's good graces or a prince charming who carries her away from a cruel stepmother and sisters. In the third book, *Sink or Swim* (2013), the children try to convince the Little Mermaid to keep her tail while still having a royal wedding. In *Dream On* (2013), Robin accompanies Abby and Jonah into Sleeping Beauty and pricks her finger. The children only have ten hours to save her. When Abby and Jonah fall into the tale of Rapunzel in *Bad Hair Day* (2014), they get the story all tangled up and have to untwist it. All five books are very funny, easily read by younger students, and present strong female characters. What do students think of these plot twists? Are there other wimpy girls or princesses in the tales they know who would do well to rely on their own resources instead of waiting for rescue? Make a list of such characters and next to each name, write how she might solve her problem without magic.

When she receives a book entitled *The Art of Being a Princess* from her mother, Princess Imogene, heroine of Vivian Vande Velde's novel *Frogged* (2013), begins to wonder if she is really as good as she can be. She'd really rather do rough and tumble things than be a sedate princess, but mothers are pretty insistent beings. So when a frog who claims to be a prince cursed by a witch approaches her and asks for a kiss to break the spell, she doesn't ignore him, rude though he is and sketchy though his story seems to be. Instead she grants his request. What he has failed to tell her, however, is that the kiss will pass the curse on to her. Sure enough, Imogene is now a frog, and the so-called enchanted prince is merely a mischievous boy who had pelted the witch with apples and was punished for it. Not only that, he leaves Imogene to fend for herself and figure out a way to become human again. She can, of course, trick someone into kissing her as she had been tricked herself. But she takes the high road, instead, suffering several near-death experiences and ending up in a traveling circus where she becomes the talking-frog attraction. There she meets Luella. Will this new friend be able to save Imogene from her froggy fate? Readers will not only keep reading to find out, but they will also have an opportunity to think about class distinctions, gender roles, and more along the way.

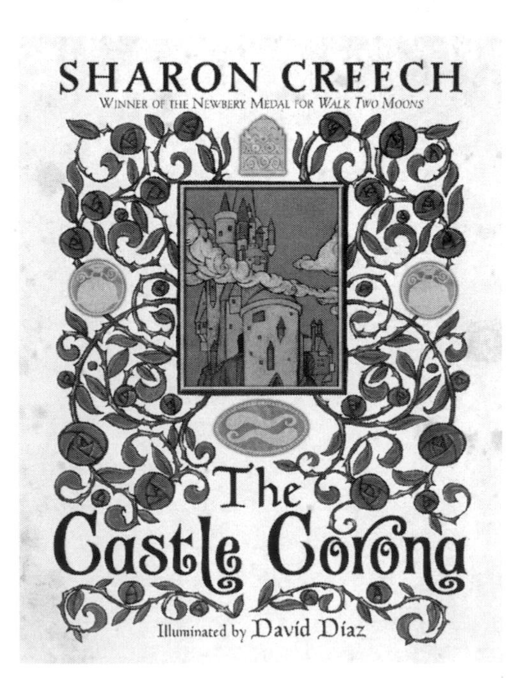

"Long Ago and Far Away" is the first section of Sharon Creech's *The Castle Corona* (2007), an original fairy tale about King Guido, Queen Gabriella and their three children, inhabitants of a sumptuous castle that glitters and sparkles in sun or moonlight high above the banks of a river, and two peasant children, Pia and Enzio. The peasant children often wonder what their lives would be like if they lived in that splendid castle amidst its gold objects and finery, and the royals wonder, "If only I could be a poor, anonymous peasant . . . If only I didn't have to wear these heavy golden clothes . . . If only I didn't have to always smile and be polite and make decisions . . . If only, if only" (6). Royal and peasant lives intertwine when Pia and Enzio find a royal pouch and end up in that castle as the king's tasters. And because this is a fairy tale, secrets are revealed that have a transforming effect on everyone. Told in very short chapters adorned with rich illustrations by David Diaz, this tale is perfect for young readers who will relish unraveling its intricate plot. While the large type and lovely illustrations might simply signal easy reading, this story has weighty themes that will require students to think beneath the words.

The fairy tales *Sleeping Beauty*, *Cinderella*, *Snow White*, and *Rapunzel* are all about their leading women, right? Sleeping Beauty pricks her finger on a spindle and falls into an enchanted sleep for 100 years. Cinderella needs to escape hard work and her evil stepmother and sisters. Snow White flees a wicked queen who wants to kill her. And Rapunzel needs to get out of that tower. We know nothing about the princes who show up in these stories—not even their names. In Christopher Healy's hilarious *The Hero's Guide to Saving Your Kingdom* (2012) (see also *The Hero's Guide to Storming the Castle*, 2013), this void is filled when the four Princes Charming (yes, that's what they want to call themselves) take center stage. We now know their names: Liam (Sleeping Beauty), Frederic (Cinderella), Duncan (Snow White), and Prince Gustav (Rapunzel), and we get to know each one with his unique personality, strengths, and weaknesses. When Frederic sets off to find Ella who has left him (he's a dainty wuss) to seek adventure, he meets up with the three other princes, also cast aside by their princesses. Together, as the League of Princes, they set out to rescue Ella who has been captured by a witch. To make matters worse, Zaubera, the witch in Rapunzel, is so angered that she was nameless in that story she vows to wreak so much havoc that she will surely be remembered this time. Each of the princes' kingdoms is threatened and they brave giants, dragons, trolls, and more in their quest to become rescuing heroes. As they undergo these trials, the men must call on resources within themselves they never realized they had and become transformed in the process. This story is a great romp and boys, especially who are reluctant readers, will easily be won over by the funny dialogue and illustrations. But there is more to this fractured tale than jokes. The princes are fully developed characters who, as divergent thinkers do, attempt tasks well beyond their comfort zone. Inspired by this story, students might:

a) Make a list of things they feel they could never do (meet a new friend, play an instrument, take up a sport, etc.) and choose one thing from the list they might attempt. What qualities do they possess that might make them successful in this task? What shortcomings might hold them back? What can they do to make up for these shortcomings?

b) Choose a fairy tale character about whom we know nothing and write an original character sketch or description of that person. Give the person a task to perform and write what happens based on the traits the character possesses.

b) Novels for Older Readers

East of the Sun West of the Moon is a haunting fairy tale from Northern lands—one that may be less familiar to students but certainly well worth exploring for its theme of love and the courage to brave repeated hardships to right a wrong. A huge white bear comes to the door on a blustery cold evening and promises riches to the poor family within if the youngest daughter will come away with him. She eventually agrees to do so, and the family prospers. After coming back to the bear from a visit home several months later, the girl, in spite of the bear's warnings not to do so, lights a candle to see him during the night. This causes the bear/prince, instead of being released from a spell, to be banished to a distant land east of the sun and west of the moon by the witch who enchanted him. What follows is an arduous journey and many encounters as the girl tries to find her prince and free him. Once students are familiar with the original tale (available in older picture book editions and collections of Scandinavian tales), they can compare it to Jackie Morris's *East of the Sun West of the Moon* (2013). Morris follows the old tale closely, but sets it in modern times. In this slim volume the girl is the eldest child of poor immigrants seeking asylum. The bear who comes to the door promising security for the family in exchange for their daughter Rose is vaguely familiar to her as the creature who has haunted her dreams. The language and plentiful illustrations in this story are gorgeous, but what is most striking is the twist in the ending. There is so much to discuss here. Some risks are worth taking, and divergent thinkers often take on what others fear to try. But there are certain risks that are foolhardy. Is Rose's going off with the bear a sensible risk to take? Why or why not? Discuss Rose's courage in undertaking a journey to an unknown land with no directions and little resources. From whence does such courage spring? Finally, what do the students think of the unexpected ending? Do they agree with Rose's decision? Why or why not? Which do they prefer—the original ending or the one created by Morris? Why?

Cinder, the heroine of Marissa Meyer's (2012) fantasy/science fiction novel that bears her name is a far cry from the passive Cinderella of the familiar fairy tale. Living in New Bejing in a future time after World War IV in a world where millions are dying of a plague called letumosis, Cinder is an ace mechanic. She is also a cyborg, reviled as a second class citizen by her stepmother and the citizenry as well and, of course, unable to attend the upcoming royal ball. When handsome Prince Hal comes to Cinder's shop to have her fix his android, though, her life changes. She does get to the palace, and becomes involved with him and with a palace doctor who is trying to develop an antidote to the plague by using the most expendable subjects in New Bejing for his experiments—cyborgs. When her stepmother volunteers Cinder for these experiments, the tests in the lab reveal Cinder's true identity and her value as someone immune to letumosis. "With your help, we could save hundreds of thousands of lives . . . we could—well, we could stop the cyborg draft, to start with" (102), the doctor tells her. Cinder has to decide whether to risk her life to save others. But even worse, she learns that only she can stop the Lunar Queen Levana from controlling the world. This first of a five-part series has suspense, adventure, and even some romance—ingredients certain to keep readers turning the pages. They will enjoy finding elements from the Cinderella tale that cross over here—Cinder's ill-fitting prosthetic foot and Cinderella's ill-fitting slipper, for example.

Anne Ursu's *Breadcrumbs* (2011) is a haunting novel inspired by Han Christian Andersen's *The Snow Queen* (see Bagram Ibatoulline's (2013) beautifully illustrated retelling of this tale) and filled with references to the fantastical worlds of *Narnia*, Philip Pullman's *The Golden Compass*, and so much more. Hazel and Jack have been best friends since they were six years old. Hazel's "mother [is] white with blue eyes and light brown hair. Hazel [has] straight back hair, odd big brown eyes, and dark brown skin" (17)—different, a misfit, so she thinks, and so even now that they are eleven and should be hanging out with kids of their own gender, Jack is still Hazel's best and only friend—Jack, who even though his mother is suffering from depression, keeps his creativity intact and whose imagination ushers them into fantastical play places like Wonderland and the Arctic. So it is particularly horrible when, unknown to Hazel or anyone "He got a piece of an enchanted mirror in his eye . . . he changed" (88), stopped speaking to her, and eventually "got in [a] sled and drove into the woods" with a woman who "was all white and silver and made of snow" (144–45). So

> a boy got a splinter in his eye, and his heart turned cold. Only two people noticed. One was a witch, and she took him for her own. The other was his best friend. And she went after him in ill-considered shoes, brave and completely unprepared. (155)

Hazel's journey into the forbidding woods, where she must follow the cold to find Jack, brings her in touch with fairy tale creatures like wolves and woodsmen, Ravens, and even the Little Match Girl; in and out of fairy tales and into contact with people, both helpful and harmful, who offer her talismans along her way. The dangers and adventures are many, and readers follow the breadcrumbs of the stories within story to a deeper look at the false security taking the easy way out can bring, and the pain involved in dealing with changing relationships and loss.

Adam Gidwitz has written two brilliant novels, each based on fairy tales, with characters weaving in and out of several stories as they undertake their fantastic journeys. In the first, *A Tale Dark and Grimm* (2010), he takes the story of Hansel and Gretel to new and gory heights students have likely never explored before. The story begins with the bloody Grimm tale, *Faithful Johannes*, which is the story of how, in trying to save Hansel's and Gretel's mother and father from death, the faithful servant Johannes is turned to stone. Only by cutting off the heads of Hansel and Gretel and rubbing their blood on the stone can Johannes be brought back to life. The king does this awful deed and Johannes, newly restored to life, places the children's heads back on their shoulders and they live once more. But they have heard how their parents, without knowing they would eventually be brought back to life, were willing to sacrifice them for Johannes. So they run away into the forest where they meet a baker woman who tries to roast Hansel only to end up in the oven herself. That is just the beginning of adventures in which they escape one disaster after another, and even become separated, until they receive their final challenge from Johannes:

> There is an evil thing . . . in the kingdom. Because of their weakness and their sadness, a dragon has come to the Kingdom of Grimm. . . . The dragon has taken possession of one of the people. It lives inside him like a disease. . . . You must kill it. You and Gretel. . . .
>
> Why us? (asks Hansel).
>
> Because there is a time when a kingdom needs its children. (155)

The children do succeed and live happily ever after—eventually! *In a Glass Grimmly* (2013) Gidwitz again meshes several fairy tales into a clever story of self-discovery. It begins with a beautiful girl who refuses to keep her promise after a frog has rescued her ball from a well. The girl grows into a gorgeous queen, Jill's mother, who is the cause of Jill parading naked, without knowing it, before all their subjects after being duped by a silk merchant. Humiliated, Jill runs away to her cousin Jack's house. But the boy is the object of bullying by a gang he would love to be a part of and, besides, has just disappointed his father by selling their cow for a magic bean. The two go off and finally undertake a quest for a special mirror. Fairy tale references are sprinkled throughout, largely manipulated by the author's inventive talents. The story's narrator sums up their adventures this way:

> They had climbed an enormous bean stalk . . . killed murderous giants . . . evaded an evil mermaid . . . outwitted a kingdom of goblins . . . made friends with an enormous, fire-breathing salamander . . . and they had won a mirror . . . rare and powerful. (247)

But more important than all that, their journey through the woods and their many life-threatening experiences help them discover who they really are and what they are capable of—a new realization that helps transform their families as well.

Both of Gidwitz's novels demonstrate the power of fairy tales to instruct; to reveal the inner resources required to overcome trial and adversity; and to illustrate how misfortune can be turned to good. Divide the students into groups and ask each group to make a list of the things they understand about fairy tales after reading one or both of these books. The narrator of *A Tale Dark and Grimm* states, "There is a certain kind of pain that can change you. Even the strongest sword, when placed in a raging fire, will soften and bend and change its form" (122). What does he mean? What do students think Johannes's statement, "there is a time when a kingdom needs its children," means? What do they make of the relationship between parents and children in these stories? Again, the narrator of *A Tale Dark and Grimm*: "Maybe in real life there are perfect parents and amazing adults who will never, ever disappoint you. But Once Upon a Time, no grown-up was perfect" (123). Why did the tellers of these tales choose to present so many unreliable, even cruel, adults?

Tom McNeal's *Far Far Away* (2013) is infused with the tales of the Brothers Grimm. Jacob Grimm is a ghost caught in the Zwischenraum, a place between life and death, seemingly because he is troubled by something left undone. Jeremy Johnson Johnson (his real name) can hear Jacob when he presses his hand to his temple; Jacob is his constant companion whose mission is to keep him safe from the Finder of Occasions, urge him to study, and stay out of trouble. Jeremy could use the help. His father has remained in his room for years since the death of his mother, the family store and business is about to be foreclosed, and Jeremy is ridiculed and shunned by the townsfolk. To make matters worse, the energetic Ginger Boultinghouse talks Jeremy into playing a prank that eventually leads them right into the hands of the Finder of Occasions, the person who has been making some of the children in Never Better disappear. Grimm stories, along with the lives of their collectors, populate this novel, and Jeremy and Ginger use them to try to make sense of their lives. At one point, Jacob Grimm, lamenting the death of his young nephew muses: "The tales we collected are not merciful. [They] are full of terrible punishments . . . but they follow just cause. But a Creator who takes a child so small, so kind, so tender? What can be made of that" (229)? How do students reply to Jacob's question, and what do they make of similar injustices today? What is the meaning of the title? This is a thought-provoking novel about the power and meaning of story, and the role of appearances, for few things in the town of Never Better are as they seem.

More Divergent Thinking and Creative Activities Inspired by Folk and Fairy Tales

There are some general activities students can undertake at any point in their study of fairy tales. Here are just a few suggestions:

1. Marilyn Singer's incredible *Mirror Mirror: A Book of Reversible Verse* (2010) contains poems about fairy tale characters. Each poem is written twice with only slight changes in punctuation, and each is the reverse of the other, creating a totally different point of view. She now has a companion volume entitled *Follow Follow: A Book of Reverso Poems* (2013). Again, these poems are the exact reverse of each other. For example, a poem entitled "Birthday Suit" refers to the tale of the *Emperor's New Clothes*. The first version reads:

Behold his glorious majesty:
Me.
Who dares say he drained the treasury

On
Nothing?
Ha!
This emperor has
Sublime taste in finery!
Only a fool could fail to see.

When read in reverse, these same words read, in part:

Only a fool could fail to see.
Sublime taste in finery?
This emperor has—
ha!—
nothing
on!

It is obvious that in the first instance, it is the emperor speaking, proud of his marvelous outfit and feeling the money he lavished on it well spent. In the second poem, a bystander using the same words in reverse, states the obvious—the emperor has no clothes! After older students spend considerable time with these wonderful poems, and/or the poems in *Mirror Mirror* (2010), and understand how they work, challenge them to create reverso poems of their own about fairy tale characters not in either book. Funny illustrations or caricatures will enhance their work.

2. Jane Yolen and Rebecca Kai Dotlich have also written a book of poems about fairy tales entitled *Grumbles from the Forest: Fairy-Tale Voices with a Twist* (2013). For each of the fifteen tales represented, the poets have written two poems, each one in a different character's voice, presenting alternative points of view. For *Gingerbread Boy*, a poem entitled "Gingerbread Boy: A Haiku" presents the boy's view that the whole world is a mouth. In the accompanying poem, "From the Kitchen," the parents express their sorrow at the loss of their son: "It broke our hearts / when he ran away." The first poem related to The Princess and the Pea, "Just One Pea," is written in the pea's voice as he talks about having to endure the princess's snoring and how he misses "my dear pod." The second, "The Pea Episode," is in the princess's voice as she informs us that it was that pile of mattresses, not the lone pea that kept her awake.
   It will likely be a bit easier for students to create their own pairs of poems about fairy tales than it would be to write reverso poems, so this might be a fine alternative for some of them. Here is a challenge from the authors themselves:

Why not try writing a fairy-tale poem yourself? Pick a character or an object—maybe the bridge in Three Billy Goats Gruff, or Beauty's father, or the chair that Goldilocks broke. Imagine. Enchant. Write a poem that rewrites the tale. Make a little magic. (Author note)

3. Jane Yolen has retold twenty folk and fairy tales and her daughter, Heidi Stemple, has created recipes to accompany them, in *Fairy Tale Feasts: A Literary Cookbook for Young Readers and Eaters* (2009). What is especially delightful about

this volume is that the tales represent a great variety, from a Brer Rabbit tale originating in the American South, to tales from different European countries, to one from China, to Aesop fables, Andersen tales, and even to a tale related to folk music. Yolen gives sources for each story. All the recipes are connected to the tales in some way, and Stemple provides ideas for serving and for creating variations on a recipe. Perhaps there are tales students especially liked from this collection or others they have enjoyed since the onset of this study of fairy tales. In addition, provide an ample selection of stand-alone tales as well as several volumes of collected stories for students to peruse so that they become familiar with other tales not read in class. Is food mentioned in any of them or can students connect a food to any of the stories? What tales have the students selected? Divide the students into groups and ask each group to create an original recipe related to food in a specific tale or to the country from which the tale originated. Keep in mind that this is not simply a cooking activity—read *The Gingerbread Man* and make gingerbread cookies, for instance. Divergent thinking leads to original ideas, to *creating*. The recipes, therefore, should be the students' own creations (having several cook books on hand can give them an idea of how recipes work), and if it is not possible to test them in class to determine whether they work and actually taste good, perhaps individual students or groups could meet at home to work on each recipe. (Or perhaps the cafeteria staff would be willing to help?) When the recipes are finalized, type them into a book, add illustrations, and place it in the school or class library. The students may wish to dramatize one of the tales for another class and then serve food made with their recipe. They might also be interested in posting their original recipes in a blog or other online venue.

Further Thoughts to Ponder

As stated in the Introduction (p. xiii) divergent thinkers are characterized as having logical thinking skills and a tolerance for ambiguity. Carefully considering all the fairy tales they have read thus far will certainly provide students with an opportunity not only to think logically, but also to deal with the unresolved issues that might arise from their pondering. What are they to make of all these stories, many of which were not even originally meant for them—hence the "scrubbing" of many of the unsavory elements out of them to make them suitable for young audiences? In her article, "When Stories Had Sharp Teeth" (November 5, 2010), Marjorie Ingall writes about the day she discovered an old copy of the original Grimm fairy tales. "These stories were sick, serious and bloody. Cinderella's sisters did *what* to their feet? . . . I felt both thrilled and duped—why had no one told me that fairy tales were creepily delicious?" In *A Tale Dark & Grimm* discussed earlier, Adam Gidwitz tells readers, "Grimm's stories—the ones that weren't changed for little kids—are violent and bloody . . . You see, the land of Grimm can be a harrowing place. But it is worth exploring. For, in life, it is in the darkest zones one finds the brightest beauty and the most luminous wisdom." (unpaged) Do they agree with Gidwitz that there is beauty and wisdom to be found amidst the gore? Ask students to explain his statement. Older students can compare some original Grimm tales with the versions they know, discuss the differences, and decide whether or not "cleaning up" the stories is a good idea. They might also discuss some modern fractured tales, such as those by Gidwitz, that do include bloody and horrific elements. What do these works add to or subtract from the original tales the students have grown up with? Bruno Bettelheim, in his book, *The Uses of Enchantment* (1976), argues that the dark, scary, evil episodes in fairy tales actually help children come to terms with their own dark fears—fears of abandonment, of death, of disappointment, and so on—in a nonthreatening way since the children are far removed from the episodes in the stories. Do the students agree with this view? Why or why not?

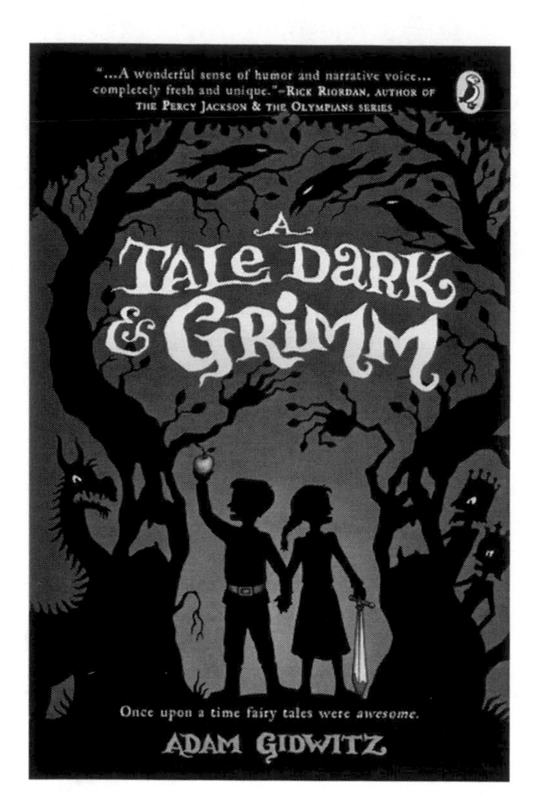

Another consideration: Surely many tales appeal to young people's sense of justice since often enough, the wicked are punished and the good rewarded. The greedy wife who wanted ever bigger houses and eventually even demanded to become God in the story of the *Fisherman and His Wife* ends up back in the shack she so wanted to escape because she refused to be satisfied with the magic fish's gifts. Such is also the fate of *The Old Woman Who Lived in a Vinegar Bottle* who moans "Oh what a pity, what a pity, pity, pity," as she complains about her tight quarters. But when a kind fairy provides her with ever grander houses, the woman is still not satisfied, until the fairy, fed up with her greed, sends the woman back to her vinegar bottle. The wolf who tries to eat the three pigs ends up in a hot kettle himself. The troll who wants to devour the Billy Goats Gruff is "crushed to bits, body and bones" by the biggest goat. Anansi the Spider, that lazy trickster character in many tales of African origin, often gets his comeuppance when he tries to fool the other animals into doing work for him. The Gingerbread Boy is punished both for running away from his parents, for his continual boasts, and for his miscalculation of the fox's intentions. But Jane Yolen, in an in sightful chapter of *Touch Magic* entitled "Killing the Other," discusses several tales in which it is the good or the innocent who are punished, intimating that if the character is "not one of us," then it is alright to cheat or destroy him or her. In Rumplestiltskin, a miller lies about his daughter's ability to spin straw into gold, his daughter is complicit in his lie, and a king believes the outlandish claim. Rumplestiltskin, on the other hand, never lies about his intentions—"I'll spin the straw into gold, but you must give me your first-born child." The girl uses his services to save herself, becomes queen, then sends out spies to help her get out of her promise. She is rewarded and poor Rumplestiltskin ends up being torn in two! To benefit his impoverished master in the story of *Puss 'n Boots*, Puss robs an ogre of his land and possessions and eventually kills him. Nowhere does the tale mention that the ogre is cruel to the inhabitants of his land, or that he goes about pillaging and killing for sport. He is simply an "ogre," one not like us, and therefore, expendable. He can be robbed and eventually killed to advance the fortunes of Puss's master. Goldilocks enters the bears' home without permission, steals their food, breaks furniture, and goes unpunished. Some writers of fractured tales, such as *Rump* discussed earlier, attempt to explain such injustices, while Jacob in *Far Far Away* questions them. Robust discussions can take place among older students as well. Are there different tiers in society, with the rich or powerful justified in cheating or harming those "beneath" them? Are there any instances of this behavior students have encountered online, in newspapers, or on news broadcasts? What steps are students aware of that wronged people have taken to improve their situation? Were these steps justified? What ideas do students have to deal with a particular situation that has come to their attention—in the community, in their school? What are our responsibilities toward others? In considering one or more of these puzzling fairy tales, students may wish to engage in any of the following activities:

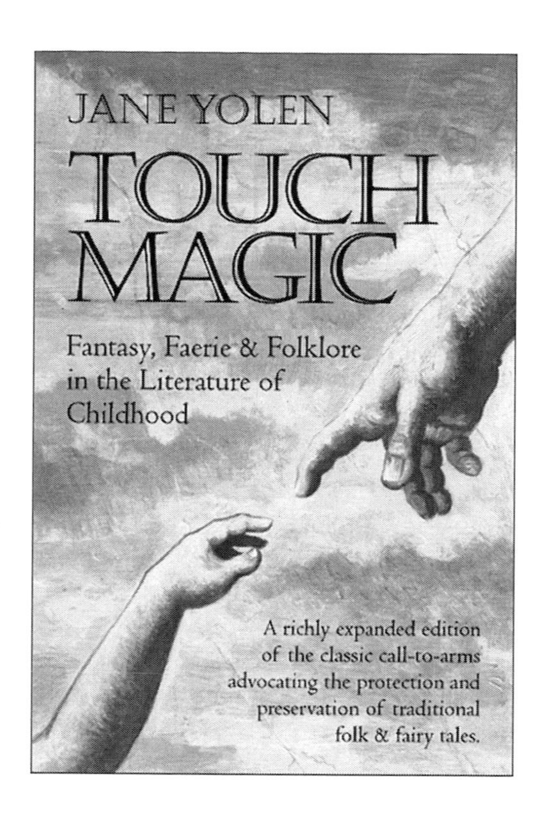

1. Rewrite the tale so that those who inflict harm on an undeserving victim are themselves punished or see the error of their ways.
2. Pick up the tale many years after a character has unjustly wronged another. Write about how his or her life has been affected by these actions.
3. Write and/or engage in an interview with a "relative" of a wronged fairy tale character to obtain that person's point of view.
4. Working in groups, write two newspaper articles about an event recounted in a fairy tale: one from the vanquished character's point of view and one from the victorious protagonist's point of view. (For example, from Cinderella's and one from one of her stepsister's vantage points.) Provide time for the groups to share their articles. Then compare newspaper articles about the same event in two different current newspapers and two different television broadcasts. What are the differences and similarities? How can the students, as consumers of today's news, obtain objective information about what is happening in their community, in the world?

Fairy Tales—Root of Contemporary Fantasy Novels

Even fantasy novels outside the realm of fractured fairy tales or those directly derived from them borrow elements of these stories in the yarns they spin. Well-known fantasy writer, Patricia C. Wrede, writes:

> Modern fantasy books take the raw materials of myths and fairy tales—the deserving younger sons and beautiful princesses, the dark woods and brilliant palaces, the unicorns and dragons, the magic of fairy gifts and curses, the heroic quests—and make new tales.
>
> —In *Facts about Fantasy*, "The Raw Material," unpaged

Those children who are familiar with fairy tales, then, will enjoy these modern stories to the full as they discover how today's writers use fairy tale elements to develop their characters and plots. But authors must do more than rely on fairy tale motifs to write their stories. Writing fantasy involves the creation of alternate worlds—worlds alien to readers, worlds with their own sets of rules and creatures. If readers are to suspend disbelief, to become convinced, at least while they are engrossed in the pages of a fantasy novel, that such a world really does exist, writers must make that world as real as readers' own neighborhoods. We enter into such secondary worlds, as Patricia Gauch (1994) says, "so easily we forget that people really can't fly, or mice really can't talk, or trees really can't transport . . . we believe so completely in the world that the author has created for us" (165). Only when readers are wrapped in these wondrous worlds with their magical creatures and heroes and villains, can they begin to ask themselves that all-important question: "what if." What if we, like the characters in this particular story, could get inside the minds of others and overtake them? What would happen? What if we could use our powers for our own gain or to harm others as the villain in this story does? What if we were called upon to take the incredible risks the hero of this story is asked to take? Would we? Should we? Could we? What if we lived in such a world with this particular set of rules—how would we fare? Or, perhaps more important, how could such a world come to be in the first place? Only when we ask the right questions will we be able to seek answers and solutions—solutions that call for deep thinking, unusual ideas, and even risk. Susan Lehr (1991) puts it well:

> Fantasy is a genre in which the imagination parallels the play worlds children enter. Reader response is critical. No passive readers are allowed. Authors and illustrators who invite the reader into the game, into the action, and ask something of the reader are highly successful. ("Fantasy: Inner Journeys for Today's Child," 99)

Modern Fantasy and Science Fiction Novels

Laura Amy Schlitz's historical fantasy, *Splendors and Glooms* (2012), takes place in 1860 and features children, a witch, magic, and an evil puppeteer. Clara Wintermute, the only surviving child of her wealthy parents (her siblings died because they ate cholera-invested watercress) enjoys a street puppet performance done by Gaspare Grisini and his two apprentices, Lizzie Rose and Parsefall, and insists they be hired for her birthday. After the performance, Clara mysteriously disappears and the authorities suspect Grisini is responsible. But he has disappeared as well, leaving Lizzie Rose and Parsefall abandoned in a dismal boarding house. When the witch Cassandra lures the children to her sumptuous home with the promise of leaving all her wealth to them at her death, they go, unaware that she means to trick them into stealing an opal and saving her from its curse—"almost everyone who possess[es] it die[s] of fire" (131). To make matters worse, Grisini is in hiding at Cassandra's home and is determined to make a slave of the child who steals the opal. At the beginning of the story these three children look out for their own interests but in the end break out of what might be expected of them to achieve a greater good. Lizzie Rose, who misses the warmth of her family, does everything in her power to keep the children safe and together and even tends to the witch in her dying days. Parsefall, an orphan who doesn't hesitate to steal anything he can lay his hands on, tries to protect the others from Grisini's evil intentions and determines to make an honest living running his own puppet theater. Clara, shy, overcome with loneliness and guilt because she gave her watercress portion to her twin, risks her own life to keep the opal from Grisini: "For a fraction of a second, she considered surrendering the fire opal [to Grisini]. Then she imagined what he might do, given its magical powers, and she steeled herself to outwit him" (129). Venturing out on a pond's thin ice, she hurls the opal out of his reach as the ice beneath her begins to crack. In the end, they all learn the hard truth that "magic power cannot be had for nothing. There must always be sacrifice" (129). It takes all three of them, willing to sacrifice and work together, to save not only themselves, but Clara's bereft parents as well.

Kathi Appelt's marvelous fantasy, *The True Blue Scouts of Sugar Man Swamp* (2013), involves two raccoon brothers, Bingo and J'Miah, who live in a swamp near the Gulf of Mexico in an abandoned 1949 DeSoto; Chap Brayburn and his mom who are trying desperately to keep their café afloat in the face of their landlord's desire to turn the swamp into an adventure theme park featuring a female alligator wrestling champion; the Sugar Man, protector of the swamp but asleep lo these sixty years and sure to be full of wrath if unexpectedly awakened; Chap's grandfather Audi (after James Audubon) who, though recently deceased, is very much alive in the hearts of those who loved him; and a stampeding herd of wild hogs. Sound confusing? It isn't, because Appelt is a masterful writer who holds these plot lines together and neatly wraps them to a satisfying conclusion. Students will love this fantasy and will keep reading to discover whether the raccoon scouts can awaken Sugar Man for his help and whether the café and the swamp itself will be saved. This story is a natural springboard for discussion about protecting habitats and species. Can the students identify the real cause of the problem faced by the swamp inhabitants? Research a threatened habitat and create a wiki (see wikispaces .com) to present your findings and their sources. Invite another class to join the wiki and add whatever information those students uncover. How can the students share what they have learned with agencies that might be able to take corrective action?

Zach, Poppy, and Alice, the three friends in Holly Black's *Doll Bones* (2013), have been playing a continuous game of pirates and adventures and quests since forever. But when Zach's father throws out the action figures that are central to the game believing that twelve is too old for such nonsense, Zach decides, unwillingly, to quit the game rather than tell his friends what really happened. But then Poppy reveals a strange ghostly appearance related to her mother's valuable antique porcelain doll the three have dubbed the Queen. Poppy tells her friends that Eleanor Kerchner, who actually lived and who died under questionable circumstances is now a ghost possessing the doll. "[The doll], Poppy says, is made from [Eleanor's] bones . . . That hair threaded through the scalp is the little girl's hair. And the body of the doll is filled with her ashes" (63). Unless they bury the doll, Eleanor will never be at peace. While not really believing Poppy's ghost story, Zach and Alice reluctantly agree to this one last adventure together, which means traveling to Eleanor's home in East Liverpool, Ohio via bus and boat in the middle of the night. The journey is fraught with difficulties and dangers that include being vandalized in the park (was it the doll expressing displeasure?), strange happenings in a restaurant and more, until a librarian reconnects them with their families. But this is much more than a difficult journey undertaken with limited resources and without permission. The entire venture is actually a metaphor for the friends' life journey from childhood into budding adolescence; from pretend games with action figures to managing new relationships and first crushes; to dealing with the rules laid out by their families while trying to assert their increasing desires for more independence. All three children are dealing with serious issues: Zach's strict father has returned after three years' absence; Alice lives with an overbearing grandmother whose unreasonable rules and penchant for grounding her granddaughter for lengthy periods make life miserable; and Alice feels ignored by a mother who seems to care more for her precious porcelain doll than her own child. Divide the students into groups and ask each group to discuss what they feel this story is about. Do they believe Poppy's ghost story? Why or why not? Do they believe Poppy is sincere or is she just trying to entice her friends into another game? How do they feel this journey has changed each of the three children? Encourage the groups to discuss the journey as metaphor and connect it to their own life's journey.

Mrs. Tootie Tickham is the, well, questionably happy recipient of a Ulysses Super-Suction, Multi-Terrain 2000X vacuum cleaner—a birthday present from her husband in Kate DiCamillo's wonderful, hilarious Newbery-award-wining *Flora & Ulysses* (2013) "It is indoor / outdoor. It goes everywhere. It does everything" (2). In fact, the machine is so powerful it scoops up everything in sight, drags Mrs. Tickham out into the yard, and vacuums up a squirrel. The only witness to this horror is young Flora Buckman, a "natural-born cynic" (6) who believes in almost nothing except janitor Alfred T. Slipper, hero of the comic *The Illuminated Adventures of the Amazing Incandesto!*, her regular reading matter. Whenever trouble is afoot, Slipper cries out, "This malfeasance must be stopped," and is transformed into the amazing Incandesto, "a towering, crime-fighting pillar of light" (7). But the amazing Incandesto isn't around to save the squirrel. There is only Flora, who runs into the yard to assess the damage. Incredibly, the squirrel is still alive, though minus lots of fur. She names him Ulysses and declares, contrary to her cynical bent, that he now has a new life with super hero powers. "Together she and Ulysses could change the world. Or something" (39). So far, though, Ulysses is behaving like a regular squirrel, and Flora determines, as her book, *Terrible Things Can Happen to You!* advises, not to hope but instead, to observe. Eventually the squirrel does demonstrate his super powers with his ability to fly and to write poetry! Flora wants to keep him, but her romance-novel-writing mother wants no part of this plan and saddles her estranged husband, Flora's comic-loving soul mate, with the task of bringing about Ulysses's demise.

But Flora and her dad team up to defeat their arch-nemisis, wife and mother, along with some help from Tootie, Tootie's nephew William, who feels he is temporarily blind, and Dr. Meescham. Their quest to save the squirrel transforms everyone involved, and these transformations as well as other aspects of the book are grist for meaningful class discussion and projects:

1. Flora eschews hope in the unseen and intangible for observation of what is in front of her. Yet Dr. Meescham advises, "All things are possible. When I was a girl in Blundermeecen, the miraculous happened every day . . . Actually, sometimes it did not happen at all . . . But still, we expected it" (130). What roles do hope and observation play in the life of a divergent thinker? How can they work together? What else might be required to effect change?
2. How are each of the characters in the story changed? What brought about these transformations?
3. The text in this story is interspersed with comic book layouts. Is this a good choice? Why or why not? Does the class have any other suggestions for accompanying illustrations for this story?
4. Continue writing the story where DiCamillo leaves it. What will life in the Buckman family be like now? Why?

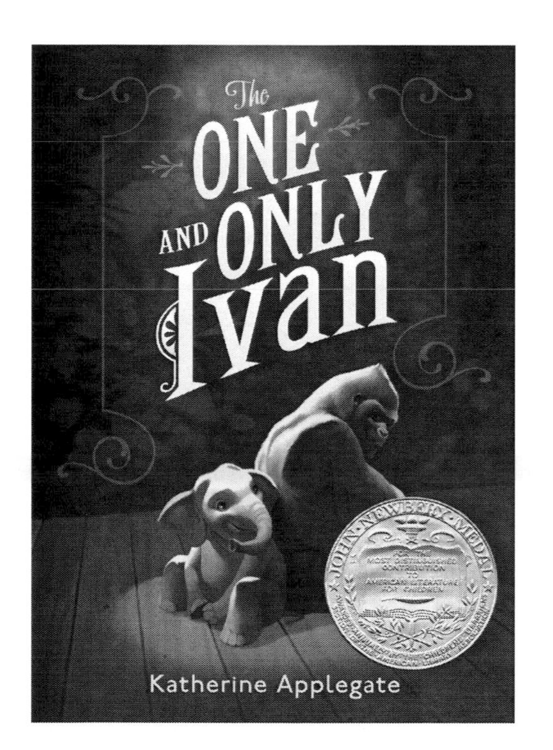

Katherine Applegate's Newbery-award-winning *The One and Only Ivan* (2012) is a charming fantasy featuring, among others, Ivan, a gorilla who lives in a habitat (really, a cage) made of "thick glass and rusty metal and rough cement" (7) in the Big Top Mall and Video Arcade. Next to Ivan's habitat, in a domain of metal bars, lives Stella, an elephant. Stella and a dog named Bob are Ivan's friends, but these friends cannot make up for the loneliness and terrible fate of living in a small enclosure to be stared at by fewer and fewer shoppers in a mall that has seen better days. To relieve his boredom, Ivan draws and his owner, Mack, sells the drawings to humans who, while not quite sure what the drawings represent, will pay for them since they were made by a gorilla. Stella was once a circus elephant but was sold to Mack when her foot was injured. Because Mack won't spend the money needed to care for Stella's foot, Stella dies, but before she does, she extracts a promise from Ivan—that he will care for the new baby elephant, Ruby, recently purchased by Mack. "If she could have a life that's . . . different from mine. She needs a safe place, Ivan." "Not here," says Ivan (112, 113). After Stella's death, Ivan begins to regret his promise. How will he ever get Ruby out of the Big Top Mall? But when an idea finally comes to him, it takes all his artistic talent, working far into the night, and ultimately, facing the horror of the cruel murder and dismemberment of his family, to finally rouse the public to do something about releasing caged animals in a mall. This is a lovely story, and Applegate tells readers that it is based on a news story about the real Ivan, who "spent twenty-seven years of his life alone in a cage" (303) in a circus-themed mall in Washington state without ever seeing another of his own kind until public opinion eventually effected his release. It is a fine example of how fantasy stories can help us realize important truths about ourselves and about our capacity to affect change. "Humans," says Stella, "can surprise you sometimes. An unpredictable species" (104).

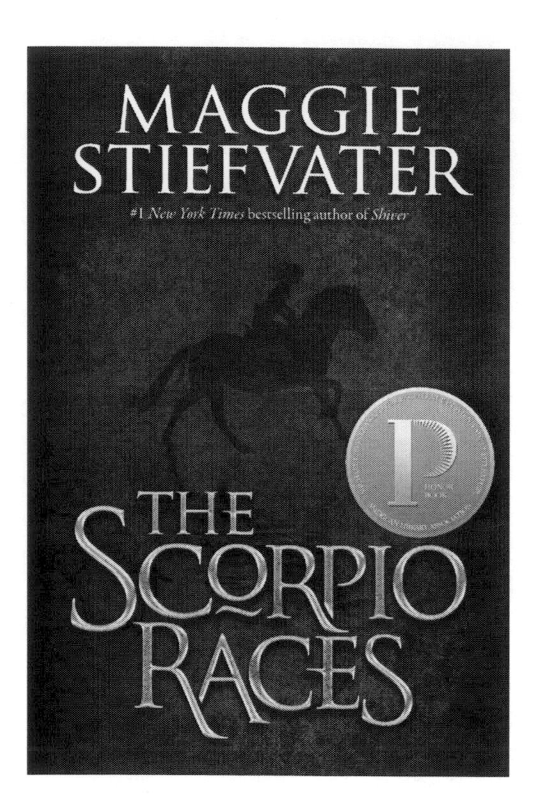

Maggie Stiefvater's *The Scorpio Races* (2011) begins, "It is the first day of November and so, today, someone will die" (1). That's because on the island of Thisby, those who have managed to control a *capaill uisce*, one of the huge, flesh-eating water horses that come up out of the sea each year, will race them on the beach. It is a fierce, vicious race, and, inevitably, there is death. Nineteen-year-old Sean has raced successfully in the past, and this year, he is desperate to win and thereby own Corr, the magnificent capaill uisce he has trained. But Katherine, called Puck, wants to win, too, to earn enough money to avoid losing the family home. Two huge complications stand in her way though: her island pony can't possibly compete with the powerful capaill uisce, and "No woman's ridden in the races since they began" (195). The determination with which she fights against both obstacles, and the growing friendship between Puck and Sean, both orphaned because of the races, make for a simply marvelous read for older students. In her author's note, Stiefvater states she got the idea for this fascinating story from a Scottish myth about kelpie horses. Students can go to http://www.lizaphoenix.com/encyclopedia/horses.shtml for an extensive list of legendary horses from different civilizations. After the class reads the descriptions of the creatures on the list, ask different groups to choose a horse and collaborate to write a short fantasy story about it.

Paolo Bacigaluipi has written a post-apocalyptic science fiction thriller for older students in *Ship Breaker* (2010). Nailer lives in a bleak world on the Gulf Coast. There are no more fossil fuels, and coastal cities have been drowned by rising waters due to global warming. The community ekes out a living by salvaging whatever it can from old wrecked oil tankers. Nailer works on the light crew, trying to salvage his daily quota of copper and enduring the brutal beatings of his drug-addicted father. So when he discovers a modern ship-wrecked clipper ship, he sees a way out of his poverty and miserable life—if only he can keep it secret and sell its many riches. But then he discovers an injured girl aboard. It would be so easy to kill her and keep the treasures for himself. It turns out, though, that she is the rich daughter of the shipping company's owner, and she promises him a better life if only he will save her and return her to her people. Really? Can he trust her? And even if he tries to save her, his cruel father will surely find out. Nailer's decision is not an easy one, and when he makes it, he faces unimaginable hardships, betrayals, and cruelty. Older middle graders and teens will love this adventure, and they will encounter a great deal to ponder. It might be interesting to stop reading before Nailer makes his decision and discuss what they would do in his situation and why. Ask them to visualize Nailer's world. Do they think such a society is possible? What do they believe about global warming and the depletion of natural resources? What are their creative ideas for preserving the natural environment? Challenge the students to find instances in the local papers or on the internet in which decisions are being made that harm the environment, or where current environmental laws are being rolled back. Stage a debate for and against such decisions.

High Fantasy

Nestled within the world of fantasy literature is an extremely important subgenre called high fantasy. In this genre are all the characteristics we have already seen in fantasy novels, and more. High fantasy most often involves a huge problem: a kingdom is about to be destroyed, a plague will wipe out everyone, an evil character is working to control an entire population to do his or her bidding, and so on. Enter the hero—usually a young or unimportant person (or insignificant animal) without power or means, who is called upon to undertake a quest to right this grave wrong. A threshold guide usually calls the unlikely hero to enter into the fight against evil. The hero often receives help along the way—from the threshold guide and others—but the mission will not be easy. There will be continuous trials that test the hero's courage and skills. Entering into dangerous situation after dangerous situation, maneuvering through an alligator-infested swamp or the deep, forbidding forest, finding ways to solve each crisis as it arises—all these trials transform the hero from a powerless, sometimes even selfish, individual into someone with inner strength and courage. The hero moves from consideration of him or herself to concern for the community and brings back a boon—victory over the evil person or group, or whatever powerful artifact will save the people. The hero never battles dark forces for his or her own glory, but for the good of the community. It is easy to see, then, how works of high fantasy that explore "real struggles, real dilemmas, and real depictions of evil [can] provide frameworks for children to grow as individuals and make choices about how they will live" (Lehr, 1991, 100).

Many believe that high fantasy, while rooted in ancient folklore, began its modern life with *The Hobbit* and *The Lord of the Rings* trilogy by J.R.R. Tolkien. In these books, we have all the ingredients for excellent fantasy. If students have not read them (though many may have seen the films), they should certainly be introduced to *The Hobbit* (older students can enjoy *The Lord of the Rings* as well). Bilbo Baggins, the unlikely hero, enjoys his life in Hobbitown and wants nothing more than the comfort of his hobbit hole and good food. But a threshold guide, the wizard Gandalf, talks him into joining a band of dwarves who are setting out to reclaim lost treasure guarded by the dragon Smaug at Lonely Mountain. The group encounters trolls, goblins, giant spiders and all manner of other menacing creatures on their quest. There's even "The Battle of Five Armies" to be waged. Tolkien has created such a vivid Middle Earth world that students will easily lose themselves in it, and it is a tale against which they can evaluate modern works of high fantasy. While it is the goal of this text to introduce teachers and parents to the most recent works of literature for children, it is important to ground students in the masters, and it is fortunate that many of their books have been reissued for today's children. Lloyd Alexander's *The Book of Three* and the other *Prydian Chronicles*; Ursula LeGuin's *Earthsea Cycle*; Susan Cooper's *The Dark Is Rising Sequence*; Terry Prachett's *Discworld* books (see www.orderofbooks.com/characters/discworldfor a complete listing and description); and

Philip Pullman's *His Dark Materials* trilogy should all be part of students' high fantasy reading and thoughtful discussion.

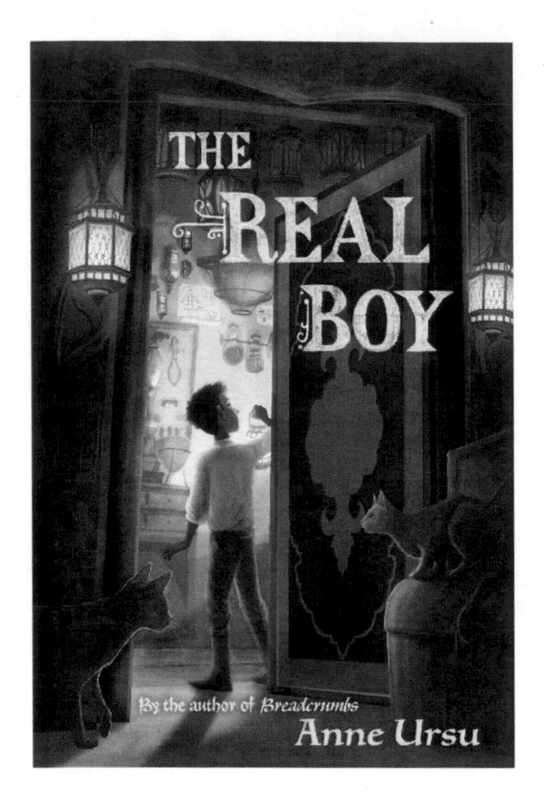

In the Barrow, a vast forest of ancient trees that feed magic into the earth, Oscar, hero of Anne Ursu's lovely *The Real Boy* (2013), works as a magician's hand grinding herbs and mixing potions in the basement with only cats for company. He has no idea how to deal with people, so when the magician's apprentice is killed, the magician himself disappears, and he must run the magician's shop, Oscar is distraught. He can't speak to the customers nor can he read their faces to judge their needs and reactions. To add to his distress, Callie, a local healer's apprentice, whose mistress has also disappeared, brings news that children in Asteri, a city saved by magic from a destroying plague over 100 years ago, are becoming seriously ill. Asteri and its children, however, are supposed to be perfect, beneficiaries of powerful magic. There's more. The glass house in which Oscar's herbs grow is "broken. Shattered." (127), And the shops in the market along with the magician's shop are attacked by a huge mud-covered giant. What's going on? When Callie and Oscar piece together some of the answers, the truth is more terrible than they ever realized. Together, at Callie's urging: "these children need us . . . We're the best they have right now" (170). they try to help the children, and alone, Oscar enters into the forest, willing to offer his life to fight the monster who threatens to destroy them all. Filled with metaphor, there is much to uncover in this multilayered fantasy. Here are some thoughts and questions that might spark discussion:

1. There are numerous references in the book to the futility of magic. Some examples: "Small enchantments make us dream of big ones" (121), "you cannot look to magic to solve your problems" (122), and "Magic is not ours to use . . . We think it serves us, but that is only magic playing tricks. Magic only makes us hungry for more magic" (217). What do students understand by these and other similar statements? What connections, as divergent thinkers, can they make to other fantasies they've read and even more importantly, to the world in which they live? What original ideas can they come up with to counteract a culture that seems to want "something for nothing?" How can they disseminate these ideas?
2. What do students think of Oscar's character? Is he just shy or is something more involved? How does he change as the story progresses? What are their experiences of relating to someone who seems different from themselves? Connect their responses to the earlier discussion of *Puss in Boots*.
3. The wooden cat Oscar keeps in his pocket is a metaphor. Uncover its meaning.
4. What do students think about the people of Asteri wanting perfect children? Again, what connections can they make to their own lives?

Like Oscar in *The Real Boy*, Tommy Pepper of Plymouth, MA, the protagonist of Gary D. Schmidt's *What Came from the Stars* (2012) is as unlikely a hero as it is possible to be. He is grieving because of his mother's sudden death—a death that has left his little sister a selective mute. The siblings and their father live in a small home by the sea, and even that is being threatened by a real estate agency trying to claim it for development. And to compound his troubles, Tommy is the victim of constant bullying at school. But Tommy's life will soon change. Unknown to him, the peaceful civilization of Valorim is about to fall into the hands of the dark Lord Mondus. To preserve Valorim's extraordinary beauty, a few of its heroes bind it all into a necklace and fling it to Earth where it lands in Tommy's lunch box. From the moment Tommy dons the necklace, he begins to speak a strange language, to make drawings that seem to move, and to see things others can't. When the dark forces that wish to control Valorim come to Earth to get the necklace, leaving messages like the one on the school walls, "Pepper give us what we want" (135), life gets even more complicated. Tommy's teacher disappears and a strange substitute takes his place. Much worse than that is the disappearance of Tommy's father and sister, victims of that strange substitute. He threatens Tommy: "You must give [the chain] to me, for the sleep that closes the eyes of your sister and your father will be only sleep for another day. Then . . . it will be death" (238). What is Tommy to do? It would be so easy to give up the necklace and save his family—but the consequences for others are dire. Stop the reading at this point and ask the students what they think he should do and why? Should Tommy trust Mr. Pilgrim Way to save his father and sister in return for the necklace? Why or why not? Can they figure a way out of his dilemma without sacrificing the people of Valorim?

Some other suggestions for related discussion and activities:

a) As divergent thinkers, what connections can they make between Tommy's situation and that of the people of Valorim?
b) Like many writers of fantasy, Schmidt has created a new language for the alternate universe in this tale. Can the students create a story involving two different groups of people, and devise a new language for the group living in an alternate universe? A wiki that provides clear instructions, tips, and different methods for creating a language is available at http://www.wikihow.com/Create-a-Language.
c) Discuss Mr. Pilgrim Way's statement: "There is no Art made without power, and there is no reason for Art to be made except for power" (182). What does he mean, and do students agree with him? Why or why not?

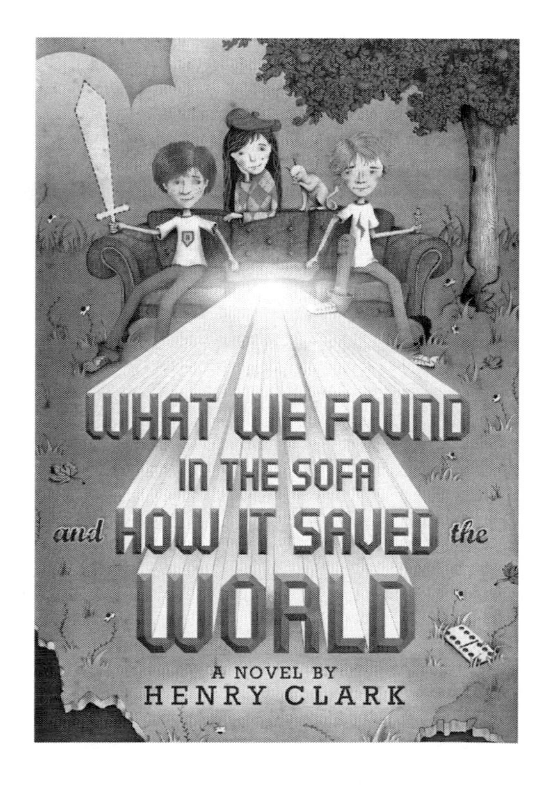

Henry Clark's zany, cleverly funny fantasy/science fiction novel, *What We Found in the Sofa and How It Saved the World* (2013), features River and his friends, Freak and Fiona. They live in the only remaining houses in Hells boro—so called because of the coal-seam fires that have been burning underground for years, destroying homes and the landscape. One day a sofa appears at their bus stop—a fine place for lounging as they wait for their transportation to arrive—until they discover a rare zucchini-colored crayon beneath its cushions. This discovery leads them to the spooky Underhill House and its weird occupant, Alf, who, it turns out, is trying to prevent Disin, an evil dictator from another universe, Indorsia, from taking over Earth and forcing its people to do his bidding. Alf's plan is to lure Disin, whose surprising identity readers discover later in the story, to Underhill by auctioning the zucchini crayon, a prize the dictator covets for his crayon collection. Once Disin is identified at the auction and apprehended by FBI agents Alf has arranged to be there, the threat to Earth will be over. Simple. But nothing ever is in the world of setbacks and advances that is fantasy, and saving Earth requires more than just a crayon. It requires brave children who, at risk of their lives, dare to enter an abandoned coal plant to go through to Disin's universe and stop him before it's too late. As they are chased by spies wearing dog heads and face mind-control serums and even cloning, they receive some help from an artificial intelligence hidden in a domino. It's a wild ride that will have readers turning pages, but it raises some questions as well. There is mind control through the use of cell phones and food additives, greed, and that coal fire ("It's never been proven . . . but a lot of people think the factory had been dumping some sort of waste chemicals into the soil, and after a while they somehow cause the coal to ignite" (76).) and the risks of being a whistle blower—all fodder for interesting discussion.

Grace Lin's *Starry River of the Sky* (2012) is a story that takes places centuries before the events in her *Where the Mountain Meets the Moon* (2009). In *Starry River*, Rendi, a self-centered, petulant boy runs away from home by hiding in a merchant's cart, disembarking in the Village of Clear Sky where the absence of the moon is causing drought and scorching heat. He becomes a chore boy at an inn where he seems to be the only one who hears the sad moans of the sky each night as it grieves the loss of the moon. The inn is empty, as is most of the village, but wise old Mr. Shan takes his meals there, and one day mysterious Madame Chang arrives. She is a gifted storyteller and enchants everyone with her stories at meals, insisting that for every story she tells, Rendi tells one as well. These stories begin to piece together the incidents of Rendi's past and the reason for the moon's disappearance. But even more important is their effect on the listeners. Rendi begins to change from a selfish boy whose only wish is to leave the village, to one with a better understanding of his father and an awareness of his destiny to recover the moon and save the village. He begins to be concerned about the moans he hears nightly: "Ever since he started hearing the cries, all he had thought about was himself, never about who was suffering or how he could help. Well, he would find out and help now" (212). He sets out on a journey, a quest, across the forbidding Stone Pancake where he ultimately finds the moon and undertakes the strenuous task of lifting it back into the sky. This story is filled with Chinese folklore, enriched with Grace Lin's beautiful illustrations, and includes a magic toad, bandits, and a kidnapping—a great recipe for garnering student interest. Can they unravel the folktales imbedded with the fantasy, each one cycling back to its teller, before Rendi does? The key to the mystery at the heart of this book lies in remembering the folktales and putting them together, that is, making the connections characteristic of the divergent thinker. Explore the themes of forgiveness that abound throughout the tale. Older students might accept the challenge to create a mystery with hints contained in a series of interweaving original stories. Discuss a plan as a class and then ask the students to work in groups to write each story. Come together to make sure the stories fit together. Present them to another class to solve.

Matthew J. Kirby has taken actual historical events and people from the 18th century—the design of an aeroship by Francesco Lana de Terzi; a Philosophical Society; the rumor of a tribe of Welsh-speaking Indians; and Benjamin Franklin and the famous botanists John Bartram and his son; and woven them into an exciting high fantasy adventure entitled *The Lost Kingdom* (2013). Members of the American Philosophical Society, each with a special expertise, set off into the American wilderness on an aeroship to seek a kingdom inhabited by Welsh Indians, descendants of the Welsh Prince Madoc. Their aim is to make allies of them against the French who will soon make war on the colonies. Only with this help can the colonies prevail against a powerful French army intent upon claiming land for France. Along with their noble intentions to save their people via this diplomatic mission, however, it slowly becomes clear that several members, with the exception of young Billy Bartram who accompanies his father John, have hidden agendas that ultimately wreak disaster. In spite of the unprecedented speed of their aeroship, the group faces constant danger from a fierce bear-wolf that seems to be stalking them, and the pursuing French army. There is seemingly no end to the surprises, unpleasant and otherwise, visited upon the members of this expedition. To complicate matters further is John Bartram's intense hatred of Indians, even the one who is guiding them, and his son's defiance of his father's views. What is striking in this fantasy is the self-serving goals of some members of the Philosophical Society—so contrary to the spirit of high fantasy in which danger is faced to save others. Discuss with students the effects this self-centeredness has on the expedition. Young Billy's view of Indians is very different from that of most of his contemporaries. How does his different point of view ultimately affect others, especially his father ? Discuss why openness to different viewpoints plays a significant role in arriving at innovative ideas. Another fantasy with a similar theme, while not fitting into the high fantasy category, is Susan Cooper's *Ghost Hawk* (2013). When Little Hawk returns from a three-month ordeal in the woods in winter to prove his manhood, he discovers everyone in his village except his grandmother has died of the white man's small pox. Greater numbers of ships bring even more white people to his land, one of whom is young John Wakeley. John's views of Indians, like Billy's, are very different from those in his settlement and his bond with Little Hawk puts his life in danger. This is a wonderful read that will raise many questions among students as they ponder the treatment of these first Americans.

A genocidal spore has wiped out everyone except the young and the very old in the not-too-distant- future community featured in Lisa Price's haunting *Starters* (2012). The wealthy elderly, who live to very advanced ages, rent out the bodies of the young so they can engage in vigorous activities once again. But when Callie, forbidden by law to get a job and must constantly flee lest she be institutionalized along with other youth, rents

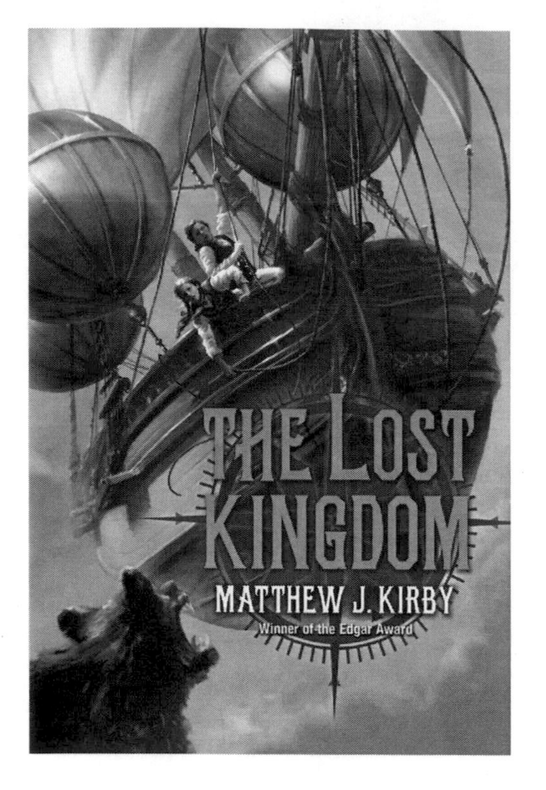

out her body to obtain money to care for her younger brother, she discovers a horrible plan and realizes that unless she can stop this plan from becoming reality, many young people will die. During a conversation with Lisa Price, she mentioned that she got the idea for this book when she went to the Costco pharmacy to obtain a flu shot. She was told there wasn't enough vaccine and it was only being given to children and the elderly. She then began to wonder what a society would be like if its middle-aged population disappeared. After reading the book, tell students how Price germinated the idea for this novel. While fantasy, especially high fantasy, builds worlds none of us have ever seen, the ideas for the creation of these worlds are often rooted in our own society. Ask the class, working in groups if they wish, to generate a list of real-world scenarios that, if carried forward by an imaginative author, could become the seed of a fantasy novel. Ask each group to choose one item on its list and, in conversation, talk about its possibilities as a meaningful story.

Melina Marchetta's *Finnikin of the Rock* (2010) is an excellent high fantasy novel for older students. When he was just a boy, Finnikin dreamt that he would have to sacrifice a pound of his flesh to save the royal house of Lumatere. When he relates the dream to his friends Balthazar, the king's son and heir, and Lucian, the three pledge by offering their own blood, to serve the house of Lumatere as defender, protector, and guiding light. And "they were indeed blessed as no other kingdom in the land. Until the five days of the unspeakable" (unpaged). During these five days, the king, queen, and their daughters are murdered and Balthazar is believed dead as well; the king's cousin leads an army and burns the Forest Dwellers; Trevanion, Finnikin's father and captain of the guards, is arrested for treason; and a curse effectively locks Lumatere shut along with all those who could not flee while forcing those outside into exile. During the ten years he is in exile himself, Finnikin meets Evanjalin who claims to be able to read people's dreams. She delivers the shocking news that Balthazar is actually alive and that it is Finnikin's destiny to find him and free Lumatere. Evanjalin, Finnikin, and his mentor, Sir Tropher, sojourn from kingdom to kingdom, freeing exiled leaders and gathering an army. Facing multiple dangers as they journey to carry out their mission, the two young people gain inner strength and skills and Finnikin calls forth courage he never knew he had. This is an amazing novel and comparisons to our current world situation are unavoidable. In their need for power, so many of today's leaders wreak havoc on their own land and people, killing hundreds of thousands and forcing many more into refugee camps where they linger for years and even die. At one point in the story Evanjalin says, "our kingdom was cursed. Damned. Taken away from us, because good people stood by while evil took place. Let that be our lesson" (235). What do the students, actually the good people who read her words, make of her message? Do they feel moved to do anything, however limited it may seem, to respond to unjust power-seeking activity in the world? Are they

aware of any instances of the use of power in their school community to control others? Can they devise an original campaign, complete with posters, suggestions for dealing with unjust situations, and so on?

"My mother left me a complicated and burdensome inheritance. My father hid the dreadful details from everyone, including me" (1). So says Seraphina, heroine of Rachel Hartman's book that bears her name (2012). The inheritance is that she is half human, half dragon, anathema to the citizens of Goredd, even though they and the dragons have lived an uneasy truce—humans may not enter dragon kind lands and dragons can only enter human lands if they assume human form—for the last forty years. So she dresses to hide the scales on her arms and stomach and tries to remain unobserved in her father's house. But she is a talented musician and when she plays a solo for the funeral of the murdered prince, she becomes well known. To make matters worse, a dragon is suspected of killing the prince and anti-dragon sentiment is increasing. Seraphina, like Prince Lucian and his betrothed, Princess Glisselda, wants to keep the peace by extending the treaty, but there are those who are thirsting for war. The queen expresses her distress to a meeting of dragons and humans:

> I believed, perhaps erroneously, that our peoples would simply grow accustomed to each other . . . Are we oil and water, that we cannot mix? Have I been remiss in expecting reason and decency to prevail, when I should have rolled up my sleeves and enforced them? (103)

Seraphina has some suspicions about who has murdered the prince and she and Lucian set off to uncover the culprit and possibly avoid war. But will he want to join forces with her if he discovers her secret? And what is she to do with her feelings for him? There are fantasies about dragons aplenty, but this one is truly unique. And it has much to say about living among those who are different from oneself.

When the Harry Potter books hit library and book store shelves, the series created a revolution in children's book publishing. Captivated by Harry, young people began to look for and demand similar heroes, and the result was an explosion in the number of fantasy and science fiction books and series—far too many to include here. You and the young people in your care will discover many more. What is essential, though, is that you do discover and savor them together. No other genre offers as powerful an opportunity for students to think in big ways about decisions and actions and their ramifications. No other genre offers as many heroes for young people to emulate—heroes who consider the needs of the community before their own and often risk all for its sake. No other genre feeds young people's imaginations as deeply as they read about imaginary worlds and creatures, even newly created languages. No other genre says quite so powerfully, because the trials are often so huge, that hardship and suffering make us stronger and able to do more than we ever envisioned we could. Gifted author and editor Patricia Lee Gauch says it best:

> If literature does, in fact, provide a map for living, there is no map more powerful for the developing individual, more full of humanity . . . than fine fantasy. And for that revelation, I do not have to suspend disbelief. I believe.
>
> —"A Quest for the Heart of Fantasy," *The New Advocate*, 1994, 166

Note

1. Myths and legends are, of course, an important part of fantasy literature, and students may be familiar with many of them, especially those of Greek and Roman origin. But myths and legends and their various gods inhabit the literature of cultures throughout the world, and the genre is so all-encompassing it cannot be given the treatment it deserves here. Most likely, students will read some myths and become introduced to the ancient gods that form an important part of different peoples' history as part of their curriculum. Certainly they will encounter the roots of myths and legends in the novels of Lloyd Alexander, Rick Riordan, and other fine writers of modern fantasy and science fiction. A selected bibliography of such works appears below and will help your students select books that appeal to them.

References

Ahlberg, Allan. 2012. *The Goldilocks Variations*. Illustrated by Jessica Ahlberg. Somerville, MA: Candlewick. ISBN 978-0-7636-6268-4. This innovative book, with its tabs and pop-ups, contains different stories involving Goldilocks's visit to a cottage in the woods.

Alexander, Lloyd. 2011. *The Chronicles of Prydian Boxed Set*. New York: Square Fish/Macmillan. ISBN 978-1-25000093-4. pb reissue. Recipients of both a Newbery medal and honor, this series about the adventures of Taran, the assistant pig keeper, sets the standard for high fantasy. The titles are available individually as well.

Appelt, Kathi. 2013. *The True Blue Scouts of Sugar Man Swamp*. Illustrated by Jennifer Bricking. New York: Atheneum/Simon & Schuster. ISBN 978-1-4424-2105-9. A developer and a marauding herd of wild hogs threaten a swamp and it's up to two raccoon scouts to awake Sugar Man and avert the crisis.

Applegate, Katherine. 2012. *The One and Only Ivan*. Illustrated by Patricia Castelao. New York: Harper/HarperCollins. ISBN 978-0-06-199225-4. Ivan, a gorilla caged in a mall, tries to save the baby elephant Ruby from remaining at the mall for the rest of her life.

Bacigaluipi, Paolo. 2010. *Ship Breaker*. New York: Little Brown Books for Young Readers. ISBN 978-0-31605621-2. Nailer, who lives in a bleak world under a cruel father, must decide whether to take the riches in a sunken vessel for himself or risk everything to save a girl he discovers within the ship.

Baleman, Teresa. 2011. *Paul Bunyan vs. Hals Halson: The Great Lumberjack Challenge!* Illustrated by C. B. Canga. Park Ridge, IL: Albert Whitman. ISBN 978-0807563670. Hals challenges Paul to determine who is the most powerful lumberjack.

Barnett, Mac. 2012. *Extra Yarn*. Illustrated by Jon Klassen. New York: Balzer + Bray/HarperCollins. ISBN 978-0-06-195338-5. A girl finds a box of magic yarn and knits sweaters for everyone in town until an evil archduke tries to take the box from her.

Bettelheim, Bruno. 1976. *The Uses of Enchantment*. New York: Knopf. ISBN 978-0394497716. Bettelheim discusses the dark aspects of fairy tales as a way of helping children cope with their fears. There are more recent paperback editions of this text.

Black, Holly. 2013. *Doll Bones*. Illustrated by Eliza Wheeler. New York: Simon & Schuster. ISBN 978-14169-6398-1. Three friends undertake a dangerous journey to bury a porcelain doll they believe to be haunted by a girl who died under mysterious circumstances.

Blackwood, Sage. 2013. *Jinx*. New York: Harper/HarperCollins. ISBN 978-0-06-212990-1. Left by his parents to die in the forest, Jinx is rescued by a wizard whom he serves for many years. But is this wizard good or evil? Jinx's exciting adventures continue in *Jinx's Magic* (2014).

Breslin, Theresa. 2012. *Illustrated Treasury of Scottish Folk and Fairy Tales.* Illustrated by Kate Leiper. Harrison Gardens, Edinburgh: Floris Books. ISBN 978-086315-907-7. This is a collection of eleven beautifully illustrated Scottish tales.

Brett, Jan. 2011. *Beauty and the Beast.* New York: Putnam/Penguin. ISBN 978-0-39925731-5. To save her father, Beauty agrees to live with a Beast and learns to love him.

Bruchac, Joseph, and James Bruchac. 2003. *How Chipmunk Got His Stripes.* Illustrated by Jose Aruego and Ariane Dewey. New York: Puffin/Penguin. ISBN 978-0142500217. pb reprint. When squirrel teases Big Bear, the bear claws his back leaving the stripes we now recognize as the characteristic markings of the chipmunk.

Carle, Eric. 2008. *The Rabbit and the Turtle.* New York: Orchard/Scholastic. ISBN 978-0-545005418. Ten Aesop's fables from Carle's previous collection appear in this redesigned edition with larger, more vibrant illustrations.

Catchpool, Michael. 2012. *The Cloud Spinner.* Illustrated by Alison Jay. New York: Knopf/Random House. ISBN 978-0-375-87011-8. A boy can spin cloth from the clouds, but a greedy king causes the clouds to disappear until his daughter helps solve the problem.

Clark, Henry. 2013. *What We Found in the Sofa and How It Saved the World.* Illustrated by Jeremy Holmes. New York: Little, Brown. ISBN 978-0-316-20666-2. Three children, with the help of a crayon, a sofa, and artificial intelligence, try to keep a dictator from Indorsia from taking over Earth.

Cooper, Susan. 2013. *The Dark Is Rising Sequence.* New York: Margaret McElderry/Simon & Schuster. ISBN 978-1-4424-1253-8. This set contains all six books about the quest of Will Stanton and his companions to keep humans free from the Dark. pb reissue.

Cooper, Susan. 2013. *Ghost Hawk.* New York: Margaret K. McElderry/Simon & Schuster. ISBN 978-1-4424-8141-1. John Wakeley, child of strict pilgrims, and Little Hawk, an East Coast Indian, are bound in a friendship that endangers both their lives.

Creech, Sharon. 2007. *The Castle Corona.* Illustrated by David Diaz. New York: HarperCollins. ISBN 978-0-06-084621-3. Two peasant children find a pouch that changes their lives as well as the lives of those who live in the Castle Corona.

David, David, and Jan Peck. 2011. *The Green Mother Goose: Saving the World One Rhyme at a Time.* New York: Sterling. ISBN 978-1-40276525-4. The authors rewrite thirty rhymes and children's songs to reflect an ecological theme.

DiCamillo, Kate. 2013. *Flora & Ulysses.* Illustrated by K. G. Campbell. Somerville, MA: Candlewick. ISBN 978-0-7636-6040-6. After a squirrel gets sucked up into a vacuum cleaner, he survives with new superhero powers. Flora tries to save his life after her mother declares she wants to get rid of him.

Divakaruni, Chitra Banerjee. 2013. *Grandma and the Great Gourd: A Bengali Folktale.* Illustrated by Susy Pilgrim Waters. New York: Neal Porter/Roaring Brook/Macmillan. ISBN 978-1-59643-378-6. Grandma escapes being eaten by three jungle animals by using her wits.

Duffy, Chris, editor. 2013. *Fairy Tale Comics: Classic Tales Told by Extraordinary Cartoonists.* New York: First Second/Macmillan. ISBN 978-1-59643-823-1. Seventeen cartoonists retell and illustrate seventeen fairy tales in comic format.

Duffy, Chris, editor. 2011. *Nursery Rhyme Comics.* New York: First Second/Macmillan. ISBN 978-1-59643-600-8. Fifty cartoonists illustrate fifty nursery rhymes as comics.

Dusíková, Maja. 2012. *Sleeping Beauty.* New York: NY: North-South Books. ISBN 978-0735840874. This familiar fairy tale is a straightforward retelling accompanied by lovely illustrations.

Emberley, Rebecca, and Ed Emberley. 2012. *The Ant and the Grasshopper.* New York: Neal Porter/Roaring Brook/Holzbrinck. ISBN 978-1-59643-493-6. The music played by Grasshopper and his band relieves Ant's weariness as she carries food back to the nest. (See also *Chicken Little* (2009), *The Red Hen* (2010), and *The Crocodile and the Scorpion* (2013), all available from the same publisher.)

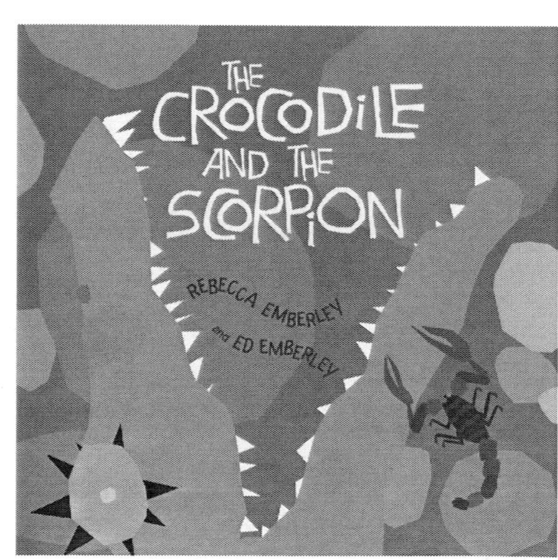

Enersen, Adele. 2013. *When My Baby Dreams of Fairy Tales*. New York: Balzer + Bray/HarperCollins. ISBN 978-0-06-207177-4. The author dresses her sleeping baby in outfits resembling characters in fairy tales.

Fleischman, Paul. 2007. *Glass Slipper, Gold Sandal: A Worldwide Cinderella*. Illustrated by Julie Paschkis. New York: Henry Holt. ISBN 978-0-8050-7953-1. In both text and illustrations, this book combines Cinderella stories from around the world into one fascinating tale.

Gauch, Patricia Lee. Summer 1994. "A Quest for the Heart of Fantasy." *The New Advocate* 7(3): 159–67. Gauch discusses the qualities of fine fantasy writing.

Gidwitz, Adam. 2010. *A Tale Dark & Grimm*. New York: Dutton/Penguin. ISBN 978-0-525-42334-8. Hansel and Gretel leave home and encounter characters, both good and evil, from eight other fairy tales as they discover their destiny.

Gidwitz, Adam. 2013. *In a Glass Grimmly*. New York: Dutton/Penguin. ISBN 978-0-525-42581-6. Jack and Jill leave their parents and encounter characters from Grimm tales as well as those of Hans Christian Andersen.

Goldman, Judy. 2013. *Whiskers, Tails & Wings: Animal Folktales from Mexico*. Illustrated by Fabricio Vanden Broeck. Watertown, MA: Charlesbridge. ISBN 978-1-60734-617-3. This collection includes tales from five different indigenous peoples of Mexico.

Gray, Luli. 2011. *Ant and Grasshopper*. Illustrated by Giuliano Ferri. New York: Margaret McElderry/Macmillan. ISBN 978-1416951407. Luli extends this fable by having the ant eventually take in and care for the starving grasshopper.

Guarnaccia, Steven. 2014. *Cinderella: A Fashionable Tale*. New York: Abrams. ISBN 978-1-419709869. Ball gowns and accessories worn by the characters in this tale are modeled on the work of famous 20th- and 21st-century fashion designers.

Guarnaccia, Steven. 2010. *Goldilocks and the Three Bears: A Tale Moderne*. New York: Abrams. ISBN 978-0-8109-8966-5. When Goldilocks enters the bears' home, she finds furnishings created by famous designers.

Guarnaccia, Steven. 2010. *The Three Little Pigs: An Architectural Tale*. New York: Abrams. ISBN 978-0-8109-8941-2. The interiors and exteriors of the three pig residences created by Guarnaccia pay homage to three famous architects.

Harrington, Janice N. 2013. *Busy-Busy Little Chick*. Illustrated by Brian Pinkney. New York: Farrar Straus Giroux. ISBN 978-0-374-34746-8. Because mama hen is too distracted to build a much-needed new home, Busy Chick does it himself.

Hartman, Rachel. 2012. *Seraphina*. New York: Random House. ISBN 978-0-375-86656-2. Seraphina, half dragon, teams up with Lucian to discover who killed the prince and avoid a new war between dragons and humans.

Healy, Christopher. 2012. *The Hero's Guide to Saving Your Kingdom*. Illustrated by Todd Harris. New York: Walden Pond Press/HarperCollins. ISBN 978-0-06-211743-4. The princes who appeared in Sleeping Beauty, Cinderella, Snow White, and Rapunzel set out to save their kingdoms and brave many dangers along the way.

Healy, Christopher. 2013. *The Hero's Guide to Storming the Castle*. Illustrated by Todd Harris. New York: Walden Pond Press/HarperCollins. ISBN 978-0-06-211845-5. The four princes set off again, along with a group of compatriots, to escape the destructive wiles of Briar Rose.

Hoberman, Mary Ann. 2010. *You Read to Me, I'll Read to You: Very Short Fables to Read Together*. Illustrated by Michael Emberley. Boston/New York: Little Brown. ISBN 978-0-316-04117-1. These thirteen fables are humorously told and enable child and adult to take turns reading.

Ibatoulline, Bagram. 2013. *The Snow Queen: A Retelling of the Fairy Tale* by Hans Christian Andersen. New York: Harper/HarperCollins. ISBN 978-0-06-220950-4. Kai and Gerda are separated when Kai is enchanted by a Snow Queen and carried away to the land of ice and snow.

Ingall, Marjorie. November 5, 2010. "When Stories Had Sharp Teeth." *The New York Times Book Review*. 26. Ingall discusses modern fantasy novels and their roots in ancient fairy tales.

Isaacs, Anne. 2010. *Dust Devil*. Illustrated by Paul O. Zelinsky. New York: Schwartz & Wade/Random House. ISBN 978-0-375-86722-4. When woods woman Angelina Longrider moves to Montana, she meets up with the bandit Backwards Bart, with hilarious results.

Isaacs, Anne. 2014. *Meanwhile, Back at the Ranch*. Illustrated by Kevin Hawkes. New York: Schwartz & Wade/Random House. ISBN 978-0-375-96745-3. The widow Tulip Jones buys a ranch in Texas, outwits 1,000 suitors, and captures the Hole in the Pants gang.

Isaacs, Anne. 2000. *Swamp Angel*. Illustrated by Paul O. Zelinsky. New York: Puffin/Penguin. ISBN 978-0140 559088. Angelica Longrider, famous Tennessee woodswoman, saves a wagon train at age twelve and defeats the great bear Thundering Tarnation.

Isadora, Rachel. 2008. *The Fisherman and His Wife*. New York: Putnam/Penguin. ISBN 978-0-39924771-2. A greedy wife asks greater and greater gifts from a magic fish until she ends up with nothing.

Isadora, Rachel. 2009. *Hansel and Gretel*. New York: Putnam/Penguin. ISBN 978-0-39925028-6. After their parents leave them in the woods, Hansel and Gretel come upon a house made of candy and encounter a witch who plans to eat them.

Isadora, Rachel. 2007. *The Princess and the Pea* New York: Putnam/Penguin. ISBN 978-0-39924611-1. A queen puts a pea under a pile of mattresses on which a young woman will spend the night to determine whether she is a real princess.

Isadora, Rachel. 2008. *Rapunzel*. New York: Putnam/Penguin. ISBN 978-0-39924772-9. Rapunzel is locked in a tower by a sorceress. When a prince enters the tower and she becomes pregnant, the sorceress blinds him.

Jolley, Dan. 2009. *Pigling: A Cinderella Story*. Illustrated by Anne Timmons. Minneapolis: Lerner. ISBN 978-1580138253. Pear Blossom's life is made miserable by her stepmother and stepsisters in this Korean version of Cinderella.

Kasbarian, Lucine. 2011. *The Greedy Sparrow*. Illustrated by Maria Zaikina. Allentown, PA: Two Lions. ISBN 978-0-76145821-0. A sparrow who starts out with a thorn in his foot ends up the same way because of his greed.

Kellogg, Steven. 2000. *Paul Bunyan*. New York: Harper Trophy/HarperCollins. ISBN 978-06-88058005. Paul Bunyan, a strong lumberjack, and his companion Blue Ox, are responsible for creating many famous geological formations.

Kimmel, Eric. 2001. *Anansi and the Magic Stick*. Illustrated by Janet Stevens. New York: Holiday House. ISBN 978-0823414437. Anansi steals a magic stick so he will not have to water his garden, but the plan backfires.

Kimmel, Eric. 2009. *Anansi's Party Time*. Illustrated by Janet Stevens. New York: Holiday House. ISBN 978-0823422418. Anansi invites Turtle to a party but plays so many tricks on him that Turtle never gets there.

Kimmel, Eric. 2007. *The Three Cabritos*. Illustrated by Stephen Gilpin. Allentown, PA: Two Lions. ISBN 978-0-761453437. Three goats fool a monster under the bridge as they head off to Mexico to play their instruments at a fiesta.

Kirby, Matthew J. 2013. *The Lost Kingdom*. New York: Scholastic Press. ISBN 978-0-545-27426-5. John Bartram and his son Billy set out with others across the American wilderness in an aeroship to seek a lost kingdom on the eve of the French and Indian War. (See also Kirby's wonderful fantasy *Icefall*, 2011, Scholastic.)

Kojo, K.P. 2011. *The Parade: A Stampede of Stories about Ananse, the Trickster Spider*. Illustrated by Karen Lilje. London: Frances Lincoln. ISBN 978-1847801630. This book contains seven Ananse tales, including one that tells why Ananse became a trickster.

Krensky, Stephen. 2007. *John Henry*. Illustrated by Mark Oldroyd. Minneapolis: Millbrook/Lerner. ISBN 1-57505-887-1. Krensky tells of the deeds of this African American hero for beginning readers.

Krishnaswami, Uma. 2013. *The Girl of the Wish Garden: A Thumbelina Story*. Illustrated by Nasrin Khosravi. Toronto: Groundwood. ISBN 978-1-55498-324-7. Lina is no bigger than a thumb, but she can provide for her own safety.

Laird, Elizabeth. 2010. *Pea Boy and Other Stories from Iran*. Illustrated by Shirin Adl. London: Frances Lincoln. ISBN 978-1-845079123. The seven tales in this collection are beautifully illustrated and reveal aspects of the Iranian culture.

Lee, H. Chuku. 2014. *Beauty and the Beast*. Illustrated by Pat Cummings. Amistad/HarperCollins. ISBN 978-0-688-14819-5. Cummings illustrates this straightforward retelling with lovely pictures inspired by West African culture.

LeGuin, Ursula. 2012. *A Wizard of Earthsea*. New York: Houghton Mifflin/Houghton Mifflin Harcourt. ISBN 978-0-547-72202-3. Ged, once known as the irresponsible Sparrow hawk, embarks on a quest to right a wrong he has set in motion. See the other five books in this wonderful cycle.

Lehr, Susan. January 9, 1991. "Fantasy: Inner journeys for today's child." *Publishing Research Quarterly* 7(3): 91–101. Lehr divides fantasy into five categories and discusses each one.

Lester, Julius. 1999. *John Henry*. Illustrated by Jerry Pinkney. New York: Puffin/Penguin. ISBN 978-014056622-2. This is a beautifully illustrated picture book version of this African American hero's heroic deeds.

Lester, Julius. 2006. *Tales of Uncle Remus*. Illustrated by Jerry Pinkney. New York: Puffin. ISBN 978-0-142407202. Lester retells forty-eight of Harris's tales updating the language.

Lin, Grace. 2012. *Starry River of the Sky*. New York: Little Brown. ISBN 978-0-316-12595-6. Rendi, a runaway from his father's home, discovers that the stories Madame Chang tells hold the key to returning the missing moon into the Starry River of the Sky.

MacDonald, Margaret Read, and Nadia Jameel Taibah. 2009. *How Many Donkeys? An Arabic Counting Tale*. Illustrated by Carol Liddiment. Park Ridge, IL: Albert Whitman. ISBN 978-0-8075-3424-3. A silly merchant counts a different number of donkeys each time, depending upon whether he is riding or walking.

Marchetta, Melina. 2010. *Finnikin of the Rock*. Somerville, MA: Candlewick. ISBN 978-0-7636-4361-4. After his kingdom is overtaken by the king's evil cousin, Finnikin, aided by Evangelin and others, embarks on a quest to free its people and restore the rightful heir to the throne.

Marshall, James Vance. 2008. *Stories from the Billagong*. Illustrated by Francis Firebrace. London: Frances Lincoln. ISBN 978-1845077044. The ten stories in this collection are taken from the pourquoi tales of the Yorta-Yorta people, an Australian aboriginal tribe.

McNeal, Tom. 2013. *Far Far Away*. New York: Knopf/Random House. ISBN 978-0-375-84972-5. The ghost of Jacob Grimm tries to save Jeremy Johnson Johnson from harm.

Medbery, Jennifer. 2012. *Co. Exist*. "Reinventing Education to Teach Creativity and Entrepreneurship." http://www.fastcoexist.com/1679771/reinventing-education-to-teach-creativity-and-entrepreneurship (accessed April 14, 2014). Medbery argues that instead of teaching students to regurgitate facts, we should be teaching them to "tinker, create, and take the initiative."

Meyer, Marissa. 2012. *Cinder*. New York: Feiwel and Friends/Macmillan. ISBN 978-0-312-64189-4. Cinder, a cyborg living in a plague-infested future world, is a mechanic who joins Prince Hal in an effort to save the world from being controlled by the Lunar queen.

Miller, Bobbi. 2009. *Davey Crockett Gets Hitched*. Illustrated by Megan Lloyd. New York: Holiday House. ISBN 978-0-8234-1837-4. Davey and Sally Ann Thunder are so impressed with each other's dancing that they decide to get married.

Miller, Bobbi. 2012. *Miss Sally Ann and the Panther*. Illustrated by Megan Lloyd. New York: Holiday House. ISBN 978-0-8234-1833-6. Sally Ann and a red-eyed panther wrestle for possession of a fur coat but eventually become friends.

Mlynowski, Sarah. 2014. *Bad Hair Day*. New York: Scholastic. ISBN 978-0-545-62728-3. Abby and Jonah fall into the tale of Rapunzel and have to untangle themselves.

Mlynowski, Sarah. 2013. *Dream On*. New York: Scholastic. ISBN 978-0-545-41571-2. Abby's and Jonah's friend Robin accompanies them into Sleeping Beauty's story where Robin pricks her finger and requires rescuing pronto.

Mlynowski, Sarah. 2012. *Fairest of All*. New York: Scholastic. ISBN 978-0-545-40330-6. Abby and Jonah enter Snow White's realm through a mirror they find in the basement and foil the wicked queen's plot to poison the princess.

Mlynowski, Sarah. 2013. *If the Shoe Fits*. New York: Scholastic. ISBN 978-0-545-41567-5. In trying to discover why they were sent into a fairy tale, Abby and Jonah find themselves in Cinderella's world where they help her become a self-reliant person.

Mlynowski, Sarah. 2013. *Sink or Swim*. New York: Scholastic. ISBN 978-0-545-41569-9. Abby and Jonah try to convince the Little Mermaid to keep her tail when they enter into her story.

Mora, Pat. 2005. *Doña Flor: A Tale about a Giant Lady with a Great Big Heart*. Illustrated by Raúl Colón. New York: Random House. ISBN 0-375-82337-9. In this tall tale, the giant Doña Flor searches for the menacing creature that seems to be threatening her village.

Morris, Jackie. 2013. *East of the Sun West of the Moon*. London: Frances Lincoln. ISBN 978-1-84780-294-1. This modern retelling of the old tale has a new twist at the end.

Naidoo, Beverley. 2011. *Aesop's Fables*. Illustrated by Piet Grobler. London: Frances Lincoln. ISBN 978-1847800077. This collection of sixteen fables is beautifully illustrated to place them in an African setting.

Nelson, Scott Reynolds, with Marc Aronson. 2007. *Ain't Nothing but a Man: My Quest to Find the Real John Henry*. Washington, DC: National Geographic Books for Children. ISBN 978-1-4263-0000-4. The author explains his methods as a historian and his use of the ballad about his subject to trace the real man.

Nolen, Jerdine. 2003. *Thunder Rose.* Illustrated by Kadir Nelson. San Diego: Harcourt. ISBN 0-15-216472-3. Thunder Rose, first free child of her African American parents, has powers to control the elements.

Opie, Iona, and Peter Opie. 1997. *The Oxford Dictionary of Nursery Rhymes.* 2nd ed. Oxford: Oxford University Press. ISBN 978-0-19860088-6. The authors present over 500 rhymes, along with illustrations and how the rhymes have changed over the years.

Osborne, Kate. 2005. *Kate and the Beanstalk.* Illustrated by Giselle Potter. New York: Aladdin/Simon & Schuster. ISBN 978-1-416-90818-0. Kate, feisty and adventurous, climbs a beanstalk, recovers stolen magical items, and kills a giant.

Osborne, Mary Pope, and Will Osborne. 2005. *Sleeping Bobby.* Illustrated by Giselle Potter. New York: Anne Schwartz/Atheneum. ISBN 978-0-689-87668-4. Prince Bobby falls asleep for 100 years under a Wise Woman's curse until an adventurous princess awakes and marries him.

Pichon, Liz. 2008. *The Three Horrid Pigs.* Wilton, CT: Tiger Tales Books. ISBN 978-1-58925-423-7. Three lazy, badly behaved pigs and a kindly wolf find a way to live together.

Pinkney, Jerry. 2000. *Aesop's Fables.* San Francisco: Chronicle Books. ISBN 978-1587170003. This beautiful collection features sixty-one familiar and lesser-known fables.

Pinkney, Jerry. 2007. *Little Red Riding Hood.* New York: Little Brown. ISBN 978-0-316-01355-0. On the way to her grandmother's, Red Riding Hood meets a wolf who later eats both the girl and her grandmother until a woodsman saves them.

Pinkney, Jerry. 2012. *Puss in Boots.* New York: Dial/Penguin. ISBN 978-0-80371642-1. By tricking a sorcerer, Puss obtains the favor of the king and enables his master to marry the princess.

Pinkney, Jerry. 2009. *The Lion & the Mouse.* Boston/New York: Little Brown. ISBN 978-0-316-01356-7. A lion lets a mouse go free and, contrary to expectations, the little mouse is able to return the favor.

Pinkney, Jerry. 2013. *The Tortoise & the Hare.* Boston/New York: Little Brown. ISBN 978-0-316-18356-7. A slow turtle manages to win a race against a fleet-footed hare.

Price, Lisa. 2012. *Starters.* New York: Delacorte/Random House. ISBN 978-0385742375. When Callie rents out her body to obtain money to care for her younger brother, she accidentally discovers that those who run the rental operation plan to destroy young people unless she can stop them. (See Price's sequel, *Enders* (2014) to discover Callie's new challenges.)

Pullman, Philip. 2012. *Fairy Tales from the Brothers Grimm: A New English Translation.* New York: Viking. ISBN 978-0670024971. This is a collection of fifty familiar and lesser-known tales, complete with commentary and sources.

Pullman, Philip. 2007. *His Dark Materials Omnibus.* New York: Knopf/Random House. ISBN 978-0-375-94722-3. All three books in this amazing series about the adventures of Lyra Belaqua are included here, with additional art and commentary by Pullman.

Randolph Caldecott's Picture Books. 2008. Edited by Susan Green. San Marino, CA: Huntington Library Press. ISBN 978-0-87328-223-0. This is a beautiful reproduction of nine of Caldecott's most popular books for children.

Ray, Jane. 2010. *Ahmed and the Feather Girl.* London: Frances Lincoln. ISBN 978-1845079888. A feathered girl hatches from an egg and is imprisoned in a circus until Ahmed frees her and is eventually rewarded by her.

Ray, Jane. 2008. *The Apple-Pip Princess.* Cambridge, MA: Candlewick. ISBN 978-0-7636-3747-7. The youngest of three princesses plants an apple pip and brings the kingdom joy after the gloom induced by her mother's death.

Santore, Charles. 2012. *Aesop's Fables.* New York: Sterling. ISBN 978-1402784125. The fables in this collection are arranged according to different animal protagonists.

Schlitz, Laura Amy. 2007. *The Bearskinner.* Illustrated by Max Grafe. Cambridge, MA: Candlewick. ISBN 978-0-7636-2730-0. A soldier must wear a rotting bear skin and not bathe or cut his hair for seven years or belong to the devil.

Schlitz, Laura Amy. 2012. *Splendors and Glooms.* Somerville, MA: Candlewick. ISBN 978-0-7636-5380-4. When Clara vanishes after a puppet performance, suspicion of kidnapping drives her and the two orphaned puppeteer assistants from London. They are soon caught in a trap by a witch with a deadly inheritance to shed before it is too late.

Schmidt, Gary D. 2012. *What Came from the Stars.* New York: Clarion/ Houghton Mifflin Harcourt. ISBN 978-0-547-61213-3. When a necklace from Valorim falls into Tommy Pepper's lunch box, he discovers a planet that is about to fall into an evil lord's hands just as his own world seems to be falling apart.

Schwartz, Corey Rosen. 2012. *The Three Ninja Pigs*. Illustrated by Dan Santat. New York: Putnam/Penguin. ISBN 978-039925514-4. Three pigs attend Ninja school to develop the skills they need to defeat the bad wolf, but only one succeeds.

Scoggins, Liz. 2010. *The Fairy Tale Book: Classic Tales from Childhood*. New York: Scholastic. ISBN 978-0545134064. This collection contains twenty stories from both Grimm and Andersen.

Sharpe, Leah Marinsky. 2009. *The Goat-Faced Girl*. Illustrated by Jane Marinsky. Boston: David R. Godine. ISBN 978-1-56792393-3. A girl who is punished for her laziness by being inflicted with a goat's head learns her lesson and becomes an industrious, independent woman.

Shaskan, Trisha Speed. 2011. *Honestly, Red Riding Hood Was Rotten! The Story of Little Red Riding Hood as Told by the Wolf.* Illustrated by Gerald Claude Guerlais. North Mankato, MN: Picture Window/Capstone. ISBN 978-1-4048-7046-8. Because Red Riding Hood and her grandmother are so vain and the wolf is so hungry, he eats them both.

Shaskan, Trisha Speed. 2011. *Seriously, Cinderella Is SO Annoying!: The Story of Cinderella as Told by the Wicked Stepmother!* Illustrated by Gerald Claude Guerlais. North Mankato, MN: Picture Window/Capstone. ISBN 978-1-4048-7048-2. The "kind" stepmother tells her side of the Cinderella story.

Shurtliff, Liesl. 2013. *Rump: The True Story of Rumpelstiltskin*. New York: Knopf/Random House. ISBN 978-0-307-97793-9. Shurtliff tells the story of Rumpelstiltskin's youth, how he came to spin straw into gold, and the vital importance of his name.

Sierra, Judy. 2000. *The Gift of the Crocodile: A Cinderella Story*. Illustrated by Reynold Ruffins. New York: Simon & Schuster Books for Young Readers. ISBN 978-0-68982188-2. This version of Cinderella is from the Spice Islands.

Singer, Marilyn. 2013. *Follow Follow: A Book of Reverso Poems*. New York: Dial/Penguin. ISBN 978-0-803703769-3. This collection of poems is based on fairy tales and are mirror images of themselves, reading from top to bottom or bottom to top.

Singer, Marilyn. 2010. *Mirror Mirror: A Book of Reversible Verse*. Illustrated by Josee Massee. New York: Dutton/Penguin. ISBN 978-0525479017. This collection of poems is based on fairy tales and are mirror images of themselves, reading from top to bottom or bottom to top.

Souhami, Jessica. 2013. *Foxy*. London: Frances Lincoln. ISBN 978-1-84780-218-7. A fox tricks everyone he meets until he is finally tricked himself.

Stampler, Ann Redisch. 2012. *The Wooden Sword: A Jewish Folktale from Afghanistan*. Illustrated by Carol Liddiment. Park Ridge, IL: Albert Whitman. ISBN 978-0-8075-9201-4. An Afghani shah tests a shoemaker's bright outlook by giving him several challenges the man overcomes through perseverance and wit.

Stewig, John Warren. 2013. *Nobody Asked the Pea*. Illustrated by Cornelius Van Wright. New York: Holiday House. ISBN 978-0-8234-2224-1. In this fractured retelling of "The Princess and the Pea," ten characters express their opinions in a series of monologues.

Stiefvater, Maggie. 2011. *The Scorpio Races*. New York: Scholastic. ISBN 978-0-545-22490-1. Sean competes against Puck, the first girl to ever ride in the dangerous Scorpio Races on the island of Thisby.

Tarnowska, Wafa. 2010. *The Arabian Nights*. Illustrated by Carole Henaff. Cambridge, MA: Barefoot Books. ISBN 978-1-84686568-8. pb. Eight tales comprise this collection translated from a 14th-century Syrian manuscript and beautifully illustrated.

Teague, Mark. 2013. *The Three Little Pigs and the Somewhat Bad Wolf.* New York: Orchard/Scholastic. ISBN 978-0439915014. Three pigs who have been ousted from their farm have dealings with a wolf who turns out to be nicer than expected.

Thomson, Sarah L. 2012. *Cinderella*. Illustrated by Nicoletta Ceccoli. Allentown, PA: Two Lions. ISBN 978-0761461708. This retelling is set in the era of King Louis XIV, with its elaborate costumes and furnishings.

Tolkien, J.R.R. 2012. Rev. ed. *The Hobbit or There and Back Again*. New York: Del Rey/Random House. ISBN 978-0-345-53483-5. Bilbo Baggins, a hobbit, helps a band of dwarves in their quest to recover lost treasure and encounters many obstacles on the journey.

Tolkien, J.R.R. n.d. *Readings*. "On Fairy Stories." http://brainstorm-services.com/wcu-2004/fairystories-tolkien.pdf (accessed April 14, 2014). This is a pdf version of an important essay in which Tolkien defines fairy stories, traces their origins, and states their importance.

Tulien, Sean Hamman. 2010. *Pecos Bill, Colossal Cowboy: The Graphic Novel*. North Mankato, MN: Stone Arch Books/Capstone. ISBN 978-1-43421896-4. Pecos Bill's extraordinary exploits are told in graphic novel format.

Ursu, Anne. 2013. *Breadcrumbs*. Illustrated by Erin McGuire. New York: Walden Pond/HarperCollins. ISBN 978-0-08-201505-1. pb. When a witch dressed in white takes her best friend away, Hazel makes the dangerous journey to the land of cold to rescue him.

Ursu, Anne. 2013. *The Real Boy*. Illustrated by Erin McGuire. New York: Walden Pond/HarperCollins. ISBN 978-0-06-201507-5. A magician's hand and a healer's apprentice, though possessing no magic themselves, face danger as they try to save their world and the children of the city from destruction.

Vande Velde, Vivian. 2013. *Frogged*. New York: Houghton Mifflin Harcourt. ISBN 978-0-547-94215-5. When Princess Imogene kisses a frog who claimed to be an enchanted prince, she turns into a frog herself and has to find a way to become human again.

Weulersse, Odile. 2013. *Nasreddine*. Illustrated by Rébecca Dautremer. Grand Rapids, MI: Eerdsmans. ISBN 978-0-8028-5416-2. After being criticized several times by onlookers, Nasreddine learns that he must trust his own judgment.

Wiesner, David. 2001. *The Three Pigs*. New York: Clarion/Houghton Mifflin. ISBN 978-0-618-00701-1. When the wolf huffs and puffs, he blows the pigs right out of the illustrations and into the margins where they engage in adventures of their own.

Willems, Mo. 2013. *Goldilocks and the Three Dinosaurs*. New York: Balzer + Bray/HarperCollins. ISBN 978-0-06-210418-2. Dinosaurs ready their home to entice an "innocent little succulent child" visitor.

Wrede, Patricia C. 1994, 1993. "The Raw Material," in *Facts about Fantasy*. New York: Harcourt Brace & Company/Jane Yolen Books. In this small pamphlet, fourteen authors talk about the importance of fantasy literature. Wrede's article discusses the roots of modern fantasy.

Yolen, Jane. 2000. *Touch Magic: Fantasy, Faerie & Folklore in the Literature of Childhood*. Little Rock, AR: August House. In this classic, Yolen, a writer of fantasy herself, offers essays on the importance of fantasy and its various aspects.

Yolen, Jane, and Heidi E. Y. Stemple. 2009. *Fairy Tale Feasts: A Literary Cookbook for Young Readers and Eaters*. Illustrated by Phillipe Béha. Northampton, MA: Crocodile Books/Interlink Publishing Group. ISBN 978-1-56656-643-8. Twenty folk and fairy tales are accompanied by appropriate recipes.

Yolen, Jane, and Rebecca Kai Dotlich. 2013. *Grumbles from the Forest: Fairy-Tale Voices with a Twist*. Illustrated by Matt Mahurin. Honesdale, PA: Wordsong/Highlights. ISBN 978-1-59078-867-7. Two poems are written about each of fifteen fairy tales, each poem presenting a point of view that gives the tale a new twist.

Selective Bibliography of Mother Goose Rhymes

Engelbreit, Mary. 2008. *Mary Engelbreit's Mother Goose Book and CD*. New York: HarperCollins. ISBN 978-0-06-143153-1. One hundred rhymes are beautifully illustrated and accompanied by a CD.

Long, Sylvia. 1999. *Sylvia Long's Mother Goose*. San Francisco: Chronicle. ISBN 978-0-81182088-2. Long's intention with this book was to make it unique, and she has done so not only by including lesser-known rhymes, but also by providing surprising twists through her illustrations. In addition, each illustration has something in it that connects it to the illustration to follow—a good visual literacy practice.

Mathers, Petra. 2012. *The McElderry Book of Mother Goose: Revered and Rare Rhymes*. New York: McElderry/Macmillan. ISBN 978-06-8985605-1. The fifty-seven rhymes are beautifully illustrated and include familiar as well as lesser-known ones. An author's note contains some information about the real-life situations that inspired the rhymes.

Opie, Iona. 2007. *Mother Goose's Little Treasures*. Illustrated by Rosemary Wells. Cambridge, MA: Candlewick. ISBN 978-0-763636555. This book contains twenty-two less familiar rhymes.

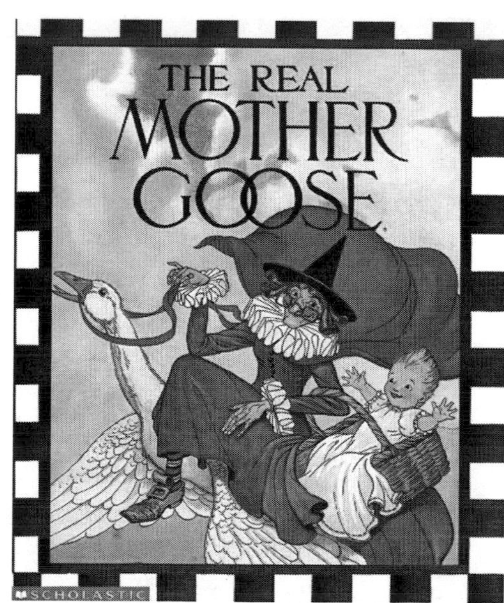

Thorpe, James (Introduction). 2006. *Kate Greenaway's Mother Goose*. Illustrated by Kate Greenaway. San Marino, CA: Huntington Library Press. ISBN 978-0873282161. Kate Greenaway was one of the most popular Victorian illustrators in England. Here her 1881 illustrations of many Mother Goose rhymes are beautifully reproduced.

Wright, Blanche Fisher. 2013. *Mother Goose Nursery Rhymes*. New York: Fall River/Sterling. ISBN 978-1-454 909804. Beautiful illustrations accompany this collection of favorite rhymes.

Wright, Blanche Fisher. 1994. *The Real Mother Goose*. New York: Cartwheel/Scholastic. ISBN 978-0-59022517-5. This classic contains over 200 rhymes, illustrated in a charming old-fashioned style. A must-have.

Selective Bibliography of Cinderella Stories from around the World

Climo, Shirley. 2000. *The Irish Cinderlad*. Illustrated by Loretta Krupinski. New York: Harper-Collins. ISBN 978-0064435772. pb reprint.

Climo, Shirley. 2001. *The Persian Cinderella*. Illustrated by Robert Florczak. New York: HarperCollins. ISBN 978-006443853-7. pb reprint.

dePaola, Tomie. 2004. *Adelita: A Mexican Cinderella Story*. New York: Puffin/Penguin. ISBN 978-0142401873. pb reprint.

Hickox, Rebecca. 1999. *The Golden Sandal: A Middle Eastern Cinderella Story*. Illustrated by Will Hillenbrand. New York: Holiday House. ISBN 978-0-82341513-7. pb

Jolley, Dan. 2009. *Pigling: A Cinderella Story*. Illustrated by Anne Timmons. Minneapolis: Lerner. ISBN 13: 978-0-7613-4647-0.

Lowell, Susan. 2000. *Cindy Ellen: A Wild Western Cinderella*. Illustrated by Jane Manning. New York: Harper-Collins. ISBN 978-0-06-027446-7.

Manna, Anthony L., and Soula Mitakidou. 2011. *The Orphan: A Cinderella Story from Greece*. Illustrated by Giselle Potter. New York: Schwartz & Wade/Random House. ISBN 978-0-375-98500-3.

Quoc, Minh. 2006. *Tam and Cam: The Ancient Vietnamese Cinderella Story*. Illustrated by Mai Long. Manhattan Beach, CA: East West Discovery Press. ISBN 978-0970165442. bilingual.

San Souci, Robert D. 2002. *Cendrillon: A Caribbean Cinderella Story*. Illustrated by Brian Pinkney. New York: Aladdin/Simon & Schuster. ISBN 978-0689848889. pb

San Souci, Robert D. 2000. *Little Gold Star: A Spanish American Cinderella Tale*. Illustrated by Sergio Martinez. New York: HarperCollins. ISBN 978-0-688147808.

San Souci, Robert D. 2010. *Sootface: An Ojibwa Cinderella Story*. Illustrated by Daniel San Souci. Logan, IA: Perfection Learning. ISBN 978-0780772335.

Schroeder, Alan. 2000. *Smoky Mountain Rose: An Appalachian Cinderella*. Illustrated by Brad Sneed. New York: Puffin/Penguin. ISBN 978-0140566734. pb reprint.

Sierra, Judy. 2000. *The Gift of the Crocodile: A Cinderella Story*. Illustrated by Reynold Ruffins. New York: Simon & Schuster. ISBN 978-0689821882.

Steptoe, John. 2008. *Mufaro's Beautiful Daughters: An African Tale*. New York: Puffin/Penguin. ISBN 978-014 0559460. pb

A Selective Bibliography of Fantasy and Science Fiction Novels That Weave Threads of Myths and Legends

Armstrong, K. L., and M. A. Marr. 2014. *Odin's Ravens*. New York: Little Brown. ISBN 978-0-316-20498-9. Thirteen-year-old Matt Thorsen, a modern day descendant of the Norse god Thor, is chosen to represent Thor in an epic battle to prevent the apocalypse.

Barrett, Tracy. 2010. *King of Ithaka*. New York: Henry Holt. ISBN 978-0-80508969-1. In this young adult (YA) retelling of the Odyssey from the point of view of Telemachos, Odysseus's teenage son, the boy sets out to find the father he has never met before the people of the small island of Ithaka demand his mother remarry so they will have a new king.

Henrichs, Wendy. 2011. *I am Tama, Lucky Cat: A Japanese Legend*. Illustrated by Yoshiko Jaeggi. Atlanta: Peachtree. ISBN 978-1-56145589-8. Based on the Lucky Cat legend from Japan's Edo period, this is the story of Tama, a stray cat who comes to live with a poor monk and ends up saving the life of a samurai warlord.

Holub, Joan, and Suzanne Williams. 2010–2013. *The Goddess Girls Series*. New York: Aladdin/Simon & Schuster. At this writing there are about 13 book including titles such as *Artemis the Brave, Pandora the Curious, Athena the Brain, Cassandra the Lucky*, and others, in this series for younger readers. Preteen goddesses or mortals with special powers attend Mount Olympus Academy and are involved in adventures with various gods. This series will introduce students to the Greek gods, or prompt them to know more about the gods after this introductory taste.

Holub, Joan, and Suzanne Williams. 2012–2014. *Heroes in Training Series*. New York: Aladdin/Simon & Schuster. In this series, consisting of seven titles at this writing, younger readers meet the Greek gods as youngsters and follow their heroic adventures. Titles include *Poseidon and the Sea of Fury* (2012); *Zeus and the Thunderbolt of Doom* (2012); *Hades and the Helm of Darkness* (2013); *Hyperion and the Great Balls of Fire* (2013); *Tryphon and the Winds of Destruction* (2013); and *Apollo and the Battle of the Birds* (2014).

Joyce, William. 2011. *The Man in the Moon*. New York: Atheneum/Simon & Schuster. ISBN 978-1442430419. Taking on the legends of those guardians of childhood like the Man in the Moon and the Sandman, Joyce begins with this one in which Mim (Man in the Moon), inspired by his old friend Nightlight, goes against Pitch, King of Nightmares, to guard the dreams of children. In *The Sandman: The Story of Sanderson Mansnoozie* (2012, ISBN 978-1442430426), we learn the origins of The Sandman, who becomes Mim's backup in protecting the dreams of children when the moon is now shining brightly. These picture books eventually spawned the Guardians, a series of novels featuring these childhood guardians and their fight against evil.

McCaughrean, Geraldine. 2003. *Gilgamesh the Hero*. Illustrated by David Parkins. Grand Rapids, MI: Eerdmans. ISBN 0-8028-5262-9. When his friend Enkidu dies, Gilgamesch searches the world for the gift of immortality only to find at home, the real secret to an immortal life.

McCaughrean, Geraldine. 2005. *Hercules*. Chicago: Cricket. ISBN 0-8126-2737-7. Hercules has killed his family in a drunken stupor and is enslaved by a cousin as punishment. For twelve years he must perform impossible tasks.

McCaughrean, Geraldine. 2004. *Odysseus*. Chicago: Cricket. ISBN 0-8126-2721-0. McCaughrean recounts Odysseus's epic journey from Troy to his wife, Penelope, in Ithaca, and his many dangerous adventures en route as he tries to appease the god Poseidon.

McCaughrean, Geraldine. 2004. *Perseus*. Chicago: Cricket. ISBN 0-8126-2735-0. Perseus undertakes a quest to kill the hideous Medusa and save his mother from a bad marriage.

McCaughrean, Geraldine. 2005. *Theseus*. Chicago: Cricket. ISBN 0-8126-2739-3. Theseus travels to his father to claim his right to the throne, and conquers many gruesome creatures along the way. But when he must appease the gods after causing a plague in Athens, he must perform a horrible deed.

Meyer, Carolyn. 2013. *Beauty's Daughter: The Story of Hermione and Helen of Troy*. Boston: Houghton Mifflin Harcourt. ISBN 978-0-544-10862-2. When Helen runs off to Troy with Prince Paris, her husband, King Menelaus, starts the Trojan War, leaving their daughter, Hermione, alone to witness the deaths of heroes on both sides. Historical notes.

Napoli, Donna Jo. 2011. *Treasury of Greek Mythology: Classic Stories of Gods, Goddesses, Heroes & Monsters*. Illustrated by Christina Balit. Washington, DC: National Geographic Children's Books. ISBN 978-1426308444. While this is not a novel, it is an essential collection of wonderfully written and illustrated stories, each enhanced with sidebars of information about the culture, geography, and history involved in the tale.

O'Connor, George. 2013. *Aphrodite Goddess of Love*. New York: First Second. ISBN 978-1-596-43947-4. This is the story of Aphrodite's dramatic birth and her role in the Trojan War.

O'Connor, George. 2013. *Poseidon Earth Shaker*. New York: First Second. ISBN 978-1-596-43738-8. Many stories of the Olympian gods are folded into this first person account of how Poseidon became god of the sea. An Olympian family tree is included.

Riordan, Rick. 2005. *The Lightning Thief*. New York: Hyperion. ISBN 978-0786856299. In this first of Percy Jackson's adventures, he discovers he is a demigod, son of Poseidon, and he is sent on a quest to the underworld to prevent a war among the gods of Olympus. Highly popular, this novel was followed by four others: *The Sea of Monsters, The Titan's Curse, The Battle of the Labyrinth,* and *The Last Olympians*. All five books are available in a boxed set (2010) from Hyperion and as individual titles.

Riordan, Rick. 2011. *The Red Pyramid*. New York: Hyperion. ISBN 978-1423113454. Two siblings, Carter and Sadie, have been separated since their mother's death but are reunited in London where they accompany their father to the British Museum. There the Rosetta Stone is destroyed, their father disappears, powerful Egyptian gods are unleashed. In trying to rescue their father, Carter and Sadie discover their powers as descendants of the pharaohs and become involved in trying to stop ancient forces from taking over the world. The *Throne of Fire* (2011) and *The Serpent's Shadow* (2012) continue the saga.

4

Nonfiction: Igniting Curiosity, Inquiry, and Divergent Thinking

Under the Common Core, a report will not be three or five key facts, it will be facts plus sources that yield more than one point of view, or a comparison of approaches, or what one source presents against another. "Good for reports" (a phrase commonly used in reviews of non-fiction texts) is now understood to mean "good for thinking, questioning, and examining."

—Marc Aronson (2013)

In an interview with Adam Bryant of the *New York Times* (2013), Daniel T. Hendrix, president and CEO of Interface, Inc., a designer and maker of carpet tile, described the kind of person he wants to hire: "I look for that person who thinks on a different level . . . when you find that person, and I've found a few in my career, they are gold. They are the people whom you really want to keep and build your company around. They see implications, they see around corners, they see other possibilities. They'll come up with a different way to think about the problem, a different solution to the problem" (2). Of course, education is about much more than getting a job, but since they will eventually need to earn a living, and since we hope they will make a difference in their chosen fields, we have to ask ourselves, "What can we do in our classrooms now to ensure that our students grow into the kind of thinkers people like Hendrix are anxious to hire?" One answer is to ground them in excellent nonfiction texts, texts that, as Aronson says, lead students to "thinking, questioning, and examining"; texts that demonstrate the out-of-the-box thought and behavior we strive to make part of our students' daily lives. And lest we need any further motivation to share nonfiction with our students, let us consider that the Common Core State Standards require that up to 50 percent of reading in elementary schools, 55 percent in middle schools, and 70 percent in high schools be nonfiction. The following sections of this chapter illustrate the specific characteristics of the genre that make reading nonfiction, along with careful analysis and related activities, a powerful way to develop divergent thinkers. We begin with the authors of these nonfiction works.

Nonfiction Writers Demonstrate Curiosity about and Passion for Their Subject

When we read excellent nonfiction written for young people, it becomes evident early on that the authors of these works really care about their topic. We know this because they tell us so, describing an itch that began, in many cases, even in childhood and has grown more intense with the passing of years. We know this because they tell us about the years they've spent studying and observing—study that often involves travel to difficult locations and living under adverse conditions for extended periods of time; researching written, online, and media sources; and consulting with experts in the field. We know this, most especially, because we can sense their passion in their writing. It's as if they want every reader to fall in love with the subject just as they have.

Why is it important for young people to be exposed to such passionate inquiry? Because it models the kind of investigation we want students to undertake as we explore various units of study with them. What knowledge would they gain, what contributions could they make, if they approached each subject with interest strong enough to sustain them over weeks of research and writing, even though it may sometimes lead to dead ends; with curiosity strong enough to prompt them to ask difficult questions, to "see around corners," rather than cut corners, to uncover even the least known facts; and with passion strong enough to prompt them to keep going even when no solution is readily within reach? The following writers are fine models for this kind of intense inquiry.

HP Newquist describes himself as a "monster enthusiast" (Acknowledgements), and the back flap of his book, *Here There Be Monsters: The Legendary Kraken and the Giant Squid* (2010) states that he "traveled all the way to Australia to view a frozen giant squid and then handled architeuthis arms at Yale University" in the process of studying these giants of the sea. The author talks about researchers who have been studying giant squids over several decades and how they helped him achieve a greater understanding of these elusive creatures. He talks about photographs taken by a scientist at the National Science Museum in Tokyo and how Eric Lazo-Wasem of the Peabody Museum at Yale University walked him through Yale's giant squid history and allowed him to touch actual specimens. He thanks the staffs of the American Museum of Natural History in New York, the Te Papa museum in New Zealand, the Melbourne Aquarium, and the Smithsonian Institution for their help. Just reading his book is clear evidence that Newquist is enthralled by his subject. "Imagine you are on {a ship}," he writes. All is quiet, and then an eye "rise[s] up from the rippling sea. It is ghostly and round, and it gets brighter as it nears the water's surface." He then brings the eye closer and describes the reader's first view of the beast's tentacles on this imaginary voyage: "You look down and see a long dark tentacle reach out of the water and feel its way across the deck" (1–2). Finally, the tentacle grabs the poor reader's foot, and he is saved only by the quick action of fellow sailors. Surely, Newquist wants readers to become as wrapped in the wonder and intrigue surrounding the giant squid as he is, so enthralled that he or she will eagerly peruse the many references and sources of additional information he provides at the conclusion of his riveting book.

Chris Demarest witnessed his father's burial in Arlington National Cemetery. Some years later, he became an artist for the U.S. Coast Guard and documented a Coast Guard burial at Arlington. Little wonder, then, that his book, *Arlington: The Story of Our Nation's Cemetery* (2010), is a fulfillment of his long-time desire "to do a book on this special place" (Author's Note). Demarest writes about the 200-year history of the cemetery; the famous heroes buried there; the guarding of the Tomb of the Unknowns; and the several ceremonies that take place on holidays honoring those who died for their country. The author concludes,

> Each day at Arlington fills the senses. From the distant noise of mowers and trimmers to the soft clip-clop of horses pulling caissons; from the smell of blossoms in spring to fallen leaves in the fall; from the sharp report of rifle and cannon volleys to the heart-stopping sound of taps.

Reading his words, it is not hard to determine that this sacred ground is a very special place for the author, a place he is passionate about.

Hudson Talbott's *River of Dreams* (2009) is a love song to New York's Hudson River. He begins,

> When I was growing up in Kentucky, I used to dream about New York, the great city on the river that bore my name—Hudson . . . At night I would end my prayers with "God bless Mommy and Daddy, may I please have a horse and go to New York? Amen." It was a place of wonder and possibilities. A magnet for dreamers like me.

But the magnet's power actually came from the river. Hudson's book is more than just a history of the river and its discovery, though. He tells readers about all the river has given: transportation, ice in the days before refrigeration, trade, fish, cement for buildings, inspiration for stories, and paintings. But then, he writes, "New York didn't seem to need the river anymore, except as a sewer." Companies began dumping their waste into the river, the fish died, and the fishing industry collapsed until Pete Seeger and others began agitating for a clean-up effort. Talbott's song ends,

> I live in the Hudson Valley now, grateful to all those who came before me, following their dreams to this river, building this nation, sharing its beauty, securing its future. It's now my turn to help in keeping the river of dreams flowing, for all those dreamers yet to come.

Passion? Oh, yes!

Phillip Hoose is a conservationist who has worked for the Nature Conservancy since 1977. So of course, he cares deeply about the environmental health of our planet and the preservation of the creatures that inhabit it. In *Moonbird* (2012) he tells how he followed the year-long migration of the very endangered rufa, beginning in Argentina, to Las Grutas on San Antonio Bay, and on to Reeds Beach,

Delaware Bay, and participated in efforts to save it. "To become extinct is the greatest tragedy in all nature. Extinction means that all the members of an entire genetic family are dead and gone, forever" (107), he writes. So in his book, Hoose tells the rufa's story with great feeling, almost as if to say, "See how wonderful this tiny creature is. How can we possibly, possibly bear to see it disappear?" To give the story power, he tells it by focusing on a single rufa known as B95, the number on the band he wears. "Meet B95 . . . Weighing a mere four ounces, he's flown more than 325,000 miles in his life—the distance to the moon and nearly halfway back" (3). Hoose describes how changes in the bird's migratory route and breeding grounds have led to greatly diminished numbers and profiles individuals who are working to bring those numbers back. One such person is Mike Hudson, who fell in love with birds at age six and who founded the Friends of the Red Knot (another name for the rufa) at age ten, testifying at hearings and getting legislation passed to protect the birds. He ends with a section in which he suggests things readers can do to help shore birds. After reading such an impassioned account, how can we not act?

Ellen Bryan Obed grew up on a farm in Waterville, Maine, and her brief memoir, *Twelve Kinds of Ice* (2012), is a delicious celebration of ice in all its forms—ice that played a central role in family fun throughout the long Maine winters of her youth. There's the anticipation of that fun with the discovery of thin and then thicker ice forming in sheep pails in fall; faces pressed against school bus windows, eager to announce the appearance of ice across the fields; skating along stream ice and then black ice on Great Pond; and finally, the family's own ice pond, formed where their summer garden once stood, the product of many ice-making sessions. It had "lights and music; it had stands; it had schedules; it had hockey games and an ice show . . . it had just about everything" (26). And when only grainy last ice was all that remained, there was always the dream ice of sleep, where "we could skate anywhere we wanted—down roads, in and out of yards, and over the tops of tress. We could do any jump we pleased without practicing" (60), until that first thin ice formed once again on the surfaces of the sheep pails. Students writing personal narratives and memoir pieces could never hope for a more glorious model than this.

Enjoy some or all of these books, or any others you feel are wonderfully written, with students. (See also chapter 5 in Saccardi, *Books that Teach Kids to Write*, 2011.) They make wonderful read-aloud choices and are also interesting enough to hold students' attention on their own. Talk about the ways in which the authors convince readers that their subject is important, interesting, or exciting. Compare the authors' techniques over several books and generate a list of examples as a class. Save the list for future reference. Then:

1. Provide time for students to free-write in order to get in touch with an everyday activity or a local place that means a great deal to them. Perhaps it's a sport, a volunteer activity, playing an instrument, a hobby, time with a friend, a quiet place in a park or other locale. Why is it special? What are some things that come to mind when they think of this special place or activity?
2. Ask students to figure out a way to convince the rest of the class how special this place or activity is. They may wish to create a slide show of pictures with accompanying text and/or music; write a poem; write a convincing piece of prose. Consulting the list of techniques they have generated may help inspire their work.

3. After students have had several days to complete their task, bring them together to share their work, either in groups if time is short, or before the entire class.
4. Talk about the things that made the students' presentations convincing. Add their techniques to the previously generated list.

Why spend time on such a lengthy activity when it may have very little to do with a science or social studies unit in the curriculum? Because students need to get in touch with what it is like to feel strongly about something and try to convince others to appreciate it as well. Later, when the class is busily engaged in the study of a topic, hopefully one the class agrees is interesting—or one that at least provides opportunities for individual students to investigate aspects of the topic that interest them—they will engage in real research instead of opting for an easy way out, and they will try to present their information in an engaging and interesting way. Francisco D'Souza, CEO of the information technology company Cognizant, sums it up. When asked by Adam Bryant of *The New York Times* about his hiring practices, D'Souza said, "I'm looking for passion. The person I'm hiring needs to have passion for what they're doing, and they need to understand where that passion comes from. They need to be in touch with that" (2013).

Everything's Just Fine . . . or Is It? (Taken from Jacket Flap, Wooldridge, 2011)

What would our 21st-century lives be like if everyone remained content with the status quo? We might still be scrubbing clothes on rocks or washboards, performing surgery without anesthesia, taking a horse and buggy to the store, and so on. But divergent thinkers, as stated in the Introduction, have the ability to escape entrenchment. They see a need and figure out new ways to answer it; see what already exists and see ways to improve it; they make connections that result in new creations. An excellent book that will get students, even younger ones, thinking about alternatives is Connie Nordhielm Wooldridge's *Just Fine the Way They Are* (2011), a sweeping 200-year history of transportation improvements, told in a series of appealing vignettes pitting those who are against change with those who see new and better ways of moving people from place to place. It sets the stage for the movers and shakers we will meet in the books that follow. In 1805, a tavern keeper was happy with the dirt road that ran past his establishment. Wagon drivers who got stuck in the mud on rainy nights stayed at his inn overnight and dug out the next day. But Congress authorized the building of the National Road anyway. Folks thought that road was just fine, so why would there be a need for a railroad? But transportation continued to evolve with the Baltimore and Ohio, the bicycle, Henry Ford's motor car, and eventually an Interstate Highway. Everyone was finally happy with all this progress, right? Well, no, there were naysayers who complained "there might be an end to how much oil can be pulled out of the earth to make into gasoline" and "cars are dirtying up the breathing air." Disquieting consequences, surely—but insurmountable crises? Maybe not, as the surprising ending of the book hints.

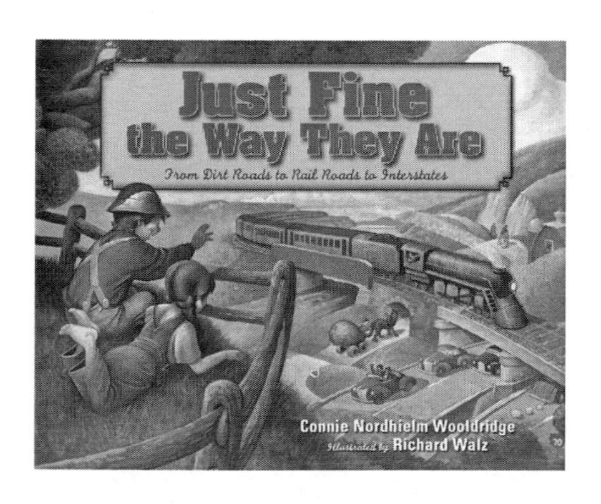

Courageous Innovators Transform Obstacles into Action

Problems such as those resulting from advances in modes of transportation discussed in Wooldridge's book are difficult enough to solve. But what about obstacles people face just because of who they are or their physical limitations? They can't change the color of their skin or their gender—and most would not want to anyway—so what are they to do? It would be tempting for them simply to follow the prevailing laws or societal norms, or to allow their physical challenges to relegate them into the background. But the courageous people students will meet in the stories that follow, despite tremendous odds, did just the opposite. In their "willingness to take risks" and their "ability to escape entrenchment and consider things in new ways" (see Characteristics of Divergent Thinkers, Introduction, p. xiii), they not only lived their own lives with courage, they made the lives of others better as well. They are the heroes about whom T. A. Barron (2002) speaks in *The Hero's Trail*: those "who, faced with a tough challenge, reach[ed] down inside and find[s] the courage, strength, and wisdom to triumph" (3). To avoid interrupting the flow of books discussed in each paragraph included in this section, relevant activities follow at the end.

People met obstacles and discrimination because of the color of their skin even before the birth of the United States as settlers claimed Native American lands and the government enacted laws that treated them unfairly. Two picture book biographies of Indian women, Sarah Winnemucca, a Paiute born in Nevada in 1844 (Ray, 2012, *Paiute Princess*) and Betty Mae Jumper, a Seminole born in 1923 (Annino, 2010, *She Sang Promise*) examine how, although both women suffered prejudice by whites and even their own tribes, they were able to make huge improvements in the lives of their people. Sarah lived during the period of westward expansion when thirst for native lands was at its peak. Although the Paiutes were the victims of broken government promises, wars, and constant resettlement, Sarah was educated for a time at the Academy of Notre Dame until parents complained about "dirty savages" attending the school and she and her sister had to leave. But her ability to speak and read and write English became invaluable later as she wrote letters of protest denouncing corrupt Indian agents and gave speeches across the country arousing public sympathy for the plight of Native Americans. In 1885, she founded the Peabody Institute for Paiute children. Ray's book contains quotes from her subject's original writings and extensive back matter. Annino's biography of Jumper uses the metaphor of song, songs through which she learned the legends and stories of her people; the song of her healing as she returns to her people after studying nursing at the Kiowa Teaching Hospital; and astoundingly, the song of her powerful leadership voice as she's elected the first female tribal leader in Seminole government—elected by a people that once wanted to throw her into the swamp because her father was white!

Students learn a great deal about the history of slavery in the United States, and there are many fictional works that hone in on the physical and emotional suffering endured not only by the slaves themselves but by the entire nation—a toll that has consequences even now. But there are nonfiction accounts of those whose courage even at the risk of their lives brought freedom to some and equal treatment under new laws for millions. Students may be aware of Harriet Tubman's trips to the South, even after she won her own freedom, to lead other slaves to safety. However, they might not know about the other accomplishments of this remarkable woman. In his biography for older students, *Harriet Tubman and the Underground Railroad* (2013), David A. Adler includes chapters about Tubman's work as a nurse and spy for the Union army during the Civil War, and how she brought hundreds of newly freed slaves behind Union lines for food, clothing, and shelter. Even after the war, she was active in helping needy African Americans and became involved in the women's suffrage movement. In one of her speeches, after recounting her work on the Underground Railroad and during the Civil War she asked, "If those deeds do not place woman as man's equal, what do?" This and the many other well-documented quotes directly from Tubman and those who knew her make this an especially enjoyable biography. Andrea Davis Pinkney's stunning collective biography, *Hand in Hand* (2012) features ten African American men presented in chronological order, beginning with Benjamin Banneker who was born in 1731 during the colonial period and ending with Barack Obama. All of them faced hardships and prejudice, and all of them broke barriers. Among those included in the book, Martin Luther King Jr., Malcolm X, Booker T. Washington, Jackie Robinson, and Barack Obama, will probably be familiar to students. But they might not know Benjamin Banneker who wrote to and received a letter from Thomas Jefferson, became an astronomer, and published yearly almanacs; or Frederick Douglass, who escaped slavery by fleeing North dressed as a sailor and became a powerful orator, even traveling to England and Ireland to press for emancipation despite the risk of recapture his fame might bring. It is likely they may not have heard of A. Philip Randolph who engaged in a dangerous twelve-year fight to obtain the right to unionize and to receive just wages and working conditions for African American railroad porters, even though "going up against Pullman was like hurling train-track pebbles at a locomotive" (97). This unique and beautifully written book begins each biography with a moving poem that encapsulates the person's achievements as well as a beautiful full-page portrait. The book concludes with a timeline and a bibliography of print and DVD resources. Whether they meet these men first the first time or after many exposures, readers will find new information about each and become engrossed in Pinkney's marvelous storytelling style. While Pinkney's book presents African American men of great courage, Cynthia Levinson's *We've Got a Job: The 1963 Birmingham Children's March* (2012), demonstrates indefatigable courage among the young.

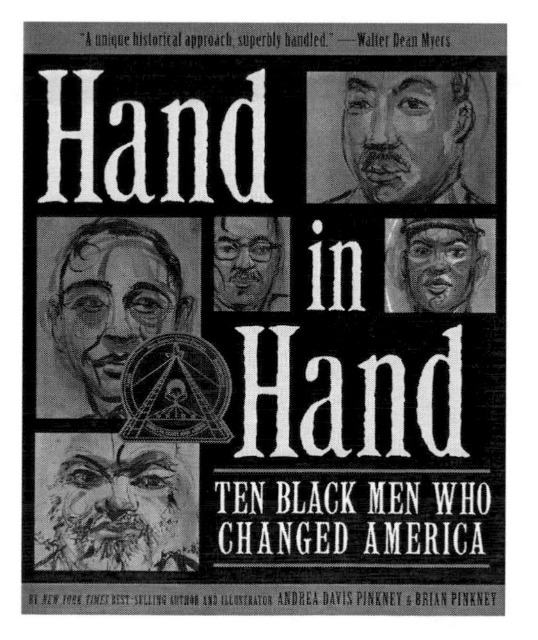

Demonstrations and sit-ins in other Southern cities had resulted in desegregated buses and lunch counters, but "despite seven years of boycotts, protests,

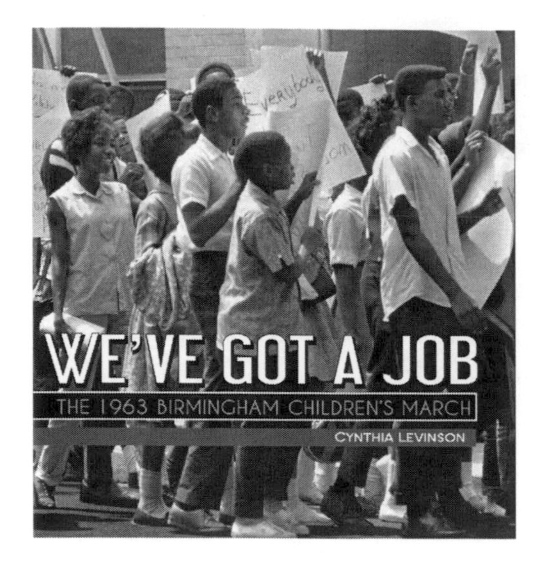

lawsuits, and sit-ins . . . Birmingham's blacks remained dismally segregated from the city's whites" (11). Finally, Martin Luther King Jr. initiated "Project Confrontation," calling on the African American community to go to places forbidden to them, get arrested and fill the Birmingham jails to overflowing. When few adults took up the challenge, young people "began to heed the call" (59). Thousands of young black students left their schools in the spring of 1963 to participate in marches and protests to end segregation. Among them were Audrey Faye Hendricks, who at age nine told her parents, "I want to go to jail" (2), Washington Booker III, James W. Steward, and Arnetta Streeter. The story of the famous Birmingham marches, the attacks by police dogs, the fire hosing, the arrests, is told through their eyes in this awe-inspiring book. It is filled with period photos, extensive quotes and sources, and a bibliography of additional materials for more information. (See also Elizabeth Partridge's *Marching for Freedom*, 2009, which recounts young people's five-day march from Selma to Montgomery that led to the passage of the Voting Rights Act in 1965.) Add works of fiction, which can provide rich insight and context, to a study of this historical period. A powerful novel about the Freedom Summer of 1964 during which buses carried young people from the North to register African Americans to vote in Mississippi is Don Mitchell's *The Freedom Summer Murders* (2014). It is about three young men, two white and one black, who were on one of those buses, disappeared, and were found murdered over a month later. Pair it with Deborah Wiles's *Revolution* (2014), a fictional account of that same summer from the point of view of a girl living in Greenwood, Mississippi.

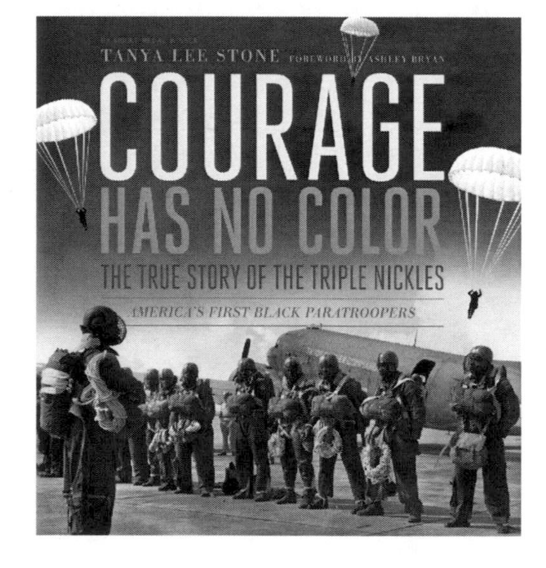

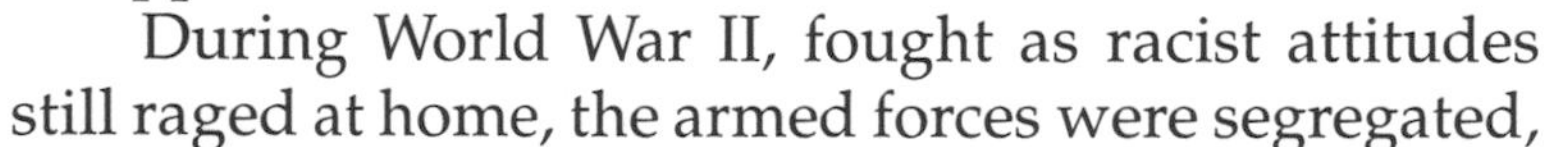

During World War II, fought as racist attitudes still raged at home, the armed forces were segregated, with African American soldiers relegated to service jobs. Such was the case at the Parachute School in Fort Benning, Georgia, where white soldiers trained to be paratroopers while their black counterparts served as guards and performed menial tasks. Tanya Lee Stone's *Courage Has No Color* (2013), is the story of Sergeant Walter Morris who tried to convince army brass to allow his men to train as well. When he couldn't get permission, he had a seemingly outlandish idea worthy of the best divergent thinkers: his men would mimic the training of the paratroopers to boost their morale. After seeing the men in action, though, General Gaither authorized Morris to form them into a "new, all-black unit of paratroopers: the 555th Parachute Infantry Company" (24). They were called the Triple Nickles. Men made bets that the Nickles would never have the courage to actually jump, but jump they did, and they excelled in every task required of them. Yet they were never allowed to see combat. Instead, the Nickles were sent to fight fires set in the west by Japanese balloon bombs. Their courage and outstanding performance there set the stage for future integration of the armed forces. Stone's book is a captivating account, enlivened by interviews of actual participants, period photographs, and drawings made by children's author/illustrator Ashley Bryant during his military service in World War II. Conditions were no better in the navy during that war. In *The Port Chicago 50: Disaster, Mutiny, and the Fight for Civil Rights* (2014), Steve Sheinkin tells the harrowing story of African American sailors stationed at a navy base called Port Chicago in San Francisco in 1944. Unlike their Caucasian comrades, these African American men were forbidden to go to sea. Instead, they remained at the base cooking, cleaning, and performing other service jobs. Most horrific of all, they were forced to load ammunition onto ships as quickly as possible with no training in how to handle explosives. No white sailors had to do this work. After a massive explosion killed 320 men and injured hundreds of others, the men were afraid to return to work, though they were ordered to do so. Two hundred refused. Most backed down, but fifty held firm and were actually tried for mutiny, a crime punishable by death. Sheinkin's book will have older students buzzing with indignation.

Nelson Mandela was born in South Africa in 1918 and learned at an early age that his people were conquered by Europeans who claimed the country for themselves. Later as a lawyer he defended the poor and eventually organized rallies to fight apartheid, a system of segregation, and spent twenty-seven years in prison during which apartheid was finally declared illegal. Winner of the Nobel Peace Prize, Mandela was overwhelmingly elected the first black president of South Africa. Kadir Nelson tells the African leader's story in *Nelson Mandela* (2013), a simply gorgeous book that even younger children can enjoy.

Another stunning book by Nelson, *Heart and Soul* (2011), sets the story of the United States in the context of the injustices suffered and enormous contributions made by African Americans throughout the country's history. What is exceptional about this book, in addition to the gorgeous full color paintings in every chapter, is that the story is told by an anonymous woman who warns readers at the outset that the story of her people is full of "things that might make you cringe, or feel angry. But there are also parts that will make you proud, or even laugh a little" (7). She concludes, "Our centuries-long struggle for freedom and equal rights had helped make the American promise of life, liberty, and the pursuit of happiness a reality for all Americans" (99). In this book students will meet African American slaves, cowboys, entertainers, scientists, and the ordinary folk who joined in the struggle to eliminate segregation and obtain equal rights. Even very young children can enjoy the paintings as they listen to an adult retell the stories. The book contains a helpful timeline, author note, and bibliography. While the African American struggle for equality and an end to segregation is well known, almost ten years before the landmark Brown versus Board of Education decision, a Mexican-American family fought for their children's right to attend their neighborhood school with white children rather than the far inferior Mexican school. The story of the Mendez versus Westminster School District is movingly told in Duncan Tonatiuh's *Separate Is Never Equal* (2014). The story contains Spanish phrases throughout and includes a glossary, sources, and a lengthy author note.

Women have faced enormous obstacles for centuries, not because they are not smart or talented, but simply because they are female. Only in recent decades, in most cases, were women even allowed formal schooling, and in some countries, they are still forbidden to go to school or get jobs. Yet many women have overcome these difficulties. Living at a time when conditions were far more difficult for females than they are today, these brave women paved the way for the opportunities many women currently enjoy. Only a few of the many picture book biographies that feature these women, accessible even for younger students, appear here.

Susan B. Anthony, whose life and amazing accomplishments are engagingly told by Alexandra Wallner (2012) in a picture book bearing her subject's name, was born in 1820 in Massachusetts. Although her parents allowed her to receive a good education, the same was not true for other women of her time. "Women were not treated as the equals of men. They could not get a good education, own property, get equal pay, or vote." After several years as a teacher, Susan quit to devote herself to all of these causes, giving speeches around the country. She faced heckling, and even endured rotten eggs and lawsuits in her efforts to effect legislation in favor of women. In her later years, she devoted herself exclusively to women's suffrage, although she never received the right to vote in her lifetime. But her battle was won fourteen years later with the passage of the Nineteenth Amendment, proving her conviction, "Failure is impossible."

In Ann Malaspina's *Touch the Sky* (2011), beautifully written in free verse, readers meet Alice Coachman. She was born in 1923 in Albany, Georgia, where, although she dreamed of jumping high as the sky, "fields shut. / Tracks shut. / Doors shut / to girls like Alice." But she practiced with ropes tied to sticks, came to the notice of school coaches, and eventually made the 1948 Olympic team. In London, during the high jump event, she became the first African American to win an Olympic gold medal. When she returned home to Albany for a ceremony at the Albany Municipal Auditorium, the audience was segregated and Alice was not invited to speak. Her incredible accomplishments were honored in 1996 when she was inducted into the United States Olympic Hall of Fame and named one of the hundred best athletes in Olympic history.

Florence Nightingale was born in Italy in 1820 to wealthy parents who were horrified when she expressed a desire to become a nurse. Though they initially refused to let her study, they relented, and Florence learned nursing and doctoring techniques by watching doctors and surgeons. In her beautiful book, *Florence Nightingale* (2014), Demi recounts the many incredible accomplishments of this dedicated woman. Florence was responsible for improving sanitary conditions in institutions for the poor; cared for injured British soldiers in the Crimean War, and "shar[ed] her knowledge about army field medicine with the Union government during the American Civil War." Demi concludes, "We remember Florence Nightingale today as the driving force behind improvements in nursing during her time and as a woman of extraordinary vision, who believed that no problem, however big it seemed, was ever too big for her to solve."

"Back in the 1830s, there were lots of things girls couldn't be . . . Being a doctor was definitely not an option." Thus begins Tanya Lee Stone's lively story of Elizabeth Blackwell, the first woman doctor in America. In *Who Says Women Can't Be Doctors?* (2013), she shows young readers an exceptional girl who slept on the floor with no covers "to toughen herself up" and stretched out on the roof with a spyglass to "see what was happening on the other side of town." So, even when she hadn't thought of doing so before, when it was suggested that she become a doctor, Elizabeth was ripe for the challenge. Twenty-eight medical schools turned her down, but one said yes, as a joke, really. After graduation, no one would hire her, even though she had graduated at the top of her class. Still she persevered, and succeeded in opening a free clinic, and starting her own hospital and medical school for women. Young children will love the comical illustrations filled with jeering onlookers and pages of "no, no, no's" and "ha ha ha's."

Another woman who was one of the first to practice medicine was Mary Walker. Cheryl Harness tells her story in *Mary Walker Wears the Pants* (2013). Unlike the women of her day, Mary dressed in a suit consisting of a top coat and pants, served as a physician during the Civil War treating both Union and Confederate soldiers, was imprisoned during that war, and eventually won the Medal of Honor. Throughout her life she championed women's rights through her writings and speeches.

Henrietta Leavitt is not very well known, yet she was responsible for many important discoveries about measuring the solar system. And she made these discoveries in the early 1900s at a time when, as Robert Burleigh writes in his biography *Look Up!* (2013), "almost all astronomy teachers and students were men." After graduation she worked in the Harvard College Observatory for many years where she and other women were forbidden to use the giant telescope but worked instead as "human 'computers', recording, measuring, and calculating." In spite of this, however, she continued to study and observe photographs taken with the telescope until she discovered differences in the brightness of stars as a way to measure their distance from Earth. Because of her work, we now know that the Milky Way is not the only galaxy and that the universe is expanding.

In the first years of the 20th century, Clara Lemlich arrived in New York with a horde of other immigrants. She's "got grit . . . knows in her bones what is right and what is wrong," states Michelle Markel in *Brave Girl: Clara and the Shirtwaist Makers' Strike of*

1909 (2013). Hired to work in a garment factory, Clara soon realized conditions were definitely wrong. Workers, many of them teenage girls, endured long hours, received inadequate pay, and were fired with little provocation. Clara couldn't even speak English, but she studied evenings, and soon proved the men who felt "ladies are not tough enough" wrong. She led a strike, was beaten, and arrested seventeen times. When the strike had no effect, Clara, a lone woman who was not even invited to the podium with the men, called for a general strike. This eventually resulted in fairer conditions and spurred factory workers in other cities to strike as well. Clara proved that "warriors can wear skirts and blouses, / and the bravest hearts / may beat in girls / only five feet tall."

Louise Borden's *Fly High!* (2004) is the story of Bessie Coleman, the first African American pilot. From her rural roots in Texas where she had to pick cotton instead of attending school, Bessie educated herself and vowed to become successful. When no flight schools in the United States would accept her, her determination to fly led her to France where she earned an international pilot's license in 1921. Bessie performed at many U.S. air shows and served as a model for African American children, constantly urging them to "fly high" and "be somebody."

The horrors men suffer in war are well documented, but there is precious little written about women in war, especially about the women who voluntarily leave home to serve as nurses. Mary Cronk Farrell's *Pure Grit* (2014) fills the gap wonderfully with the story of the U.S. army nurses who served in the Philippines treating wounded and dying soldiers while bombs exploded around them. The women served in jungle hospitals on the Bataan Peninsula and in underground tunnels on Corregidor Island. Later, when most of them were captured by the Japanese as prisoners of war, they suffered disease and near-starvation for three years. This story of sisterhood and suffering is a perfect choice for older students studying World War II. To bring consideration of women's work and accomplishments right up to the present, share Ilene Cooper's *A Woman in the House (and Senate)* (2014) with older students. Beginning with the women's suffrage movement and going all the way through the results of the 2012 election, Cooper covers more than a century of U.S. history, highlighting a diverse group of female leaders who opened doors for women in politics. Featured women include Hattie Caraway, Patsy Mink, Shirley Chisholm, Nancy Pelosi, and Hillary Clinton. The book is filled with illustrations and archival photographs and includes a glossary, index, and chart of all the women who have served in Congress.

"There is a tendency among human beings to take people with diagnostic labels and put them as far away as possible," says Thomas Armstrong, an advocate for neuro diversity, in Sy Montgomery's fascinating biography of Temple Grandin (2012) who was diagnosed with autism at age three. Her father wanted to put her into an institution, but her mother found her tutors, therapists, and special schools where Temple flourished. Temple used her

own sensitivities to understand the fears of cattle, and her designs are responsible for new worldwide practices in raising and slaughtering animals humanely. Written off by some as a child, Temple Grandin is now a scientist and professor of animal science at Colorado State University and advocate for people with autism.

"As of 2012, he remains one of only three outfielders to record three assists to home plate in one game and is the only outfielder ever to lead a major league in assists, putouts, and fielding percentage in the same season . . . He scored 100 runs or more in a single season nine times, stole thirty or more bases in a season eleven times, and registered more than 2,000 career hits." Who is this outstanding player? Bill Wise tells his story in *Silent Star: The Story of Deaf Major Leaguer William Hoy* (2012). Born in 1862, Hoy contracted meningitis at age three, an illness that left him deaf. William was taunted by his classmates until his parents sent him to a special school for the deaf. There he fell in love with baseball, was discovered by a scout as he played pick-up games after work, and was eventually hired by the Washington Nationals where he excelled as an outfielder for fourteen years. After he retired, Hoy ran a successful farm, became a personnel director for deaf employees at Goodyear, and coached and umpired in deaf leagues. This unlikely hero "overcame numerous obstacles to become the first deaf player to have a long and distinguished career in the major leagues," and paved the way for the deaf players who would come after him.

Deborah Hopkinson's *Annie and Helen* (2012) offers a new twist on what might be a familiar story to students—Helen Keller's triumph over her deafness and blindness to become a well-educated woman who made considerable contributions to society—because it is her teacher, Annie Sullivan's story as much as it is Helen's. Hopkinson emphasizes Sullivan's enormous patience as she helps transform Helen from a tantrum-throwing child unable to communicate into an enthusiastic learner thrilled by language and ways to use it to express herself. The transformation entailed countless hours of patiently spelling words into Helen's palm day after day until the girl finally made the connection between the spelled words and the actual objects they represented. Young children will enjoy excerpts from Annie's letters to her teacher in Boston detailing Helen's progress, the actual photographs of the two women on the endpapers, and a copy of Helen's first letter home.

Many young girls dream of becoming ballerinas, but when the girls have cerebral palsy and other muscle disorders, have "trouble raising their arms, holding themselves upright . . . keeping their balance," and even need "wheelchairs or walkers to get around," that dream seems well beyond reach. But in *Ballerina*

Dreams (2007), Lauren Thompson tells how Joann Ferrara, who runs a ballet school for children with muscular problems, make five little girls' (ages 3–7) dancing dreams come true. The book has brief text and large photographs, perfect for very young children. While including information about the years of practice it takes for the five girls to be able to control their movements, the book emphasizes their tremendous joy in overcoming the seemingly impossible and Ferrara's patience and vision as she sees beyond the girls' challenges to what they will be able to accomplish.

Suggested Activities

1. The many books discussed in this section provide students with powerful models—women, men, and children—who exhibited many of the characteristics of divergent thinkers to overcome their own difficulties and/or serve others. Make a large copy of these characteristics (See the Introduction, p. xiii) or display them on a white board. Engage the students in conversation about the subjects of those books they were able to read or listen to. Ask them to consider the actions of these biographical subjects or those who helped them and align their actions and decisions with the relevant characteristics. The students may wish to collaborate in groups as they form three columns: person; actions, decisions, or difficulties overcome; and divergent thinking characteristic demonstrated. As the class learns about innovators in other sections of this chapter, they may wish to add names to their lists.
2. After enjoying *She Sang Promise* together, divide the students into groups and ask them to discuss the "songs" of their elders—teachings handed down to them by grandparents, parents, and other family members. Bring the class together and make a list of some of these "songs." Some teachings may have to do with treatment of others, how to work conscientiously, how to act in public, manners, among others. Make a class list of the most popular and meaningful teachings as students comment on them. Do any of the "songs" inspire service to others, ways of engaging in relationships with others? Ways to know themselves better? Reconvene the groups and ask each group to incorporate the list in whole or in part into an original creative work: a poem, an illustrated book, a slide presentation, a song with musical accompaniment, and so on. They might even find a way to fold the "songs" into a unit they are currently studying if applicable. The groups may need several days to work on this project. Have each group present its creation so that the class is surrounded by the wisdom of its elders and what that accumulated wisdom has to teach them about their engagement with their school or wider community. The students might also wish to incorporate some of their creative works into a mural for the hall or school lobby.
3. Reading about the lives of any or all of the exceptional African American leaders discussed earlier is inspiring for all students, but especially appropriate for those studying the history of slavery, the Civil War or the Civil Rights era. An activity that would be a meaningful culmination of such units would be to create a board game highlighting some of the people they've encountered in these books or other study materials. The design of the game should be completely their own with students working in pairs or groups to accomplish the different tasks necessary. One suggestion might be to have the game consist of cards, each with a person's accomplishment on it. The player that draws the card must name the person connected to that accomplishment. A correct answer advances a player; an incorrect answer moves him or her back. Correct answers for checking appear on a separate sheet. Students may wish to devise a large illustration to cover the board and an illustration for the area players are striving to

reach to "win" the game. An excellent simple book for beginners at game-making is Greg Austic's *Game Design* (2014). What is especially valuable about this book is that it gets readers thinking carefully before plunging into making their game. "The next time you play a game, think about the emotions you are feeling. Are you happy? Excited? Proud? Something else? Now try to figure out why the game is making you feel this way" (7). Austic also emphasizes the importance of failure, for information about why people don't like a game helps the designer make it better. (For more information on how to create a board game, go to http://www.wikihow.com/Make-Your-Own-Board-Game)

4. In his article, "Syria, Spain, and the Eternal Present | Consider the Source" (June 13, 2013), noted nonfiction writer Marc Aronson states,

> As we investigate the past, as we ask new questions, as we line up cause and effect in new ways, our present changes. Indeed, as we begin to see how easily events could have been different or altered, we begin to see that we can influence the present and craft a new future. We study history not out of reverence for the past, but to give us the tools to make a better future.

Use several books featuring the contributions and struggles of African Americans during the slavery, Civil War, or Civil Rights eras previously discussed, along with other excellent books about these historical periods such as Elaine Landau's *Fleeing to Freedom on the Underground Railroad: The Courageous Slaves, Agents, and Conductors* (2006); Doreen Rappaport's *No More! Stories and Songs of Slave Resistance* (2005); *The Civil War: A Visual History* (2011), a DK Publication; Tonya Bolden's *Emancipation Proclamation: Lincoln and the Dawn of Liberty* (2013); Linda Tarrant-Reid's *Discovering Black America: From the Age of Exploration to the Twenty-First Century* (2012); Phillip Hoose's *Claudette Colvin: Twice Toward Justice* (2009); and others you and your students discover, to create a unit of study on one era of African American history required by the curriculum. Add poetry books as well. The "Dare to Dream . . . Change the World" section of chapter 1 contains many relevant suggestions. You may also wish to use films, original sources from such sites as the Smithsonian (see http://www.smithsoniansource.org/display/primarysource/search.aspx), and other websites.

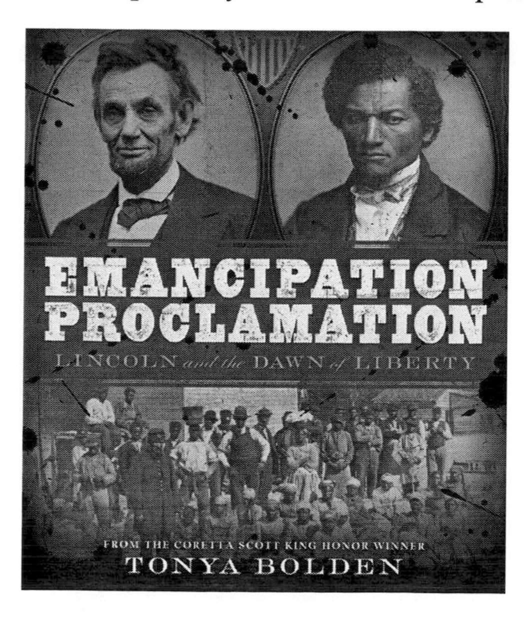

a) Ask questions—See discussion of questioning later. At the outset, ask the students what questions they have about this period. As you explore the material together, do more questions arise? Do any of the books on the same subject contradict one another? How might the students resolve these differences and discover the truth?
b) What are the authors' stances in each of the books? Their point of view?
c) Apply lessons and insights—Engage in a conversation with the students about the ways in which the events of the period being studied may shed light on one or more current events. For example, what might we learn from the enslavement of Africans in the United States that would inform our response to the enslavement of people in countries throughout

the world in our own day? What original ideas can students bring to the current situation?

d) Rewrite history—Ask students to rewrite an event from the period of history they are studying. For example, solve the slavery issue and other problems that resulted in Civil War without a war. Put together a detailed plan that involves how the president, the Congress, and leaders from both sides would proceed. How might this rewritten plan inform the resolution of a current-day conflict?

e) Create a wiki—Go to http://www.wikispaces.com/ or use a site already in place in your school to create a class wiki about the historical period being studied. In it, students can contribute their research on the period; list websites containing primary source documents, films, among others, relevant to the period; ask questions they might have about what they are studying; contribute ideas, and so on. Invite another class studying the same period to enter the wiki and contribute their own research and information and/or comment on your class's work. How has collaboration with another class informed and/or modified, changed your students' views?

5. Kadir Nelson's paintings in *Heart and Soul* (2011) are not just beautiful, but also contain metaphors that help tell the story of the African American people in the United States. See pages 22, 78, and 98 for some examples. Discuss their meaning and look for other metaphors within the art. What other visual metaphors can the students create that would add information and depth of meaning to the unit they are studying?
6. The women featured in the biographies discussed earlier were pioneers who created a smoother path for women who come after them, but conditions for women in the developing world and even in the United States are far from perfect.

   a) Ask students to make a list of rights still denied women. Encourage research to arrive at their choices. Create a color-coded map indicating, in degrees of prevalence, the areas of the world where the greatest numbers of women are denied a particular right (red for highest numbers, for example).

   b) After determining what students consider to be the most serious infringements of women's rights, create an advertising campaign to convince government bodies, employers, and other leaders to grant women these rights. Why would this be advantageous to the women involved? To society?

7. *Look Up!*, the biography of astronomer Henrietta Leavitt, is an excellent accompaniment to a unit on the solar system since it features a woman in the field (an inspiration to future female astronomers, perhaps?) and demonstrates the rewards of patient study. There are several other recent nonfiction books to use as well, along with whatever science text is employed in the school. In addition to the planets with which students are likely familiar, David A. Aguilar's *13 Planets: The Latest View of the Solar*

System (2013) brings the most up-to-date information about the solar system to both younger- and middle-grade students, introduces them to dwarf planets, and helps them understand how our solar system was formed and will likely end. Fine illustrations and captions add information and interest. Younger students will learn a good deal from Catherine D. Hughes's *National Geographic Kids First Big Book of Space* (2013). *The Solar System through Infographics* by Nadia Higgins (2013) helps readers understand the huge numbers and concepts related to our solar system by presenting them visually, through charts, maps, timelines, among others. There are two books on the solar system in Scholastic's Discover More series: *Planets* (Arlon and Gordon-Harris, 2012) and *Night Sky* (Sparrow, 2012) Both books offer readers key symbols for obtaining information and the pages are full of charts, photos, captions, and more to enhance understanding. A special code enables readers to access a free digital book that contains additional information. *Planets* is targeted for children as young as six, and its digital book provides information on space machines, definitions of terms, and even periodic quizzes. Older students will enjoy *Night Sky* along with its digital book explaining the zodiac and much more. Scholastic also publishes *Level 2 Reader: Solar System* (Vogt, 2012) for K-2 students. Students in grades 4 and up will enjoy Elizabeth Rusch's *The Mighty Mars Rovers* (2012). Rusch relates the launching of rovers Spirit and Opportunity in 2003 through the eyes of Steve Squyres of the Jet Propulsion Lab as a heart-stopping adventure. Side bars and colored photos add interesting information. Mary Kay Carson's *Beyond the Solar System* (2013) is an excellent book that provides a history of astronomy from the beginning to the present day, including the contributions of some female astronomers; breakthrough discoveries; hints for successful viewing of the night sky; and twenty-one activities. Jason Chin's *Gravity* (2014) makes the concept of gravity, an important one to understand when learning about space, very accessible for young children. Chin explains gravity through basic examples such as why objects do not float out of our hands. *Feel the Force!* (2011) by Tom Adams makes physics fun through the use of pop-ups and experiments. There is a section on gravity and how space ships are able to blast into space. Win reluctant space observers over with Carolyn Cinami De Cristofano's *A Black Hole is NOT a Hole* (2012). In this slim book, the author makes difficult concepts easy to understand, and the lovely illustrations along with many NASA photos will ignite awe in readers. See the discussion of Amy Sklansky's *Out of This World: Poems and Facts about Space* (2012) in chapter 1 to add poetry to the unit. Douglas Florian sings the wonder of the universe in the twenty poems in his glorious *Comets, Stars, the Moon and Mars* (2007). Some related fiction books such as Steve Metzger's *Pluto Visits Earth* (2012) in which Pluto demands reinstatement as a planet, might inspire students to incorporate what they know about the solar system into a fiction piece of their own. An important project that stems from this fictional look at Pluto's chagrin would be to compare the books on the solar system suggested here as well as others and determine what the writers' criteria are for declaring a body a planet or for removing that designation. On what do they base their criteria? Do students agree with the change in Pluto's designation? Why or why not? Depending

upon their ages, there are several creative projects students can undertake in addition to the ones suggested in these books:

a) Young children can create a slide show with each slide containing a sentence and perhaps accompanying picture about something they learned during the unit and present it to another class.
b) Create a crossword puzzle using some terms learned during this unit.
c) See directions in *Beyond the Solar System* for building some objects related to space study. Then write original directions for building an object not contained in the book.
d) Students can download three free 3D modeling programs to design their own telescope and have it printed on a 3D printer in the school or local library. Trimble Sketch Up at sketchup.com is the easiest one to use; 123D Catch at 123dapp.com includes an iPad app; Blender at blender.org is more advanced. Another option is to go to the thingiverse website, view telescope designs others have made, download them as STL files (a format used by Stereolithography software to generate the information needed to produce 3D models on Stereolithography machine) and then use a program called Replicator G to slide the design into layers for printing. Stereolithography is a technology that enables one to build 3D plastic prototypes. Download Replicator G from replicat.org/download. (See Terence O'Neill and Josh Williams's *3D Printing* (2014) for more detailed instructions, as well as other fascinating books in the Makers as Innovators series, all published by Cherry Lake Publishing, Ann Arbor, MI.)

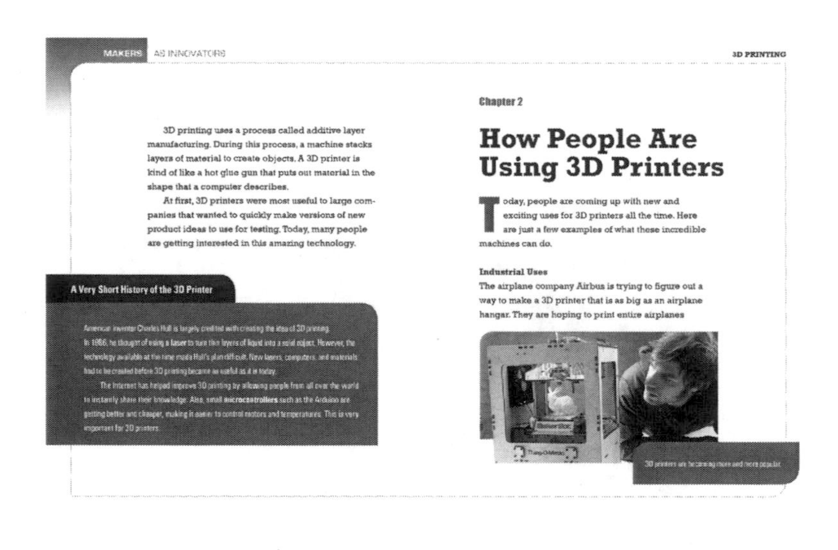
MAKERS AS INNOVATORS

3D PRINTING

3D printing uses a process called additive layer manufacturing. During this process, a machine stacks layers of material to create objects. A 3D printer is kind of like a hot glue gun that puts out material in the shape that a computer describes.

At first, 3D printers were most useful to large companies that wanted to quickly make versions of new product ideas to use for testing. Today, many people are getting interested in this amazing technology.

A Very Short History of the 3D Printer

American inventor Charles Hull is largely credited with creating the idea of 3D printing. In 1986, he thought of using a **laser** to turn thin layers of liquid into a solid object. However, the technology available at the time made Hull's plan difficult. New lasers, computers, and materials had to be created before 3D printing became as useful as it is today.

The Internet has helped improve 3D printing by allowing people from all over the world to instantly share their knowledge. Also, small **microcontrollers** such as the Arduino are getting better and cheaper, making it easier to control motors and temperatures. This is very important for 3D printers.

Chapter 2

How People Are Using 3D Printers

Today, people are coming up with new and exciting uses for 3D printers all the time. Here are just a few examples of what these incredible machines can do.

Industrial Uses

The airplane company Airbus is trying to figure out a way to make a 3D printer that is as big as an airplane hangar. They are hoping to print entire airplanes

3D printers are becoming more and more popular.

8. Identify the children in class and throughout the school who have physical challenges and the nature of these challenges. Then present an innovative plan to the principal for

something that is not currently being done but would make life easier for these students.

9. Read pages 131–133 in Sy Montgomery's biography, *Temple Grandin*, which offers advice for "Kids on the [Autism] Spectrum." Discuss her seven points with students. Do they agree that doing these things or having these attitudes would help kids become successful? While Grandin's advice is geared toward young people trying to manage various forms of autism, other challenges, such as making friends or learning something that is difficult for them, face students as well. Make a list of such challenges with the students. Then divide them into groups, ask each group to choose a specific challenge, and write a list of ways to overcome that challenge. As Grandin did, encourage the students to explain each point on their lists and/or give examples of how a particular suggestion might be implemented. Students should strive for originality and come up with suggestions that have never been presented to them or discussed before in class.

Invention Born of the Observation and Investigation of Nature (Adapted from Marcus Tullius Cicero)

The importance of observation has been stressed often in this volume. The divergent thinker is curious and ready to pay close attention to whatever information his or her senses provide. So very many of the inventions that have revolutionized the way we live and the ideas that have had global impact are the result of close and prolonged observation by inquisitive, patient individuals. The ideas spawned by the innovators discussed in this section bear this out. But observation by itself is not enough. As Bernard Baruch once famously said, "Millions saw the apple fall but Newton was the one who asked 'why'." (Quoted in *New York Post* (June 24, 1965.) So in addition to teaching our students to be alert observers of the world around them, we need to encourage them to continually question what they are seeing and to make connections between what they already know, what they observe, and what they want to know more about. In an article entitled "How a Radical New Teaching Method Could Unleash a Generation of Geniuses" (October 15, 2013), Joshua Davis describes how allowing students to take the lead in their learning, to ask their own questions, has been producing remarkable results. Instead of showing students how to find answers in math or other subjects, teachers have left students to find their own solutions to difficult math problems or figure out how to research information on a particular topic. "The bottom line is," he states, "if you're not the one controlling your learning, you're not going to learn as well" (http://www.wired.com/business/2013/10/free-thinkers/). Teachers can learn more about setting up a Student Organized Learning Environment, or SOLE, by going to http://tedsole.tumblr.com/ and by downloading a free SOLE Tool Kit at http://www.ted.com/pages/835#public. Watching Sugata Mitra, a founder of the movement and winner of a TED prize, give his TED talk at http://www.ted.com/talks/sugata_mitra_the_child_driven_education.html is inspiring.

In chapter 2 we discussed several fiction books that could encourage students to ask questions. But questioning is so vital to learning, that we stress it through the use of nonfiction literature as well. Kingfisher publishes a series that will not only get the questioning started but will even prompt students to ask questions about their questions. The big philosophical, moral, and scientific questions contained in them will have students grappling with things that may have been on their minds but either not formulated or not given any attention. Dr. Stephen Law's *Really, Really Big Questions about Life, the Universe, and Everything* (2009) questions, among other things, the origins of the universe, what "stuff" is made of, the workings of the mind, and the nature of right and wrong. Mark Brake's *Really, Really Big Questions about Space and Time* (2010) asks about heavenly bodies, the possibility of time travel, and how one might make a time travel machine. Julian Baggini's *Really, Really Big Questions about God, Faith, and Religion* (2011) contains questions about the meaning of religion, and even whether miracles exist. Stephen Law's *Really, Really Big Questions about Me and My Body* (2012) questions where people come from, how our bodies work, how we know things, and much more. All the books contain interesting quotes and even more perplexing boxed questions called "Brain Burns" that are sure to fuel spirited discussions. If the class is studying mammals, a good book to prompt young children to ask questions is Gilda and Melvin Berger's *Why Do Zebras Have Stripes?* (2013). Each of the twenty questions in the book appears in large print in a green box along with a picture of the animal to which it refers. This provides an opportunity for children to try answering the question themselves before turning the page to discover the authors' response. The children might wish to create their own question and answer book about animals they are studying, following the same format. The questions in Catherine Ripley's *Why?* (2010), another book suitable for very young children, are divided into categories: bath time, supermarket, nighttime, outdoor, kitchen, and farm animal questions. Most questions are answered in one paragraph, and there are diagrams and amusing illustrations as well. Students can continue the questions by drawing up an original list of school questions along with related answers and illustrations.

Perhaps the quintessential observer and questioner is Charles Darwin who, after years of travel, observations, and meticulous note-taking (and twenty years of silence about his findings), published his *On the Origin of Species*, a theory of evolution that, Rosalyn Schanzer writes in *What Darwin Saw* (2009), "will forever change the way people think about our planet and every single thing that lives here" (3). Darwin arrived at this revolutionary idea because, the flyleaf of the book states, "All the time he was traveling, he was asking himself questions. Why do we find seashells at the tops of mountains? Why do different versions of similar animals live in such different places?" Schanzer's book is filled with Darwin's own words, describes how evolution works, and has a map that follows the scientist's journey on the HMS Beagle. During that journey from 1831 to 1836, Darwin found some unusual pointy-nosed frogs with a flap of skin on their noses, and saved some in specimen jars. When a French zoologist examined a specimen in 1841, he discovered tadpoles in its mouth. Questions about how this could be came from every direction, and scientists are still looking for some answers today. Marty Crump describes this strange frog and the work of scientists who are trying to uncover its mysteries in *The Mystery of Darwin's Frog* (2013). It is a fine example of scientific inquiry and

an examination of the threats to frog habitats. (Go to http://www.youtube.com/watch?v=IAF5N-HwgOc to see this frog in action.)

Johannes Gutenberg's invention of the printing press in 1450 changed the world. Book-making was transformed from a tedious process of hand lettering a relatively small number of books to a method that allowed for far larger numbers of books to become available. Literacy eventually became possible for greater numbers of people as books reached even those who were not wealthy. In *From the Good Mountain: How Gutenberg Changed the World* (2012), James Rumford takes readers on a poetic journey through the step-by-step process of Gutenberg's invention, emphasizing the materials used and its impact on the world. He depicts lovely hand-lettered books made before the printing press as well as a book produced by Guttenberg. Rumford also reveals what little is known about the inventor's life and provides key search words for students who want to find additional information on the Internet. What he doesn't say in this brief account is how Gutenberg came up with the idea of the printing press in the first place. An excellent film at http://www.youtube.com/watch?v=Y1vl2j24Mtk provides some answers. Gutenberg lived at a time during which woodblock printing was a similar, though much more labor intensive, way of producing pictures and books. He also grew up in Mainz, the center of Germany's wine-producing industry. Surely he must have seen many wine presses in his youth. By observing how the screw press worked in wine making, Gutenberg was able to design a press that could successfully press impressions from inked moveable letters onto paper, much the way pressing on inked woodblock impressions produced images on paper or other materials. "An important part of Gutenberg's genius," writes Steven Johnson (2010), "lay not in conceiving an entirely new technology from scratch, but instead from borrowing a mature technology from an entirely different field, and putting it to work to solve an unrelated problem" (153). At the end of his book, Rumford asks, "Will all of tomorrow's books be made of silicon and light and be connected by the Internet to the world, or will they be something we can't even imagine today?" In a film at ow.ly/n47uu, Valerie Hill has gone further than the book Gutenberg made ubiquitous to ask what information will look like in the years to come. E-books are more and more popular, but will it end there? Ask students to grapple with this question. Can they take what they observe in their world, what they see taking place on the Internet and on the many electronic devices currently in use and push the idea further as Gutenberg did in his time? What do they imagine obtaining information will look like when they are adults?

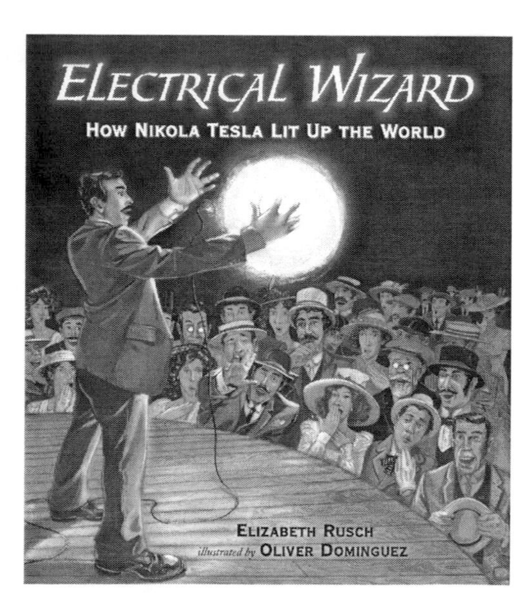

"If you play with a remote-control car, flick on a fluorescent or neon light, get an X-ray . . . check the speedometer in a car, call someone on a cell phone, or even just turn on the radio, you are using Nikola Tesla's inventions," writes Elizabeth Rusch in *Electrical Wizard: How Nikola Tesla Lit Up the World* (2013). Tesla was born in Serbia in 1856 and later emigrated to the United States. He started observing and questioning even as a very young boy. When, at age three, he received an electric shock after stroking his cat, he wanted to know what the tiny sparks were. When he felt how fast water in a nearby brook moved across his fingers, he poked a hole through a wooden disk and held it over the moving water. As he had surmised, the powerful water flow spun the disk. "Nikola began to notice invisible energy everywhere." Rusch describes Tesla's tireless efforts to prove AC and not DC current was a more efficient way to provide electricity despite strong opposition and sabotage from Thomas Edison; his triumph in lighting the Chicago World's Fair; his harnessing the power of Niagara Falls to provide electricity for the region; and more. Students can learn, among other things, through the diagrams and explanations in the book, how AC and DC current work, how Tesla survived some of his experiments with electricity, and how he harnessed the power of the falls. After reading this book, younger children can have an opportunity to think about Tesla's work by performing an experiment. Provide the class with a comb, a piece of woolen material, and a fluorescent light bulb. Darken the room. Ask a student to rub the comb many times over the material and then touch the comb to the metal part of the bulb. What happens? Ask the children to explain this result. Older children can devise several experiments with magnets to demonstrate Tesla's work with AC current. Young middle-grade students might enjoy seeing how two children use their knowledge of electricity and gadgets to solve a mystery in Bob Pflugfelder's and Steve Hocken Smith's *Nick and Tesla's High-Voltage Danger Lab* (2013). When the two children are sent to live with their uncle, an eccentric scientist, they discover an abandoned house, a mysterious girl in an upstairs window, and a black SUV that seems to be following them around. What do the children make of the female protagonist's name? Another fiction book to tie into a study of electricity and/or Tesla's work is Neal Schusterman's *The Accelerati Trilogy Book One: Tesla's Attic* (2014). Objects in an attic lead four teens into a dangerous plan concocted by Nikola Tesla.

Very young children will not only enjoy David A. Kelly's *Miracle Mud: Lena Blackburne and the Secret Mud that Changed Baseball* (2013), they will readily be able to see how making a connection between what a person observes and a pressing problem that needs a solution can have amazing results. Kelly's biography, printed in large type with brief text, begins, "Lena Blackburne wanted to be a famous baseball player. But instead, he discovered mud . . . His special, secret mud changed the game of baseball." When umpires complained to Lena, the team coach, that new baseballs were too soft and soggy, he observed that the mud near a river at home was both smooth and gritty—just the thing to rub the shine out of new baseballs without the soaking that made them soggy. Today Lena's family carries on the business of harvesting and selling the mud to baseball teams, and his mud is displayed in the Baseball Hall of Fame! Ask students to think hard about what they see in their classroom. What problems need solutions that might be solved by close observation? Is there a better way to arrange particular materials so that they are more accessible, for example?

Another book suitable for young children is *On a Beam of Light* (2013), Jennifer Berne's biography of Albert Einstein. A late talker, Einstein, nevertheless, exhibited many characteristics of the divergent thinker as he observed and questioned everything he saw. With curious eyes he "looked and wondered. Looked and wondered." When he saw beams of light from the sun, he wondered whether he could race "through space on a beam of light." He saw sugar dissolve in his tea and asked, "How could this happen?" He watched smoke disappear into the air and asked, "How could one thing disappear into another?" Einstein's continual out-of-the-box thinking lead him to figure out that everything is made up of atoms and eventually, to the famous $E = mc^2$ formula. Provide learning journals for young students (and older ones as well) and ask them to write down at least one question they have about what they learned during a particular lesson or at the end of the day. Discuss the questions and their possible answers often in class. The genius of Berne's book is that she is able to explain some of Einstein's most complex ideas, both in the text and her author's note, in a way that is understandable for young children. She read fifty books to write this one simple picture book text. Ask older students to follow her example in a special challenge: take a complex topic they are studying or a complicated idea they are grappling with and make it understandable for younger children. They can do this with a song, slides, a film, a picture book, play, among others.

Dora Lee's *Biomimicry: Inventions Inspired by Nature* (2011), Bridget Heos's *Stronger than Steel* (2013), and Helaine Becker's *Zoobots* (2014), books for middle and upper-grade students, are a perfect way to conclude this look at the power of making connections through observation. Heos describes the work of Randy Lewis, who has been studying the largest web-making spider in the world, the golden orb weaver. It can weave webs up to three feet wide in less than an hour. Lewis has been transplanting the orb weaver's DNA into goats that will then produce milk containing proteins that can be spun into stronger material for airbags, parachutes, medical sutures, and other products. Readers are asked to think deeply about the ethics of genetically engineered foods and experiments with animals. They can be part of an ethics discussion by turning to page 59 in the book, answering the questions posed, and coming up with their own original list of rules for animal testing. Lee's *Biomimicry* provides a fascinating look at the many inventions as well as engineering and scientific breakthroughs that have come about as a result of looking closely at nature. "Nature," Lee asserts, "has had approximately 3.8 billion years' worth of inventing experience . . . What works, stays. What doesn't, goes" (8). Not only does nature invent what it needs, it does so without destroying the planet, so inventors, engineers, and scientists are studying nature to solve our problems in sustainable ways as well. Swiss inventor George de Mestral noticed how cocklebursstuck to his pant legs when he went walking in the woods. The result: Velcro. When a crack develops on the outside of a pipevine stem, the cells inside swell to plug it. Scientists are working to develop a similar foam to make a strong, yet light-weight building beam. Da Vinci studied the flight of birds, as did the Wright brothers and others, to invent a successful flying machine. Engineers changed the front of the bullet train in Tokyo to resemble a kingfisher's pointy beak, "so it [can] 'slice' through the air [the way the bird's beak slices through water in search of fish] in a more streamlined way" (21). Nature even has something to tell us about making ever better computers as scientists study single-celled creatures to discover how to make computer chips without using toxic chemicals. This is a book to pour over and marvel at. Becker describes twelve of the "creepiest, crawliest, and downright weirdest real-life robots ever invented." (5) All of them are modeled to resemble animals that actually exist in the wild and are designed for specific important applications. The animal model for each robot appears on one page along with a discussions of its particular skills and attributes. On the opposite page is the robot engineered to perform like that animal along with a discussion of what it can do and how it is used. Whatever units students are currently studying—botany, the human body, insects, mammals—they can find something scientists have learned from nature and used to make our lives better. Students can do the same. Consider a problem that needs to be solved, a building that could be designed, or a machine that would make life easier. Can the behavior of an insect, animal, or plant, the functioning of a human organ, among others, shed light on that problem or design? To motivate them even further, watch the very enjoyable Nova film, *Making Stuff Wilder*, part of the Making More Stuff series. It is available at http://www.pbs.org/wgbh/nova/tech/making-more-stuff.html#making-stuff-wilder. In the film host David Pogue shows how scientists are inventing things based on what they observe in nature. Challenge older students to create a Making Stuff design event in their school or community, inviting others to join in design projects modeled after nature. Go to http://www.pbs.org/wgbh/nova/tech/making-more-stuff.html#mep-related-links for links to more information and the possibility of obtaining materials to get students involved in creative projects.

Dare Mighty Things (From the Title of Rappaport's Biography of Theodore Roosevelt)

While not necessarily taking their cue from the natural world as the divergent thinkers highlighted in the previous section did, the innovators we focus on here, through their insight and farsighted vision achieved far-reaching results. Even more remarkable, many did so largely as *single individuals* who dared to risk everything.

Bonnie Christensen enlists the famous astronomer's own voice to recount his life in her biography, *I, Galileo* (2012). Born in Pisa, Italy in 1564, before inventions now commonly used by scientists, Galileo was, nevertheless, a curious boy who joined his father in exploring the relationship between mathematics and music. "A person must be allowed to ask questions [his father] insisted, "and seek answers in search of truth." Eventually young professor Galileo began studying the motion of pendulums and the effects of gravity, and invented a compass "capable of complex mathematical calculations." But it was his invention of the telescope, an improvement upon the Dutch spyglass, that enabled him to see heavenly bodies more clearly than anyone before him. What he saw forced him to contradict the long-held theory proposed by Aristotle that the "sun, moon, planets, and all the stars circled a motionless Earth." This new idea enraged Catholic Church hierarchy who declared, in 1616, that Galileo's idea was heresy! Although he was forced to remain silent, the scientist continued to work. He invented the microscope and worked on his book, *Dialogue on the Two Chief World Systems*. The book was received enthusiastically in Florence, but the pope halted distribution, put Galileo on trial, and condemned him to imprisonment within the walls of his house for life. Yet Galileo's contributions have been so monumental that he has been called the Father of Science. Enjoy this biography together and discuss Galileo's work. What difference does Galileo's theory of a revolving Earth make to our understanding of the universe? What character traits did he possess that enabled him to continue his work despite strong, even life-threatening opposition? (See Peter Sis's marvelous *Starry Messenger* (2000) for additional information.) Engage in the following activities:

a) Make tubes (paper towel rolls, larger PVC tubes, etc.) available to young students and ask them to roll objects such as marbles or small cars through them. How do the students think they can make the objects move through the tubes faster? Why?
b) Divide students into groups and ask them to plan a settlement on the moon or another planet. They would first have to research the atmosphere there and decide what they would need in order to survive under those conditions. A group might be responsible for drawing up a training regimen, another for planning a list of supplies, another for designing (and even building with Lego bricks or other materials) the building or space station in which they would live, and so on.

Robert Byrd's *Electric Ben: The Amazing Life and Times of Benjamin Franklin* (2012) is as full of energy as its title. Byrd manages to condense the main aspects of Franklin's eventful life without losing a sense of the tremendous impact his subject had, not only on his contemporaries, but on generations to come. Curious and adventuresome from his youth, Franklin was a master at what Steven Johnson (*Where Good Ideas Come From*, 2010) calls finding the "adjacent possible," that is, finding "the edges of possibility that surround you" (41). For example, although the Almanac was already the most popular reading material of his day, Ben made it unique by taking it a step further—inventing a character, Poor Richard Saunders, whose opinions filled its pages and made it "the most successful publication in America," selling today's equivalent of 2,000,000 copies annually. Students probably know Franklin best for his discovery of electricity and his vital role in the founding of the country. (For an informative and amusing look at the important contributions women were making while the men were founding the country, look at Cokie Roberts's wonderful *Founding Mothers: Remembering the Ladies* [2014]. Along with a timeline and additional resources, Roberts describes the vital roles these women played as they fought, spied, and wrote alongside the men to form the colonies into a new nation.) Franklin was "curious about all manner of things and he loved to tinker." "Working until he was eighty . . . Ben invented among other things his stove, the lightning rod, odometer, a library chair (with ladder), a chair with a writing arm, a twenty-four-hour clock, a four-sided streetlamp, the armonica, bifocals, and the long-armed pole to reach objects on a high shelf." Make Byrd's fascinating book as well as other readily available Franklin biographies for children available to the class and ask them to write and dramatize a brief play about his life. A small group of children can take the part of a Greek chorus, calling out a characteristic of the divergent thinker while other groups enact a scene that exemplifies that characteristic. Franklin is an excellent subject for such a play since he embodied just about every one of these characteristics during his long life. This biography is an invaluable addition to a study of the colonial period and/or the American Revolution. For older students see Russell Freedman's masterful *Becoming Ben Franklin: How a Candle-Maker's Son Helped Light the Flame of Liberty* (2013) and Kathleen Krull's *Benjamin Franklin* (2013). Compare all three books about Franklin. How are they the same? Different? What are the different authors' points of view? What evidence do they give for the information they provide? How do they incorporate the society in which Franklin lived into his life and its effect on his accomplishments?

"Perseverance, drive, and commitment to a task," certainly describes a characteristic of the divergent thinker General Henry Knox had in spades. During the American Revolution, 9,000 British troops occupied Boston. Washington's meager army had no chance against such a well supplied and trained force—not without cannons. But the nearest cannons were at Fort Ticonderoga, NY, and "300 miles of lakes and rivers, hills and glades, and mountain forests" separated them from Boston. Washington feared it would be impossible to get them in the dead of winter, but Henry Knox was confident he could do it. Don Brown's *Henry and the Cannons* (2013) describes Knox's arduous 40-mile-a-day journey to the fort, and the trip back over land and sea he and his men undertook with 120,000 pounds of cannon: the setbacks, heavy treks through snow, overturned boats, the final delivery of all fifty-nine cannon, and Washington's ultimate victory. It is such an incredible journey that students might at first think it fiction. After discussing this remarkable feat, students can learn more about General Knox at the Maine Historical Society website: http://www.mainememory.net/bin/Features?f=lb;album_id=2687;supst=Album. Once there, they can create their own album of pictures from the site and use them to narrate a slide show or imovie about General Knox for another class studying the American Revolution.

How can we sum up the legacy of Theodore Roosevelt? His almost larger-than-life laughing image looks out at readers from the cover of Doreen Rappaport's *biography To Dare Mighty Things* (2013), revealing a man who not only lived life, but attacked it full on to accomplish his goals despite opposition even from his own political party. Born in 1858, Roosevelt was a sickly child but built his strength through exercise and strenuous outdoor adventures. Rappaport's book is filled with his sayings and stories of his accomplishments. Fearless soldier, outdoorsman, conservationist, police commissioner, governor, congressional leader, and president—Roosevelt did it all. Students, especially those studying civics, will be fascinated by this account of a big man with big ideas.

a) After reading the book, ask students to make a list of things Roosevelt did as a member of Congress and as president. Do they feel his actions were justified? Why or why not? Compare Roosevelt's actions with the way politicians in Washington, D.C., and/or their own state legislators conduct business. How would Roosevelt's views shape congressional conduct today? Would it be a good or bad thing for Congress persons to follow Roosevelt's philosophy? Why?
b) Choose some of Roosevelt's sayings from the book or from other sources. Print each on a large sheet of paper. Surrounding each saying, students should paste headlines, pictures, summaries of articles, among others, that they feel relate to each saying.

Mohandas Gandhi was born in India in 1869. He became a lawyer to advocate peacefully for the rights of his people. The British forced native Indians to buy cloth and salt from them at high prices and taxes instead of spinning their own yarn and gathering their own salt from the sea. In *Gandhi: A March to the Sea* (2013), Alice B. McGinty describes in lovely free verse Gandhi's brave 24-day march to the Arabian Sea to collect salt. This heroic act of peaceful disobedience was a signal to all Indians, Hindus, Muslims, and untouchables alike, as Gandhi insisted, to do the same. "They [were] arrested, / sent to jail, / until the prisons overflow[ed], / and the British let them go." After this victory, Gandhi worked for the next seventeen years, fasting and protesting peacefully not only to free India from 200 years of British rule, but also to gain equal treatment for those considered untouchables. His patience and determination to obtain justice peacefully instead of through violence was an inspiration to Martin Luther King Jr. as he led the Civil Rights Movement, and to other leaders around the world. A moving book written by Gandhi's grandson, Arun with Bethany Hegedus and beautifully illustrated is *Grandfather Gandhi* (2014). At age 12, Arun leaves his home in South Africa to live in Sevagram, his grandfather's village, for two years. When he becomes angry enough to hurl a stone at an older boy who has treated him unfairly in soccer, Arun feels he will never be able to live up to expectations that he live a life of nonviolence as his grandfather has. In his meeting with Gandhi, his grandfather explains that anger is not wrong as long as we use it for good instead of harm. The authors' note describes how the book was born out of the grief and anger experienced in the wake of the 9/11 attacks. "Each time we choose to act rather than react, to sit instead of strike, to listen instead of shout, we work to create peace. We help

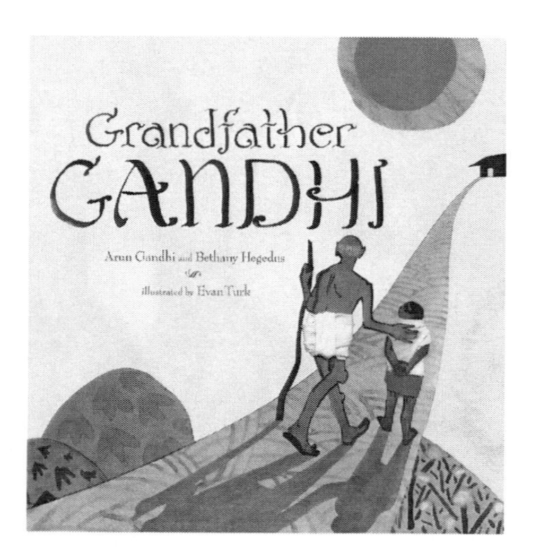

our world heal," the authors tell readers. As students read about Gandhi, encourage them to take a global view in considering his life, work, and philosophy. (They can go to http://www.wartgames.com/themes/people/gandhi.html to find out more about him, including actual photographs of this frail leader, letters he has written, and much more.)

Ask older students to research trouble spots around the world, for example, the conflict between the Palestinians and the Israelis. They can communicate their information visually using graphs, pictograms, icons, and so on, and code them to indicate problem areas from greatest to least volatile. Two very interesting books that will give students examples of how to do this are Jon Richards's and Ed Simkins's *Plant Earth: The World in Infographics* (2013) and *The Natural World: The World in Infographics* (2013). Once they determine these trouble spots, students might wish to choose one and discuss what the countries involved are currently doing to solve their problems and what nonviolent steps might be taken to resolve the conflict. Younger students might want to review conflicts that have taken place in the school yard, classroom, or neighborhood during the week. What creative ways can they think of that might have resolved these issues. Perhaps they can contribute a list of ideas for a chart on how to resolve conflicts peacefully for display in the school lobby.

Rachel Carson was born in Pennsylvania in 1907 and became interested in the natural world at an early age. Following her undergraduate work, she attended Johns Hopkins University on scholarship and received a master's degree, one of only a handful of women to do so. Carson became a marine biologist, worked for the Bureau of Fisheries, and eventually devoted herself to research and writing about the effects of pollution and insecticides on water, air, and animal life. Laurie Lawlor tells Carson's story in *Rachel Carson and Her Book that Changed the World* (2012). In it she describes the incredible opposition Carson received from a chemical company that threatened to sue *The New Yorker* and Houghton Mifflin for publishing her work, from several government agencies, and even from the secretary of agriculture. Many called her an alarmist and "an hysterical woman" (31), but her book, *Silent Spring*, eventually led to the banning of DDT and "opened the minds of millions to what was considered to be a new concept at the time: what we do to the air, water, and soil directly affects us, future generations, and animals and plants that share the earth with us" (31). Suggested activities following this reading:

a) Rachel Carson called her ground-breaking book *Silent Spring*. She envisioned a spring in which there would be no bird song because pollution and insecticides would have killed off the avian population. The title conjures up a stark result of human disregard for the environment. Ask students to think of other powerful titles for publications about environmental issues—titles that will capture people's attention and inspire them to take action. Create a hall bulletin board with these titles and invite other classes to write responses to them.
b) Rachel Carson wrote several books and articles. Read from some of these sources and compare them to current articles about the environment. Do Carson's views still hold up? What are some similarities and differences?

"The families used to be hungry. / Their animals were hungry too. / But then things began to change / all because of a tree." In *The Mangrove Tree* (2011), Susan L. Roth and Trumbore describe how Dr. Gordon Sato, a Japanese-American cell biologist, helped to relieve poverty and famine in Hargigo, a village in Eritrea, Africa, by planting mangrove trees in salt water. Tended mainly by women, the trees flourish and multiply, supplying food for animals and fish that, in turn, provide food for the people. A lengthy afterward contains additional information about Dr. Sato and photos of him working with the local people on the planting project. Another environmental story set in Africa is Jen Cullerton Johnson's *Seeds of Change: Planting a Path to Peace* (2012), the story of Wangari Maathai who, after being educated in the United States, returned to her home in Kenya where she found that the trees that had sustained her people for generations had been cut down "as her government sold more and more land to big foreign companies." "No longer held in place by tree roots, the soil streamed into the rivers. The water that had been used to grow maize, bananas, and sweet potatoes turned to mud and dried up. Many families went hungry." Refusing to accept such a dire situation, Wangari traveled from village to village urging the women to plant trees. Although 30,000,000 trees were planted thanks to the Green Belt Movement she started, powerful businessmen who wanted the land for themselves had Wangari arrested. However, she was freed, elected to parliament, and became minister of the environment. In 2004, Wangari Maathai received the Nobel Peace Prize. Donna Jo Napoli also tells the environmentalist's story in her lyrical *Mama Miti* (2010) along with illustrations by Kadir Nelson.

Born in Massachusetts in 1959, Dr. Paul Farmer decided while in medical school at Harvard that he wanted to cure infectious diseases among the poor throughout the world. Tracy Kidder has chronicled Farmer's work in *Mountains Beyond Mountains*, now adapted for young people by Michael French (2013). Kidder traveled extensively with Farmer to the poorest areas of Lima, Peru; prisons in Russia and Siberia; and especially to Haitii where Farmer has worked extensively among the poor for decades. Kidder describes Farmer's seemingly tireless energy and his founding of Partners in Health, an organization now working among the poor throughout the world. This is an inspiring account and evidence that even one person can make an important difference. It would be an excellent accompaniment to a unit on health, contagious diseases, among others.

Stories of children who have the inventiveness and courage to dare to make change can inspire students to come up with unique ways to make a difference in the world. In 1950, in Virginia, fifteen-year-old Barbara Johns and other African American children in her community had to travel fifteen miles to attend a high school consisting of shacks covered in tar paper while white students attended a nearby modern school with excellent amenities. In *The Girl from the Tarpaper School* (2014), Teri Kanefield tells the riveting story of how Barbara single-handedly marshaled the students in her school to strike to protest conditions and petition for a new school. The strike finally got the NAACP (The National Association for the Advancement of Colored People) involved in seeking an end to segregation. The Virginia case along with those in several other states went to the Supreme Court as Brown versus the Board of Education. Segregation was declared unconstitutional in 1954, but schools in Farmville, VA, were not integrated until 1980. Barbara's parents' home was

burned to the ground and her life was threatened, but she never backed down. When he read a newspaper article about Iqbal Masih, an escaped child slave worker who was speaking out against child slavery and was murdered by those who wished to silence him, Craig Kielburger, then 12, took action. He gathered a small group of classmates who were willing to join him in working to end child slavery. He visited areas of the world where young children were forced to work to learn more about their plight and eventually founded Free the Children, a worldwide organization. Students can read or listen to stories in Kielburger's book *Free the Children: A Young Man Fights against Child Labor* and *Proves that Children Can Change the World* (1999) and learn more about the organization through its official site, freethechildren.com, and by viewing YouTube films. They can even start a group in their school. In 2001, Malawi, Africa was experiencing severe drought. Maize crops failed and people were living on a handful of food a day. William Kamkwamba, fourteen years old, had to leave school because his parents couldn't pay the fees. But he walked to a library established by Americans, taught himself English so he could understand the science books, and determined to build a windmill modeled after those in the books, to bring water from the earth. As a divergent thinker, he could "visualize what was unseen": "He closed his eyes and saw a windmill outside his home, . . . drawing cool water from the ground, sending it gushing through the thirsty fields, turning the maize tall and green." To build his machine William scoured the junk yard, picking up pieces he felt would be useful—despite the taunts of villagers who called him "misala"—crazy. He cut down trees to build a tower for his windmill, succeeded in lighting bulbs and eventually, in creating enough electricity to pump underground water into the fields. William, along with Bryan Mealer, tells how he saved his village in *The Boy Who Harnessed the Wind* (2012). Students will enjoy seeing William himself describe his experiences in a TED talk. Go to: http://www.ted.com/talks/william_kamkwamba_how_i_harnessed_the_wind.html.

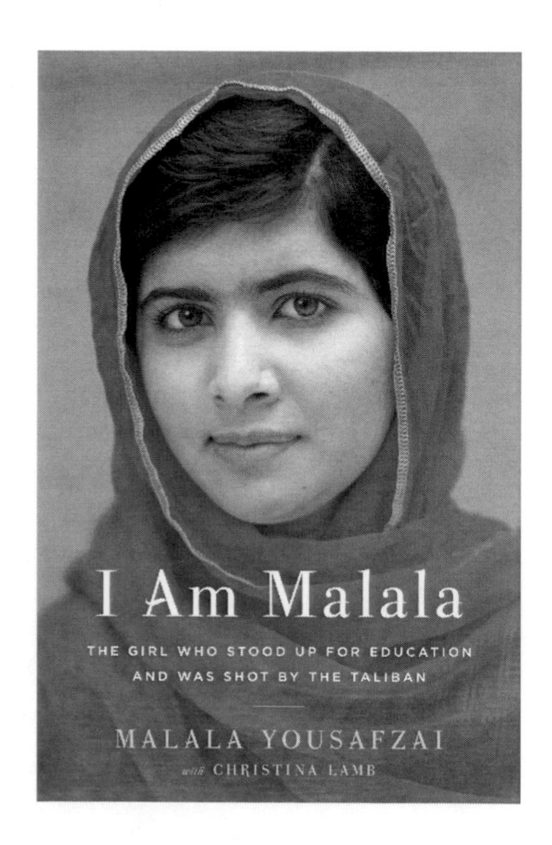

In 2009, Malala Yousafzai, an eleven-year-old living in Pakistan, wrote a blog for the BBC under a pseudonym, describing her life under Taliban rule and her advocacy for the education of girls. The following year the *New York Times* filed a documentary about her life and she was nominated for the Children's Peace Prize. Because of her outspoken views against Taliban prohibition of education for women, a young Talib entered the school bus in which she was riding on October 9, 2012, and shot her point blank in the face. The bullet missed her brain, and Malala was rushed to England for medical treatment. Now recovered, Malala continues to speak out, even though the Taliban still seek to kill her. Her story, cowritten by Patricia McCormick, is told in *I Am Malala: How One Girl Stood Up for Education and Changed the World* (2014). It is inspiring reading for older students seeking the courage to stand up for a cause or promote an idea.

Elizabeth Suneby's *Razia's Ray of Hope* (2013), a book for younger students, while not strictly nonfiction, is based on the true experiences of students at the Zabuli Education Center for Girls in Kabul, Afghanistan. Razia, a young girl, wants desperately to attend a school for girls that is being built in her village, but to do so, she needs permission from her father and oldest brother. When they refuse, she walks to the school herself to enlist the help of the teacher, who then visits the family. Only when Razia convinces her brother that her ability to read and write will help the whole family does he agree to let her attend school. Before sharing the author's note at the end of her story, ask students to write a list of arguments Razia and the sixty-nine million children like her throughout the world who do not have access to education can use to make a case to their elders to send them to school.

Powerful Collaboration

In *Where Good Ideas Come From?* (2010), Steven Johnson discusses research done by Stanford Business School professor Martin Ruef who found that "the most creative individuals . . . consistently had broad social networks that extended outside their organization and involved people from diverse fields of expertise" (166). A recent article, "Car Mechanic Dreams Up a Tool to Ease Births," by Donald G. McNeil Jr. of the *New York Times* (Nov. 14, 2013) confirms Ruef's research most convincingly. McNeil writes about Jorge Odón, an Argentine car mechanic who made the leap from viewing a YouTube video on extracting a lost cork from a wine bottle to the problem of extracting a baby stuck in the birth canal. Using the Odón Device, first built as a prototype in Mr. Odón's kitchen, "an attendant slips a plastic sleeve around the head, inflates it to grip the head and pulls the bag until the baby emerges." The device, now in production, has "enormous potential to save babies in poor countries." Because he is a mechanic used to dealing with tools, Mr. Odón was able to make a connection to solve a problem that has eluded medical personnel for years. Encouraging such collaborations can result in improving lives around the globe.

Several children's books describe fruitful collaborations that bore results greater than what the individuals might have accomplished working alone. Martin Luther King Jr. was a political leader; Mahalia Jackson was a singer. Yet, as Andrea Davis Pinkney describes in *Martin & Mahalia* (2013), when they appeared on the stage together in the famous March on Washington in 1963, her singing and her urging, "Tell them about your dream, Martin!" transformed his ordinary speech into an unforgettable call to freedom and equal justice for all. In *When Stravinsky Met Nijinsky* (2013), Lauren Stringer describes how the dancer and musician influenced one another so dramatically that both their dance and the music changed. Dolores Huerta was a teacher. César Chávez was a migrant farm worker. Monica Brown describes how they worked together for thirty years to win fair treatment for migrants in California in her bilingual book *Side by Side* (2010). Together, through speeches, marches, hunger strikes, and determination, they motivated workers to stand up to powerful bosses and fight for their rights. Reading any or all of these books and others like them can motivate students to collaborate with other students in their learning. Imagine students in the northeast sharing their learning about the Civil War with students in the South. Or students studying global warming in Alaska obtaining feedback from students who live there. Might ideas change, become richer? Might students think of aspects of the topic they had never considered before? Collaboration would be especially powerful if students are studying immigration and/or the Farm Worker Movement and can connect with migrant workers or other immigrants. With today's advances in technology, such collaborations are becoming easier and easier to accomplish, and students will likely be more aware of ways to do this than their teachers. We have discussed collaboration possibilities throughout this text. Here are a few more suggestions:

1. Create a blog about a topic and invite another class to comment as well as contribute their own learning. Teachers can also sign their class up on http://quadblogging.net/. They are then linked with three other schools to provide an opportunity for elementary and secondary students to blog with each other.
2. Go to EduClipper.net, set up an account, and clip items of interest related to a particular study. Invite another class studying the same topic to clip items they find useful. Students can clip videos, their own original writing and research, articles from the Internet, and more. A class can create a profile that describes what they are studying and asking others to contribute to their learning. EduClipper has recently (2014) announced the addition of new features: whiteboard recording capability, new annotation tools, new animations, and a new notification system.
3. If students have access to iPads, they can download the Google Drive app for free and obtain 15 GB of storage. They can use Google Documents to publish a research document on a subject two or more classes are studying at the same time. Google Docs enables collaborating classes to see and make changes in real-time or at different times. Once a document is created and shared, students can access it from any Internet-enabled device such as a laptop, tablet, or smartphone. Rather than emailing multiple drafts to numerous participants, Google Documents allows a master version to be continually updated. A chat room provides students with the ability to comment either on the entire document or specific passages. Discussions and comments can be marked "resolved" to indicate group consensus. Groups of students can also incorporate other types of documents into their shared Google Drive folders. According to Greg Kulowiec, 6 Ways Students Can Collaborate with Ipads at http://www.edudemic.com/6-ways-students-can-collaborate-with-ipads/, "Students working in collaborative groups now have the ability to create not only a Google Document to collaborate on the writing process, but they can also upload PDF files to a collaborative folder. Students conducting collaborative research can convert web-based articles and blog posts to PDF documents."
4. Create a class wiki to gather information and research and invite another class to contribute and/or comment.

5. Share research gathered during a project by creating an online slide show. To do this, go to animoto.com.
6. Go to http://inkthinktank.com/authors-on-call and collaborate with nonfiction authors on call. Learn how these authors do their research and make decisions about what to include and exclude in their texts. This would be a great school-wide project. (Also, check out authors' websites. Many of them show their drafts, note-taking, etc.)

Examining Nonfiction Authors' Angles or Points of View (Marc Aronson)

The Common Core requires more of students than any previous set of standards. The emphasis on nonfiction has already been stated. But even more, Common Core assessments ask students, not simply *what* is in a particular text, but *how* it is said, and the *evidence* the author used for building that particular case or argument. Teachers have been putting "text sets" together for years. The Common Core standards take reading these collections to a new level, asking students not simply to read from a variety of such texts but to "analyze multiple accounts of the same event or topic, noting important similarities and differences in the point of view they represent." Therefore, it is essential that students read not just one source, such as a textbook, on a topic, but several different approaches to the same subject. And they need to examine that topic through as many different kinds of texts and visuals as possible: primary sources, nonfiction books, historical pictures, articles in print and on the Internet, film, among others. In addition, since fiction and poetry writers present their stories and poems from a particular angle or view, it would be useful to include these as well. Often throughout this chapter we have clustered books on a topic to enable this kind of in-depth analysis. Two more book clusters follow later and contain a range of books to suit both younger and older students. You may wish to use only those geared to your students' ages and abilities. However, it might be useful for older students to study books meant for younger ones to determine the differences in layout and content and to serve as models should they wish to create books of their own for a younger class. As students study the books in these collections and others you provide, these are some things they should consider or activities they might undertake, depending upon their ages:

1. For what age group is each book suitable? How do students know this?
2. What is the author's point of view? What specific evidence from the text leads students to determine this is the author's stance in writing the book? How does the author build his or her argument/point of view throughout the book?
3. Compare the different authors' points of view across the set of books. How are they the same? Different? Is one stance more effective or powerful than another? Why or why not?
4. What are the most important things students have learned from each book? Why do they think these things are the most important? How has the author emphasized or called attention to the most important aspects of the topic?
5. Compare the information provided in all the books. What is included in all of them? What is unique to a particular book? Why do they think some information is omitted by certain authors and included by others? Does the information in one or more books contradict the information in others? Be specific. What evidence do the authors give for the information they provide? Do they demonstrate cause and effect? Do they use graphs,

maps, statistics? How can students determine which information is accurate? What sources will they use?

6. What kinds of study aids do the authors provide: table of contents, index, author's notes, additional back matter, list of additional resources? How do such elements help in the study of the topic? Does it matter if any of these elements are not included? Why or why not? What are some additional things students have learned from author's notes and/or back matter that wasn't in the body of the book? Why do students believe the authors did not include this information within the book?
7. Do the books contain pictures? If so, are they illustrations or photographs? Which do students prefer? Why? How do the pictures add to the information gleaned from the text? Would it matter if the pictures were not included? Why or why not? What roles do captions and headings play in providing or focusing information? (A series of books published by Compass Point/Capstone, 1710 Roe Crest Drive, North Mankato, MN 56003, called *Capturing History* may help students develop their visual literacy skills. Each 64-page book discusses one photograph, such as the Migrant Mother of the dust bowl; the African American girl shown walking into an all-white school, etc.; and how it galvanized public opinion and action.)
8. How have the authors of the different books presented their material? Are there side bars, speech bubbles, direct quotes, references within the text from other books? Do the authors present the very same information in different ways? Do the authors use humor, a conversational tone, a scholarly tone? What kinds of presentations do the students feel are the most effective? Why?

Drawing on Nonfiction in Units of Study

A. Frogs and Toads

Science writer Laurence Pringle's *Frogs! Strange and Wonderful* (2012) provides a wealth of information about these creatures. In addition to the beautiful illustrations, students will learn about the frogs' habitats, food, camouflage, mating, and more. In *Frog Song* (2013), Brenda Z. Guiberson categorizes different frogs by the unique sounds they make. Children who think all frogs say ribbit! ribbit! are in for a surprise. The text within the book is large and suitable for young children, while additional information in smaller print appears as end matter. Children can explore the many suggested websites for additional information. The illustrations are stunning. After enjoying this book, students can go to http://animaldiversity.ummz.umich.edu/collections/frog_calls/ to listen to various frog calls.

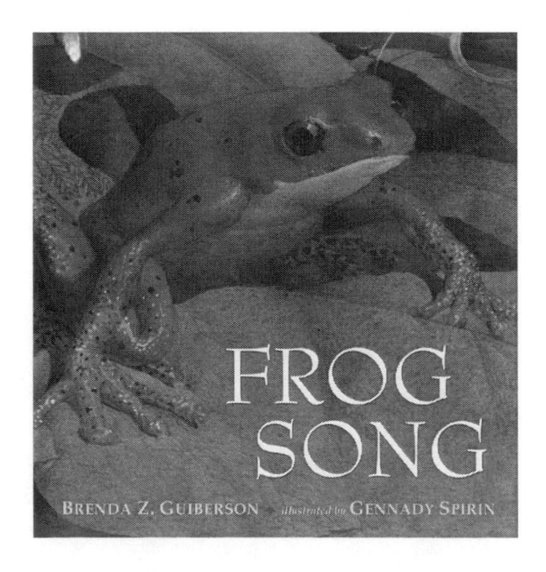

The tiny golden frog is the national symbol of Panama, and hence very special. But as Sandra Markle discusses in *The Case of the Vanishing Golden Frogs* (2012), for the last fifteen years, these little creatures have been disappearing. Her book reads like a detective story, chronicling the work of scientists who have been trying to isolate the cause of the frog's demise. Finally, in a section entitled "Frog Killer Found" (18) Markle relates how the culprit was discovered and what is being done to try and save the frogs. Back matter provides suggestions for helping local frogs as well as information about global rescue efforts. The little golden frogs are not the only ones in trouble. Pamela S. Turner follows the work Dr. Hayes and his students did to find out what was happening to these creatures in her fine book, *The Frog Scientist* (2009). Students can see many young college students of different ethnicities out in the field and in the lab with their mentor working to uncover this mystery. There are colored photos showing many different kinds of frogs as well as, unfortunately, frogs with malformations due to exposure to pesticides and other environmental problems. The work has implications, not only for frogs, but also for human food and water supply. After reading this book, students may wish to hear Hayes speak about his work, his disturbing findings and his suggestions for action. They can go to: http://www.youtube.com/watch?v=z4lijvIjp Rw. Shannon Zemlicka's *From Tadpole to Frog* is a book for beginning readers that focuses solely on the development of a frog from egg to adult stage. There are a glossary and summary questions. Add some poetry to the collection. A good choice is Douglas Florian's *Lizards, Frogs and Poliwogs* (2005). (See chapter 1.) Youtube.com has several excellent films about frogs for young people. An interesting page is http://allaboutfrogs.org/weird/weird.html, which supplies facts about frogs and toads.

B. Insects

Penelope Arlon's and Tory Gordon-Harris's *Bugs* (2012) is an excellent book to initiate students into the world of insects. There are larger-than-life photos, a Hall of Fame of bug record holders, and lots of facts. What makes the book especially valuable is that it can serve many age groups. There is information in large type on each page, as well as facts in smaller type for older readers. Pictures depict life cycles as well as insects going about their daily work. In addition, the book has an interactive website that will get students involved in spotting bugs on their own. In *Insects: Biggest! Littlest!* (2009), Sandra Markle persuades readers that there are good things about being a small insect as well as good things about being a big one. In addition to the text printed in large type, questions and additional information appear in yellow boxes throughout. Jim Arnosky, a hands-on nature explorer, presents readers with a larger-than-life view of insects in *Creep and Flutter: The Secret World of Insects and Spiders* (2012). The book is filled with information from his field notes and has eight spectacular gatefolds that show the insects up close. Steve Voake's *Insect Detective* (2009) is an interactive book that will encourage readers to follow the prompts and explore on their own. Students enamored with anything yucky will love Jody Sullivan Rake's *Why Bedbugs Bite and Other Gross Facts about Bugs* (2012). Although only twenty-four pages, it still provides a good number of interesting facts, many of them deliciously gross. Three-dimensional glasses accompany Barry and Betsy Rothstein's *Eye-Popping 3-D Bugs* (2011). This large book contains a full page of information, separated into sections, for each bug with a large colored image on the opposite page that readers view with the glasses. Eye-popping is an apt description! Several books, while not nonfiction, provide interesting information about insects in very enjoyable ways. Does it matter that honey bee colonies are in danger, with millions of these insects dying every year? Sandra Markle discusses the importance of these insects and the attempts to solve the mystery of their strange fatal illness in *The Case of the Vanishing Honeybees: A Scientific Mystery* (2013). Students can also read the latest information about the cause of these bee deaths in a *New York Times* article by Michael Wines entitled "Bee Deaths May Stem From Virus, Study Says" (Jan. 21, 2014). Younger students can follow the journey of a honey bee as it gathers nectar and returns to the nest in Raymond Huber's beautiful *Flight of the Honey Bee* (2013). Linds Glaser, in *Not a Buzz to be Found* (2012), tells readers what they would do in winter if they were a particular bug. The delightful verbs in Angela Diterlizzi's *Some Bugs* (2014) gives readers an idea of bug habits: "Some bugs click. / Some bugs sing." J. Patrick Lewis's poems in *Face Bugs* (2013) are filled with metaphor and capture the characteristics of each bug perfectly. In addition to the captivating close-up photos, line drawings add humor. In David Shannon's hilarious *Bugs in My Hair* (2013), a boy laments having lice in his hair while readers learn a great deal about these pests. A sweeping overview of all kinds of bugs is Darlyne Murawski's *Ultimate Bugopedia* (2013). It contains information and photographs on bugs, beetles, wasps, bees, ants, caterpillars, butterflies, dragonflies, spiders, flies, crickets and grasshoppers, and centipedes and millipedes and includes "Did You Know" sections. Students will even see prehistoric bugs and bugs that live in different parts of the world. The National Geographic website has some wonderful images of insects, questions, and more.

Moving Forward

The world of nonfiction for young people is vast, covering as many topics as there are curricula and beyond—and it will only grow as publishers try to provide the materials teachers need to fulfill the Common Core State Standards. Only a few topics and book clusters are possible in this brief space. You can take any topic discussed here, add additional books for discussion and activities, or set about collecting different clusters of books to meet the needs of your curriculum. Hopefully some ideas presented here will fuel your own discoveries.

References

Adams, Tom. 2011. *Feel the Force!* Illustrated by Thomas Flintham. Designed by the Templar Company. Somerville, MA: Templar/Candlewick. ISBN 978-0-7636-5566-2. Pop-ups and experiments help readers understand the physics of how things work.

Adler, David A. 2012. *Harriet Tubman and the Underground Railroad.* New York: Holiday House. ISBN 978-0-8234-2365-1. Adler recounts Tubman's heroic efforts to bring slaves North to freedom, her work as nurse and spy during the Civil War, and her last years. Extensive notes and sources.

Aguilar, David A. 2013. *13 Planets: The Latest View of the Solar System.* Washington, DC: National Geographic. ISBN 978-1426307706. This completely revised work brings the latest information about the solar system to students.

Annino, Jan Godown. Afterward by Moses Jumper Jr. 2010. *She Sang Promise: The Story of Betty Mae Jumper, Seminole Tribal Leader.* Illustrated by Lisa Desimini. Washington, DC: National Geographic Society. ISBN 978-1-4263-0592-4. This biography of the Seminole leader tells of her work as nurse, alligator wrestler, and spokesperson for her people.

Arlon, Penelope, and Tory Gordon-Harris. 2012. *Discover More: Bugs.* New York: Scholastic. ISBN 978-0-545-36574-1. Many bugs appear close-up in this fact-filled book that is accompanied by a digital edition.

Arlon, Penelope, and Tory Gordon-Harris. 2012. *Discover More: Planets.* New York: Scholastic. ISBN 978-0-545-33028-2. Readers explore the planets, moons, asteroids, space machines, and more, using this print edition as well as its digital companion.

Arnosky, Jim. 2012. *Creep and Flutter: The Secret World of Insects and Spiders.* New York: Sterling Children's Books. ISBN 978-1402777660. Arnosky provides information on many different insects and spiders. Includes eight gatefolds.

Aronson, Marc. 2013. "The Road Ahead: Common Core Insights," Consider the source *School Library Journal.* Available online at http://www.slj.com/2013/05/opinion/consider-the-source/the-road-ahead-common-core-insights-consider-the-source/ (accessed April 15, 2014).

Austic, Greg. 2013. *Game Design.* Ann Arbor, MI: Cherry Lake Books. ISBN 978-1624312748. Austic provides simple instructions and ideas for designing a game.

Baggini, Julian. 2011. *Really, Really Big Questions about God, Faith, and Religion.* Illustrated by Nishant Choksi. New York: Kingfisher/Macmillan. ISBN 978-0-7534-6678-0. This book helps readers question the meaning of belief by raising philosophical and ethical questions.

Barron, T. A. 2002. *The Hero's Trail: A Guide for a Heroic Life.* New York: Puffin/Penguin. ISBN 978-0-14-240760-8. Barron describes the qualities of true heroes and gives examples of real-life heroes, both young people and adults.

Becker, Helaine. 2014. *Zoobots: Wild Robots Inspired by Real Animals.* Illustrated by Alex Ries. Toronto: Kids Can Press. ISBN 978-1-55453-971-0. Becker describes twelve robots modeled after actual animals living in the wild.

Berger, Gilda, and Melvin Berger. 2013. *Why Do Zebras Have Stripes?* New York: Scholastic. ISBN 978-0-545-56323-9. pb A question about one of twenty sea or land mammals appears by itself on a page, and a page turn reveals the answer.

Berne, Jennifer. 2013. *On a Beam of Light: A Story of Albert Einstein.* Illustrated by Vladimir Radunsky. San Francisco: Chronicle Books. ISBN 978-0-8118-7235-5. Through constant questioning and wondering about the world around him, Einstein came up with some of the most revolutionary ideas known to science.

Bolden, Tonya. 2013. *Emancipation Proclamation: Lincoln and the Dawn of Liberty.* New York: Abrams. ISBN 978-1-4197-0390-4. Everything about this book: the writing, the stunning photos, the quotes from the people involved, and more, make this an invaluable resource for information about the document and the era in which it was written.

Borden, Louise, and Mary Kay Kroeger. 2004. *Fly High! The Story of Bessie Coleman.* Illustrated by Teresa Flavin. New York: Aladdin/Simon & Schuster. ISBN 978-0-689-86462-9. pb This appealing biography with its rhythmic text emphasizes Coleman's "can do" attitude and determination to succeed as a pilot.

Brake, Mark. 2010. *Really, Really Big Questions about Space and Time*. Illustrated by Nishant Choksi. New York: Kingfisher/Macmillan. ISBN 978-0-7534-6747-3. This book raises questions about space, heavenly bodies, and time travel.

Brown, Don. 2013. *Henry and the Cannons*. New York: Holtzbrinck Publishing Holdings. ISBN 978-1-59643-266-6. This is the dramatic story of Henry Knox's 300-mile journey from Fort Ticonderoga, NY, to Boston, MA, to deliver cannons to George Washington.

Brown, Monica. 2010. *Side by Side Lado a Lado*. Illustrated by Joe Cepeda. New York: Rayos/HarperCollins. ISBN 978-0-06-122781-3. This bilingual book describes the efforts of Dolores Huerta and Cesar Chavez to obtain better working conditions and pay for migrant workers.

Bryant, Adam. 2013. "Corner Office: Daniel T. Hendrix." *The New York Times*, Sunday Business, February 17, BU2. Bryant interviews Daniel T. Hendrix about his managing practices and his criteria for hiring employees.

Bryant, Adam. 2013. "Corner Office: Francisco D'Souza." *The New York Times*, Sunday Business, September 1, BU2. Bryant interviews Francisco D'Souza about his managing practices and his criteria for hiring employees.

Burleigh, Robert. 2013. *Look Up! Henrietta Leavitt, Pioneering Woman Astronomer*. Illustrated by Raúl Colón. New York: Paula Wiseman/Simon & Schuster Books for Young Readers. ISBN 978-1-4169-5819-2. Henrietta Leavitt, an early female astronomer, discovered a way of measuring a star's distance from Earth.

Byrd, Robert. 2012. *Electric Ben: The Amazing Life and Times of Benjamin Franklin*. New York: Dial/Penguin Group. ISBN 978-0-8037-3749-5. Byrd's account of Franklin's life and his accompanying illustrations provide a fascinating look at the man, his times, and his contributions to future generations.

Carson, Mary Kay. 2013. *Beyond the Solar System: Exploring Galaxies, Black Holes, Alien Planets, and More; A History with 21 Activities*. Chicago: Chicago Review Press. ISBN 978-1-61374-544-1. Carson provides a history of astronomy, helps readers explore heavenly bodies, and provides activities to enhance learning.

Chin, Jason. 2014. *Gravity*. New York: Roaring Brook/Macmillan. ISBN 978-1596437173. In this book, enhanced with beautiful illustrations, readers will learn about gravity and its effects on the planet.

Christensen, Bonnie. 2012. *I, Galileo*. New York: Knopf/Random House. ISBN 978-0-375-86753-8. This biography contains an account of the scientist in his own voice, a timeline, list of Galileo's experiments, inventions, and astronomic discoveries.

Cooper, Ilene. 2014. Foreward by Olympia Snowe. *A Woman in the House (and Senate): How Women Came to The United States Congress, Broke Down Barriers, and Changed the Country*. Illustrated by Elizabeth Baddeley. New York: Abrams Books for Young Readers. ISBN 978-1-41971036-0. This is a lively history of the brave women who broke barriers to serve in Congress over the last 128 years.

Crump, Marty. 2013. *The Mystery of Darwin's Frog*. Illustrated by Steve Jenkins and Edel Rodriguez. Honesdale, PA: Boyds Mills/Highlights. ISBN 978-1-59078-864-6. Scientists try to determine why and how a male frog discovered by Darwin carries its young live in its mouth.

Davis, Joshua. October 15, 2013. "How a Radical New Teaching Method Could Unleash a Generation of Geniuses." http://www.wired.com/business/2013/10/free-thinkers/all/ (accessed April 15, 2014). Davis discusses how allowing students to take charge of their own learning produces incredible results.

DeCristofano, Carolyn Cinami. 2012. *A Black Hole is NOT a Hole*. Illustrated by Michael Carroll. Watertown, MA: Charlesbridge. ISBN 978-1-57091-783-7. DeCristofano's humor, engaging text, and the many illustrations and photos in this book make a difficult concept easy to understand.

Demarest, Chris. 2010. *Arlington: The Story of Our Nation's Cemetery*. New York: Flash Point/Roaring Brook. ISBN 978-1-59643-517-9. Demarest writes about the history of Arlington, some of the heroes buried there, the ceremonies performed there, and the care of this special place.

Demi. 2014. *Florence Nightingale*. New York: Henry Holt. ISBN 978-0-8050-9729-0. Demi recounts Nightingale's untiring efforts to improve nursing conditions in field hospitals and for the general public as well.

Diterlizzi, Angela. 2014. *Some Bugs*. Illustrated by Brendan Wenzel. New York: Beach Lane/Simon & Schuster. ISBN 978-1-4424-5880-2. Different bugs "glide," "hop," "swim," and more as they make their way through this enjoyable book.

DK Publishing. *The Civil War: A Visual History*. New York: DK Publishing. ISBN 978-0756671853. With pictures from the Smithsonian's collection, this large format pictorial history of the Civil War is stunning.

Farrell, Mary Cronk. 2014. *Pure Grit: How American World War II Nurses Survived Battle and Prison Camp in the Pacific*. New York: Abrams. ISBN 978-1-4197-1028-5. This story, filled with archival photos, glossary, end notes, and timeline, relates the heroic service and imprisonment of U.S. army nurses serving in the Philippines during World War II.

Florian, Douglas. 2007. *Comets, Stars, the Moon, and Mars: Space Poems and Paintings*. San Francisco: Harcourt. ISBN 0-15-205372-7. Florian's twenty poems sing the praises of the universe.

Florian, Douglas. 2005. *Lizards, Frogs, and Polliwogs*. Boston: Sandpiper/Houghton Mifflin Harcourt. ISBN 978-0152052485. Among these twenty-one poems about reptiles and amphibians are "The Tortoise" (9), who wears a helmet on its back and "The Wood Frog" (38), "a frozen frogsicle."

Freedman, Russell. 2013. *Becoming Ben Franklin: How a Candle-Maker's Son Helped Light the Flame of Liberty*. New York: Holiday House. ISBN 978-0-8234-2374-3. Freedman's brilliant biography describes how Franklin's ingenuity and hard work helped him rise from a poor boy to one of the most important men of his era. Filled with period photos and art.

Gandhi, Arun, and Bethany Hegedus. 2014. *Grandfather Gandhi*. Illustrated by Evan Turk. New York: Atheneum/Simon & Schuster. ISBN 978-1-4444-2365-7. Arun Gandhi tells the story of how he learned to use his anger for good when he lived in his grandfather's village for two years.

Glaser, Linda. 2013. *Not a Buzz to Be Found: Insects in Winter*. Illustrated by Jaime Zollars. Minneapolis: Millbrook. ISBN 978-0-7613-5644-8. This book shows what twelve different insects do to survive the winter.

Guiberson, Brenda Z. 2013. *Frog Song*. Illustrated by Gennady Spirin. New York: Henry Holt. ISBN 978-0-8050-9254-7. Guiberson identifies frogs by their different songs in this beautiful book.

Harness, Cheryl. 2013. *Mary Walker Wears the Pants: The True Story of the Doctor, Reformer, and Civil War Hero*. Illustrated by Carlo Molinari. Chicago: Albert Whitman & Company. ISBN 978-0-8075-4990-2. Mary Walker, one of the first female doctors, served during the Civil War and was not afraid to shock people by her dress and lifestyle.

Higgins, Nadia. 2013. *The Solar System through Infographics*. Minneapolis: Learner Publishing Group. ISBN 978-1-4677-1289-7. This book helps students understand the concepts related to the solar system by presenting them visually.

Hopkinson, Deborah. 2012. *Annie and Helen*. Illustrated by Raul Colón. New York: Schwartz & Wade/Random House. ISBN 978-0375857065. Hopkinson relates Annie Sullivan's role in helping Helen Keller, deaf and blind, succeed.

Hughes, Catherine D. 2013. *National Geographic Kids First Big Book of Space*. Illustrated by David A. Aguilar. Washington, DC: National Geographic. ISBN 978-1-42631014-0. This is a fine overview of the solar system for younger students.

Heos, Bridget. 2013. *Stronger than Steel: Spider Silk DNA and the Quest for Better Bulletproof Vests, Sutures, and Parachute Rope*. Photographs by Andy Comins. New York: Houghton Mifflin Books for Children. ISBN 978-0-547-68126-9. Heos describes the work of scientist Randy Lewis who is studying how goats genetically implanted with golden orb weaver spider DNA can produce milk with proteins strong enough to be spun into better and stronger products.

Hoose, Phillip. 2009. *Claudette Colvin: Twice Toward Justice*. New York: Melanie Kroupa/Farrar Straus Giroux. ISBN 978-0-374-31322-7. Hoose recounts Colvin's role in the Montgomery bus boycott and the injustices suffered by African Americans in the South during the 1940s and 1950s.

Hoose, Phillip. 2012. *Moonbird: A Year on the Wind with the Great Survivor B95*. New York: Farrar Straus Giroux. ISBN 978-0-374-30468-3. Hoose describes the year he spent following the migration of B95, a tiny rufa shore bird.

Huber, Raymond. 2013. *Flight of the Honey Bee*. Illustrated by Brian Lovelock. Somerville, MA: Candlewick. ISBN 978-0-76366760-3. This engaging book follows a honey bee out of its nest as it gathers nectar, escapes from a predator, and returns home to share its nectar and alert other bees to where the good flowers are.

Johnson, Jen Cullerton. 2010. *Seeds of Change*. Illustrated by Sonia Lynn Sadler. New York: Lee & Low. ISBN 978-1-60060-367-9. Wangari Maathai started the Green Belt movement in Kenya to plant millions of trees, eventually was elected to parliament and received the Nobel Peace Prize.

Johnson, Steven. 2010. *Where Good Ideas Come From: The Natural History of Innovation*. New York: Riverhead Books/Penguin Group. ISBN 978-1-59448-771-2. Johnson examines seven key patterns behind innovation.

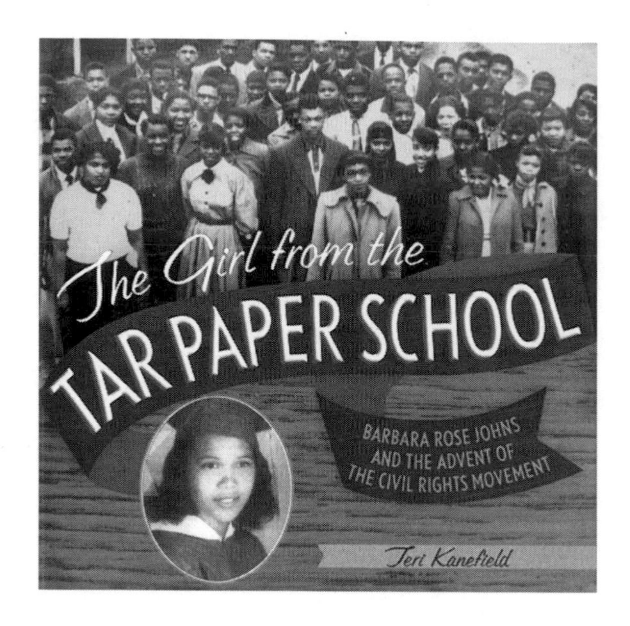

Kamkwamba, William, and Bryan Mealer. 2012. *The Boy Who Harnessed the Wind*. New York: Dial/Penguin. ISBN 978-0-8037-3511-8. William Kamkwamba, age fourteen, built a windmill out of scraps to pump water into a drought-starved field to save his village in Malawi, Africa.

Kanefield, Teri. 2014. *The Girl from the Tarpaper School*. New York: Abrams Books for Young Readers. ISBN 978-1-4197-0796-4. In 1950, Barbara Johns organized a student strike for a new school equal to what white students had. This led to the Brown versus the Board of Education decision.

Kelly, David A. 2013. *Miracle Mud: Lena Blackburne and the Secret Mud that Changed Baseball*. Illustrated by Oliver Dominguez. Minneapolis: Millbrook Press. ISBN 978-0-7613-8092-4. Lena Blackburne, a major league baseball coach, discovers a special mud near a river close to his home that removes the shine from new baseballs without making them soggy.

Kidder, Tracy. 2009. *Mountains Beyond Mountains*. Adapted for young people by Michael French (2013). New York: Delacorte/Random House. ISBN 978-0-385-74318-1. Kidder describes Dr. Paul Farmer's work to cure the sick poor throughout the world and his founding of the organization Partners in Health.

Kielburger, Craig. 1999. *Free the Children: A Young Man Fights against Child Labor and Proves that Children Can Change the World*. New York: Harper Perennial. ISBN 978-0060930653. Kielburger relates how his Free the Children movement is transforming lives around the world.

Krull, Kathleen. 2013. *Benjamin Franklin*. Illustrated by Boris Kulikov. New York: Viking/Penguin Young Readers Group. ISBN 978-0-670-01287-9. Krull emphasizes Franklin's scientific contributions and injects her biography with humor.

Landau, Elaine. 2006. *Fleeing to Freedom on the Underground Railroad: The Courageous Slaves, Agents, and Conductors*. Minneapolis: Twenty-First-Century Books. ISBN 978-0-82253490-7. Landau describes the escape route used by fugitive slaves and the work of those who helped them.

Law, Dr. Stephen. 2009. *Really, Really Big Questions about Life, the Universe, and Everything*. Illustrated by Nishant Choksi. New York: Kingfisher/Macmillan. ISBN 978-0-7534-6500-4. The questions in this book help youngsters investigate the meaning of life and the world around them.

Law, Stephen. 2012. *Really, Really Big Questions about Me and My Body*. Illustrated by Marc Aspinall. New York: Kingfisher/Macmillan. ISBN 978-0-7534-6892-0. Law presents questions about where people come from, how our bodies work, how we know things, and much more.

Lawlor, Laurie. 2012. *Rachel Carson and Her Book that Changed the World*. Illustrated by Laura Beingessner. New York: Holiday House. ISBN 978-0-8234-2370-5. Lawlor describes Carson's love of the sea and all nature and how her book *Silent Spring* revolutionized thinking about the environment.

Lee, Dora. 2011. *Biomimicry: Inventions Inspired by Nature*. Illustrated by Margot Thompson. Tonawanda, NY: Kids Can Press. ISBN 978-1-55453-467-8. Lee provides many examples of the ways in which inventors, scientists, and engineers copy nature to produce the products we use.

Levinson, Cynthia. 2012. *We've Got a Job: The 1963 Birmingham Children's March*. Atlanta: Peachtree. ISBN 978-1-56145-627-7. In 1963, thousands of African American children endured beatings, attacks by dogs, dousings with powerful fire hoses, and arrests to win the end of segregation.

Lewis, J. Patrick. 2013. *Face Bugs*. Photographs by Frederic B. Siskind. Illustrations by Kelly Murphy. Honesdale, PA: Word Song/Highlights. ISBN 978-1-59078-925-4. Lewis captures the characteristics of fourteen bugs in marvelous poems illustrated with photos and funny line drawings. Additional back matter.

Malaspina, Ann. 2011. *Touch the Sky: Alice Coachman, Olympic High Jumper*. Illustrated by Eric Velasquez. Chicago: Albert Whitman & Company. ISBN 978-0-8075-8035-6. This is the inspiring story of Alice Coachman, who overcame poverty and prejudice to become the first African American woman to win a gold Olympic medal.

Markel, Michelle. 2013. *Brave Girl: Clara and the Shirtwaist Makers' Strike of 1909.* Illustrated by Melissa Sweet. New York: Balzer + Bray/HarperCollins. ISBN 978-0-06-180442-7. Clara Lemlich led a general garment workers' strike that resulted in better working conditions.

Markle, Sandra. 2012. *The Case of the Vanishing Golden Frogs: A Scientific Mystery.* Minneapolis: Millbrook Press. ISBN 978-0-7613-5108-5. Markle's book reads like a detective story as scientists work to discover why golden frogs are disappearing.

Markle, Sandra. 2013. *The Case of the Vanishing Honey Bees: A Scientific Mystery.* Minneapolis: Lerner Publishing Group. ISBN 978-1-467-70592-9. Markle discusses the importance of honey bees and the efforts being made to discover the cause of their fatal illness.

Markle, Sandra. 2009. *Insects: Biggest! Littlest!* Photographs by Dr. Simon Pollard. Honesdale, PA: Boyds Mills, 2009. ISBN 978-1-59078-512-6. Markle's text, augmented by incredible photographs, provides information about the smallest and the largest insects.

McGinty, Alice B. 2013. *Gandhi: A March to the Sea.* Illustrated by Thomas Gonzalez. Las Vegas: Amazon Children's Publishing. ISBN 978-1477816448. McGinty recounts Gandhi's heroic march to the sea to obtain salt for his people. Beautiful free verse.

McNeil, Donald G. Jr. November 14, 2013. "Car Mechanic Dreams Up a Tool to Ease Births." *The New York Times.* CLXIII (56, 320). A1, 4. McNeil describes a device invented by Jorge Odón to extract babies stuck in the birth canal.

Metzger, Steve. 2012. *Pluto Visits Earth.* Illustrated by Jared Lee. New York: Orchard/Scholastic. ISBN 978-0-545-24934-8. Pluto seeks help to be reinstated as a planet.

Mitchell, Don. 2014. *The Freedom Summer Murders.* New York: Scholastic. ISBN 978-0-545-47725-3. This powerful book takes readers from the murders of James Chaney, Andrew Goodman, and Michael Schwerner, who went South to register African American to vote, through to the conviction in 2005 of Edgar Ray Killen.

Montgomery, Sy. 2012. Foreword by Temple Grandin. *Temple Grandin: How the Girl Who Loved Cows Embraced Autism and Changed the World.* Boston: Houghton Mifflin Books for Children/Houghton Mifflin Harcourt. ISBN 978-0-547-44315-7. This fascinating biography recounts Temple's struggles with autism and how she used her talents to revolutionize the cattle industry.

Murawski, Darlyne, and Nancy Honovich. 2013. *Ultimate Bugopedia: The Most Complete Bug Reference Ever.* Washington, DC: National Graphic. ISBN 978-1426313769. This reference contains information and photographs on many kinds of bugs, even prehistoric ones.

Napoli, Donna Jo. 2010. *Mama Miti.* Illustrated by Kadir Nelson. New York: Paula Wiseman/Simon & Schuster. ISBN 978-1-4169-3505-6. Napoli's book is a lyrical telling of how Wangari Maathai planted trees in Kenya to save her people from starvation.

Nelson, Kadir. 2011. *Heart and Soul: The Story of America and African Americans.* New York: Balzer + Bray/HarperCollins. ISBN 978-0-06-173074-0. A female narrator recounts African Americans' contributions to the history of the United States, their trials and triumphs.

Nelson, Kadir. 2012. *Nelson Mandela.* New York: HarperCollins. ISBN 978-0-06-178374-6. This beautifully illustrated biography describes the life, imprisonment, and amazing contributions of this South African leader.

Newquist, HP. 2010. *Here There Be Monsters: The Legendary Kraken and the Giant Squid.* Boston: Houghton Mifflin. ISBN 978-0-547-07678-2. Newquist traces the history of belief in sea monsters and our current information about the giant squid.

Obed, Ellen Bryan. 2012. *Twelve Kinds of Ice.* Illustrated by Barbara McClintock. New York: Houghton Mifflin Harcourt. ISBN 978-0-618-89129-0. In this gorgeous memoir, Obed writes about all the ways she and her family enjoyed the ice of Maine winters in her youth.

O'Neill, Terence, and Josh Williams. 2014. *3D Printing.* Ann Arbor, MI: Cherry Lake Publishing. ISBN 978-1624311383. The authors discuss the innovations made possible by 3D printing and provide basic instructions for using a 3D printer. Other books in the series *are Makerspaces, Digital Badges, Maker Faire, Arduino, Raspberry Pi,* and *E-Textiles.*

Partridge, Elizabeth. 2009. *Marching for Freedom: Walk Together, Children, and Don't You Grow Weary.* New York: Viking/Penguin. ISBN 978-0-670-01189-6. Partridge recounts the role children played in the march from Selma to Montgomery to secure voting rights for African Americans.

Pflugfelder, "Science Bob," and Steve Hockensmith. 2013. *Nick and Tesla's High-Voltage Danger Lab: A Mystery with Electromagnets, Burglar Alarms, and Other Gadgets You Can Build Yourself.* Illustrated by Scott Garrett. Philadelphia: Quirk Books. ISBN 978-1-59474-648-2. Nick and Tesla try to solve a mystery using their knowledge of gadgetry and electricity.

Pinkney, Andrea Davis. 2012. *Hand in Hand: Ten Black Men Who Changed America.* Illustrated by Brian Pinkney. New York: Disney/Jump at the Sun Books. ISBN 978-142314257-7. Pinkney presents ten outstanding African American men in chronological order whose accomplishments and vision had a profound effect on the lives of millions.

Pinkney, Andrea Davis. 2013. *Martin & Mahalia: His Words Her Song.* Illustrated by Brian Pinkney. New York: Little Brown. ISBN 978-0-316-07013-3. Martin Luther King Jr. and Mahalia Jackson worked together to achieve civil rights for African Americans.

Pringle, Laurence. 2012. *Frogs! Strange and Wonderful.* Illustrated by Meryl Henderson. Honesdale, PA: Boyds Mills. ISBN 978-1-59078-371-9. Beautiful illustrations and fascinating facts fill this book about a large variety of frogs.

Rake, Jody Sullivan. 2012. *Why Bedbugs Bite and Other Gross Facts about Bugs.* Mankato, MN: Capstone Press. ISBN 978-1429679541. This short book provides facts, many of them deliciously gross, about insects.

Rappaport, Doreen. 2005. *Rappaport's No More! Stories and Songs of Slave Resistance.* Illustrated by Shane V. Evans. Cambridge, MA: Candlewick. ISBN 978-0-76362876-5. pb This fine book contains stories, songs, and poems about slave misery and resistance.

Rappaport, Doreen. 2013. *To Dare Mighty Things: The Life of Theodore Roosevelt.* Illustrated by C. F. Payne. New York: Disney/Hyperion. ISBN 978-142312488-7. Rappaport recounts many of Roosevelt's accomplishments as he undertook different roles throughout his life.

Ray, Deborah Kogan. 2012. *Paiute Princess: The Story of Sarah Winnemucca.* New York: Frances Foster/Farrar Straus Giroux. ISBN 978-0-374-39897-2. Sarah Winnemucca fought against government injustices toward native peoples and aroused public sympathy toward their plight.

Richards, Jon, and Ed Simkins. 2013. *The Natural World: The World in Infographics.* Ontario: Owl Kids. ISBN 978-1-926973-74-6. This book explores the natural world using a variety of icons, graphics, and pictograms.

Richards, Jon, and Ed Simkins. 2013. *Planet Earth: The World in Infographics.* Ontario, Canada: Owl Kids. ISBN 978-1-926973-75-3. This book explores our planet using a variety of icons, graphics, and pictograms.

Ripley, Catherine. 2010. *Why: The Best Ever Question and Answer Book about Nature, Science and the World around You.* Illustrated by Scot Ritchie. Toronto: Owl Kids. ISBN 978-1-926818-00-9. The many questions in this simple book for young children are divided into categories such as kitchen and outdoors.

Roberts, Cokie. 2014. *Founding Mothers: Remembering the Ladies.* New York: Harper/HarperCollins. ISBN 978-0-06-078002-9. Roberts describes the contributions many women made to aid in the founding of the United States.

Roth, Susan L., and Cindy Trumbore. 2011. *The Mangrove Tree: Planting Trees to Feed Families.* New York: Lee & Low. ISBN 978-1-60060-459-1. U.S. biologist, Dr. Gordon Sato planted mango trees in Eritrea to provide food for the people and their animals.

Rothstein, Barry, and Betsy Rothstein. 2011. *Eye-Popping 3-D Bugs.* San Francisco: Chronicle Books. ISBN 978-0-8118-7772-5. This large book is filled with information about bugs. Huge pictures viewed with accompanying 3D glasses bring the insects to life.

Rumford, James. 2012. *From the Good Mountain: How Gutenberg Changed the World.* New York: Roaring Brook/Flash Point/Neal Porter. ISBN 978-1-59643-542-1. Rumsford describes in poetic language how the printing press was invented.

Rusch, Elizabeth. 2013. *Electrical Wizard: How Nikola Tesla Lit Up the World.* Illustrated by Oliver Dominguez. Somerville, MA: Candlewick. ISBN 978-0-7636-5855-7. Rusch relates Tesla's life and the enormous impact his many inventions have had on the world.

Rusch, Elizabeth. 2012. *The Mighty Mars Rovers: The Incredible Adventures of Spirit and Opportunity.* Boston: Houghton Mifflin Books for Children. ISBN 978-0-547-47881-4. Rusch relates the launching of these rovers to Mars as one of the most daring space adventures of our time.

Saccardi, Marianne. 2011. *Books that Teach Kids to Write.* Santa Barbara, CA: Libraries Unlimited/ABC-CLIO. ISBN 978-1-59884-451-1. Saccardi discusses over 400 children's books that can serve as models for student writing in different genres. Includes reproducibles.

Schanzer, Rosalyn. 2009. *What Darwin Saw: The Journey that Changed the World*. Washington, DC: National Geographic. ISBN 978-1-4263-0396-8. Much of this story is told in Darwin's own words as readers learn about his journey and theory of evolution.

Shannon, David. 2013. *Bugs in My Hair.* New York: Blue Sky/Scholastic. ISBN 978-0-54514313-4. A boy laments having lice in his hair while readers learn a great deal about these pests.

Sheinkin, Steve. 2014. *Port Chicago 50: Disaster, Mutiny, and the Fight for Civil Rights.* New York: Roaring Brook/Macmillan. ISBN 978-1-59643-796-8. Fifty African American sailors refuse to load ammunition after an explosion kills 320 people, and they are tried for mutiny.

Shusterman, Neal. 2014. *The Accelerati Trilogy Book One Tesla's Attic.* New York: Disney/Hyperion. ISBN 978-1-42314803-6. Four teens become involved in a dangerous plan hatched by inventor Nikola Tesla.

Sis, Peter. 2000. *Starry Messenger.* New York: Square Fish. ISBN 978-0-374-47027-2. pb This marvelous biography of Galileo contains beautiful illustrations as well as panels displaying the scientist's own notes.

Sparrow, Giles. 2012. *Discover More: Night Sky.* New York: Scholastic. ISBN 978-0-545-38374-5. Middle-grade readers will discover major constellations and learn about galaxies beyond their own.

Stone, Tanya Lee. 2013. *Courage Has No Color: The True Story of the Triple Nickles America's First Black Paratroopers.* Somerville, MA: Candlewick. ISBN 978-0-7636-5117-6. Stone sets the story of the first African American paratroopers in the context of the racism prevalent in the United States during the 1940s.

Stone, Tanya Lee. 2013. *Who Says Women Can't Be Doctors?* Illustrated by Marjorie Priceman. New York: Christy Ottaviano/Henry Holt. ISBN 978-0-8050-9048-2. The picture book biography highlights Elizabeth Blackwell's indomitable spirit as she goes against societal norms to become the first female doctor in America.

Stringer, Lauren. 2013. *When Stravinsky Met Nijinsky: Two Artists, Their Ballet, and One Extraordinary Riot.* Boston: Harcourt Children's Books/Houghton Mifflin Harcourt. ISBN 978-0-547-90725-3. When the dancer and musician met, they influenced one another so dramatically that *The Rite of Spring* was born.

Suneby, Elizabeth. 2013. *Razia's Ray of Hope: One Girl's Dream of an Education.* Illustrated by Suana Verelst. Toronto: Kids Can Press. ISBN 978-1-55453-816-4. A young girl in Afghanistan tries to convince her father and oldest brother to allow her to attend school.

Talbott, Hudson. 2009. *River of Dreams: The Story of the Hudson River.* New York: G. P. Putnam's Sons. ISBN 978-0-399-24521-3. Talbott chronicles the discovery of the river, its contributions to society, how it became polluted, and successful clean-up efforts.

Tarrant-Reid, Linda. 2012. *Discovering Black America: From the Age of Exploration to the Twenty-First Century.* New York: Abrams. ISBN 978-0-8109-7098-4. This comprehensive history of African Americans is a wonderful exploration of the African American community and its contributions to the United States. It is filled with pictures, has complete sources and provides invaluable information for many topics students might study.

Thompson, Lauren. 2007. *Ballerina Dreams.* Photographs by James Estrin. New York: Feiwel & Friends/Macmillan. ISBN 978-0-312-37029-9. Five little girls with muscular challenges fulfill their dreams to dance in a ballet.

Tonatiuh, Duncan. 2014. *Separate is Never Equal: Sylvia Mendez and Her Family's Fight for Desegregation.* New York: Abrams Books for Young Readers. ISBN 978-1-41971054-4. This picture book is the story of how Sylvia Mendez and her family helped end school segregation in California in the 1940s.

Tougas, Shelley. 2011. *Little Rock Girl 1957: How a Photograph Changed the Fight for Integration.* North Mankato, MN: Compass Books/Capstone. ISBN 978-075654512-3. This short book demonstrates how a powerful photograph brought the segregation fight to the world's attention.

Turner, Pamela S. 2011. *The Frog Scientist.* Photographs by Andy Comins. New York: Houghton Mifflin Harcourt, 2009. ISBN 978-0-618-71716-3. Turner follows the work of scientist Tyrone Hayes and his students as they study frogs to determine why their populations are diminishing.

Voake, Steve. 2009. *Insect Detective.* Illustrated by Charlotte Voake. Somerville, MA: Candlewick. ISBN 978-0-7636-4447-5. Readers are encouraged to discover insects for themselves.

Vogt, Gregory. 2012. *Scholastic Reader Level 2: Solar System.* New York: Scholastic. ISBN 978-054-538267-0. Vogt provides young readers with a simple explanation of the Sun, planets, and other bodies in the solar system.

Wallner, Alexandra. 2012. *Susan B. Anthony.* New York: Holiday House. ISBN 978-0-8234-1953-1. Wallner's biography tells of Anthony's tireless efforts on behalf of women's rights. It includes sources for quotes, a timeline, and bibliography.

Wiles, Deborah. 2014. *Revolution.* New York: Scholastic. ISBN 978-0-545-10607-8. Sunny, who lives in Greenwood, MS, has to decide whose side she's on as people in her town deal with Freedom Riders who have come to register African Americans to vote.

Wise, Bill. 2012. *Silent Star: The Story of Deaf Major Leaguer William Hoy.* Illustrated by Adam Gustavson. New York: Lee & Low. ISBN 978-1-60060-411-0. William Hoy, who became deaf at age three, eventually became a star outfield for the Washington Nationals where he played for fourteen years.

Wooldridge, Connie Nordhielm. 2011. *Just Fine the Way They Are: From Dirt Roads to Rail Roads to Interstates.* Illustrated by Richard Walz. Honesdale, PA: Calkins Creek. ISBN 978-1-59078-710-6. Wooldridge traces transportation improvements from the National Road in the 19th century to the interstate in the 20th century.

Yousafzai, Malala, and Patricia McCormick. 2014. *I Am Malala: How One Girl Stood Up for Education and Changed the World.* New York: Little Brown. ISBN 978-0-316-32793-0. This is the courageous story of a young Pakistani girl who was shot by the Taliban for promoting education for girls and who continues to speak out bravely for the rights of all to receive an education.

Zemlicka, Shannon. 2012. *From Tadpole to Frog.* Minneapolis: Learner. ISBN 978-0761385776. This beginning reader focuses on the development of the frog from egg to adult.

Additional Titles

While space did not allow for detailed discussion of these books, they are, nevertheless, highly recommended.

Bailey, Gerry. 2013. *Adventure Homes.* Illustrated by Moreno Chiacchiera. New York: Crabtree. ISBN 978-0-7787-0287-0. Part of the Young Architect series, this book introduces young students to basic engineering and architecture concepts and vocabulary. Readers are encouraged to think creatively about how and why homes are built the way they are. Other books in the series are *Storybook Homes, Towering Homes,* and *Working Homes.*

Bolden, Tonya. 2014. *Searching for Sarah Rector the Richest Black Girl in America.* New York: Abrams. ISBN 978-1-4197-0846-6. Bolden tells the story of how Sarah, a freed black member of the Creek Indians, became rich and went missing.

Bone Collection: Animals. 2013. New York: Scholastic. ISBN 978-0-545-57628-4. This unusual book consists of layouts of the skeletons of various kinds of animals including humans, and what they tell us about how these animals live.

Brown, Don. 2013. *The Great American Dust Bowl.* Boston: Houghton Mifflin Harcourt. ISBN 978-0-547-81550-3. Told in graphic novel form, this is the dust bowl as never seen before. A must!

Burns, Loree Griffin. 2012. *Citizen Scientists: Be a Part of Scientific Discovery from Your Own Backyard.* Photographs by Ellen Harasimowicz. New York: Henry Holt. ISBN 978-0-8050-9062-8. Burns encourages children to try a science activity for each of the four seasons.

Cate, Annette LeBlanc. 2013. *Look Up!: Bird-Watching in Your Own Backyard.* Somerville, MA: Candlewick. ISBN 978-0-763645618. This book encourages youngsters to become aware of the avian life that surrounds them, thus emphasizing the importance of observation—a theme of this chapter. She groups birds into their different characteristics, making it easier for readers to hone their observational skills. (Would also be a great tie-in to the unit on birds in chapter 1.)

Floca, Brian. 2013. *Locomotive.* New York: Richard Jackson/Atheneum. ISBN 978-1-4424-8522-8. A steam-powered train travels across the country in 1869 and readers join in the journey as they learn about the train and the country.

Freedman, Russell. 2012. *Abraham Lincoln and Frederick Douglass: The Story of an American Friendship.* New York: Clarion/Houghton Mifflin Harcourt. ISBN 978-0-547-38562-4. Freedman shows how the lives of these two great men intersect at a pivotal moment in U.S. history.

Goldstone, Bruce. 2012. *Awesome Autumn: All Kinds of Fall Facts and Fun*. New York: Henry Holt. ISBN 978-0-8050-9210-3. Young children will learn about autumn sounds, migration, hibernation, length of days, autumn holidays, and obtain instructions for engaging in autumn crafts. Lovely.

Griffiths, Andy. 2012. *What Body Part Is That?* Illustrated by Terry Denton. New York: Feiwel and Friends/Macmillan. ISBN 978-0-312-36790-9. Griffiths explains in sixty-eight short chapters how each part of the body works. Each chapter contains an amusing illustration.

Hearst, Michael. 2012. *Unusual Creatures: A Mostly Accurate Account of Some of Earth's Strangest Animals*. San Francisco: Chronicle. ISBN 978-1-4521-0467-6. Though presented with a great deal of humor, this is a fact-filled collection of fascinating animals.

Jacobson, Ryan. 2014. *Exciting Entertainment Inventions*. Minneapolis: Lerner Publications. ISBN 978-1-4677-1094-7. Readers discover how people made the important connections that resulted in some of their favorite entertainment inventions.

Jacobson, Ryan. 2014. *Marvelous Medical Inventions*. Minneapolis: Lerner Publications. ISBN 978-1-4677-1095-4. Readers discover how people made the important connections that resulted in medical inventions we use every day.

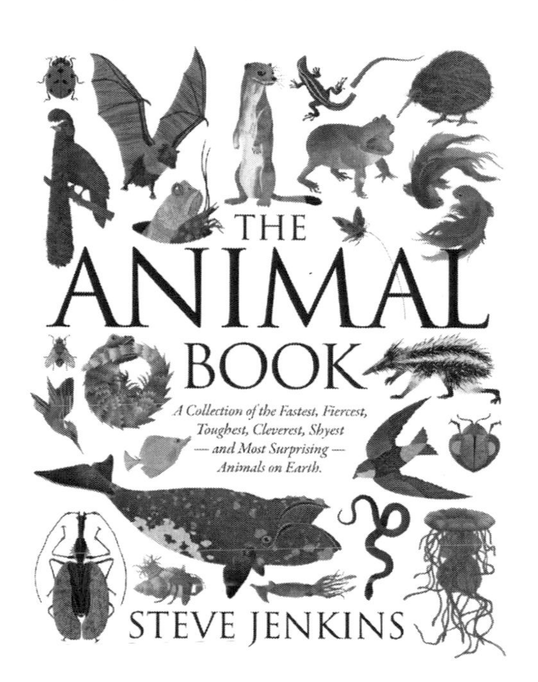

Jenkins, Steve. 2013. *The Animal Book*. Boston: Houghton Mifflin Books for Children. ISBN 978-0-547-55799-1. This big beautifully illustrated book offers information about 300 animals, past and present, along with information graphics and an appendix. Stunning.

Kerley, Barbara. 2013. *The World Is Waiting for You*. Washington, DC: National Geographic. ISBN 978-1-4263-1114-7. Kerley invites readers to go out and explore the wonders of the world around them.

Krull, Kathleen. 2013. *Lives of the Scientists: Experiments, Explosions (and What the Neighbors Thought)*. Illustrated by Kathryn Hewitt. Boston: Harcourt Children's Book/Houghton Mifflin Harcourt. ISBN 978-0-15-205909-5. In a witty, entertaining style, Krull presents short biographies of nineteen scientists from around the world.

Levy, Debbie. 2013. *We Shall Overcome: The Story of a Song*. Illustrated by Vanessa Brantley-Newton. New York: Jump at the Sun/Disney. ISBN 978-1-423-11954-8. This picture book is the story of the struggle for freedom told through the times the song played an important part.

Markle, Sandra. 2014. *The Case of the Vanishing Honeybees*. Minneapolis: Millbrook Press. ISBN 978-1-4677-0592-9. Like her book on the golden frogs, this wonderful text reads like a detective story as scientists work to discover why honeybees are disappearing.

McLeod, Elizabeth, and Frieda Wishinsky. 2013. *A History of Just about Everything: 180 Events, People and Inventions that Changed the World*. Illustrated by Qin Ling. Toronto: Kids Can. ISBN 978-1554537754. This entertaining book describes historic milestones ranging from 6,000,000 BCE to 2011.

Meissner, David, and Kim Richardson. 2013. *Call of the Klondike: A True Gold Rush Adventure*. Honesdale, PA: Calkins Creek/Highlights. ISBN 978-1-59078-823-3. In 1897, two Yale grads hear about the discovery of gold in the Klondike. Using letters, diaries, and newspaper articles, the authors tell the story of their action-packed expedition. This is a great model for using primary sources to present information gleaned from a study unit.

Nivola, Claire A. 2012. *Life in the Ocean: The Story of Oceanographer Sylvia Earle*. New York: Frances Foster/Farrar Straus Giroux. ISBN 978-0-374-38068-7. With lovely art work, Nivola writes the biography of Earle, who has dedicated her life to learning about and protecting the world's oceans.

Owings, Lisa. 2014. *Do Your Research*. Minneapolis: Learner Publications. ISBN 978-1-4677-1503-4. This book is especially valuable since it helps very young children understand how to do research. They learn such things as how to ask the right questions, what sources are, and how to share their knowledge.

Rosen, Michael J. 2013. *Let's Build a Playground.* Photographs by Ellen Kelson and Jennifer Cecil. Somerville, MA: Candlewick. ISBN 978-0-7636-5532-7. Rosen depicts how a community got together to build a playground through a Kaboom grant and shows how other communities can do the same.

Roth, Susan L., and Cindy Trumbore. 2013. *Parrots over Puerto Rico.* Collages by Susan L. Roth. New York: Lee & Low. ISBN 978-1-62014-004-8. In this gorgeous book the authors manage to give a history of Puerto Rico as well as a history of the wonderful parrots that almost became extinct.

Rusch, Elizabeth. 2013. *Eruption: Volcanoes and the Science of Saving Lives.* Photographs by Tom Uhlman. Boston: Houghton Mifflin Books for Children/Houghton Mifflin Harcourt. ISBN 978-0-547-50350-9. Rusch follows volcanologists Andy Lockhart and John Pallister as they work to predict when volcanoes will erupt and how to protect people.

Sayre, April Pulley. 2013. *Let's Go Nuts!* New York: Beach Lane/Simon & Schuster. ISBN 978-1-4424-6728-6. Perfect for units on nutrition, Sayre reveals that nuts, beans, grains, and some spices are really seeds we can eat. See also *Rah, Rah, Radishes!* (2011) and *Go, Go, Grapes!* (2012).

Sheinkin, Steve. 2012. *Bomb.* New York: Flash Point/Roaring Brook. ISBN 978-1-59643-487-5. In what reads like a breathtaking detective novel, Sheinkin in describes the race to build and steal the atomic bomb. A must for World War II units.

Thimmesh, Catherine. 2013. *Scaly Spotted Feathered Frilled.* Boston: Houghton Mifflin Harcourt. ISBN 978-0-547-99134-4. Thimmesh describes how paleoartists figure out what dinosaurs really looked like.

Thompson, Ben. 2014. *Guts & Glory: The American Civil War.* Illustrated by C.M. Butzer. New York: Little Brown. ISBN 978-0-316-32053-5. This fine book provides accounts of many heroes of the Civil War: female spies, the only female surgeon serving in the war, Southern and Northern generals, battles and much more. Filled with art work and suitable for students in middle grade and up, this would be an excellent addition to Civil War units.

5

Divergent Thinking in the Classroom

Let us think of education as the means of developing our greatest abilities, because in each of us there is a private hope and dream which, fulfilled, can be translated into benefit for everyone and greater strength of the nation.

—John F. Kennedy

Do not go where the path may lead; go instead where there is no path and leave a trail.

—Ralph Waldo Emerson

In the previous chapters we've suggested that choosing excellent books in different genres of literature written expressly for young people along with discussion and related activities and projects can lead them toward divergent thinking—thinking that helps them arrive at important questions, not just answers; that helps them look at problems, challenges, and the world around them in new ways; that gives birth to innovative ideas. Perhaps you are asking, "This sounds fine on paper, but can it happen in the real world? Can it happen in a mainstream classroom?" The answer, as demonstrated in the fourth-grade classroom of Valerie Viscome and Elizabeth McMillan, is a resounding YES!

In the fall of 2012, I approached Trish McGuire, principal of Julian Curtiss, a K-5 school in Greenwich, CT, to determine whether any of her teachers would be willing to work on a project I would later describe in this book. I explained that I wanted to feature talented teachers who, through the use of excellent children's books and the ways in which they enabled students to research a topic and apply and present their learning, would demonstrate divergent thinking in action. I emphasized that I did not want teachers to create a new curriculum but to examine the topics already scheduled for the year and to select an area of study best suited to our purposes. My goal was not to add on to the already overwhelming requirements teachers face but rather, to teach a given unit in a new way.

Students Take on the Issue of Poor Air Quality

Within a few weeks of our initial meeting, both Valerie and Elizabeth were on board, deciding that an ecology unit encompassing social studies, science, and the language arts, and slated for the spring, would be perfect. The fourth grade had, for the past several years, focused on the ecology of Long Island Sound, a body of water that graces Greenwich's shore line, focusing on threatened East Coast populations of horseshoe crabs and the need to protect them for their importance in the food chain and medical research. When the children learned that Connecticut has poorer air quality than the other New England states, they were surprised and even angered and decided they wanted to combine that issue with their study of the Sound, since air quality affects the health of the waters and its inhabitants as well. Their enthusiasm for the topic was the perfect motivation necessary for being willing to undertake the hard work involved in asking meaningful questions and arriving at innovative solutions.

Since the students would be doing a great deal of reading and research throughout the project, Valerie began the unit by discussing with them the kinds of questions readers ask themselves and even how to think more deeply about a question once it is raised. The children were encouraged to identify problems, think about them in all their complexities in order to pinpoint their causes, and, as divergent thinkers do, to make connections among different problems and their sources.

To reinforce the students' determination to do something about the quality of the air and the Sound in Connecticut and provide them with information about other young people

Valerie instructs the class in careful questioning and thinking

Valerie discusses their reading with group members

who have made a difference, we started with a collection of Citizen Kid books from Kids Can Press. The children were divided into groups called Reading Clubs, by interest, with each group reading a Citizen Kid book and taking notes. As we sat in on the Clubs and listened to their discussions and reporting to each other, we could sense the students' surprise and even awe that children as young as they could accomplish so much.

Could first grader Ryan Hreljac living in Canada really build a well in Africa, begin a worldwide network of fundraising to bring clean water to people in need, and work with his family to save Jimmy Akana, a youngster from Agweo Village, Uganda, from rebel forces? Could Kojo, a young boy in Ghana, really build a micro-lending system that he continues as an adult today from a single hen? Yes, they could, and their stories, along with examples of other child activists documented in the books the children devoured, aroused in our fourth graders a desire to become change makers themselves.

The students began a second round of Reading Clubs, this time reading a large selection of both nonfiction and fiction about the causes of and problems triggered by air and water pollution, along with earth-friendly solutions. In addition to the reading in their clubs, the children read a variety of materials during their free time and at home, so that by the end of the project, they had used all five boxes of books available to them. Valerie and Elizabeth also read related books such as the *Barefoot Book of Earth Tales* by Dawn Casey as read-alouds, thereby rounding out the children's exposure to many literary genres.

Elizabeth discusses their reading with group members

Girls expand information by perusing the internet

A student takes notes

Reading led to questions and questions to research as the students delved more deeply into the causes and effects of air pollution and thought hard about meaningful solutions. They studied nonfiction materials and websites looking for information and for solutions currently being employed, and went on field trips to clean up a shore area and to study the current health of the Long Island Sound and its horseshoe crab population. As their research notes grew, so did their questions, discoveries, and discussions. The children talked about diseases caused by air pollution and even questioned the integrity of pharmaceutical companies. Would they really want cleaner air and less instances of asthma, or would they rather keep selling asthma drugs? They talked about the relationship between the emissions generated by trucks transporting produce from long distances and pollution in the air, and how community gardens might alleviate the problem. Later in the process, a group would write and perform a play to drive home this message. Eventually the students began compiling and developing their findings by creating a wiki, an activity they accomplished completely on their own. It is filled with both internet and text resources and comments on each other's ideas. What is extremely interesting about their wiki is that they used it,

Two boys take notes gleaned from a text

not just as a computer note-taking and sharing system, but as a place to think and to generate new ideas as a result of that thinking. To cite just a few examples: One student wrote, "This page is for me to collect my ideas to solve the air pollution problem by myself!" The group that read about Ryan and Jimmy wrote a list of ideas inspired by the boys' work in Africa. They suggested that to help the people of Africa, solar panels could be placed on poles since thatch roofs would not be strong enough to hold them. They even thought the panels could ride atop donkey carts! Stella listed a series of questions she would use to interview a couple who had solar panels on their roof to determine the effectiveness, cost, and drawbacks, if any, to using them.

As research progressed, we invited Mr. Sam Sampieri, an Environmental Analyst from the Connecticut Department of Energy and Environmental Protection in Hartford to speak to the children. He spent an entire morning with the class, showing them how summer heat waves affect air quality, how the department measures and tracks air pollution, and describing other services provided by the agency. He was delighted with the depth and breadth of the children's questions, their enthusiasm for the topic, and with their ideas in progress—evidence that they had been reading, writing, and thinking about the issue seriously for many weeks. The students were able to follow Mr. Sampieri on individual computers as he showed them various graphs, maps, and other information from the agency's website.

Sam Sampieri from the CT Dept. of Energy and Environmental Protection speaks to the class

Students follow Mr. Sampieri's talk on individual computers

The time was fast approaching for the students to incorporate their research and discoveries into innovative ideas. Valerie spent some class time discussing how government works and how laws are made, since being a change maker often involves convincing government officials to take legislative action. While a letter-writing campaign is not a novel idea, embarking on one helped get the children's activist juices flowing as they wrote to different stake holders about their environmental concerns. One wrote to Greenwich Town Selectmen to advocate for the creation of a local community garden. (Progress is being made on the project at this writing.) Another letter to town officials advocated bike lanes. The gym teacher received a letter asking for exercise bikes that would be hooked up to a power source to generate energy. Even the governor received letters containing the children's ideas. From letters the students transitioned to creating inventions and designing vehicles that would provide cleaner energy. In addition, they wrote original short stories, plays, songs, and choreographed dances about cleaning the air and water.

Divergent Thinkers Present Their Innovative Projects

Shortly before the end of the school year, parents and school personnel gathered in room 4V to witness the results of the children's three-month study. On the white board as we entered the room was a quote from Anne Frank: "How wonderful it is that nobody need wait a single moment before beginning to improve the world."—the lead-in to a lovely film put together by Valerie in which she described in words and pictures the children's passionate response to the issue of air pollution in Connecticut and their determination to solve the

Girls present a radio broadcast, "Clean Air 101"

problem. The film took us through the months of work that brought the students to the projects and ideas they were about to share with us. Here are some highlights:

Three girls presented "Clean Air 101," a news broadcast they wrote along with a video they made of themselves riding exercise bicycles to generate energy.

Two boys redesigned the main thoroughfare in Greenwich to accommodate bicycle lanes.

A redesigned Main Street

Eric had studied a book of science experiments involving the properties of air and air pollution. One experiment suggested putting a jar top coated with petroleum jelly out for several hours and noting what collected in the jelly to determine the amount of the pollutants in the air. This gave him the idea of designing an air-cleaning factory using the jelly as a pollutant collector. He showed us a model of his factory (replicated in the diagram below) as he explained its operation:

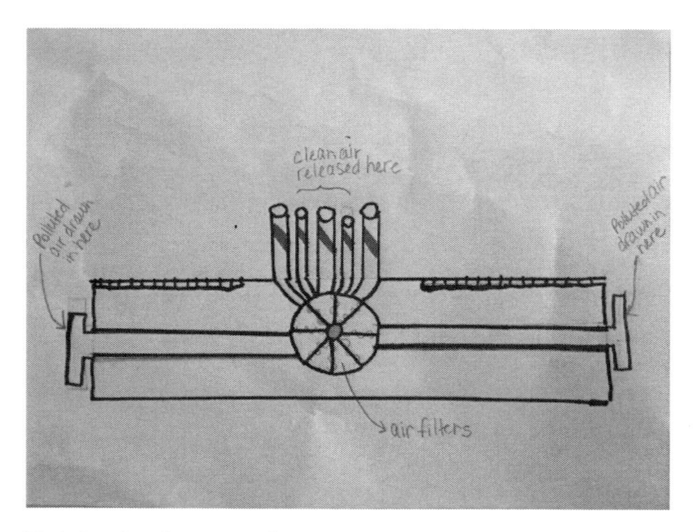

Eric's air cleaning factory

My air cleaning factory operates on solar energy so it only cleans the air, not pollutes it. Solar panels on top of the factory convert the energy from the sun into the necessary power for the factory to operate. First, the polluted air is drawn in through an opening(s) into a circular room that contains petroleum jelly-covered screens, which filter the air. A meter is used to measure the quality of the filtered air. Then, when the quality is high, the cleaned air gets moved out of the filters and into a chamber that releases it through chimneys into the atmosphere.

Kyle also showed us a factory, this one for manufacturing cars, which he constructed out of Lego. He explained:

> My car factory is powered by hydro power and solar panels. For the hydro power, there is a large paddle wheel turned by water. The wheel turns an axle, which is

Kyle's car manufacturing factory

connected to a conveyor belt. The conveyor belt moves the cars from station to station, while they are being built. The solar panels provide electricity to power the robots and tools needed to build the cars. This factory would reduce air pollution by not having to rely on any fossil fuels. Since many large factories are often already near a water source (and since global warming is contributing to fast-melting glaciers and ice caps providing even more water), it would make more sense for them to use hydro-power and solar power, instead of fossil fuels, to power their factories.

Design of an environmentally friendly car

Several children looked at vehicles we already use for travel and designed them differently to reduce their impact on air quality, and explained their newly designed cars and airplanes.

Alexander described his innovative plane: "The sun will power the solar panels on the top and the windows; and there will be small wind turbines on the bottom. This will help reduce air pollution because it won't release any CO_2." Alex even wrote a short story in which he imagined himself aboard the "first ever solar and wind powered airplane." Sena explained his environmentally friendly train:

1. Three advanced horizontal wind tubes designed after whale fins are placed at the front of the train to maximize how much energy it produces.
2. Rows of swirling solar panels are placed on top of the train.
3. Micro windmills are on the front of the train.
4. There are transparent solar panels on all windows.
5. The wheels are energy efficient.
6. There are rows of batteries under the train.
7. A cool design can be added but is not really necessary.

Sena's train

Tyler's unique idea was a billboard that cleans the air. He told us how it works while we viewed his diagram: "The billboard works by the air coming in from the vacuum on the top. The air then goes into the air pollution trap. And the petroleum jelly keeps the air from coming back out. The solar panels on the top power it so it's eco-friendly. And if there's no sun, the electric batteries will power it."

Tyler's air-cleaning billboard

Before the morning was over, we enjoyed original posters and skits, a comic strip, shortstories, and the grand finale, an original song and dance number urging us all to save the Earth.

Some Concluding Thoughts

In his wonderful book discussed in previous chapters, *Where Good Ideas Come From* (2010), Steven Johnson states, "Some environments squelch new ideas; some environments seem to breed them effortlessly" (16). The students' projects we saw and heard about during their final presentation came about, in large part, because room 4V is an environment that "breeds" new ideas. Here collaboration, so essential for innovation, is not just tolerated but required. Valerie and Elizabeth encourage students to ask questions, not just answer them, and to see connections among questions, problems, and causes. Room 4V is a place where all voices are heard, where it is safe to try new things, and even to fail in the trying.

Boys share their comic strip

Children sing and dance their passion for a healthy environment

Will any of the children's ideas actually become reality? Possibly not, although one design is already being shown to some company executives at the time of this writing. But what is even more important is that these children are thinking in big ways, seeing what is already in use—things like solar and wind power and batteries—and figuring out ways to employ them differently or more effectively. It is interesting to note that while his work was never mentioned to them, the students were following what Johnson calls "The Adjacent Possible." "We take the ideas we've inherited or that we've stumbled across," he says, "and we jigger them together into some new shape" (28–29).

What is especially gratifying is that all of the students ended the project with the conviction that, young as they are, they can truly make a difference. In fact, in our conversations to evaluate the unit, Valerie mentioned that every student was certain the publishers gave us so many books because they (the publishers) felt that only children, not adults, could solve the environmental problems facing the planet! Many of the students said they plan to continue their thinking over the summer and into the school years that lie ahead of them. Mitzi Montoya, dean of the College of Technology and Innovation, Arizona State University, writing in the September 3, 2013, issue of *Science Times*, states,

> If I could change one thing about engineering education—well, actually, all education—it would be to center it around solving real problems and making things. In other words, we ought to be creating innovators and inventors at our engineering schools. (D4)

Surely, the students in Valerie's and Elizabeth's class will grow into the tinkerers, innovators, and inventors Montoya so desires—into the thinking adults we will need to meet the challenges of the 21st century.

When we discussed the children's learning during this project, we concluded that all of their extensive reading and writing, their careful analysis and comparison of texts, their talking and listening certainly demonstrated that they had met many important Common Core Standards for the Language Arts. These are just a few examples:

CCSS.ELA-Literacy.RL.4.1 Refer to details and examples in a text when explaining what the text says explicitly and when drawing inferences from the text.
CCSS.ELA-Literacy.RI.4.2 Determine the main idea of a text and explain how it is supported by key details; summarize the text.
CCSS.ELA-Literacy.RI.4.4 Determine the meaning of general academic and domain-specific words or phrases in a text relevant to a grade 4 topic or subject area.
CCSS.ELA-Literacy.RI.4.7 Interpret information presented visually, orally, or quantitatively (e.g., in charts, graphs, diagrams, time lines, animations, or interactive elements on web pages) and explain how the information contributes to an understanding of the text in which it appears.
CCSS.ELA-Literacy.RI.4.8 Explain how an author uses reasons and evidence to support particular points in a text.
CCSS.ELA-Literacy.RI.4.9 Integrate information from two texts on the same topic in order to write or speak about the subject knowledgeably.
CCSS.ELA-Literacy.SL.4.1 Engage effectively in a range of collaborative discussions (one-on-one, in groups, and teacher-led) with diverse partners on *grade 4 topics and texts,* building on others' ideas and expressing their own clearly.
CCSS.ELA-Literacy.SL.4.4 Report on a topic or text, tell a story, or recount an experience in an organized manner, using appropriate facts and relevant, descriptive details to support main ideas or themes; speak clearly at an understandable pace.
CCSS.ELA-Literacy.SL.4.5 Add audio recordings and visual displays to presentations when appropriate to enhance the development of main ideas or themes.
CCSS.ELA-Literacy.SL.4.6 Differentiate between contexts that call for formal English (e.g., presenting ideas) and situations where informal discourse is appropriate (e.g., small-group discussion); use formal English when appropriate to task and situation.

Future Goals

It would have expanded and enriched the children's experience and perhaps even led to more innovative ideas if they had had the opportunity to share their learning with other students. With today's advanced technology, they might have engaged in face-to-face conversations via their iPads or other means and exchanged written work, films, and other materials, with other classes in the district, or even with students in other states and countries interested in the same concerns. Initially, we had intended to arrange for this, but we were not able to put this phase of the project in place in time for a meaningful exchange. Certainly, it is something we would wish to include in future units.

It would also have been wonderful to enable the students, where possible, to go beyond their drawings and designs and actually make some of their creations, in whole or in part. With the maker movement now in full swing, even very young children are becoming participants. More and more libraries and schools are investing in 3D printers and other necessary equipment so that young people can engage in hands-on learning and creating. Certainly thinking carefully about how something will work and what is necessary to make it work is a prerequisite for building it. Being able to turn their idea into a product is motivation enough for our students to engage in this kind of deep thinking. (See the Appendix for an article explaining the Maker Movement, a video of a young girl who actually has her own online maker show, and other helpful links and suggestions for becoming involved in the maker movement.)

Parent Comments

Their children's hard work and enthusiasm for this project did not go unnoticed by their parents and other caregivers. Students were bringing books home, discussing their concerns regarding air and water pollution, and talking about their ideas for solutions. Comments such as: "It was amazing to see all the children coming up with different ideas and putting in a tremendous amount of effort to gather their thoughts to present to the class"; "It was so fun to see the students use creative thinking and act out their creations. This shows how important it is to not only learn about something in an interesting way but also to have fun and be creative"; and "We think it is important for kids to be exposed to learn and understand ways to help improve air quality and protect our environment," are indicative of what parents told us throughout this study.

The Final Word

It seems right to give the students themselves the last word about what this project meant to them:

I wish I could do this all over again and stop air pollution.
Deb

I want to do this again because so I can get to learn more about one subject and trying to find new ways to solve it.
Nicole

For the whole 4th grade, I think this air pollution study was the best memory. I just can't believe it just ended. Over the summer I want to do something like this. I truly wish we can do this again next year. And I know other children would like this study.
Sofia

During the air pollution unit I had a lot of fun. I learned interesting facts, I became a change maker, and most of all, I had fun going on this adventure with everyone. I will defiantly remember this as long as I live. It is very important that people all over the world notice the huge effect Air pollution has on us all. I also liked cleaning up Tods Point. It gave me a feeling that I was making a difference in our gloomy world. It made me feel like the earth was smiling. I will imagine everything in nature will be smiling and laughing when I pass just like what the man in the book The Little Prince told the tiny prince, "I will imagine the stars will be laughing everytime I look at it." That's why this unit is important to me.
UMA

Acknowledgments

We gratefully acknowledge author T. A. Barron for supplying the video *Dream Big* and the following publishers: Kids Can Press, Toronto; Norwood House Press, Chicago; Enslow

Publishers, Inc., Berkeley Heights, NJ; Scholastic Library Publishing, New York City; Macmillan Children's Publishing Group, New York City; Lerner Publishing Group, Minneapolis; Penguin Young Readers Group, New York City; Random House Children's Books, New York City; and Candlewick Press, Somerville, MA, for their generosity in supplying the following books for use in this project:

Bang, Molly, and Penny Chisholm. 2009. *Living Sunlight: How Plants Bring the Earth to Life*. New York: Blue Sky Press/Scholastic. ISBN 978-0-545-04422-6. The sun reveals how its light is the source of energy for all living things on earth.

Bang, Molly, and Penny Chisholm. 2012. *Ocean Sunlight: How Tiny Plants Feed the Seas*. New York: Blue Sky Press/Scholastic. ISBN 978-0-545-27322-0. The sun itself narrates the story of how tiny sea plants catch its light, which then flows through them to all the ocean animals.

Barron, T. A. 2002. *The Hero's Trail: A Guide for a Heroic Life*. New York: Puffin/Penguin Young Readers Group. ISBN 978-0-13-240760-8. pb Barron explains how to live the life of a hero as differentiated from that of a celebrity, and gives examples of real-life heroes.

Becker, Helaine. 2012. *The Big Green Book of the Big Blue Sea*. Illustrated by Willow Dawson. Toronto: Kids Can Press. ISBN 978-1-55453-746-4. Becker provides stories of people around the world who are working to keep our oceans healthy and offers tips on making sustainable choices that will protect our oceans.

Bridges, Andrew. 2008. *Clean Air*. New York: Flash Point/Roaring Brook. ISBN 978-1-59643-576-6. Readers learn about the invisible gases that make up our air, the pollutants in the air, and what we can do to cleanse and protect the air we breathe.

Bourgeois, Paulette, with Kathy Vanderlinden. 2008. *The Dirt on Dirt*. Illustrated by Martha New bigging. Toronto: Kids Can Press. ISBN 978-1-55433-102-8. Readers learn the many wonders of dirt, where it comes from, and how to make the best dirt.

Bullard, Lisa. 2012. *Choose to Reuse*. Illustrated by Wes Thomas. Minneapolis: Millbrook Press/Lerner. ISBN 978-0-7613-8511-0. Readers follow Tyler as he finds ways to reuse old things. Includes directions for making reusable napkins.

Bullard, Lisa. 2012. *Go Easy on Energy*. Illustrated by Wes Thomas. Minneapolis: Millbrook Press/Lerner. ISBN 978-0-7613-8513-4. Readers learn what kinds of energy make the earth dirty and how they can use energy wisely. Includes a Power Patrol game.

Bullard, Lisa. 2012. *Power Up to Fight Pollution*. Illustrated by Wes Thomas. Minneapolis: Millbrook Press/Lerner. ISBN 978-0-7613-8515-8. Readers join Tyler to learn what makes earth's land, air, and water dirty and discover useful ways to clean up our world.

Cartlidge, Cherese. 2009. *Water from Air: Water-Harvesting Machines*. Chicago: Norwood House Press. ISBN 978-1-59953-196-0. Cartlidge discusses the invention and development of a water-harvesting machine that can pull water from the air to provide clean water in an emergency after a natural disaster.

Dávila, Claudia. 2012. *Luz Makes a Splash*. Toronto: Kids Can Press. ISBN 978-1-55453-762-4. Luz and her friends find a way to conserve water during a drought and to stop a soda company from siphoning all the ground water for its products. Graphic novel.

Dávila, Claudia. 2012. *Luz Sees the Light*. Toronto: Kids Can Press. ISBN 978-1-55453-581-1. Luz and her friends transform her fossil fuel-dependent community by creating an eco-friendly park. Graphic novel.

Donald, Rhonda Lucas. 2001. *Air Pollution*. New York: Children's Press/Scholastic. ISBN 0-516-25998-9. Donald explains what air pollution is, how it harms plants and animals, and how to help prevent it.

Donald, Rhonda Lucas. 2001. *Water Pollution*. New York: Children's Press/Scholastic. ISBN 0-516-27357-4. Donald explains what water pollution is, how it harms plants and animals, and how to help prevent it.

Dr. Seuss. 1999. Reissue. *The Lorax*. New York: Random House. ISBN 978-0-394-82337-9. The Oncler tells how he, despite the warnings of the Lorax, destroyed the trees for his own profit with disastrous results for the environment.

Drummond, Allan. 2011. *Energy Island: How One Community Harnessed the Wind and Changed Their World*. New York: Frances Foster/Farrar Straus Giroux. ISBN 978-0-374-32184-0. This marvelous book is the story of how the community on the Danish island of Samsø accept the Danish Ministry of Environment's challenge to become independent of nonrenewable energy and produced enough energy from wind and other means to power the entire island.

Feinstein, Stephen. 2011. *Solving the Air Pollution Problem: What You Can Do.* Berkeley Heights, NJ: Enslow Publishers. ISBN 978-0-7660-3347-4. Readers learn about air pollution, global warming, indoor air quality, automobiles, air quality, and public health, and what they can do to help.

Gardner, Robert. 2011. *Air: Green Science Projects for a Sustainable Planet.* Berkeley Heights, NJ: Enslow Publishers. ISBN 978-0-7660-3646-8. This book guides students through science experiments that explain the properties of air, how to conserve energy while heating and cooling air, and how to reduce air pollution.

Gray, Susan H. 2012. *Ecology: The Study of Ecosystems.* New York: Children's Press/Scholastic. ISBN 978-0-531-24675-7. Gray discusses the scientists who have contributed to the study of ecology and what we can do to help preserve earth's many ecosystems.

Greene, Carol. 2013. *I Love Our Air.* Berkeley Heights, NJ: Enslow Publishers. ISBN 978-0-7660-4037-3. This book discusses what air is, why it's important, and how to protect it.

Higgins, Matthew with Mark Stewart. 2012. *The Air Out There: How Clean Is Clean?* Chicago: Norwood House Press. ISBN 978-1-59953-451-0. This book examines the science of air pollution, its causes, and separates fact from fiction regarding man-made and natural pollution.

Horowitz, Ruth. 2004. *Crab Moon.* Illustrated by Kate Kiesler. Somerville, MA: Candlewick. ISBN 978-0-7636-2313-5. One night Daniel sees many horseshoe crabs come to shore to lay their eggs and is able to help one of them return to the sea.

Kaner, Etta. 2012. *Earth-Friendly Buildings, Bridges and More.* Illustrated by Stephen MacEachern. Toronto: Kids Can Press. ISBN 978-1-55453-570-5. This wonderfully readable book employs comics, letters, stories, and graphics to show how innovative engineers and architects are actually designing earth-friendly buildings.

Lichtenheld, Tom. 2011. *Cloudette.* New York: Christy Ottaviano/Henry Holt. ISBN 978-0-8050-877-5. Cloudette, the littlest cloud, finds a way to do something big and important like the other clouds do.

Mara, Wil. 2013. *Environmental Protection.* New York: Children's Press/Scholastic. ISBN 978-0-531-23603-1. This book presents the history of environmental protection in the United States, the writers that have influenced Americans' views on the environment, and what the U.S. government is doing to protect the environment today.

Mason, Adrienne. 2013. *Planet Ark: Preserving Earth's Biodiversity.* Illustrated by Margot Thompson. Toronto: Kids Can Press. ISBN 978-1-55453-753-2. Mason describes how every species on earth is linked and the importance of this rich biodiversity. She presents the dangers that threaten its destruction and offers ways we can help and sustain the planet.

Milway, Katie Smith. 2010. *The Good Garden: How One Family Went from Hunger to Having Enough.* Illustrated by Sylvie Daigneault. Toronto: Kids Can Press. ISBN 978-1-55453-488-3. Maria Luz and her family are poor farmers in Honduras who can't make a living until a teacher arrives and shows them how to farm wisely, how to grow cash crops, and how to avoid becoming victims of middlemen.

Milway, Katie Smith. 2008. *One Hen: How One Small Loan Made a Big Difference.* Illustrated by Eugenie Fernandes. Toronto: Kids Can Press. ISBN 978-1-55453-028-1. Kojo, a young boy living in Ghana, West Africa, is given a small loan. He uses it to buy a hen, which provides eggs to sell. From this he develops a thriving business that enables him to attend school. Now an adult, he obtains loans for others through a microcredit lending program.

Mooney, Carla. 2010. *Sunscreen for Plants.* Chicago: Norwood House Press. ISBN 978-1-59953-344-5. Mooney discusses how the problem of too much sun exposure for plants was solved by the development of a new, environmentally friendly plant sunscreen.

Muldrow, Diane. 2010. *We Planted a Tree.* Illustrated by Bob Staake. New York: Random House Children's Books. ISBN 978-0-375-86432-2. Two families in different parts of the world plant a tree and reap its many benefits such as cleaner air, enriched soil, and better crops.

Murphy, Wendy. 2011. *USA Today Health Reports: Diseases and Disorders: Asthma.* Minneapolis: Twenty-First Century Books/Lerner. ISBN 978-0-7613-5457-4. Murphy provides case studies of people suffering from asthma, the diagnosis and treatment of the disease, and risk factors associated with it.

Petersen, Christine. 2004. *Alternative Energy.* New York: Children's Press/Scholastic. ISBN 0-516-22804-8. Petersen discusses various forms of energy derived from renewable resources, such as wind power, solar power, water power, geothermal energy, and biofuels.

Rapp, Valerie. 2009. *Protecting Earth's Air Quality.* Minneapolis: Lerner. ISBN 978-0-7613-3878-9. Rapp shows how many of the things we use every day hurt air quality and what steps we can take to protect it.

Shoveller, Herb. 2006. *Ryan and Jimmy and the Well in Africa that Brought Them Together.* Toronto: Kids Can Press. ISBN 978-1-55337-967-6. Hearing how difficult it was to obtain water in Africa, six-year-old Ryan Hreljac determined to earn enough money to build a well there, even if it took him years. A newspaper article brought in much-needed donations and eventually brought Ryan and a Ugandan boy named Akana Jimmy together to share the gift of water.

Smith, David J. 2011. *This Child, Every Child: A Book about the World's Children.* Toronto: Kids Can Press. ISBN 978-1-55453-466-1. Readers learn that children live differently in different parts of the world and that many of them do not have access to clean air and water, adequate food, health care, education, and other basic needs.

Sohn, Emily, and Barbara M. Linde. 2011. *Environments: Beetles in the Garden.* Chicago: Norwood House Press. ISBN 978-1-59953-423-7. This book presents readers with the problem of a beetle-infested rose garden and, through the study of various environments and what makes them thrive, are offered five possible solutions. Readers must decide which of the solutions is best.

Strauss, Rochelle. 2007. *One Well: The Story of Water on Earth.* Illustrated by Rosemary Woods. Toronto: Kids Can Press. ISBN 078-1-55337-954-6. This beautiful book provides information on the sources of water and how all living things depend upon it, threats to water supply, and constructive suggestions for water conservation.

Strauss, Rochelle. 2004. *Tree of Life: The Incredible Biodiversity of Life on Earth.* Illustrated by Margot Thompson. Toronto: Kids Can Press. ISBN 978-1-55337-669-9. This beautifully illustrated book describes the interconnectedness and diversity of life on earth and how even the largest life forms depend upon the smallest ones for existence.

Tilmont, Amy, and Jeff Garside. 2012. *Man vs. Animal: Species at Risk.* Chicago: Norwood House Press. ISBN 978-1-59953-460-2. This book discusses the problem of animal extinction due to habitat destruction, climate change, land management and introduction of invasive species, and offers viable solutions.

Tilmont, Amy, and Jeff Garside, with Mark Stewart. 2011. *Trash Talk: What You Throw Away.* Chicago: Norwood House Press. ISBN 978-1-59953-459-6. This book looks at the waste products humans create, how they affect the environment, and what innovative steps young readers can take now and in the future to make a difference.

Tocci, Salvatore. 2004. *Oxygen.* New York: Children's Press/Scholastic. ISBN 0-516-27851-7. Tocci explains what oxygen is, why it is important, and some problems caused by its use.

Venezia, Mike. 2010. *Luis Alvarez: Wild Idea Man.* New York: Children's Press/Scholastic. ISBN 978-0-531-23703-8. This is the story of Luis Alvarez, born in 1911, who became a famous experimental physicist, helped unlock important secrets about the atom, and made many other great contributions to science.

Venezia, Mike. 2010. *Rachel Carson: Clearing the Way for Environmental Protection.* New York: Children's Press/Scholastic. ISBN 978-0-531-20778-9. This biography covers Carson's early life and education, how she became interested in environmental issues, and the groundbreaking work she did to rid the world of harmful pesticides.

Wines, Jacquie. 2007. *You Can Save the Planet: 50 Ways You Can Make a Difference.* Illustrated by Sarah Horne. New York: Scholastic. ISBN 978-0-545-05332-7. This book is filled with practical things students can do to make their home, school, neighborhood, and planet more environmentally friendly.

Wyatt, Valerie. 2009. *How to Build Your Own Country.* Illustrated by Fred Rix. Toronto: Kids Can Press. ISBN 978-1-55453-310-7. Readers learn how to build their own country, complete with national anthem, laws, citizens, services, and responsibilities.

Yezerski, Thomas F. 2011. *Meadowlands: A Wetlands Survival Story.* New York: Farrar Straus Giroux. ISBN 978-0-374-34913-4. Yezerski chronicles how the 20,000 acres of wetlands in New Jersey became so polluted that this ecosystem was almost destroyed and how it is making a comeback through the efforts of activist groups, government organizations, and concerned citizens.

References

Casey, Dawn. 2009. *The Barefoot Book of Earth Tales.* Illustrated by Anne Wilson. Cambridge, MA: Barefoot Books. ISBN 978-1-84686-224-3. Stories and complementary craft activities help readers appreciate and respect nature and its many gifts.

Johnson, Steven. 2010. *Where Good Ideas Come From: The Natural History of Innovation.* New York: Riverhead Books/Penguin Group. ISBN 978-1-59448-771-2. Johnson examines seven key patterns behind innovation.

Montoya, Mitzi. September 3, 2013. "Voices." *The New York Times.* Science Times. D4. Montoya voices her opinion about how to improve education.

Coda: Going Places

In *Going Places* (2014) by Peter H. Reynolds and Paul A. Reynolds, each student in the class is given an identical Going Places Kit that will enable them to build a go-cart for the Going Places race. Everyone follows the directions carefully, and everyone ends up with an identical go-cart—all except Maya. Instead of following the directions that came with her kit, she spends time observing and sketching a bird. The next morning, she starts building something with wings. "That's not a go-cart," objects Rafael. "Who said it HAD to be a go-cart?" she replies. The two then team up to build a plane that, while a subject of ridicule at first, wins the race.

May the teachers and students who have read the books in these chapters and engaged in the activities and projects they suggest continue to go to unchartered places; may they create for each other an atmosphere where risk-taking is the norm; where no one marches to the same tune; where no idea is too outlandish; and where everyone is convinced that even one person, thinking divergently, can make a difference.

It is time for us to wake . . .
you and I,
who rant about in justice,
who see all that is wrong in this world
but believe we are shackled
and powerless . . .
Open your eyes.
Feel your strength . . .
Join hands.
Right here.
Our moment:
starting now.
(From "Starting Now" in *What the Heart Knows* by Joyce Sidman, 31)

References

Reynolds, Peter, and Paul Reynolds. 2014. *Going Places*. New York: Atheneum/Simon & Schuster. ISBN 978-1-4424-6608-1. Instead of following the directions in the identical kit everyone receives, Maya and Rafael build their own kind of machine and win the Going Places race.

Sidman, Joyce. 2013. *What the Heart Knows: Chants, Charms & Blessings*. Illustrated by Pamela Zagarenski. Boston: Houghton Mifflin Books for Children. ISBN 978-0-544-10616-1. This gorgeous collection of poems will help readers through any trying moments they might face.

Appendix: Useful Websites to Encourage Student Creativity

3D Printing for Dummies
http://www.independent.co.uk/life-style/gadgets-and-tech/features/3d-printing-for-dummies-how-do-3d-printers-work-8668937.html
Andrew Walker explains how 3D printers work.

19 Pencils
19 pencils.com
This is an easy-to-use online platform for locating and sharing PreK–6 educational resources. The Basic Classroom section is free.

Activities for Kids from Smithsonian
http://www.mnh.si.edu/education/studentactivities.html
This site that provides activities for young people.

Admongo
admongo.gov
This is a game and curriculum designed to educate preteens about Internet advertising.

Building Big
http://www.pbs.org/wgbh/buildingbig/index.html
Students learn what it takes to build big as they explore structures such as skyscrapers, tunnels, domes, among others. Use the site in conjunction with a five-part PBS series.

Capstone
http://www.capstonepub.com/content/RESOURCES
Provides many teacher resources to support different areas of the curriculum including interactive books, maps, and much more. The Pebble Go data base obtained from this site provides bios and other information on well-known figures.

Choose What Happens Next
ow.ly/n3VB8
A series of linked videos in a choose-your-own-adventure style that requires students to make choices and reveals the consequences of those choices.

Code Monster
www.crunchzila.com/cide-monster
This site contains fifty-eight short lessons that teach kids to program, from basic resizing objects to more complex animation.

Crypto Kids
http://www.nsa.gov/kids/
At this site from the National Security Agency, you can learn all about codes and ciphers and even create your own. Many games and activities are included.

Digital Inspiration
http://www.labnol.org/internet/old-newspaper-articles/18689/
This extremely valuable site offers several ways to obtain articles from old newspapers online.

The Digital Shift: Great Websites
http://www.thedigitalshift.com/2013/07/k-12/ten-websites-added-to-alscs-great-websites-for-kids/
This site provides links to the Association for Library Services to Children's picks for the best websites for children. There are many other links to educational resources as well.

The Digital Shift: Meet the Makers
http://www.thedigitalshift.com/2013/06/k-12/meet-the-makers-can-a-diy-movement-revolutionize-how-we-learn/
The great article on this site explains how encouraging children to become "makers" and "tinkerers" is revolutionizing education. Examples of student makers, a list of materials needed, and a link to a video of an online maker show hosted by an amazing young girl, Awesome Sylvia, is a must-see.

EduClipper
educlipper.net
Once you create an account, you can set up virtual pin boards where you can "pin" anything that you find on the Internet for your classes. You can "clip" images, websites, videos, documents, audio files, and downloads. You can add your own original materials to your boards and share them with colleagues or the public. Students can share their learning with other classes on this site. EduClipper now has an app for the iPad that enables teachers to invite students to a class, create and share assignments with students, provide feedback to students, and create a portfolio of their best work.

Educreations
http://www.educreations.com/
This site enables teachers/students to view and share video lessons with other classes either on a browser or on a free app for the iPad. There are math, science, social studies, English, world languages, and arts videos available.

Evernote
http://evernote.com/evernote/
Students who prefer to take notes electronically can store notes here and access them on hand-held devices as well.

First Robotics
http://www.usfirst.org/roboticsprograms/frc/
The FIRST Robotics Competition is an international high school robotics competition that gives students real-world engineering experience.

Foldit: Solve Puzzles for Science
http://fold.it/portal/info/science
Students and even whole classes can play this online game in which they fold proteins and aid scientific research.

Future City
Futurecity.org
According to the website, "The Future City Competition is a national, project-based learning experience where students in sixth, seventh, and eighth grade imagine, design, and build cities of the future."

How a Radical New Teaching Method Could Unleash a Generation of Geniuses
http://www.wired.com/business/2013/10/free-thinkers/
This very worthwhile article documents the startling results when teachers let students lead their own learning.

Invention Convention
http://www.eduplace.com/science/invention/overview.html
This site provides an overview of an invention convention and how educators might set up and involve their students in such a project.

Kids Science Experiments
http://www.lovemyscience.com/
This site provides many links to kid-friendly experiments and games in different areas of science.

Kidwatching in a Digital World
https://www.smore.com/3sxe-kidwatching-in-a-digital-world
These teachers present many ways they keep track of their students' learning and report to parents. Their ideas are excellent.

The Learning Network
http://learning.blogs.nytimes.com/
This site features articles in the *New York Times* and ways to get students involved in the news by asking them to ponder thought-provoking questions and engage in other activities.

Library of Congress
http://loc.gov/index.html
This rich site offers so much, and all of it free. There are archives of documents and pictures, educational programs, and much more to aid student learning and research.

Maker Education Initiative
http://www.makered.org/about/
To quote from the site, "Maker Ed's mission is to create more opportunities for young people to develop confidence, creativity, and spark an interest in science, technology, engineering, math, the arts, and learning as a whole through making."

National Gallery of Art
http://www.nga.gov/content/ngaweb/education/kids.html
This site provides activities related to the art in the National Gallery.

National Geographic Education
http://education.nationalgeographic.com/education/?ar_a=1
This site provides resources for teachers, information on educational programs, mapping, current events, and more.

National Geographic Kids
http://kids.nationalgeographic.com/kids/
At this site young people can watch videos, click on images to see additional information and pictures, and much more. There's also a site for little kids.

National Institute of Health Kids Pages
http://kids.niehs.nih.gov/games/illusions/index.htm
Kids are encouraged to look at many illusions to illustrate that scientists must be sure of what they are seeing and not operating under an illusion.

NASA
http://www.nasa.gov/audience/forstudents/k-4/dictionary/Gravity.html
This sit provides links to various NASA activities and projects for students from K through high school.

NASA Games
http://kids.earth.nasa.gov/games/
NASA provides several enjoyable games for young people.

Nonfiction and the Common Core
http://www.ldonline.org/article/53710/
Marc Aronson discusses the value of nonfiction and ways in which to use it at home and in the classroom.

Odessey of the Mind
www.odesseyofthemind.com
According to the site, "Odessey of the Mind is an international educational program that provides creative problem-solving opportunities for students from kindergarten through college. Team members apply their creativity to solve problems that range from building mechanical devices to presenting their own interpretation of literary classics. They then bring their solutions to competition on the local, state, and World level."

Patterns of Innovation
http://p21.org/exemplar-program-case-studies/1274
View a case study of how one school gives its students from K up a global awareness through projects.

Real World NASA Engineering Design Challenge
http://nasarealworldinworld.org/
This site provides information about an engineering challenge initiated by NASA for students.

School Lunch Hero Day
http://www.schoollunchsuperheroday.com/index.html
Jarrett J. Krosoczka, author of the Lunch Lady graphic novels, has declared May 2, 2014, School Lunch Hero Day. The site offers stories about lunch heroes and ways to celebrate the school lunch staff. Teachers and/or schools can declare such a day at any time, though, and it would be a wonderful project to tie in with a unit on nutrition or advocacy to petition for better food in the cafeteria. Writing and other learning possibilities abound.

Science Kids
http://www.sciencekids.co.nz/experiments.html
This site has many science experiments, games, quizzes, projects, and more.

Smithsonian Databases
http://collections.mnh.si.edu/search/
Students can search through many databases such as those for amphibians and reptiles, invertebrates, botany, mammals, among others, see pictures of the different creatures, and find out more about them.

Smithsonian Museum of Natural History
http://www.mnh.si.edu/education/studentactivities.html
This page contains activities and games that help make many aspects of science and social studies understandable and enjoyable.

SOLE: How to Bring Self-Organized Learning Environments to Your Community
http://www.ted.com/pages/sole_toolkit
At this site parents and educators can download a step-by-step guide that can prepare teachers and parents to ignite the fire of curiosity in kids at home, in school or at after-school programs.

TED (Ideas Worth Sharing)
http://www.ted.com/
There are links to short videos of the best TED talks by noted innovators.

Tesla Memorial Society of New York
http://www.teslasociety.com/index.html
Students can learn more about this amazing innovator's life and see additional photos, memorials. Many links.

Thingiverse
thingiverse.com
After signing in to this site, viewers can search for 3D objects others have made, download them onto their computers, tweak them, and print them on a 3D printer.

ThinkB4U
thinkb4u.com
A series of Web-safety videos and tutorials from Google in partnership with others. It has sections for students, parents, and educators and addresses safe and responsible use of the Internet and cell phones.

Three Cheers for School! Building a Better School Day
http://www.parade.com/62420/michaelbrick/three-cheers-for-school-building-a-better-school-day/
Michael Brick offers seven ways to deepen students' learning and prepare them to be productive adults in the 21st century.

Touch Press
touchpress.com
If students have access to iPads, this marvelous site provides downloadable apps for a variety of subjects such as the Elements, Shakespeare, the Orchestra, and more.

VoiceThread
http://voicethread.com/about/features/
This is such a valuable tool that quoting from the site is the only way to do it justice:
VoiceThread is a cloud application, so there is no software to install. The only system requirement is an up-to-date version of Adobe Flash. VoiceThread will work in any modern web browser and on almost any Internet connection.

> **Creating**
> Upload, share and discuss documents, presentations, images, audio files and videos. Over fifty different types of media can be used in a VoiceThread.
>
> **Commenting**
> Comment on VoiceThread slides using one of five powerful commenting options: microphone, webcam, text, phone, and audio-file upload.
>
> **Sharing**
> Keep a VoiceThread private, share it with specific people, or open it up to the entire world. Learn more about sharing VoiceThreads.

Webmaker
https://webmaker.org/en-US/tools/
This site provides three web-making tools with directions for getting started.

Wonderopolis
wonderopolis.org
According to the site, Wonderopolis is "a place where natural curiosity and imagination lead to exploration and discovery in learners of all ages." There are many topics to explore, videos to watch, and even an educators' sandbox where teachers share ideas.

Youngzine
http://www.youngzine.org/
Youngzine is a child-centered website that provides articles, images, and videos about world news, science and technology, society and arts, movies, and books. School-age children are encouraged to respond to the content and may submit articles, short stories and book reviews. All content is reviewed by Youngzine's editors and updated every two weeks. Grades K–8.

Most publishers have educational materials related to their books on their websites. They also provide connections to the Common Core and other teacher resources.

Cover Credits

Chapter 1

Give Yourself to the Rain. Jacket illustration copyright © 2002 by Teri Weidner from *Give Yourself to the Rain: Poems for the Very Young* written by Margaret Wise Brown. Used with permission of Margaret K. McElderry Books, an imprint of Simon & Schuster Children's Publishing.

A Children's Treasury of Poems. Reprinted with permission from *A Children's Treasury of Poems* © 2008 Linda Beck, Sterling Children's Books, an imprint of Sterling Publishing Co., Inc. Illustration by Linda Beck.

Yum! ¡Mmmm! ¡Qué Rico! Americas' Sproutings, copyright 2007, by Pat Mora and illustrated by Rafaél Lopez. Permission arranged with Lee & Low Books, Inc., New York, NY 10016.

Face Bugs by J. Patrick Lewis, illustrated by Kelly Murphy, photographs by Fred Siskind. Copyright © 2013 by J. Patrick Lewis, Kelly Murphy, and Fred Siskind. Published by Wordsong, an imprint of Boyds Mills Press, Inc. Used by permission.

Outside Your Window: A First Book of Nature. Text copyright © 2012 by Nicola Davies. Illustrations copyright © 2012 by Mark Hearld. Reproduced by permission of the publisher, Candlewick Press, Somerville, MA, on behalf of Walker Books, London.

A Foot in the Mouth. Text copyright © 2009 by Paul Janeczko. Illustrations copyright © 2009 by Chris Raschka. Reproduced by permission of the publisher, Candlewick Press, Somerville, MA.

Twist Yoga Poems. Jacket illustration copyright © 2007 by Julie Paschkis from *Twist: Yoga Poems* written by Janet S. Wong. Used with permission of Margaret K. McElderry Books, an imprint of Simon & Schuster Children's Publishing.

The Underwear Salesman. Jacket illustration copyright © 2009 by Serge Block from *The Underwear Salesman* written by J. Patrick Lewis. Used with permission of Atheneum Books for Young Readers, an imprint of Simon & Schuster Children's Publishing.

Hip Hop Speaks to Children: A Celebration of Poetry with a Beat by Nikki Giovanni. © 2008 by Sourcebooks. All Rights Reserved.

Birds of a Feather by Jane Yolen, photographs by Jason Stemple. Copyright © 2011 by Jane Yolen and Jason Stemple. Published by Wordsong, an imprint of Boyds Mills Press, Inc. Used by permission.

The Seldom-Ever Shady Glades by Sue VanWassenhove. Copyright © 2008 by Sue VanWassenhove. Published by Wordsong, an imprint of Boyds Mills Press, Inc. Used by permission.

Cover from Antarctic Antics: A Book of Penguin Poems by Judy Sierra. Text copyright © 1998 by Judy Sierra. Reprinted by permission of Harcourt Children's Books, an imprint of Houghton Mifflin Harcourt Publishing Company. All rights reserved.

Heroes and She-Roes: Poems of Amazing and Everyday Heroes by J. Patrick Lewis, illustrations by Jim Cooke. © 2005 Penguin Young Readers Group.

Cover from *Roots and Blues: A Celebration* by Arnold Adoff. Illustrations copyright © 2011 by R. Gregory Christie. Reprinted by permission of Clarion Books, an imprint of Houghton Mifflin Harcourt Publishing Company. All rights reserved.

Cover from *Emma Dilemma* by Kristine O'Connell George, illustrated by Nancy Carpenter. Text copyright © 2011 by Kristine O'Connell George. Illustrations copyright © 2011 by Nancy Carpenter. Reprinted by permission of Clarion Books, an imprint of Houghton Mifflin Harcourt Publishing Company. All rights reserved.

Cover from *His Shoes Were Far Too Tight* Illustrations © Calef Brown Introduction © Daniel Pinkwater from *His Shoes Were Far Too Tight* published by Chronicle Books.

I've Lost My Hippopotamus. Cover used with permission of HarperCollins Publishers.

Stardines Swim High Across the Sky and Other Poems. Cover used with permission of HarperCollins Publishers.

Dreaming Up: A Celebration of Building, copyright 2012, written and illustrated by Christy Hale. Permission arranged with LEE & LOW BOOKS, INC., New York, NY 10016.

Cover from *Tap Dancing on the Roof: Sijo (Poems)* by Linda Sue Park. Text copyright © 2007 by Linda Sue Park. Reprinted by permission of Clarion Books, an imprint of Houghton Mifflin Harcourt Publishing Company. All rights reserved.

I Lay My Stitches Down: Poems of American Slavery. Illustration © Michele Wood from *I Lay My Stitches Down* used by permission, Eerdman's Books for Young Readers.

The Arrow Finds Its Mark: A Book of Found Poems. Used by Permission of Roaring Brook Press.

Paint Me a Poem: Poems Inspired by Masterpieces of Art by Justine L. Rowden. Copyright © 2005 by Justine L. Rowden. Published by Wordsong, an imprint of Boyds Mills Press, Inc. Used by permission.

Side by Side © Jan Greenberg 2008 used with permission of Abrams Publishers.

Dinothesaurus: Prehistoric Poems and Paintings. Jacket illustration copyright © 2009 by Douglas Florian from *Dinothesaurus: Prehistoric Poems and Paintings* written by Douglas Florian. Used with permission of Beach Lane Books, an imprint of Simon & Schuster Children's Publishing.

The Monarch's Progress: Poems with Wings written and illustrated by Avis V. Harley. Copyright © 2008 by Avis V. Harley. Published by Wordsong, an imprint of Boyds Mills Press, Inc. Used by permission.

Cat Talk cover used with permission of HarperCollins Publishers.

Cover from *Dark Emperor & Other Poems of the Night* by Joyce Sidman, illustrated by Rick Allen. Text copyright © 2010 by Joyce Sidman. Illustrations copyright © 2010 by Rick Allen. Reprinted by permission of Houghton Mifflin Harcourt Publishing Company. All rights reserved.

Chapter 2

I'm Bored. Jacket illustration copyright © 2012 by Debbie Ridpath Ohi from *I'm Bored* written by Michael Ian Black. Used with permission of Simon & Schuster Books for Young Readers, an imprint of Simon & Schuster Children's Publishing.

Marisol McDonald and the Clash Bash/Marisol McDonald y la fiesta sin igual, copyright 2013, by Monica Brown and illustrated by Sara Palacios. Permission arranged with LEE & LOW BOOKS, INC., New York, NY 10016.

Get Dressed ©Seymour Chwast 2012 used with permission of Abrams Publishers.

An Awesome Book Cover used with permission of HarperCollins Publishers.

Material from *Ten Birds Meet a Monster* is used by permission of Kids Can Press Ltd., Toronto. Text © 2013 Cybèle Young. Illustrations © 2013 Cybèle Young.

Cindy Moo. Cover used with permission of HarperCollins Publishers.

Young Frank, Architect © Frank Viva 2013 used with permission of Abrams Publishers.

Awesome Dawson © Chris Gall, published by Little Brown and Company.

Rosie Revere, Engineer © Andrea Beaty 2013 used with permission of Abrams Publisher.

Boy Wonders. Jacket illustration copyright © 2011 by Calef Brown from *Boy Wonders* written by Calef Brown. Used with permission of Atheneum Books for Young Readers, an imprint of Simon & Schuster Children's Publishing.

The Museum © Susan Verde 2013 used with permission of Abrams Publishers.

The Hero of Little Street Used by Permission of Neal Porter Books/Roaring Brook Press.

Robot Zombie Frankenstein! Copyright © 2012 by Annette Simon. Reproduced by permission of the publisher, Candlewick Press, Somerville, MA.

The Quiet Place. Used by Permission of Margaret Ferguson Books/Farrar Straus Giroux BFYR.

Imagine. Copyright © 2005 by Norman Messenger. Reproduced by permission of the publisher, Candlewick Press, Somerville, MA, on behalf of Walker Books, London.

Grumpy Goat. Cover used with permission of HarperCollins Publishers.

That Is Not a Good Idea! Cover used with permission of HarperCollins Publishers.

Material from *Toads on Toast* is used by permission of Kids Can Press Ltd., Toronto. Text © 2012 Linda Bailey. Illustrations © 2012 Colin Jack.

Cows for America by Carmen Agra Deedy and Wilson Kimeli Naiyomah, illustrated by Thomas Gonzalez. Text Copyright © 2009 by Carmen Agra Deedy. Illustrations Copyright © 2009 by Thomas Gonzalez. Afterword Copyright © 2009 by Wilson KimeliNaiyomah. Published by arrangement with Peachtree Publishers.

The Monsters' Monster © Patrick McDonnell, published by Little Brown and Company.

Freedom Song!: The Story of Henry "Box" Brown. Cover used with permission of HarperCollins Publishers.

The Dark ©Lemony Snicket, published by Little Brown and Company.

A Mango in the Hand © Antonio Sacre 2011 used with permission of Abrams Publishers.

My First Book of Proverbs/Mi primer libro de dichos, copyright 1995, written and illustrated by Ralfka Gonzalez and Ana Ruiz. Permission arranged with LEE & LOW BOOKS, INC., New York, NY 10016.

Tap the Magic Tree. Cover used with permission of HarperCollins Publishers.

Grandpa Green. Used by Permission of Roaring Brook Press.

Chopsticks by Jessica Anthony and Rodrigo Corral. © 2012 Penguin Young Readers Group.

Look! Another Book! © Bob Staake, published by Little Brown and Company.

Black Meets White. Text copyright © 2005 by Justine Fontes. Illustrations copyright © 2005 by Geoff Waring. Reproduced by permission of the publisher, Candlewick Press, Somerville, MA.

Night Light Cover used with permission of Scholastic.

A Long Way Away © Frank Viva, published by Little Brown and Company.

Open This Little Book Illustrations © Suzy Lee from *Open This Little Book* published by Chronicle Books.

The Spider and the Fly. Jacket illustration copyright © 2002 by Tony DiTerlizzi from *The Spider and the Fly* written by Mary Howitt. Used with permission of Simon & Schuster Books for Young Readers, an imprint of Simon & Schuster Children's Publishing.

Cover from *More* by I. C. Springman, illustrated by Brian Lies. Text copyright © 2012 by I. C. Springman. Illustrations copyright © 2012 by Brian Lies. Reprinted by permission of Houghton Mifflin Harcourt Publishing Company. All rights reserved.

Pancho Rabbit and the Coyote: A Migrant's Tale © Duncan Tonaliuth 2013 used with permission of Abrams Publishers.

The Templeton Twins Illustrations © Jeremy Holmes from *The Templeton Twins Have an Idea* published by Chronicle Books.

Hold Fast Cover used with permission of Scholastic.

P.S. Be Eleven Cover used with permission of HarperCollins Publishers.

Code Name Verity by Elizabeth Wein (New York: Disney • Hyperion Books, an imprint of Disney Book Group, LLC, 2012). Reprinted by permission.

Hero on a Bicycle. Copyright © 2012 by Shirley Hughes. Reproduced by permission of the publisher, Candlewick Press, Somerville, MA, on behalf of Walker Books, London.

A Soldier's Secret: The Incredible True Story of Sarah Edmonds, a Civil War Hero © Marissa Moss 2012 used with permission of Abrams Publishers.

Dodger Cover used with permission of HarperCollins Publishers.

Chapter 3

Nursery Rhyme Comics. Used by Permission of First Second Books an imprint of Roaring Brook Press.

Reprinted with permission from *The Green Mother Goose* © 2011 Jan Peck and David Davis, Sterling Children's Books, an imprint of Sterling Publishing Co., Inc. Illustration by Carin Berger.

Grandma and the Great Gourd: A Bengali Folktale—Chitra Banerjee Divakaruni. Used by Permission of Neal Porter Books/Roaring Brook Press.

Busy-Busy Little Chick. Used by Permission of Farrar Straus and Giroux BFYR.

How Many Donkeys? An Arabic Counting Tale by Margaret Read MacDonald and Nadia Jameel Taibah Illustrated by Carol Liddiment Published by Albert Whitman & Company (2009).

Illustration copyright © 2013 by Fabricio Vanden Broeck from *Whiskers, Tails & Wings: Animal Folktales from Mexico* by Judy Goldman.

The Tortoise and the Hare © Jerry Pinkney, published by Little Brown and Company.

The Ant and the Grasshopper. Used by Permission of Neal Porter Books/Roaring Brook Press.

Cover from *Thunder Rose* by Jerdine Nolen, illustrated by Kadir Nelson. Text copyright © 2003 by Jerdine Nolen, illustrations copyright © 2003 by Kadir Nelson. Reprinted by permission of Houghton Mifflin Harcourt Publishing Company. All rights reserved.

John Henry by Julius Lester, illustrations by Jerry Pinkney. © 1994 Penguin Young Readers Group.

Ain't Nothing but a Man by Scott Reynolds Nelson and Marc Aronson. © 2007 National Geographic Society.

Stories from the Billabong by James Vance Marshall, Illustrated by Francis Firebrace published by Frances Lincoln Ltd, copyright © 2010. Reproduced by permission of Frances Lincoln Ltd.

Fairy Tale Comics. Used by Permission of First Second Books an imprint of Roaring Brook Press.

When My Baby Dreams of Fairy Tales Cover used with permission of HarperCollins Publishers.

Cover from *Beauty and the Beast* by Jan Brett. Copyright © 1989 by Jan Brett Studio, Inc. Reprinted by permission of Clarion Books, an imprint of Houghton Mifflin Harcourt Publishing Company. All rights reserved.

Cover image of *The Girl of the Wish Garden: A Thumbelina Story*, by Uma Krishnaswami. Groundwood Books, 2013. Illustration © by Nasrin Khosravi. Design by Michael Solomon. Reproduced with permission of Groundwood Books Limited. www.groundwoodbooks.com.

Glass Slipper, Gold Sandal: A Worldwide Cinderella. Used by Permission of Henry Holt BFYR.

Goldilocks and the Three Dinosaurs. Cover used with permission of HarperCollins Publishers.

Goldilocks and the Three Bears: A Tale Moderne © 2010 Steven Guarnaccia used with permission of Abrams Publishers.

The Three Little Pigs and the Somewhat Bad Wolf Cover used with permission of Scholastic.

Jinx Cover used with permission of HarperCollins Publishers.

Fairest of All Cover used with permission of Scholastic.

The Castle Corona Cover used with permission of HarperCollins Publishers.

The Hero's Guide to Saving Your Kingdom Cover used with permission of HarperCollins Publishers.

Cinder Used by Permission of Feiwel&Friends.

In a Glass Grimmly by Adam Gidwitz, illustrations by Hugh D'Andrade. © 2012 Penguin Young Readers Group.

Follow Follow: A Book of Reverso Poems by Marilyn Singer, illustrations by Josee Masse. © 2013 Penguin Young Readers Group.

Grumbles from the Forest: Fairy-Tale Voices with a Twist by Jane Yolen and Rebecca Kai Dotlich, illustrated by Matt Mahurin. Copyright © 2013 by Jane Yolen, Rebecca Kai Dotlich, and Matt Mahurin. Published by Wordsong, an imprint of Boyds Mills Press, Inc. Used by permission.

A Tale Dark & Grimm by Adam Gidwitz, illustrations by Hugh D'Andrade. © 2010 Penguin Young Readers Group.

Touch Magic. Cover art by Don Bell. Used by permission, August House, Inc.

Splendors and Glooms. Text copyright © 2012 by Laura Amy Schlitz. Illustrations copyright © 2012 by BagramIbatoulline. Reproduced by permission of the publisher, Candlewick Press, Somerville, MA.

The True Blue Scouts of Sugar Man Swamp. Jacket illustration copyright © 2013 by Jennifer Bricking from *The True Blue Scouts of Sugar Man Swamp* written by KathiAppelt. Used with permission of Atheneum Books for Young Readers, an imprint of Simon & Schuster Children's Publishing.

Flora & Ulysses: The Illuminated Adventures. Text copyright © 2013 by Kate DiCamillo. Illustrations copyright © 2013 by Keith Campbell. Reproduced by permission of the publisher, Candlewick Press, Somerville, MA.

The One and Only Ivan Cover used with permission of HarperCollins Publishers.

The Scorpio Races Cover used with permission of Scholastic.

The Real Boy Cover used with permission of HarperCollins Publishers.

What We Found in the Sofa and How It Saved the World © Henry Clark, published by Little Brown and Company.

Starry River of the Sky © Grace Lin, published by Little Brown and Company.

The Lost Kingdom Cover used with permission of Scholastic.

Finnikin of the Rock. Copyright © 2010 by Melina Marchetta. Reproduced by permission of the publisher, Candlewick Press, Somerville, MA.

The Crocodile and the Scorpion. Used by Permission of Neal Porter Books/Roaring Brook Press.

The Real Mother Goose Cover used with permission of Scholastic.

Treasury of Greek Mythology: Classic Stories of Gods, Goddesses, Heroes & Monsters by Donna Jo Napoli and Christina Balit. © 2011 National Geographic Society.

Chapter 4

Arlington. Used by Permission of Flash Point, an imprint of Roaring Brook Press.

Moonbird: A Year on the Wind with the Great Survivor B95. Used by Permission of Farrar Straus and Giroux BFYR.

Just Fine the Way They Are: From Dirt Roads to Rail Roads to Interstates by Connie Nordhielm Wooldridge, illustrated by Richard Walz. Copyright © 2011 by Connie NordhielmWooldrige and Richard Walz. Published by Calkins Creek Books, an imprint of Boyds Mills Press, Inc. Used by permission.

Paiute Princess: The Story of Sarah Winnemucca. Used by Permission of Frances Foster Books/Farrar Straus and Giroux BFYR.

Hand in Hand by Andrea Davis Pinkney, illustrated by Brian Pinkney (New York: Disney Jump at the Sun Books, an imprint of Disney Book Group, LLC, 2012). Reprinted by permission.

We've Got a Job: The 1963 Birmingham Children's March by Cynthia Y. Levinson. Text Copyright © 2012 by Cynthia Y. Levinson. Published by arrangement with Peachtree Publishers.

Courage Has No Color. Copyright © 2013 Tanya Lee Stone. Jacket photos copyright © 1944 and 1945, courtesy of US Army Air Forces. Reproduced by permission of the publisher, Candlewick Press, Somerville, MA.

Nelson Mandela cover used with permission of HarperCollins Publishers.

Touch the Sky: Alice Coachman, Olympic High Jumper by Ann Malaspina Illustrated by Eric Velasquez Published by Albert Whitman & Company (2012).

Look Up! Henrietta Leavitt, Pioneering Woman Astronomer. Jacket illustration copyright © 2013 by Raúl Colón from *Look Up! Henrietta Leavitt, Pioneering Woman Astronomer* written by Robert Burleigh. Used with permission of Paula Wiseman Books, an imprint of Simon & Schuster Children's Publishing.

Fly High! The Story of Bessie Coleman. Jacket illustration copyright © 2001 by Teresa Flavin from *Fly High! The Story of Bessie Coleman* by Louise Borden and Mary Kay Kroeger. Used with permission of Margaret K. McElderry Books, an imprint of Simon & Schuster Children's Publishing.

Silent Star: The Story of Deaf Major Leaguer William Hoy, copyright 2012, by Bill Wise and illustrated by Adam Gustavson. Permission arranged with LEE & LOW BOOKS, INC., New York, NY 10016.

Ballerina Dreams. Used by Permission of Feiwel&Friends.

Emancipation Proclamation: Lincoln and the Dawn of Liberty © Tonya Bolden 2013 used with permission of Abrams Publishers.

Heart and Soul Cover used with permission of HarperCollins Publishers.

The Solar System through Infographics © 2014 by Lerner Publishing Group, Inc.

3D Printing © Terence O'Neill and Josh Williams, Published by Cherry Lake Publishing.

How People Are Using 3-D Printers from 3D Printing © Terence O'Neill and Josh Williams, Published by Cherry Lake Publishing.

Cover from *Temple Grandin* by Sy Montgomery. Copyright © 2012 by Sy Montgomery. Reprinted by permission of Houghton Mifflin Harcourt Publishing Company. All rights reserved.

From the Good Mountain: How Gutenberg Changed the World. Used by permission of Flash Point an imprint of Roaring Brook Press.

Electrical Wizard. Text copyright © 2013 by Elizabeth Rusch. Illustrations copyright © 2013 by Oliver Dominguez. Reproduced by permission of the publisher, Candlewick Press, Somerville, MA.

Nick and Tesla's High-Voltage Danger Lab. Cover used with permission of Quirk Books.

On a Beam of Light Illustrations © Vladimir Radunsky from *On a Beam of Light* published by Chronicle Books.

Electric Ben: The Amazing Life and Times of Benjamin Franklin by Robert Byrd. © 2012 Penguin Young Readers Group.

Henry and the Cannons: An Extraordinary True Story of the American Revolution. Used by Permission of Roaring Brook Press.

To Dare Mighty Things by Doreen Rappaport, illustrated by C. F. Payne (New York: Disney • Hyperion Books, an imprint of Disney Book Group, LLC, 2013). Reprinted by permission.

Grandfather Gandhi. Jacket illustration copyright © 2014 by Evan Turk from *Grandfather Gandhi* written by Arun Gandhi and Bethany Hegedus. Used with permission of Atheneum Books for Young Readers, an imprint of Simon & Schuster Children's Publishing.

Seeds of Change: Planting a Path to Peace, copyright 2010, by Jen Cullerton Johnson and illustrated by Sonia Lynn Sadler. Permission arranged with LEE & LOW BOOKS, INC., New York, NY 10016.

The Boy Who Harnessed the Wind by William Kamkwamba and Bryan Mealer, illustrations by Elizabeth Zunon. © Penguin Young Readers Group.

I Am Malala: How One Girl Stood Up for Education and Changed the World © MalalaYousafzai and Patricia McCormick, published by Little Brown and Company.

Martin &Mahalia: His Words, Her Song © Andrea Davis Pinkney, published by Little Brown and Company.

Little Rock Girl 1957: How a Photograph Changed the Fight for Integration. Used with permission.

Frog Song by Brenda Guiberson. Cover used by permission of Henry Holt BFYR.

Bugs cover used with permission of Scholastic.

Bugs in My Hair Cover used with permission of Scholastic.

The Girl from the Tar Paper School: Barbara Rose Johns and the Advent of the Civil Rights Movement © Teri Kanefield 2014 used with permission of Abrams Publishers.

Cover from *The Animal Book* by Steve Jenkins. Reprinted by permission of Houghton Mifflin Harcourt Publishing Company. All rights reserved.

Chapter 5

Going Places. Jacket illustration copyright © 2014 by Peter H. Reynolds from *Going Places* written by Paul A. Reynolds. Used with permission of Atheneum Books for Young Readers, an imprint of Simon & Schuster Children's Publishing.

Cover from *What the Heart Knows* by Joyce Sidman, illustrated by Pamela Zagarenski. Text copyright © 2013 by Joyce Sidman, illustrations copyright © 2013 by Pamela Zagarenski. Reprinted by permission of Houghton Mifflin Harcourt Publishing Company. All rights reserved.

Index

About the Author

MARIANNE SACCARDI, MS, has taught at the elementary and college levels for over thirty-five years. Her published works include Libraries Unlimited's *Art in Story: Teaching Art History to Elementary School Children* and *Books That Teach Kids to Write*, as well as numerous articles and teacher guides. Saccardi is a children's literature consultant and a book reviewer for *School Library Journal*.